BATTLES OF THE GREEK
AND ROMAN WORLDS

To the memory of C.H.T. Hayman ('Chi Theta')
A great teacher

BATTLES OF THE GREEK AND ROMAN WORLDS

A Chronological Compendium of 667 Battles to 31 BC, from the Historians of the Ancient World

John Drogo Montagu

Greenhill Books, London
Stackpole Books, Pennsylvania

Battles of the Greek and Roman Worlds
first published 2000 by
Greenhill Books, Lionel Leventhal Limited, Park House, 1 Russell Gardens, London NW11 9NN
and
Stackpole Books, 5067 Ritter Road, Mechanicsburg, PA 17055, USA

British Library Cataloguing in Publication Data
Montagu, John Drogo
Battles of the Greek and Roman worlds : a chronological compendium of 667 battles to 31 B.C., from the historians of the ancient world
1.Battles – Greece – History 2.Battles – Rome – History 3.Rome – History, Military 4.Greece – History, Military
I.Title
355′.02′0938

ISBN 1-85367-389-7

Library of Congress Cataloging-in-Publication Data available

Typeset by DP Photosetting, Aylesbury, Bucks
Printed and bound in Great Britain by
The Bath Press, Bath

Contents

List of Maps and Battle Plans

Preface

Even war can have a comic aspect on occasions. Anyone who visualizes the naval antics of Philopoemen off Gytheum (p. 128) can hardly fail to suppress a chortle. On a different note, the Roman victory at Beneventum in 214BC (p. 184) reads like pure black comedy – with a happy ending for the slaves. Episodes such as these have considerably lightened my self-imposed task.

The purpose of this book is to bring together in one volume the ancient literature about the battles of the Greek and Roman worlds from the start of recorded history to the end of the Roman Republic. No attempt has been made to treat this material critically, apart from an occasional comment when this seemed to be warranted. The work is intended primarily as a source of reference. As far as I am aware, there has been no previous publication with a similar purpose and scope.

A battle is here defined as any armed engagement, greater than a minor skirmish, which occurred in the open and to which it is possible to assign a known or approximate date and a topographical name. Names of sites that are now entirely unknown have been included on the grounds that they might be identified in time to come. Sieges, which may involve specialized methods and equipment and which are a major subject for study in their own right, have been excluded except in so far as sallies bring the conflict into the open.

In the interest of completeness this broad definition of a battle has been applied with further laxity. Some battles within walls have been included, as also have one or two abortive confrontations which never fully materialized. If there was any doubt about inclusion, I have erred on the side of acceptance. Regrettably, many actions – even major ones of great interest – cannot be included for lack of information about their date or place or both. Such, for example, are some of the victories of Spartacus over Roman armies, the whereabouts of which are quite unknown. For these reasons the battles listed in these pages represent only a fraction of those that actually took place.

The entries in the text have been kept as concise as possible while preserving the essential military material. In general, the causes and effects of an action have been stated only briefly and then only if they were considered noteworthy. The historical context of a war has usually been outlined in connexion with the first episode in the war. Some of the entries may seem to be inordinately scanty. This is not the result of over-zealous pruning on my part but reflects only the paucity of information in the sources consulted.

The references appended at the foot of each entry do not pretend to be exhaustive, but they cover all the major ancient sources which provide the basis for existing knowledge in the field. The conventional presentation of the usual three-figure reference denoting book, chapter and 'verse' has been slightly modified, notably by quoting the 'verses' in brackets. In general, reference has only been made to the extensive modern literature when a contribution has reconstructed obscure events in the light of recent evidence and deduction. In this, I have given the credit to the first source which propounded the new wisdom. After that, the subject becomes a matter of modern dissertation, which is outside the scope of this work and could fill another volume.

Greek and Roman chronological tables are entered before the relevant texts. Apart from their obvious role as indexes, they display the battle content of the various wars. The warlike instincts of man have not always led to a 'neat' result in the eyes of the annalistic chronicler. A string of battles with a connecting theme may have been interrupted in its chronological continuity by some irrelevant act of aggression in a distant land. The tables may help the reader to extract a war from the extraneous events.

The total contents of this book – tables and text – have been divided sharply between the Greek and Roman Worlds. History is seldom so categorical. When the two worlds meet, in the late third and second centuries when Rome became involved with the Hellenistic states and Greece itself, there are problems of classification. The problem has been dealt with here by including all the 'mixed' battles, such as those of the Macedonian Wars and the war against Antiochus, in both the Greek and Roman tables. In the text, on the other hand, they have been described under the Greek World but with a cross-reference under the Roman World. Their inclusion in both tables is intended to assist those readers who are interested in the chronological relationships between events in either sphere. There were also a couple of similarly 'mixed' battles at a much earlier period of history, at Aricia in 506 for example, but it is considered that these were essentially Greek affairs and they have been treated accordingly.

In the table of Roman battles, generals such as Scipio Africanus and Pompey the Great have been entered with their honorific *cognomina* whenever their names appear. The title may therefore be shown prospectively in relation to battles which took place before the honour was actually accorded – a liberty which facilitates recognition of the individual concerned.

The maps at the end of this book are devoted almost exclusively to those known places and geographical features which are named in this work, notably those which have given their names to battles. Only one known battle site has been intentionally omitted, namely Noreia [*Neumarkt*] in what is now Austria. The remoteness of this place from the other entries would have necessitated a map to itself, assigning to the battle a degree of unwarranted importance. A few of the places and features entered in the maps have been accorded question marks indicating uncertainty as to their site or, in the case of rivers, their identity. These are not the only dubious entries. More extensive guidance is supplied in Index of Places, in which the modern name representing an ancient place may be noted as questionable or probable. Specific comments such as 'site disputed' are appended where appropriate. The index also cites the name of the relevant present-day province or department. These divisions, being many times smaller than the ancient ones, are correspondingly more informative. Terms such as 'Hispania Tarraconensis' and 'Gallia Celtica' tell one virtually nothing.

There is a body of opinion which favours the use of Greek spellings for Greek proper names. Although in agreement with these sentiments, I have adopted the more commonly used Latinized versions in conformity with many classical books of reference and all of the classical atlases in my possession. The Greek islands are usually, although not invariably, treated as exceptions. Chius, Samus and Lesbus are intolerable!

* * * * *

This book is dedicated to the man who taught me Greek and Latin, with frequent digressions into classical history. These 'asides' instilled a lifelong interest in the field but a career in medicine left no time for such indulgences. This project was undertaken only in retirement and primarily for my own edification and enjoyment.

To my friendly publisher, Lionel Leventhal, I express my admiration of his patience with a raw and sometimes awkward newcomer. He tells me that in his opinion this work should be of wide interest in view of its scope and its usefulness as a source of reference. His positive attitude and the encouragement which went with it did much to help me see the job through.

I also thank my wife for her tolerance of my prolonged absences in my bedroom/study/library where for many years I was living in another world.

J. D. M.
2000

GALLIA

Iberus

Calagurris Nassica •

Intercatia •

Numantia •

Termantia? •

Sicoris

Ilerda • • Cissis

Emporiae •

Bilbilis •

Cauca •

Segontia • Contrebia •

Idubeda Ms

Tarraco •

Segovia •

TARRACONENSIS

Intibili • • Ibera

BALEARES Is

LUSITANIA

Toletum •

Turba •

Iliturgi

Tagus

Aebura •

Turia

Saguntum

Ana • Alce

Valentia •

Sucro

PITYUSAE Is

Lauro? •

BAETICA

Baecula •

Ilorci •

Iliturgi • • Castulo

Tader

Ana

Corduba • • Castulo

Baetis

New Carthage •

Ilipa •

Italica • • Carmone

Hispalis • • Astapa

Urso •

Hasta •

Gades •

Carteia

Statute Miles

0   100

MAURETANIA

1. Spain

2. Gaul

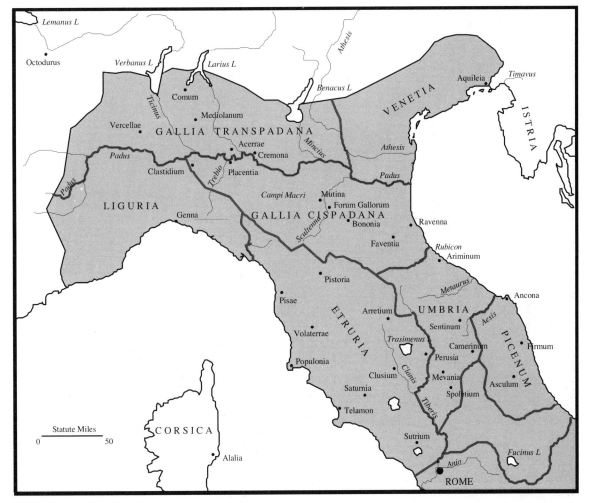

3. North Italy

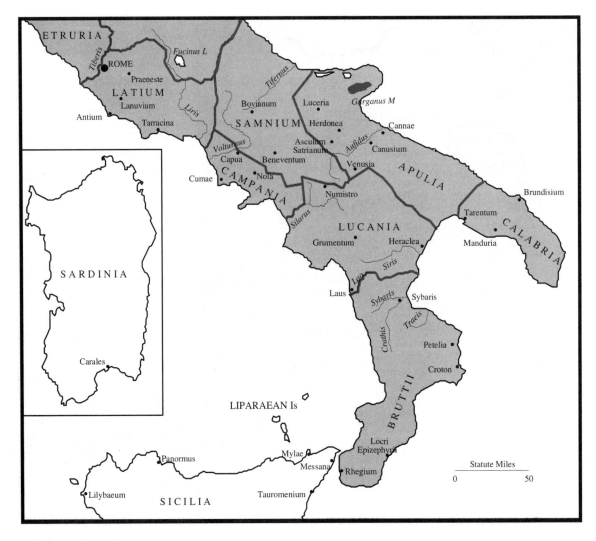

4. South Italy

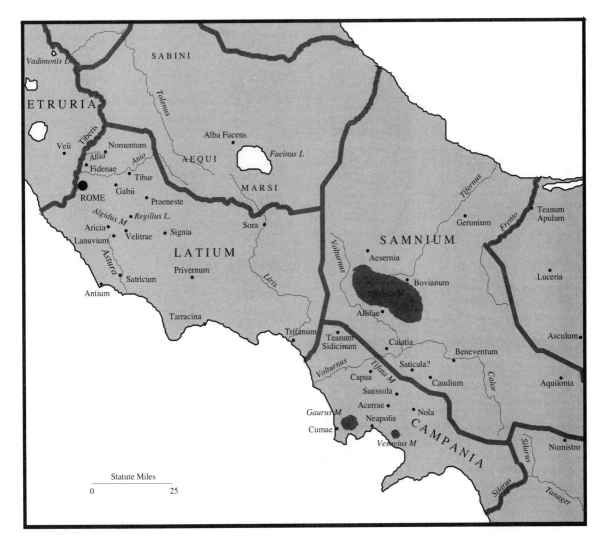

5. Latium and Campania

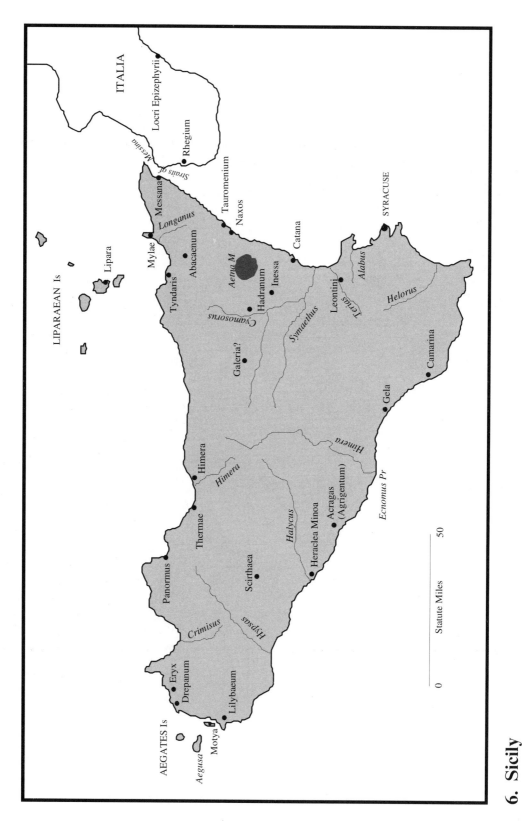

ITALIA

Locri Epizephyrii

Rhegium

Straits of Messina

Messana

Longanus

Mylae

Abacaenum

Tauromenium

Naxos

Catana

SYRACUSE

LIPARAEAN Is

Lipara

Tyndaris

Aetna M

Hadranum

Inessa

Alabus

Leontini

Terias

Helorus

Cyanosorus

Galeria?

Symaethus

Camarina

Gela

Himera

Himera

Himera

Thermae

Acragas
(Agrigentum)

Heraclea Minoa

Halycus

Ecnomus Pr

Scirthaea

Panormus

Crimisus

Hypsus

Eryx

Drepanum

Lilybaeum

AEGATES Is

Motya

Aegusa

0   50
Statute Miles

6. Sicily

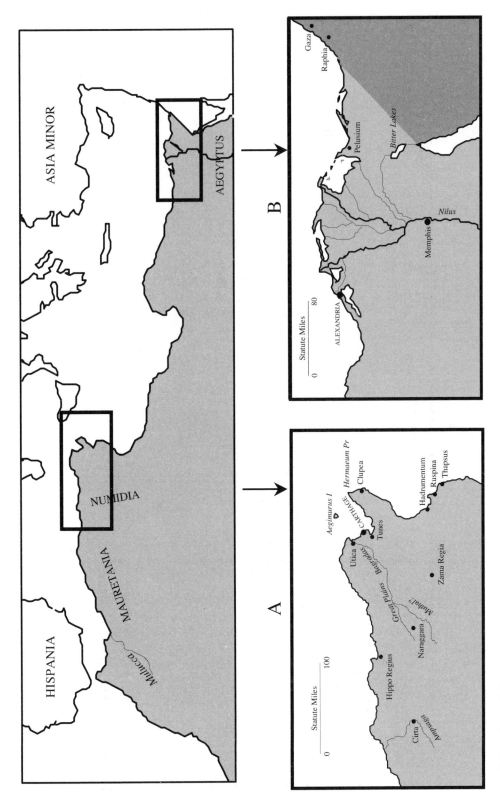

ASIA MINOR

HISPANIA

AEGYPTUS

NUMIDIA

MAURETANIA

Mulucca

B

Gaza
Raphia

Pelusium

Bitter Lakes

Nilus

Memphis

Statute Miles
0 ___ 80

ALEXANDRIA

A

Hermaeum Pr
Clupea

Aegimurus I
CARTHAGE
Tunes

Hadrumentum
Ruspina
Thapsus

Utica
Bagradas
Great Plains
Zama Regia

Muthul?

Naraggara

Hippo Regius

Cirta
Ampsaga

Statute Miles
0 ___ 100

7. North Africa

15

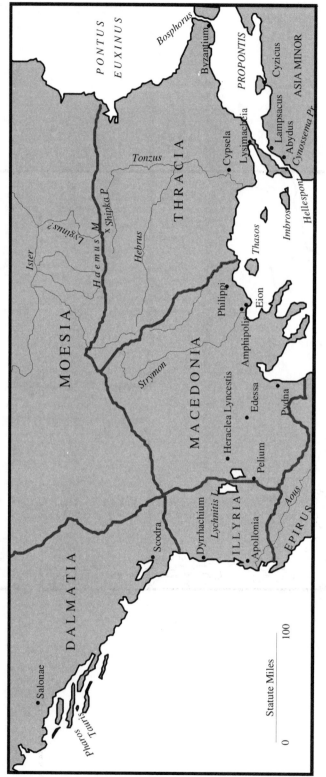

8. Illyria, Macedonia, Thrace

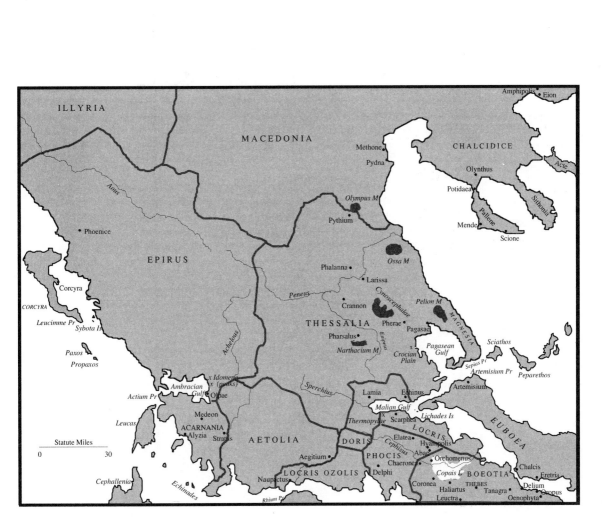

ILLYRIA

MACEDONIA

CHALCIDICE

Amphipolis
Eion

Acte

Methone

Pydna

Olynthus

Potidaea

Sithonia

Olympus M

Pallene

Pythium

Mende

Scione

Phoenice

EPIRUS

Ossa M

Phalanna

Larissa

Corcyra

Cynoscephalae

Pelion M

CORCYRA

Peneus

Crannon

Pherae

MAGNESIA

Leucimme Pr

THESSALIA

Pagasae

Sybota Is

Sciathos

Pharsalus

Empeus

Pagasean
Gulf

Paxos

Narthacium M

Crocian
Plain

Sepias Pr

Propaxos

Artemisium Pr

Peparethos

Achelous

Ambracian
Gulf

Idomene
(peaks)

Sperchius

Lamia

Echinus

Artemisium

Actium Pr

Olpae

Malian Gulf

Lichades Is

Medeon

Thermopylae

Scarphea

EUBOEA

Leucas

ACARNANIA

LOCRIS

Alyzia

Stratus

AETOLIA

DORIS

Elatea

Hyampolis

Cephisus

PHOCIS

Abae

Orchomenus

Chalcis

Statute Miles

Aegitium

Chaeronea

Copais L

BOEOTIA

Eretria

0   30

LOCRIS OZOLIS

Delphi

Coronea

THEBES

Delium

Naupactus

Haliartus

Tanagra

Oropus

Cephallenia

Echinades

Leuctra

Oenophyta

Rhium Pr

9. North Greece

17

10. South Greece

11. The Aegean World

12. Asia Minor

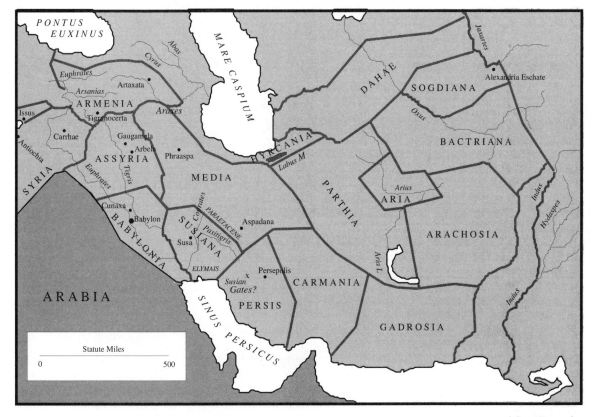

PONTUS EUXINUS

MARE CASPIUM

Euphrates

Abas

Cyrus

Artaxata

Arsanias

ARMENIA

Araxes

Issus

Tigranocerta

Carrhae

Gaugamela

Arbela

Phraaspa

DAHAE

SOGDIANA

Alexandria Eschate

Jaxartes

Oxus

BACTRIANA

HYRCANIA

Labus M

Antiochia

ASSYRIA

MEDIA

SYRIA

Euphrates

Tigris

Cunaxa

Babylon

BABYLONIA

Conates

PARAETACENE

Aspadana

SUSIANA

Pasitigris

Susa

ELYMAIS

PARTHIA

Arius

ARIA

ARACHOSIA

Indus

Hydaspes

Aria L.

ARABIA

Susian Gates?

x

Persepolis

CARMANIA

Indus

PERSIS

SINUS PERSICUS

GADROSIA

Statute Miles

0   500

13. Persia

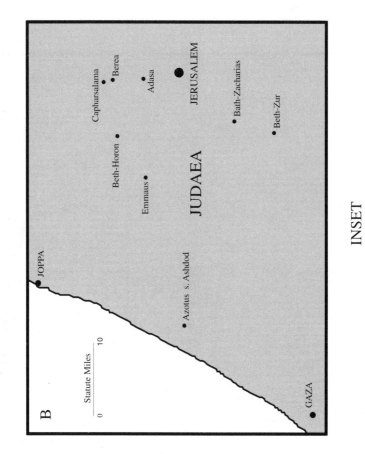

INSET

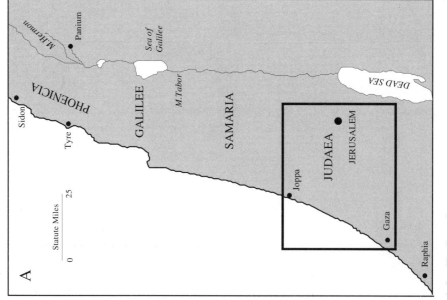

14. Palestine

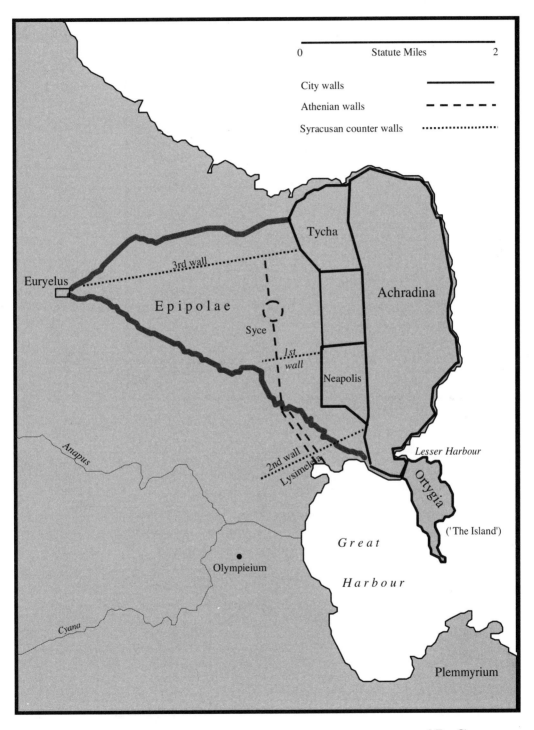

15. Syracuse

PART ONE

INTRODUCTION TO GREEK
AND ROMAN WARFARE

Greek Armies
Roman Armies
Naval Warfare
Reliability of Data
Principal Sources
Glossary

Greek Armies

HOPLITE ARMIES
The hoplite seems to have made his debut on the
martial stage at some point in the seventh century
BC. He became the cardinal unit in Greek armies;
indeed, at the battle of Marathon, the Athenian
army was composed entirely of hoplites. He
survived until near the end of the third century BC,
by which time those foot soldiers who still
possessed hoplite equipment were continuing to
use it alongside infantrymen who were otherwise
equipped.

Hoplites were equipped with helmet, corslet,
greaves and an unusual shield (*hoplon* or usually
aspis) which was their hallmark. This was a
circular shield which had two straps, one in the
centre through which the hand was passed to grip
the second one near the periphery. The double-
grip arrangement transferred the weight of the
shield away from the wrist muscles. The hoplite's
chief weapon was a spear of 6 feet or more in
length, and he also carried a sword. This equipment was greatly superior to that of the Persians in
close combat and it accounted in no mean measure
for the Greek victories in the Persian Wars.

Troops of this type were deployed in a phalanx,
a term which existed from Homeric times and
which denoted a closely knit formation of men.
They were drawn up in columns which might be as
little as four deep but were usually eight deep. Over
the years the figure tended to rise and at Leuctra in
371BC the Boeotian phalanx was 50 deep under
Epaminondas, who relied on sheer weight of
numbers to crash through the enemy lines. With
this system of warfare, individual heroics ceased to
exist and were indeed disruptive. In the phalanx
every man depended on his neighbour. Protection
was afforded to his left side by his own shield but
he relied on his neighbour's shield to give him
protection on his otherwise exposed right flank.
For this reason there was a tendency for the
phalanx to edge to the right as the right-hand
column tended to drift further to the right to avoid
being outflanked, while every man down the line
followed suit to maintain protection from his

neighbour's shield. The disadvantage of the phalanx was its lack of manoeuvrability and therefore
its vulnerability to attack on the flanks or rear.
The Spartans developed special drills aimed at
increasing flexibility. One such manoeuvre was the
'countermarch',[1] by means of which the phalanx
was inverted from front to back virtually *in situ* in
such a way that the original front line became the
new front line at what had been the rear, the whole
phalanx facing in the direction from which it had
come.

The hoplite phalanx was sometimes accompanied in battle by 'light' troops and cavalry,
although both of these arms played a subsidiary
role in the major battles of classical Greece. The
light troops were armed with javelins, bows or
slings. The peltasts were a special case, so called
because they carried a *pelta* (light shield), which
originated in Thrace, but the word 'peltast' has
sometimes been applied loosely to other javelin-
eers. In the fourth century an Athenian general,
Iphicrates, introduced new concepts of tactical
warfare, which made full use of peltasts as a flying
squad.

In action, the opposing phalanxes usually closed
to a spear's length, after which it seems that there
was much shouting and shoving until one side or
the other was overwhelmed by force of weight and
numbers, and began to give way. The hoplite was
too heavily encumbered with armour to be able to
pursue a routed enemy for any great distance.

HELLENISTIC ARMIES
Conventionally the Hellenistic era commenced in
323 with the death of Alexander the Great, but
from a military angle it may be said to have begun
with the reorganization of the Macedonian army
by his father, Philip II. His highly trained and
efficient fighting machine overran the Greeks at
Chaeronea (338) and formed the backbone of the

1. J. Lazenby, in J. Hackett (ed.), *Warfare in the Ancient World*,
Sidgwick & Jackson, 1989.

army which, under Alexander, conquered Persia and beyond.

The core of the army was the Macedonian phalanx, a formidable weapon comprising the foot companions (*pezhetairoi*) and a smaller élite band of hypaspists (shield bearers) formed up 16 deep. The basic organizational unit of the foot companions was the *dekad*, originally of 10 men but later increased to 16, i.e. one file of a 16-deep phalanx. The tactical unit was the *taxis* with a strength of around 1,500. The principal weapon was the *sarissa*, a thrusting spear up to 22 feet in length. It was gripped with both hands at a point one third of the distance up the shaft from the butt and was carried underarm. The phalangites in the front rank held their sarissas level, while the next few ranks kept their weapons parallel with those of the front rank but held them at progressively higher levels. In this way the sarissas of the first three, four or even five ranks projected in front of the phalanx to present a bristling hedge of spearheads in depth. Because of the weight of his spear the Macedonian phalangite was rather less encumbered defensively than the hoplite. He carried a small round shield suspended from his neck, a helmet, a linen (sometimes leather or occasionally bronze) corslet, and greaves. The hypaspists carried a shorter spear up to 10 feet long, which increased their mobility.

Philip set great store on cavalry and developed this arm to a pitch previously unknown, helped by a large supply of horses in his land. The cavalrymen, called the Companions, were supplied by the Macedonian aristocracy. They were usually led by Philip in person and later by Alexander. In Alexander's day the Thessalian cavalry, reputedly the finest in the land, also followed him.

After Alexander's time the Hellenistic armies of the third and second centuries deteriorated in a number of ways. In the first place cavalry was expensive to maintain and became reduced in numbers. Against this, the generals enlisted large numbers of orientals as foot soldiers, who swelled the ranks of the phalanx into an ill-trained heterogeneous horde. Quality gave way to quantity; the emphasis was on weight of numbers. At best, a phalanx always lacked manoeuvrability, but in the days of Philip and Alexander it retained some flexibility by virtue of its division into a number of units or *taxeis* which retained a certain degree of individual freedom of movement. In addition, the Macedonian phalanx was more open than its predecessors. When the phalanx degenerated into a huge block of tightly packed humanity armed with pikes of inordinate length, it became incapable of turning in any direction and could only plod inexorably forward. In consequence, it was vulnerable to any attack on the flanks or in the rear. At Cynoscephalae in 197 an unknown military tribune saved the day by taking 20 maniples from the victorious Roman right and attacking the Macedonian phalanx in the rear. There was nothing that the enemy could do but raise their pikes in token of surrender or drop them and flee. To protect the flanks and rear from such an attack a phalanx was sometimes followed by another phalanx, the so-called double phalanx. But the customary form of protection was provided by the cavalry. In the Macedonian army of Philip and his son, the phalanx was invariably central with a strong force of horse on either wing. The rundown of the cavalry arm reduced that defence. The other principal disadvantage of the phalanx was its need of suitably even terrain. On rough ground the columns tended to separate and the formation lost cohesion. This factor won the day for Aemilius Paulus at Pydna in 168 when he spotted the opportunity of infiltrating his men into gaps in the enemy lines and attacking their flanks.

Roman Armies

SERVIAN ARMY

During the period of Etruscan domination the military machine seems to have consisted basically of a phalanx, which was supported by native troops on the wings. The army was entirely patrician, each man providing his own equipment. In the middle of the sixth century it was reorganized by Servius Tullius, the penultimate king, strictly on a wealth basis with a view to increasing the numbers by extending enrolment to the poorer orders. The population was divided into seven groups. The wealthiest citizens not unnaturally formed the cavalry with its attendant expenses, while the next (first) group became fully equipped hoplites on the Greek pattern. Further down the scale the various groups sported progressively less protective equipment, the poorest having none. The lower classes formed support groups. The very lowest class was considered unfit for service. On the assumption that a century did in this case mean one hundred men, the total complement of an army might be a phalanx of 8,000, an equal number in the support groups, and a cavalry arm of 1,800. This was normally divided into four legions. The top four classes were equipped with a long spear (*hasta*); the lowest two had only slings and javelins.

After the Etruscans had been expelled, traditionally in 510, the Latin league, which had been formed for the purpose of the expulsion and which included Rome, became involved with the hill tribes such as the Volscians, the Aequians and, ultimately, the Samnites. They also had to deal with a further menace in the form of the Celtic invaders (Gauls) from the north, who had their own methods of fighting. The phalanx, which had worked well on the plains of Latium and against weapons and methods similar to its own, was not suited to warfare against either of these new enemies and it went into eclipse. In a major reorganization of the military machine, the old class system based on personal wealth was abandoned in principle, and payment of the troops was instituted. The round hoplite-type shield was discarded and replaced with the oval or oblong semicylindrical *scutum*, which had a metal band top and bottom, and offered greater protection against downward slashes from Gallic swords. Third and most important, the phalanx was replaced by a more flexible machine based on the division of the main infantry body, the legion, into small units called maniples.

THE MANIPULAR LEGION

A manipular legion was first described by Livy (**8**: 8) in connexion with the military events of 340, although it must have been evolving for some years. In a later and more detailed account, Polybius (**6**: 19ff.) describes the Roman military system at the time of the Punic Wars. Although considerable evolution had taken place in the interim, the two accounts provide similar descriptions of the basic structure of the army and its deployment in action.

There were normally four legions, two in each consular army. Each legion consisted nominally of 4,200 infantry and 300 cavalry, but it could be expanded in times of crisis. Although personal wealth still played some part as a qualification, much more emphasis was placed on age and experience. The infantry were deployed in three lines, usually either four deep or eight deep. The first line consisted of 1,200 *hastati*, the pick of the young men, who were deployed in 10 maniples with gaps between them. Instead of the old *hasta* they carried heavy javelins (*pila*). In the second line were 1,200 *principes*, who were also divided into 10 maniples. They were older and more mature than the *hastati*. The third line consisted of 600 veteran *triarii*, again in 10 maniples, who retained their *hastae* and constituted a defensive third line. The poorest and youngest men were the 1,200 light-armed skirmishers (*velites*), who were assigned to the maniples in equal numbers but usually fought in front or on the wings. The wealthiest 300 men formed the cavalry. The 10 maniples in the second line were not drawn up immediately behind those of the front line but opposite the gap between the maniples, in a checkerboard pattern (quincunx). This was a preliminary arrangement which allowed the skirmishers to withdraw through the ranks. It is assumed that the gaps were closed before a line went into action.

In action, the *hastati* threw their javelins and then charged at the disordered enemy with drawn swords. If this failed to cause a rout, the *hastati* withdrew between the *principes*, who followed up with a second similar assault. In the event of failure to break the enemy the *triarii* would rise into view from the kneeling position, close ranks and level their spears to cover the army's retreat to camp or, possibly, turn the tables.

THE PROFESSIONAL LEGION

In the preceding sections the levying of an army was based, in part at least, on an anachronistic property qualification, and military service was compulsory for those who were eligible. As a result of social changes and a decline in the middle classes, numbers available for military service were decreasing. Against this background a class of volunteers was emerging. In a paradoxical situation there were increasing numbers who wanted to serve but were excluded by lack of means, while the decreasing number of wealthy citizens who were forced to serve hated the thought. A complete reorganization was due and the name of Marius is attached to the process.

The Marian Reform is a highly controversial area and the subject of much dispute which would be out of place here. The following comments are intended only as a broad guide to the type of changes introduced. Marius abolished conscription and replaced the conscripts with volunteers who wished to make military service a profession and would serve for much longer periods. This facilitated the longer campaigns on which Rome was progressively embarking. In addition, he is credited with the virtual abolition of the property qualification in about 104BC. The tactical reforms attributed to Marius were also far-reaching. As all men were now equal in regard to the conditions of enlistment, the old classes of *hastati*, *principes* and *triarii* disappeared, as also did the *velites* and probably the cavalry. All legionaries were now heavy infantrymen and all bore the same weapons and equipment. Each man wore a mail shirt and carried the oval curved shield (*scutum*), the short sword and the heavy javelin (*pilum*). The size of the legion was increased to a nominal 6,000, (although it sometimes fell to less than half that number). It was divided into 10 cohorts, each cohort in effect incorporating three maniples, i.e. six centuries. For organizational as opposed to tactical purposes the unit remained the century, probably of a nominal 80 men. It was at this time that the eagle became the universal standard of the legion in place of the previous assortment of symbols. A small change in the *pilum* has also been attributed to Marius by Plutarch. Previously the head of the javelin was secured to the shaft by two metal pins. Marius ordered that one of the pins should be replaced by a wooden one which would break on impact so that the weapon could not be 'returned to the sender'. The term 'cohort' is not in fact a new Marian introduction. It had been in use for over a century but had been applied mainly to allied forces for a body of around 400–500 men.

In the middle of the first century BC, Julius Caesar placed greater emphasis on efficiency than on numbers so that raw recruits underwent a period of intensive training before receiving acceptance into a legion. It is partly for this reason that Caesar's legions often fell well below the nominal strength of 6,000. In action, the army was usually deployed in three lines (*triplex acies*) which were normally drawn up about eight deep. The legions fought side by side and a fully manned legion of 6,000 men would usually have four cohorts in the front line and three in each of the other two lines. Variations sometimes occurred for special reasons. For example, at the battle of Pharsalus in 48, Caesar, envisaging an outflanking attack by the enemy cavalry, withdrew one cohort from the rear line of each legion to form a fourth line which faced the threat. In the same vein, if the front line became exhausted, it was relieved by the second line which either enflanked the first or passed between the ranks. Alternatively the third line, which might have seen no action, could be brought to the front to replace exhausted troops as at Pharsalus (48), or it could turn about to face a challenge from the rear as at Bibracte (58) or be sent to assist a hard-pressed wing as happened at the Plain of Alsace (58). Such mobility was far removed from the inflexibility of the unitary phalanx.

Naval Warfare

GREEK NAVIES

The standard warship in classical Greece was the trireme, a vessel which had three banks of oars with one man to each oar. The total crew of a trireme was about 200, of whom 170 were oarsmen. The ship also carried sails but these were never used in battle, when they were either stowed or preferably left ashore. The word 'sailing' is generally used loosely to cover motion by sail or oar. A metal 'beak' was attached to the prow of the trireme and was used for ramming.

Larger ships such as quadriremes and quinqueremes were also built but the details are unknown. Owing to the logistical impossibility of adding deck upon deck of oars it seems probable that these ships carried more oarsmen rather than more oars. A configuration for a quinquereme might have been 2–2–1 with two rowers to each of the upper oars and one below. There were also smaller ships such as the penteconter, which sported a single bank of 50 oars.

In the Hellenistic era, still larger vessels were constructed, notably the 'sixes' (*hexeres*) and 'sevens' (*hepteres* or septiremes) of Demetrius. As with the quinqueremes, it was the number of oarsmen not oars that was presumably increased. Demetrius may even have reduced the number of banks to two but this is uncertain. The additional manpower made for a more powerful ship which was capable of carrying more marines, but as length was limited the increase in size was largely in the beam.

TACTICS

In the early days of Greek naval warfare the emphasis was on carrying large numbers of troops and boarding the enemy ship. This practice dropped out and the vessel itself became the weapon which was launched against the enemy ship in an effort to sink, disable or capture it. The Athenians among others became adept at this form of warfare. Under the Athenian constitution poorer citizens could find employment as paid rowers, which resulted in a good supply of well-trained crews. There were two basic tactics. The first consisted of ramming the enemy vessel, preferably amidships. In the second, which required more expertise, the attacker approached the victim head-on and then, veering to one side while shipping its own oars, it passed alongside the victim, shearing off all of the enemy's oars. Concerted manoeuvres on the part of a fleet involved these basic tactics, ramming in particular. In the *diekplous*, ships in line abreast facing a similar formation would sail between the enemy vessels and then execute a swift turn and ram the enemy craft in the flanks or stern. The manoeuvre could be forestalled by adopting a formation of two lines of ships, but this shortened the line and opened the fleet to a *periplous*. In that manoeuvre the fleet with the more extended line outflanked the enemy and rammed him amidships. The circle (*kyklos*) was a defensive measure applied to a fleet. It involved putting all the ships in a circle with the prows facing outwards. Non-combatant vessels were placed in the centre, as also were a few of the swiftest ships which acted as a flying squadron, ready to move to any point which was challenged by the enemy.

Grapnels were known to the Athenians, who used them against the Syracusans in the disastrous battles of 413. In the second century the Rhodians, who were noted for their seamanship, sometimes equipped their ships with fire equipment. This consisted of urns suspended on projecting poles and containing inflammable material which could be tipped onto any ship that ventured too close. It was a defensive measure which was remarkably effective in persuading the enemy to keep his distance.

ROMAN NAVY

Rome had no need of a navy until the beginning of the third century BC. It was the First Punic War that forced the issue when, for the first time, Rome was fighting overseas. It is said that she got hold of a damaged Carthaginian ship and copied it. Whether this was so or not, Rome produced a fleet in breathtaking time. A few triremes were included, but Rome concentrated on quinqueremes, which accounted for over 80 per cent of the fleet. These ships may have followed the Greek pattern of oars in three banks with a 2–2–1 configuration of rowers, but an alternative theory postulates a simpler arrangement with five men to each oar in a single bank. There is no certainty about the crews. They were often provided by the allies and colonies, but freedmen and occasionally slaves were used at times and it is probable that the poorest citizens may have played a part. As Romans were adept at fighting on land and inept at naval tactics, their methods differed from the established Greek tradition. They placed the emphasis on carrying marines, boarding enemy ships and, in effect, fighting a land battle on the sea, much as the Greeks had done in the early days. To this end, the Romans resorted to technical innovation and developed a device called the 'raven' (*corvus*), which made its first appearance at the battle of Mylae (260). Basically it was a 36-foot long gangplank which was hinged to the deck at the prow of the ship and was normally held upright against the mast. It could be rotated and lowered onto an enemy deck which it held fast with a spike. Unfortunately, this contraption could impair the stability of the ship and it could – and did – result in accidents. In similar vein, two centuries later Octavian's admiral Agrippa developed a successful device for grabbing an enemy craft at long range and allowing it to be hauled in. This proved successful at Naulochus (36).

The main disadvantage of the Roman ships was their weight, and hence their speed, which was usually slower than that of the enemy. Furthermore, in the early days – during the First Punic War – the Roman crews were poorly trained and greatly inferior to the skilled Carthaginians. In the second and first centuries much smaller and swifter ships began to make an appearance and became regular features. Only two of them need be mentioned. One was the Illyrian *lembos*; the other, similar to it, was the Liburnian. Both had beaks and were used as scouts and also for fighting.

Reliability of Data

GENERAL

Fact and fiction are at the two ends of a scale which ranges through all the intervening shades of grey. Close to pure invention come myths and legends, which may have had some initial factual foundation but which have accumulated a wealth of imaginary embellishment through the ages and have become incorporated in national tradition. In the early history of Greece, Sparta did overrun Messenia but there is little evidence to support Pausanias' account of the First Messenian War and virtually none for the Second. They are included in this work because there is no conclusive reason to believe that they did not happen. The reader is given the benefit of the accounts and is left to judge for himself. Likewise, the early history of Rome contains much that is purely legendary. Livy recounts it but he admits its nature. Apart from the *Fasti,* the official chronicles of magistracies, functions and the like, the Romans had very little reliable information about their history before the third century. What they had was undoubtedly padded out with tales and local 'knowledge' or pure surmise and invention.

Herodotus relied largely on oral accounts from people who had witnessed the events which he chronicled or from their families. The results of a defective memory need no elaboration. Similarly, it is said that Xenophon wrote much of his *Hellenica* as a memoir in later life. A confounding of sources, also, may introduce an unintentional falsification of history. Livy, for example, reports two pitched battles near Toletum in 193 and 192 in both of which Marcus Fulvius routed the Vettones and, in one account, other tribes. It seems probable that these accounts related to one and the same battle reported by two of Livy's sources under slightly different dates. Then there is the problem of corruption of manuscripts, which can readily occur when they are repeatedly copied through the centuries. It is suggested later in this work that *Saguntum* might have been corrupted to *Saguntia* in connexion with the Sertorian War. Other presumed instances of these sources of error at work are to be found in the text below.

A more or less subconscious bias on the part of the chronicler is another potent factor which influences perspective. It may be occasioned by patriotic feelings or for the writer's own ends. Livy was a great patriot and his desire to impress the reader with the greatness of Rome clearly shows up at times in his exaggeration of its deeds of glory. Caesar's *Gallic War* was a political document, designed to show the author himself up in a good light. Similarly, there may be a desire to please an emperor or other person who has commissioned a work or to whom it is dedicated. By the same token, a bias can operate just as easily in the other direction, resulting in the minimizing or total suppression of unfavourable events.

It is important to remember that the sources which are available to us today were sometimes compiled long after the events described. Our extant sources had their own earlier sources, to which the same considerations must have applied.

NUMBERS

Numbers present a special problem in the study of ancient warfare. In this work casualty figures or the size of armies are periodically quoted as 'alleged' numbers as a reminder of uncertainty, but in fact all numbers are open to question to a greater or lesser degree unless there is some sort of record which provides firm confirmation. The names of the 192 Athenians killed at Marathon were recorded tribe by tribe in stone. But this sort of evidence is hardly the rule.

Numbers are susceptible to all of the sources of error and distortion that influence the reliability of data in general and which have been discussed in the preceding section. In fact, they are considerably more susceptible. A chronicler who desires for any reason to impress the reader is most likely to inflate the enemy's numbers and losses and to minimize those of the 'home team'. It is easier to vary a number than a deed.

Many historians of Rome did not have access to any statistics or, in the earlier days, to any official records other than the *Fasti*, which listed the names of the magistrates and occurrence of triumphs and other functions. If it was difficult on this account for an author to assess the size of the Roman army, the problems associated with the strength of the enemy force were clearly much greater. To obtain an approximate estimate some authors resorted to deducing the size of an army from the number of units such as legions, assuming that these were reasonably consistent in size. Thus, Livy, Appian and Polybius tended to give figures for a Roman army in multiples of 5,000, which was frequently unjustified. The strength of a legion was a very variable statistic depending on circumstances.

Of all the symbols, numerals are the ones most likely to become corrupted during the copying of texts, and the effects are potentially the most damaging. One '0' more or less could change an entire scenario. Moreover, a corrupted numeral becomes just another numeral, giving no positive sign that corruption has occurred. It can only be ascertained by comparison with other copies of the text or perhaps other sources.

DATES

The system of dating which was ultimately adopted in ancient Greece for literary purposes was based on the Olympic year. The Olympic festival was first held in 776BC and thereafter in every fourth year. Thus the four years in the first Olympiad have been designated Ol.1.1 to Ol.1.4, followed by Ol.2.1 and so on. The Olympic year was adjusted to start on the Attic new year's day (not the date of the festival), which was determined by the moon and which varied from late June to early August. It is evident from this that any one Olympic year overlaps two of our modern years. Accordingly, it is necessary to define any Olympic year by two consecutive modern dates unless the season is also known, although the second figure is sometimes omitted for reasons of brevity. It follows that errors resulting from Greek chronological methodology are likely to be confined to one year in extent. In the ancient literature the name of the ruling archon in Athens is sometimes given to denote the Attic year. The names of the archons have been recorded almost without exception since the beginning of the fifth century.

The dating of Roman events in the early Republican era is subject to error from many sources. The chronological system was based largely on the *Fasti,* the listings of principal magistrates and consuls in particular. These have been the subject of much debate and dispute. In particular, there are certain years for which no magistrates have been recorded. To add to the confusion various authorities have dealt with these deficiencies in different ways. An example of the effect is the dubious date of the sack of Rome by the Gauls. On the system developed by Varro the date would be 390, but 387 seems to be as or more likely while other, more divergent, preferences have been thrown into the ring. The *Fasti consulares* appear to have been consistent since the beginning of the third century.

In Rome, events were dated from the foundation of the City (*ab urbe condita* or AUC), the date of which is itself unknown. Numerous estimates were advanced, mainly on the basis of sundry legendary happenings, until the date of 753BC became canonical. The earlier confusion undoubtedly contributed to chronological discrepancies.

For more detail on Roman chronology the reader is referred to the account by Reid.[2]

Principal Sources

Most of the works quoted below are readily available in text and English translation in the Loeb Classical Library. Many of them are also published in English in Penguin Classics. Details of recent translations are given for the few works which are not included in either of these series.

2 J.S. Reid, *Chronology*, in J.E. Sandys (ed.), *A Companion to Latin Studies*, 3rd edn, Cambridge University Press, 1943.

APPIAN (Appianos of Alexandria): Greek historian, *fl.* early second century AD. Wrote a Roman history.

ARRIAN (Lucius Flavius Arrianus): AD*c.*86 – *c.*170. Greek, born in Bithynia. Wrote *Anabasis of Alexander*.

CAESAR, Gaius Julius: 100–44BC. Dictator. Author of the *Gallic War* and the *Civil War*.

(CAESAR): Histories of the Alexandrian, African and Spanish Wars by unknown hands. Incorporated in Caesar's *Civil War* in Penguin edn.

CICERO, Marcus Tullius: Famous Roman orator. 106–43BC. Wrote numerous letters including those *ad familiares* (Letters to his Friends).

CURTIUS (Quintus Curtius Rufus): Roman historian, *fl.* probably first century AD. Wrote *History of Alexander*.

DIO CASSIUS (properly Cassius Dio): Born at Nicaea (Bithynia), *fl. c.*AD200. Wrote a *Roman History*.

DIODORUS (SICULUS) of Agyrium in Sicily: Greek historian of first century BC. Settled in Rome. Wrote *The Library of History*.

DIONYSIUS of Halicarnassus: Greek, born before 53BC. Lived in Rome from *c.*30BC. Wrote *Roman Antiquities*.

EUTROPIUS: Roman historian. Wrote his summary of Roman history AD*c.*380. Translated H.W. Bird, *Eutropius: Breviarium,* Marston Books (1993).

FLORUS, Lucius Annaeus: Roman historian, *fl.* AD*c.*140. Wrote an *Epitome of Roman History*.

FRONTINUS, Sextus Iulius: Roman consul. AD*c.*35–103. Wrote the *Stratagems* after AD84.

HELLENICA OXYRHYNCHIA: Literary papyri from Egypt. Written in middle of the fourth century BC. Texts and trans. P.R. Mckechnie and S.J. Kern, Aris & Phillips, Warminster (1988).

HERODOTUS: Greek historian, born at Halicarnassus. Lived *c.*484 – *c.*420BC. Wrote *The Histories (Persian Wars)*.

JOSEPHUS, Flavius: Jewish, became Roman citizen living in Rome. *Jewish Antiquities* published in AD 93/4. He also wrote *Jewish Wars*.

JUSTIN (Marcus Junianus Justinus): second or third century AD. Epitomized Pompeius Trogus (below). Trans. J. Yardley, Oxford University Press (1994).

LIVY (Titus Livius): Roman historian, born and died in Padua. Probably 59BC – AD17. Wrote a history of Rome in 142 books of which only 35 survive. The summaries ('epitomes' or *periochae*) of all but two books have survived.

MACCABEES: Apocryphal books in the Old Testament. Probably date from early first century BC.

NEPOS, Cornelius: Biographer from Cisalpine Gaul, *c.*110 – *c.*24BC. Lived in Rome. Wrote brief biographies of foreign generals.

OROSIUS, Paulus: *fl.* fifth century AD. Of Spanish origin, he wrote *Histories against the Pagans* in Africa. Trans. R.J. Deferrari, Catholic University of America Press, Washington, DC (1964).

PAUSANIAS: Greek from Asia Minor. Wrote his *Description of Greece* AD*c.*150–180.

PLUTARCH: Biographer, a native of Chaeronea in Greece. Lived before AD50 until after 120. Author of the *Parallel Lives*.

POLYAENUS: Macedonian rhetorician. Wrote the *Stratagems* probably late in AD161. Ed. and trans. P. Krentz and E.L. Wheeler; Ares, Chicago (1994).

POLYBIUS: Greek historian, born at Megalopolis in Arcadia. Lived *c.*200 – *c.*118BC. Much of his *Histories* has survived.

SALLUST (Gaius Sallustius Crispus): Roman historian. Probably 86–35BC. Author of *War with Catiline* and *War with Jugurtha*.

STEPHANUS of Byzantium: Greek. His *Ethnica* lost. An epitome compiled between the sixth and tenth centuries AD survives. Ed. A. Meineke, Graz (reprinted 1992). No English translation.

STRABO: Asiatic Greek geographer, born at Amasia (Pontus) *c.*64BC. Died AD*c.*25. Author of a *Geography* in 17 books.

THUCYDIDES: Athenian historian, *c.*460 – *c.*400BC. Participated in early part of the Peloponnesian War, which he chronicled in his *History of the Peloponnesian War*. This ends abruptly in the affairs of 411BC.

TROGUS, Pompeius: *Historiae Philippicae*, dated to Augustan era, are lost. Epitomized by Justin (above). Trogus' prologues survive and are included with Justin's epitome in trans. J. Yardley.

VELLEIUS PATERCULUS: Roman historian, born *c.*20BC. Wrote a summary of Roman history.

XENOPHON: Athenian, *c.*430 – *c.*355BC. His *Hellenica* begins as a continuation of Thucydides' unfinished narration. The larger second part was written much later. Also author of *Anabasis* ('the Persian expedition').

ZONARAS, Johannes: Byzantine historian in twelfth century AD. Excerpted early books of Dio Cassius (above). Text and trans. are included with Dio's *Roman History* (Loeb).

Glossary

ANABASIS: A 'going up' (expedition) into the country.

BIREME: Ship with two banks of oars.

CAETRATI: Targeteers, light troops who carried a small light shield (*caetra*).

CENTURY: The smallest Roman military unit, nominally of 100 men.

COHORT: Section of a Roman legion in the later Republic. The number of cohorts in a legion was invariably ten. Their complement varied with the strength of the legion.

COMPANIONS: Macedonian cavalry, traditionally under the king's personal leadership.

CONSUL: Chief civil and military magistrate, appointed annually. There were two consuls, each in command of his own consular army.

DEVOTION: Militarily, a religious act of self-sacrifice on the part of a Roman general, who 'devoted' himself and the enemy to the gods of the underworld.

DIADOCHI: Successors, specifically of Alexander the Great. The generals who partitioned Alexander's empire among themselves (and fought tooth and nail against each other).

DICTATOR: Supreme Roman commander appointed in time of emergency. He superseded both consuls.

FASTI CONSULARES: Listings of the consuls.

GREAVES: Armour to protect the legs from above the ankle up to and including the knee.

HASTA: Long thrusting spear.

HASTATI: Formed the front line of a Roman legion in armies of the third and second centuries. Originally armed with spears (*hastae*) but these were superseded by heavy javelins (*pila*). There were normally 1,200 *hastati* in a legion of 4,200 men.

HELOT: Spartan slave.

HOPLITE: Heavy-armed infantryman equipped with helmet, corslet, greaves and spear. He carried a round double-grip shield (*hoplon*, although usually *aspis*) which was his hallmark.

HYPASPISTS: 'Shield bearers', an élite Macedonian guard of infantry.

IMMORTALS: The Persian king's personal division of 10,000 chosen Persian troops.

LEGATE: Representative of the general, holding delegated authority but responsible to the general.

LEGION: Roman military unit, normally containing 4,200 men (third and second centuries), later increased to 6,000 although the figure was often considerably lower in practice.

MANIPLE: Roman tactical unit. There were three maniples in a cohort and two centuries per maniple.

MILITARY TRIBUNE: One of the six most senior officers in a Roman legion.

MORA: A unit of the Spartan army, probably at least 600 men, usually more.

PELTAST: Greek light-armed soldier, equipped with a small shield (*pelta*) and a throwing spear.

PENTECONTER: Ship with 50 oars in one bank.

PERIOIKOI: Literally, dwellers in the neighbourhood. Spartan *perioikoi* served in the army but could not take part in central politics.

PHALANX: Closely knit body of heavy-armed infantry.

PILUM: Heavy javelin designed to bend or break on impact.

POLEMARCH: In early Greece a leader of the generals of an army. Military command was transferred to the generals in or before 487/6 and the polemarch's functions became legal and administrative. The title also applied to the Spartan officer in charge of a *mora* (above).

PRAETOR: Chief magistrate of consular status with *imperium* (authority to command) but responsible to the consuls.

PRINCIPES: The chief troops who formed the second line of a Roman legion in the third and second centuries. There were normally 1,200 in a legion of 4,200 men.

PROCONSUL: Official of consular rank acting as consul. The title was sometimes used to prolong the appointment of a consul whose term of office had expired.

PROPRAETOR: Acting praetor.

QUADRIREME: Ship larger than a trireme, but

the number of banks of oars and the distribution of the rowers are unknown.

SACRED BAND: Élite corps of Theban infantry comprising pairs of lovers.

SARISSA: Thrusting lance of unusual length used by Macedonian phalangites.

SATRAP: Governor of a Persian province.

SCUTUM: Oval or oblong shield, curved like the section of a cylinder and covering the whole length of the bearer.

SILVER SHIELDS: 'Argyraspids'. Hypaspists (above) renamed when their shields were decorated with silver plates in 327BC.

SPOLIA OPIMA: Spoils offered by a Roman general after slaying an opposing leader in single combat.

TESTUDO: 'Tortoise' shell of overlapping shields held over their heads by a body of soldiers.

TRIARII: Veteran troops who formed the third, defensive, line in a Roman legion in armies of the third and second centuries. There were normally 600 per legion.

TRIREME: The standard Greek warship with three banks of oars.

TRIUMPH: Procession granted to a Roman general in recognition of a major victory.

TROPHY: Monument erected by a victor on the site of victory.

TYRANT: Originally meant just a ruler. The term came to signify one who had gained his power often by unconstitutional means although he was not necessarily oppressive.

VELITES: Roman light-armed troops equipped with javelins, who acted as skirmishers. Usually 1,200 in a legion of 4,200 men.

PART TWO

THE GREEK WORLD

Chronological Table of Battles of The Greek World

BC	PLACE[1]	WAR OR EPISODE	VICTORS[2]	VANQUISHED[2]
724c.	Ithome	First Messenian War	Aristodemus (Messenians)	Theopompos (Spartans)
685c.	Derae	Second Messenian War	Aristomenes (Messenians) =	Spartans =
684c.	Boar's Barrow	Second Messenian War	Aristomenes (Messenians)	Anaxander (Spartans)
682c.	Great Foss	Second Messenian War	Spartans	Aristomenes (Messenians)
669c.	Hysiae	Argive–Spartan Feud	Argives	Spartans
546	Pallene	Restoration of Tyrant	Pisistratus	Athenians
545	Thyreatis	Argive–Spartan Feud	Spartans	Argives
540c.	Alalia, off	Etruscan Expansion	Carthaginians and Etruscans	Phocaeans (Corsica)
524	Cumae	Etruscan Expansion	Aristodemus the Effeminate (Cumaeans and Aricians)	Etruscans
511	Traeis R	War of Sybaris	Milo (Crotoniates)	Sybarites
506	Aricia	Etruscan Expansion	Aristodemus the Effeminate	Etruscans
498c.	Pamphylia, off	Ionian Revolt	Athenians and Ionians	Persians
498c.	Ephesus	Ionian Revolt	Persians	Athenians and Ionians
497c.	Salamis (Cyprus)	Ionian Revolt	Artybius (Persians)	Onesilus (Cypriots and Ionians)
497c.	Keys of Cyprus	Ionian Revolt	Ionians	Phoenicians
497c.	Marsyas R	Ionian Revolt	Persians	Carians
496	Labranda	Ionian Revolt	Persians	Carians and Milesians
496	Pedasus	Ionian Revolt	Carians	Persians
494	Lade Isl, off	Ionian Revolt	Persians	Dionysius (Ionians)
494c.	Sepeia	Argive–Spartan Feud	Cleomenes I (Spartans)	Argives
493	Malene	Ionian Revolt	Harpagus (Persians)	Histiaeus (Ionians and Aeolians)
492c.	Helorus R	Sicily: Internal Wars	Hippocrates of Gela	Syracusans
490	Marathon	Persian War	Miltiades and Callimachus (Athenians, Plataeans)	Datis and Artaphernes (Persians)
480	Thermopylae P	Persian War	Leonidas (Spartans)	Xerxes (Persians)
480	Artemisium, off	Persian War	Themistocles (Athenians) =	Persians =
480	Salamis Isl	Persian War	Eurybiades (Greeks) and Themistocles (Athenians)	Xerxes (Persians)
480	Himera	Sicily: First Punic Invasion	Gelon and Theron	Hamilcar (Carthaginians)
479	Plataea	Persian War	Pausanias (Greeks)	Mardonius (Persians)
479	Mycale	Persian War	Leotychides (Greeks)	Tigranes (Persians)

[1] *Abbreviations:* C – Cape; Isl(s) – Island(s); L – Lake; M(s) – Mountain(s); P – Pass; Pr – Promontory; R – River.

[2] Equal symbols (=) after victor and vanquished denote an indecisive outcome.

BC	PLACE[1]	WAR OR EPISODE	VICTORS[2]	VANQUISHED[2]
476	Eion	Persian War	Cimon (Delian League)	Boges (Persians)
474	Cumae	Etruscan Expansion	Hieron of Syracuse	Etruscans
473c.	Tegea	Spartan Aggression	Spartans	Argives and Tegeates
472	Acragas	Sicily: Internal Wars	Hieron of Syracuse	Thrasydeus (Acragantini)
471c.	Dipaea	Spartan Aggression	Spartans	Arcadian League and Tegea
468c.	Eurymedon R	Persian War	Cimon (Delian League)	Persians
468c.	Syedra	Persian War	Cimon (Delian League)	Phoenicians
459	Papremis	Egyptian Revolt	Inaros (Egyptians and ?Athenians)	Achaemenes (Persians)
459	Halieis	'First Peloponnesian War'	Corinthians and Epidaurians	Athenians
459	Cecryphalea, off	'First Peloponnesian War'	Athenians	Peloponnesians
459	Aegina, off	'First Peloponnesian War'	Leocrates (Athenians)	Aeginetans
458	Megara	'First Peloponnesian War'	Myronides (Athenians)	Corinthians
457	Tanagra	'First Peloponnesian War'	Nicomedes (Spartan)	Athenians
457	Oenophyta	'First Peloponnesian War'	Myronides (Athenians)	Boeotians
453	Sicyon	'First Peloponnesian War'	Tolmides (Athenians)	Sicyonians
451	Motyum	Sicily: Internal Wars	Ducetius (Sicels)	Acragantini and Syracusans
451	Nomae	Sicily: Internal Wars	Syracusans	Ducetius (Sicels)
449	Salamis (Cyprus)	Resumption of Persian War	Cimon (Athenians)	Artabazus and Megabyzus (Phoenicians and Cilicians)
447	Coronea	'First Peloponnesian War'	Boeotians	Tolmides (Athenians)
446	Himera R	Sicily: Internal Wars	Syracusans	Acragantini
440	Tragia Isl, off	Samian Revolt	Pericles (Athenians)	Samians
439	Samos Isl, off	Samian Revolt	Melissus (Samians)	Athenians
435	Leucimme Pr, off	Corcyraean War	Corcyreans	Corinthians
433	Sybota Isls, off	Corcyraean War	Xenoclides (Corinthians)	Corcyraeans
432	Potidaea	Revolt of Potidaea	Callias (Athenians)	Aristeus (Corinthians)
429	Spartolus	Peloponnesian War	Chalcidians	Xenophon (Athenians)
429	Stratus	Peloponnesian War	Stratians (Acarnanians)	Cnemus (Spartans)
429	Chalcis, off	Peloponnesian War	Phormio (Athenians)	Corinthians et al.
429	Naupactus, off	Peloponnesian War	Phormio (Athenians)	Cnemus (Peloponnesians)
428	Mytilene	Peloponnesian War	Mytilenians	Cleippides (Athenians)
427	Corcyra Isl, off	Peloponnesian War	Alcidas (Peloponnesians)	Corcyraeans and Athenians
426	Tanagra	Peloponnesian War	Hipponicus, Eurymedon (Athenians)	Boeotians
426	Aegitium	Peloponnesian War	Aetolians	Demosthenes (Athenians)
426	Mylae	Peloponnesian War	Laches (Athenians)	Messanians
426	Inessa	Peloponnesian War	Syracusans	Athenians
426	Olpae	Peloponnesian War	Demosthenes (Acarnanians)	Eurylochus (Peloponnesians)
426	Idomene	Peloponnesian War	Demosthenes (Acarnanians)	Ambraciots

BC	PLACE[1]	WAR OR EPISODE	VICTORS[2]	VANQUISHED[2]
425	*Straits of Messina*	Peloponnesian War	Athenians and Rhegians	Syracusans
425	Naxos	Sicily: Internal Wars	Naxians and Sicels	Messanians
425	Messana	Peloponnesian War	Messanians	Leontinians and Athenians
425	Pylos	Peloponnesian War	Demosthenes (Athenians)	Thrasymelidas and Brasidas (Spartans)
425	Sphacteria Isl	Peloponnesian War	Cleon and Demosthenes (Athenians)	Epitadas (Spartans)
425	Solygia	Peloponnesian War	Nicias (Athenians)	Lycophron (Corinthians)
424	Cythera Isl	Peloponnesian War	Nicias (Athenians)	Cytherans
424	Delium	Peloponnesian War	Pagondas (Boeotians)	Hippocrates (Athenians)
423	Scione	Peloponnesian War	Nicias and Nicostratus (Athenians)	Peloponnesians and Scionians
423	Laodocium	Local Dispute	Tegeates =	Mantineans =
422	Amphipolis	Peloponnesian War	Brasidas (Spartans)	Cleon (Athenians)
418	Mantinea	Peloponnesian War	Agis II (Spartans *et al.*)	Argives
415	Syracuse: Olympieium	Peloponnesian War	Nicias (Athenians *et al.*)	Syracusans
414	Syracuse: Epipolae	Peloponnesian War	Athenians	Diomilus (Syracusans)
414	Syracuse: Syce	Peloponnesian War	Athenians	Syracusans
414	Syracuse: Lysimeleia	Peloponnesian War	Lamachus (Athenians)	Syracusans
414	Syracuse: Epipolae	Peloponnesian War	Gylippus (Syracusans)	Nicias (Athenians)
413	Syracuse: Plemmyrium	Peloponnesian War	Athenians =	Gylippus (Syracusans) =
413	Erineus, off	Peloponnesian War	Diphilus (Athenians) =	Polyanthes (Corinthians) =
413	Syracuse: Harbour	Peloponnesian War	Syracusans	Athenians
413	Syracuse: Epipolae	Peloponnesian War	Gylippus (Syracusans *et al.*)	Demosthenes (Athenians)
413	Syracuse: Harbour	Peloponnesian War	Gylippus (Syracusans *et al.*)	Eurymedon (Athenians *et al.*)
413	Syracuse: Harbour	Peloponnesian War	Gylippus, Pythen (Syracusans)	Demosthenes and Nicias (Athenians)
412	Spiraeum	Peloponnesian War	Athenians	Alcamenes (Peloponnesians)
412	Cardamyle	Peloponnesian War	Leon, Diomedon	Chians
412	Bolissus	Peloponnesian War	Leon, Diomedon	Chians
412	Phanae Pr, off	Peloponnesian War	Athenians	Chians
412	Leuconium	Peloponnesian War	Athenians	Chians
412	Miletus	Peloponnesian War	Athenians *et al.*	Milesians *et al.*
411	Syme Isl, off	Peloponnesian War	Astyochus (Spartans)	Charminus (Athenians)
411	Rhodes	Peloponnesian War	Leon, Diomedon (Athenians)	Rhodians
411	Chios Isl, off	Peloponnesian War	Leon (Spartans)	Athenians
411	Lampsacus	Peloponnesian War	Strombichides (Athenians)	Lampsaceni
411	Eretria, off	Peloponnesian War	Agesandridas (Lacedaemonians)	Thymochares (Athenians)
411	Cynossema Pr, off	Peloponnesian War	Thrasybulus and Thrasyllus (Athenians)	Mindarus (Peloponnesians)
411	Abydus, off	Peloponnesian War	Athenians	Mindarus (Peloponnesians)
410	Cyzicus, off	Peloponnesian War	Alcibiades *et al.* (Athenians)	Mindarus (Peloponnesians)
409	Ephesus	Peloponnesian War	Ephesians	Thrasyllus (Athenians)

BC	PLACE[1]	WAR OR EPISODE	VICTORS[2]	VANQUISHED[2]
409	Cerata Ms	Peloponnesian War	Leotrophides and Timarchus (Athenians)	Megarians
409	Himera	Sicily: Second Punic Invasion	Hannibal (Carthaginians)	Himeraeans *et al.*
409	Motye	Sicily: War of Hermocrates	Hermocrates (Himeraeans *et al.*)	Motyeans
409	Panormus	Sicily: War of Hermocrates	Hermocrates (Himeraeans *et al.*)	Panormians
408	Chalcedon	Peloponnesian War	Theramenes, Alcibiades and Thrasyllus (Athenians)	Hippocrates (Spartans)
408	Byzantium	Peloponnesian War	Alcibiades (Athenians)	Peloponnesians *et al.*
407	Gaurium	Peloponnesian War	Alcibiades (Athenians)	Andrians and Peloponnesians
406	Notium, off	Peloponnesian War	Lysander (Spartans)	Antiochus (Athenians)
406	Mytilene, off	Peloponnesian War	Callicratidas (Spartans)	Conon (Athenians)
406	Arginusae Isls, off	Peloponnesian War	Thrasyllus (Athenians)	Callicratidas (Spartans)
406	Eryx, off	Sicily: Third Punic Invasion	Syracusans	Hannibal (Carthaginians)
406	Acragas	Sicily: Third Punic Invasion	Daphnaeus (Syracusans)	Himilco (Carthaginians)
405	Aegospotami R, off	Peloponnesian War	Lysander (Lacedaemonians)	Conon (Athenians)
404	Syracuse: Neapolis	Revolt against Dionysius	Dionysius I (Campanians *et al.*)	Syracusans
403	Acharnae	Athenian Civil War	Thrasybulus (Athenians)	Thirty Tyrants of Athens
403	Munychia	Athenian Civil War	Thrasybulus (Athenians)	Thirty Tyrants of Athens
401	Cunaxa	Rebellion of Cyrus	Artaxerxes (Persians)	Cyrus (Athenians *et al.*)
397	Catana, off	Sicily: First Punic War	Magon (Carthaginians)	Leptines (Sicilian Greeks)
397	Syracuse, off	Sicily: First Punic War	Syracusans	Carthaginians
397	Syracuse	Sicily: First Punic War	Dionysius I (Syracusans)	Himilco (Carthaginians)
396	Dascylium	Campaign of Agesilaus	Agesilaus (Spartans)	Tissaphernes (Persians)
395	Sardes	Campaign of Agesilaus	Agesilaus (Spartans)	Tissaphernes (Persians)
395	Dascylium	Campaign of Agesilaus	Pharnabazus (Persians)	Agesilaus (Spartans)
395	Caue	Campaign of Agesilaus	Herippidas (Spartans)	Pharnabazus (Persians)
395	Haliartus	'Boeotian War'	Thebans	Lysander (Spartans)
395	Naryx	Corinthian War	Ismenias (Boeotians)	Alcisthenes (Phocians)
394	Nemea R	Corinthian War	Spartans *et al.*	Corinthian Confederates
394	Narthacium M	Campaign of Agesilaus	Agesilaus (Spartans)	Polycharmus (Pharsalians)
394	Cnidus, off	Spartan–Persian War	Conon and Pharnabazus (Persians)	Pisander (Spartans)
394	Coronea	Corinthian War	Agesilaus (Spartans *et al.*) =	Corinthian Confederates =
392	Abacaene	Sicily: Second Punic War	Dionysius I (Syracusans)	Mago (Carthaginians)
392	Corinth: Long Walls	Corinthian War	Praxitas (Spartans)	Iphicrates (mercenaries)
392	Phlius	Corinthian War	Iphicrates (mercenaries)	Phliasians
392	Sicyon	Corinthian War	Iphicrates (mercenaries)	Sicyonians
391	Rhegium, off	Sicilian Invasion of Italy	Italiots	Dionysius I (Syracusans)
390	Laüs	Lucanian Expansion	Lucanians	Thurians

BC	PLACE[1]	WAR OR EPISODE	VICTORS[2]	VANQUISHED[2]
390	Lechaeum	Corinthian War	Iphicrates (mercenaries)	Spartans
389	Methymna	Revolt of Lesbos	Thrasybulus (Athenians *et al.*)	Therimachus (Spartans *et al.*)
389	Elleporus R	Second Sicilian Invasion of Italy	Dionysius I (Syracusans)	Heloris (Italiots)
388	Cremaste	Command of Hellespont	Iphicrates (mercenaries)	Anaxibius (Spartans)
382	Olynthus	Olynthus Campaign	Teleutias (Spartans and Macedonians) =	Olynthians =
381	Olynthus	Olynthus Campaign	Olynthians	Teleutias (Spartans)
381	Citium, off	Revolt of Evagoras	Glos (Persians)	Evagoras of Cyprus
379	Cabala	Sicily: Third Punic War	Dionysius I (Sicilian Greeks)	Mago (Carthaginians)
379	Cronium	Sicily: Third Punic War	Carthaginians	Dionysius I (Sicilian Greeks)
376	Naxos Isl, off	Athenian–Spartan Naval War	Chabrias (Athenians)	Pollis (Spartans)
375	Alyzia, off	Athenian–Spartan Naval War	Timotheus (Athenians)	Nicolochus (Spartans)
375	Tegyra	Era of Theban Hegemony (precursor)	Pelopidas (Thebans)	Gorgoleon and Theopompus (Spartans)
371	Leuctra	Era of Theban Hegemony	Epaminondas (Thebans *et al.*)	Cleombrotus (Spartans *et al.*)
370	Orchomenus (Arcadia)	Arcadian League Feud	Lycomedes (Mantineans)	Polytropus (Spartans)
369	Corinth	Era of Theban Hegemony	Chabrias (Athenians *et al.*)	Epaminondas (Thebans *et al.*)
368	Melea ('Tearless Battle')		Archidamus (Spartans)	Arcadians, Argives
368	Drepanum	Sicily: Fourth Punic War	Carthaginians	Dionysius I
365	Lasion	Elean–Arcadian War	Arcadians	Eleans
365	Cromnus	Elean–Arcadian War	Arcadians	Archidamus (Spartans)
364	Olympia (the Altis)	Elean–Arcadian War	Pisadatans, Arcadians and Argives	Eleans and Achaeans
364	Cynoscephalae Ms	Era of Theban Hegemony	Pelopidas (Thebans and Thessalians)	Alexander of Pherae
362	Mantinea	Era of Theban Hegemony	Epaminondas (Thebans *et al.*)	Spartans and Mantineans
361	Peparethos Isl	Piratical Raid	Alexander of Pherae	Leosthenes (Athenians)
359	Methone	Rise of Macedon	Philip II (Macedonians)	Argaeus (Athenians)
358	Heraclea Lyncestis	Rise of Macedon	Philip II (Macedonians)	Bardylis (Illyrians)
357	Syracuse	Dion's Campaign	Dion	Dionysius II
357	Chios Isl	Social War	Chians *et al.*	Chares and Chabrias (Athenians)
356	Embata, off	Social War	Chians *et al.*	Chares (Athenians)
356	Delphi	Third Sacred War	Philomelus (Phocians *et al.*)	Locrians
354	Neon	Third Sacred War	Thebans	Philomelus (Phocians)
353	The Hermeum	Third Sacred War	Onomarchus (Phocians)	Boeotians
352	Crocian Plain	Third Sacred War	Philip II (Macedonians)	Onomarchus (Phocians)
352	Orchomenus (Boeotia)	Third Sacred War	Boeotians	Phayllus (Phocians)

43

BC	PLACE[1]	WAR OR EPISODE	VICTORS[2]	VANQUISHED[2]
352	Cephisus R	Third Sacred War	Boeotians	Phayllus (Phocians)
352	Coronea	Third Sacred War	Boeotians	Phayllus (Phocians)
352	Abae	Third Sacred War	Boeotians	Phayllus (Phocians)
352	Naryx	Third Sacred War	Phayllus (Phocians)	Boeotians
352	Chaeronea	Third Sacred War	Boeotians	Phalaecus (Phocians)
352	Orneae	Dispute over Megalopolis	Archidamus (Spartans *et al.*) =	Argives, Thebans =
352	Thelpusa	Dispute over Megalopolis	Thebans *et al.*	Anaxander (Spartans and Phocians)
348	Olynthus	Rise of Macedon	Philip II (Macedonians)	Olynthians
348	Tamynae	Revolt of Euboea	Phocion (Athenians)	Euboeans
347	Hyampolis	Third Sacred War	Boeotians	Phocians
347	Coronea	Third Sacred War	Phocians	Boeotians
344	Hadranum	Timoleon's Campaign	Timoleon	Hicetas of Leontini
339	Crimisus R	Timoleon's Campaign	Timoleon	Hasdrubal and Hamilcar (Carthaginians)
338	Damurias R	Timoleon's Campaign	Timoleon	Hicetas of Leontini
338	Abolus R	Timoleon's Campaign	Timoleon	Mamercus of Catana
338	Chaeronea	Rise of Macedon	Philip II of Macedon	Chares (Athenians), Theagenes (Thebans)
335	*Shipka Pass*	Alexander's First Campaign	Alexander the Great	Thracians
335	Lyginus R	Alexander's First Campaign	Alexander the Great	Triballi
335	Ister R	Alexander's First Campaign	Alexander the Great	Getae
335	Pelium	Alexander's First Campaign	Alexander the Great	Cleitus (Illyrians), Glaucias (Taulantians)
335	Thebes	Alexander's First Campaign	Alexander the Great	Thebans
334	Granicus R	Alexander's Anabasis	Alexander the Great	Arsites *et al.* (Persians)
333	Issus	Alexander's Anabasis	Alexander the Great	Darius III (Persians)
331	Megalopolis	Greek Revolt	Antipater (Macedonians)	Agis III (Spartans)
331	Gaugamela	Alexander's Anabasis	Alexander the Great	Darius III (Persians)
330	Susian Gates	Alexander's Anabasis	Alexander the Great	Ariobarzanes (Persians)
328	Jaxartes R	Alexander's Anabasis	Alexander the Great	Scythians
328	Alexandria Eschate	Alexander's Anabasis	Alexander the Great	Scythians
326	Hydaspes R	Alexander's Anabasis	Alexander the Great	Porus (Indians)

HELLENISTIC ERA

BC	PLACE[1]	WAR OR EPISODE	VICTORS[2]	VANQUISHED[2]
323	Plataea	Lamian War	Leosthenes (Greeks)	Boeotians
323	Thermopylae P	Lamian War	Leosthenes (Greeks)	Antipater (Macedonians)
322	Lamia	Lamian War	Antiphilus (Greeks)	Leonnatus (Macedonians)
322	Rhamnus	Lamian War	Phocion (Athenians)	Micion (Macedonians)
322	Abydus, off	Lamian War	Cleitus (Macedonians)	Evetion (Athenians)
322	Lichades Isls, off	Lamian War	Cleitus (Macedonians)	Athenians
322	Amorgos Isl, off	Lamian War	Cleitus (Macedonians)	Evetion (Athenians)
322	Crannon	Lamian War	Craterus and Antipater (Macedonians)	Greeks
321	Hellespont	Wars of the Diadochi	Eumenes of Cardia	Craterus and Neoptolemus
319	Cretopolis	Wars of the Diadochi	Antigonus I	Alcetas
318	Bosphorus: I	Wars of the Diadochi	Cleitus	Nicanor

BC	PLACE[1]	WAR OR EPISODE	VICTORS[2]	VANQUISHED[2]
318	Bosphorus: II	Wars of the Diadochi	Antigonus I and Nicanor	Cleitus
317	Coprates R	Wars of the Diadochi	Eumenes of Cardia	Antigonus I
317	Paraetacene	Wars of the Diadochi	Eumenes of Cardia =	Antigonus I =
316	Gabene	Wars of the Diadochi	Antigonus I	Eumenes of Cardia
315	Aphrodisias	Wars of the Diadochi	Polycleitus	Theodotus and Perilaus
314	Caprima	Wars of the Diadochi	Ptolomaeus	Eupolemus
312	Gaza	Wars of the Diadochi	Ptolemy I and Seleucus I	Demetrius 'Poliorcetes'
312	Eurymenae	Wars of the Diadochi	Lyciscus and Deinias	Alexander and Teucer
312	Apollonia (Illyria)	Wars of the Diadochi	Apollonians	Cassander
312	Galeria	Syracuse: Civil Strife	Pasiphilus and Demophilus	Deinocrates
311	Ecnomus M	Punic War of Agathocles	Hamilcar Gisgo (Carthaginians)	Agathocles
310	Tunes	Punic War of Agathocles	Agathocles	Hanno and Bomilcar (Carthaginians)
309	Syracuse: Euryelus	Punic War of Agathocles	Syracusans	Hamilcar (Carthaginians)
309	Tunes	Punic War of Agathocles	Agathocles	Carthaginians
307	Syracuse, off	Punic War of Agathocles	Agathocles	Carthaginians
307	Acragas	Sicily: Internal Wars	Leptines	Xenodocus (Acragantini)
306	Salamis (Cyprus)	Wars of the Diadochi	Demetrius I 'Poliorcetes'	Menelaus
306	Salamis (Cyprus), off	Wars of the Diadochi	Demetrius I 'Poliorcetes'	Ptolemy I (Egyptians)
305	Elatea	Wars of the Diadochi	Olympiodorus (Aetolians)	Cassander (Macedonians)
305	Torgium	Syracuse: Civil Strife	Agathocles	Deinocrates
301	Ipsus	Wars of the Diadochi	Seleucus I Nicator	Antigonus I and Demetrius I
294	Mantinea	Wars of the Diadochi	Demetrius I 'Poliorcetes'	Archidamus (Spartans)
294	Sparta	Wars of the Diadochi	Demetrius I 'Poliorcetes'	Spartans
286	Edessa	Wars of the Diadochi	Lysimachus	Pyrrhus
281	Corupedium	Wars of the Diadochi	Seleucus	Lysimachus
280c.	Hyblaeus R	Sicily: Internal Wars	Hicetas (Syracusans)	Phintias (Acragantini)
280	Terias R		Carthaginians	Hicetas (Syracusans)
279	Thermopylae P	Celtic Invasion	Greeks	Brennus (Gauls)
279	Delphi	Celtic Invasion	Greeks	Brennus (Gauls)
277	Lysimacheia	Celtic Invasion	Antigonus Gonatas (Macedonians)	Cerethrius (Gauls)
272	Sparta		Spartans	Pyrrhus
272	Argos		Antigonus Gonatas and Argives	Pyrrhus
265	Isthmus	Chremonidean War	Antigonus Gonatas (Macedonians)	Areus (Spartans)
263	Megalopolis	Local Feud	Aristodemus (Megalopolitans)	Acrotatus (Spartans)
262	Sardes		Eumenes I of Pergamum	Antiochus I Soter
246	Andros Isl, off	Third Syrian War	Antigonus Gonatas	Sophron (Egyptians)
246c.	Ephesus, off	Third Syrian War	Agathostratus (Rhodians)	Chremonides (Egyptians)
246c.	Cos Isl, off	Third Syrian War	Antigonus Gonatas	Egyptians
236	Ancyra	'War of the Brothers'	Seleucus II	Antiochus Hierax and Galatians
235	Chares R	Wars of Achaean League	Aristippus (Argives)	Aratus
235	Cleonae	Wars of Achaean League	Aratus	Aristippus

BC	PLACE[1]	WAR OR EPISODE	VICTORS[2]	VANQUISHED[2]
233	Phylacia	'War of Demetrius'	Bithys	Aratus
231	Medeon	'War of Demetrius'	Agron (Illyrians)	Aetolians
230	Phoenice	Illyrian Raids	Teuta (Illyrians)	Epirots
230	Caicus R	Galatian Invasion	Attalus I of Pergamum	Tolistoagian Galatians
230	Pergamum	Galatian Invasion	Attalus I of Pergamum	Antiochus Hierax and Galatians
229c.	Hellespont	War against Hierax	Attalus I of Pergamum	Antiochus Hierax
229c.	Coloe L	War against Hierax	Attalus I of Pergamum	Antiochus Hierax
229c	Harpasus R	War against Hierax	Attalus I of Pergamum	Antiochus Hierax
229	Paxoi Isls	Illyrian Raids	Teuta (Illyrians)	Achaeans, Aetolians
227	Lycaeus M	Cleomenean War	Cleomenes III (Spartans)	Aratus (Achaeans)
227	Ladoceia	Cleomenean War	Cleomenes III (Spartans)	Aratus (Achaeans)
227	Orchomenus (Arcadia)	Cleomenean War	Aratus (Achaeans)	Megistonous
225	Dyme	Cleomenean War	Cleomenes III (Spartans)	Aratus (Achaeans)
222	Sellasia	Cleomenean War	Antigonus Doson	Cleomenes III (Spartans)
220	Apollonia (Babylonia)	Molon's Revolt	Antiochus III	Molon
220	Caphyae	Wars of Achaean League	Dorimachus (Aetolians)	Aratus (Achaeans)
219	Pharos Isl	Second Illyrian War	L. Aemilius Paulus	Demetrius of Pharos
218	Arisba	Gallic Uprising	Prusias (Bithynians)	Gauls
217	Raphia	Fourth Syrian War	Ptolemy IV Philopator	Antiochus III
209	Larissus R	Wars of Achaean League	Philopoemen (Achaeans)	Aetolians and Eleans
209	Labus M	Anabasis of Antiochus	Antiochus III	Arsaces
208	Arius R	Anabasis of Antiochus	Antiochus III	Euthydemus (Bactrians)
208	Lamia	Wars of Achaean League	Philip V (Macedon)	Pyrrhias (Aetolians)
207	Mantinea	Wars of Achaean League	Philopoemen (Achaeans)	Machanidas (Spartans)
201	Scotitas	Wars of Achaean League	Philopoemen (Achaeans)	Spartans
201	Chios Isl, off		Attalus I (Pergamum) and Rhodians	Philip V (Macedonians)
200	Panium	Fifth Syrian War	Antiochus III	Scopas (Egyptians)
200	Athacus	Second Macedonian War	P. Sulpicius Galba Maximus	Philip V (Macedonians)
200	Ottolobum	Second Macedonian War	P. Sulpicius Galba Maximus	Philip V (Macedonians)
198	Aous R	Second Macedonian War	T. Quinctius Flamininus	Philip V (Macedonians)
197	Cynoscephalae Ms	Second Macedonian War	T. Quinctius Flamininus	Philip V (Macedonians)
197	Nemea R	Wars of Achaean League	Nicostratus (Achaeans)	Androsthenes (Macedonians)
197	Alabanda		Rhodians and Achaeans	Dinocrates (Macedonians)
195	Sparta	War against Nabis	T. Quinctius Flamininus	Nabis (Spartans)
192	Gytheum, off	War against Nabis	Nabis (Spartans)	Philopoemen (Achaeans)
192	Pleiae	War against Nabis	Philopoemen (Achaeans)	Nabis (Spartans)
192	Camp of Pyrrhus	War against Nabis	Philopoemen (Achaeans)	Nabis (Spartans)

BC	PLACE[1]	WAR OR EPISODE	VICTORS[2]	VANQUISHED[2]
191	Thermopylae P	War against Antiochus	M. Acilius Glabrio and M. Porcius Cato	Antiochus III
191	Corycus Pr	War against Antiochus	C. Livius Salinator and Eumenes II	Polyxenidas
190	Panormus	War against Antiochus	Polyxenidas	Pausistratus (Rhodians)
190	Phoenicus	War against Antiochus	C. Livius Salinator	Phoenicus
190	Pergamum	War against Antiochus	Diophanes (Achaeans)	Seleucus IV Philopator
190	Side, off	War against Antiochus	Eudamus (Rhodians)	Hannibal
190	Myonnesus Pr, off	War against Antiochus	L. Aemilius Regillus and Eudamus	Polyxenidas
190	Magnesia-ad-Sipylum	War against Antiochus	Cn. Domitius Ahenobarbus and Eumenes II	Antiochus III
189	Cuballum	Galatian Expedition	Cn. Manlius Volso	Galatians
189	Olympus M	Galatian Expedition	Cn. Manlius Volso	Galatians
189	Ancyra	Galatian Expedition	Cn. Manlius Volso	Galatians
189	Magaba M	Galatian Expedition	Cn. Manlius Volso	Galatians
188	Cypsela		Cn. Manlius Volso	Thracians
188	Tempyra		Cn. Manlius Volso	Thracians
182	Evander's Hill	Wars of Achaean League	Philopoemen (Achaeans)	Dinocrates (Messenians)
171	Callinicus	Third Macedonian War	Perseus (Macedonians)	P. Licinius Crassus
171	Phalanna	Third Macedonian War	L. Pompeius	Perseus (Macedonians)
170	Uscana	Third Macedonian War	Gentius (Illyrians)	Ap. Claudius Cento
168	Scodra	Third Macedonian War	L. Anicius Gallus	Gentius (Illyrians)
168	Elpeus R	Third Macedonian War	L. Aemilius Paulus	Perseus (Macedonians)
168	Pythium	Third Macedonian War	P. Cornelius Scipio Nasica Corculum	Milo (Macedonians)
168	Pydna	Third Macedonian War	L. Aemilius Paulus	Perseus (Macedonians)
167	Orthosia		Rhodians	Mylasa and Alabanda
166	Beth-Horon	Maccabean Revolt	Judas Maccabeus	Soron (Syrians)
166	Emmaus	Maccabean Revolt	Judas Maccabeus	Gorgias (Syrians)
165	Beth-Zur	Maccabean Revolt	Judas Maccabeus	Lysias (Syrians)
162	Bath-Zacharias	Maccabean Revolt	Lysias (Syrians)	Judas Maccabeus
161	Capharsalama	Maccabean Revolt	Judas Maccabeus	Nicanor (Syrians)
161	Adasa	Maccabean Revolt	Judas Maccabeus	Nicanor (Syrians)
160	Berea	Maccabean Revolt	Bacchides (Syrians)	Judas Maccabeus
148	Sparta	Achaean War	Damocritus (Achaeans)	Spartans
147	Azotus (Ashdod)	Maccabean Revolt	Jonathan and Simon Maccabeus	Apollonius (Syrians)
146	Alpheus R	Achaean War	Romans	Critolaus (Achaeans)
146	Scarphea	Achaean War	Q. Caecilius Metellus Macedonicus	Critolaus (Achaeans)
146	Chaeronea	Achaean War	Q. Caecilius Metellus Macedonicus	Arcadians
146	Isthmus	Achaean War	L. Mummius	Diaeus (Achaeans)
145	Oenoparas R		Ptolemy Philometor and Demetrius II	Alexander Balas

Battles of the Greek World

INTRODUCTION

Accounts of ancient military conflicts range in reality from fable to fact, although neither end of the scale may be met in pure form. Legends may have some historical basis; reported 'facts' may not be history. Both are subject to distortion from many sources, e.g. exaggeration, contamination, bias, and a failing memory. These influences have been discussed at greater length in the section, Reliability of Data (p. 32).

The recorded history of ancient Greece begins in earnest with *The Histories* of Herodotus, sometimes called 'the Father of History', who in the second half of the fifth century BC chronicled the Ionian Revolt and the Persian War of the first two decades. His chief sources of information were verbal accounts from people – and the families of people – who were alive at the time of the events which he recorded. Two centuries previously there had been struggles within the Peloponnese which had led to the First and Second Messenian Wars. The accounts of these events as told by Pausanias provide a few details of battles, with names of sites now largely unknown. Although these martial tales are almost certainly legendary or even fictitious, they may have some foundation in fact. The traditional Messenian heroes of the two wars, Aristodemus and Aristomenes, are both semi-legendary characters, but there is no conclusive reason to doubt that they were historical personalities. Their wars form the starting point for this compilation.

* * * * * * *

ITHOME (*c*.724)[1] – First Messenian War

In the early days of recorded Greek history the beginnings of Spartan growth loomed large. The first step was the conquest of the desirably fertile land of Messenia in two Messenian Wars. In the first of these, the Spartans under their king Theopompus failed to oust their opponents. After two indecisive battles in the fourth and fifth years of the war at sites unknown, in which both sides wore themselves out, the Messenians withdrew to their fortress on Mount Ithome, a hill town just north of Messene. It was six years later that the adversaries came to grips again in a pitched battle which, like its forerunners, was terminated by nightfall. After the Messenian king had been slain, the Messenians elected a distinguished citizen, Aristodemus, as their leader. He subsequently became a semilegendary hero. In the fifth year of his reign both combatants were exhausted by the war and agreed to settle matters in a pitched battle. This was waged at the foot of Mount Ithome and, under the leadership of Aristodemus, it was an overwhelming victory for the Messenians. Undeterred, the Spartans publicly 'exiled' a hundred of their people and sent them to Ithome as apparent fugitives to spy on the Messenians. But the wise and wily Aristodemus just sent them away, saying that Laconia invented new crimes but it used old tricks. Soon after this Aristodemus became depressed. Led by unfavourable omens to despair of final success, he killed himself. The Messenians were desperate. Ithome was in a state of perpetual siege and so, after 20 years of fighting, they decided to abandon the place, which was then destroyed by their enemies together with their other cities.

Pausanias, 4: 11; Tyrtaeus, fragment 5 in J.M. Edmonds (ed.), Greek Elegy and Iambus I, *Loeb*

DERAE (*c*.685) – Second Messenian War

Thirty-eight years after the fall of Ithome (above)[2] the Messenians revolted from Spartan oppression. This led to the Second Messenian War. In the first year of this war there was a minor confrontation at a place called Derae in Messenia (site unknown) in which the participants were unsupported by any allies. The outcome was indecisive, but a Messenian by the name of Aristomenes distinguished

---

[1] Bracketed figures in the subtitles are dates, all of which are BC.

[2] The word 'above' in brackets refers throughout to the immediately preceding entry.

himself to such an extent that his compatriots invited him to be their king. He refused the title but agreed to be their commander-in-chief. He became another almost legendary national hero, doing for Messenia in the second war what Aristodemus had done in the first.
Pausanias, 4: 15(4)

BOAR'S BARROW (*c*.684) – Second Messenian War

A year after the engagement at Derae there was a pitched battle between the Spartans and the Messenians with their respective allies at an unidentified site called the Boar's Grave or Boar's Barrow in Stenyclerus, the northern part of the Messenian plain. The Messenians under the indomitable Aristomenes broke the entire Spartan line and turned their retreat into a rout.
Pausanias, 4: 15(7)–16(4)

GREAT FOSS (*c*.682) – Second Messenian War

A year or so after the battle of Boar's Barrow the Spartans and the Messenians again fought it out, at an unidentified place called Great Foss or Great Trench in Messenia. It is said that the outcome of this battle was determined by trickery and treachery. The Spartans bribed Aristocrates, the king of the Arcadians, who were allies of the Messenians, with the result that Aristocrates withdrew his men just as the two sides were about to engage. This left a big hole in the Messenian line and the slaughter of many of their men was inevitable. After the battle Aristomenes gathered the survivors together and persuaded them to abandon their towns and to settle on Mount Eira. Here, they defended themselves for 11 years until their stronghold was eventually captured and destroyed. In this struggle a lame poet, Tyrtaeus, rose up to lead the Spartans and inspire his men with martial prowess and confidence as they marched to the tune of his ditties. Extant fragments of his poems provide some contemporary insight into the events of the Messenian Wars, but there is no mention of Aristomenes.
Pausanias, 4: 17(2–9)

HYSIAE (*c*.669) – Argive–Spartan Feud

The year 669 is the traditional date of a victory of Argos over Sparta at Hysiae, an Argolid city just south of modern *Akhladokambos*. This was the last in a series of Argive successes which had made her the leader among the Peloponnesian states. Within the next half century Sparta was to become the

leader, a position which she held for two centuries and more.
Pausanias, 2: 24(8–9)

PALLENE (546) – Restoration of Tyrant

In 561 Pisistratus seized power in Athens by a ruse and established a tyranny. After a few years the opposition parties united and drove him out. A year later friction developed within the coalition and Pisistratus was invited to return. Within a few years the coalition was renewed and Pisistratus was again driven out. This time he indulged in a large fund-raising campaign and used the proceeds to raise a mercenary army. In 546 he landed near Marathon and attacked his opponents at Pallene [*Pallini*], 11 miles east of Athens, while the Athenians were eating lunch or enjoying a postprandial siesta. After defeating them he advanced to the city and entered it unopposed. He was restored to power at Athens until his death.
Herodotus, 1: 62–64

THYREATIS (545, spring) – Argive–Spartan Feud

This unusual encounter is often called the Battle of the Champions. The Spartans were engaged in a quarrel with Argos over Thyreatis, the territory of Thyrea, which was about halfway between the rival cities. At that time it belonged to Argos but had been occupied by the Spartans. The Argives marched to recover their stolen land. When the two forces met, it was agreed in conference that 300 picked men from either side should fight it out. The contest was so close that by nightfall only three of the 600 survived, two Argives and one Spartan. The two Argives claimed the victory and hurried home, but the Spartan remained on the field and removed the equipment from the dead. The following day both parties claimed the victory: the Argives because they had the greatest number of survivors, the Spartans because their hero was the only survivor remaining on the battlefield. This argument led to blows and then to a full-scale battle between the two armies. After heavy losses on both sides the Spartans emerged victorious.
Herodotus, 1: 82

ALALIA (*c*.540) – Etruscan Expansion

In the early days of Greek history there were migratory movements eastwards across the Aegean to Asia Minor. One resulting settlement was Phocaea [*Foca*]. At a later date this maritime people expanded in the reverse direction, starting

new colonies as far away as Spain. One of these was Alalia [*Aleria*] on the east coast of Corsica, which presented a challenge to Carthage in what she regarded as her own Phoenician domain. The settlement had been in existence for only five years before the Carthaginians and their Etruscan allies launched a naval attack with a combined fleet of 120 ships. The Phocaeans sailed out to meet them with 60 ships. Herodotus describes the resulting debacle as a Cadmean (i.e. Pyrrhic) victory for the Phocaeans, a remarkable misrepresentation in view of his own report that 40 of their ships were sunk and the remaining 20 rendered unfit for service. In short, they were annihilated. The survivors collected their families and departed from Alalia.
Herodotus, 1: 166

CUMAE (524) – Etruscan Expansion
In the sixth century BC the Etruscans expanded their realm by conquest in all directions. At the beginning of the last quarter of the century they turned their attention to the prosperous Greek foundation of Cumae, a coastal town about 10 miles west of modern *Naples*, with its attendant fertile plain. With various barbarian tribes as allies, they tried to overthrow it. The attackers were a tumultuous horde, which has been put unrealistically at 500,000 foot and 18,000 horse, by comparison with which the 4,500 foot and 800 horse of the defenders were dwarfed. However, the place of battle was a narrow defile surrounded by mountains and lakes so that the barbarians' numbers, far from being an asset, were the cause of their destruction. Only the cavalrymen gave a good account of themselves, but they were unable to surround the Cumaeans in the confined space and eventually they fled. It was in this battle that Aristodemus, nicknamed the Effeminate, distinguished himself and came into the public eye, ultimately becoming the leader and champion of the people.
Dionysius of Halicarnassus, Roman Antiquities, 7: 3–4

TRAEIS R (511) – War of Sybaris
In the sixth century BC the Greek colony of Sybaris on the Gulf of Tarentum was a thriving and wealthy centre of commerce. Its name has since become synonymous with luxury and self-indulgence. When a man named Telys became the tyrant of Sybaris, he exiled a number of the wealthiest citizens, who took refuge in neighbouring Croton. Telys asked the Crotoniates to

expel them or else to expect war. The philosopher Pythagoras, who lived in Croton, advised his fellow citizens to grant asylum to the exiles and accept the hostilities. The Sybarites then advanced against Croton with an alleged 300,000 men and were opposed by an army of one third the strength under the command of an Olympic athlete called Milo. The numerical superiority of the Sybarites was more than offset by their affluent and unmilitary way of life. Fable has it that their cavalry were so accustomed to musical drill that they began to dance at the sound of the enemy's fifes. The Crotoniates, for their part, were in no mood to take prisoners. The end result was the slaughter of many of the Sybarites and the flight of the rest. After the battle the Crotoniates diverted the waters of the nearby river Crathis [*Crati*] over Sybaris so that not a vestige remained to mark the site. Tradition has it that this great battle was fought on the river Traeis [*Trionto*], one of many which flow into the Gulf of Tarentum [*Taranto*] along the 60-mile stretch of coast between the two warring cities.
Diodorus, 12: 9–10(1); Strabo, 6: 1, 13

ARICIA (506) – Etruscan Expansion
When the Etruscans besieged the Latin town of Aricia [*Ariccia*], 15 miles south-east of Rome, the Aricians appealed to Cumae for help. The governing aristocrats of Cumae hated their democratic opponent Aristodemus and thought that they saw a good opportunity of getting rid of him. They sent a small force of mercenaries to the aid of Aricia by sea in old ships and appointed Aristodemus as their general. One way or another he was likely to succumb! On arrival he persuaded the inhabitants of Aricia to emerge from their city and fight, and he then challenged the Etruscans to battle. The Aricians soon gave way and fled back behind their walls, but the Cumaeans remained firm. Aristodemus slew the enemy general with his own hand, subsequently gaining a glorious victory. On his return home he headed a coup, seizing power and executing all the governing aristocrats.
Dionysius of Halicarnassus, Roman Antiquities, 7: 5–6; Livy, 2: 14(5–9)

PAMPHYLIA (*c.*498) – Ionian Revolt
In 499BC the Greek colonies in Asia Minor were persuaded to revolt against their Persian masters. The instigator of the plot was Aristagoras, the tyrant of Miletus, who resigned his tyranny and persuaded other states to depose their pro-Persian

tyrants. He appealed for help to the Athenians, who responded with a squadron of 20 triremes. These duly arrived off the Asiatic coast, carrying a large force of hoplites. Plutarch has preserved a bare account of a subsequent naval engagement, in which the Ionians, reinforced with the Greek triremes, engaged the Persian fleet off Pamphylia and won the day.

Plutarch places this battle before the attack on Sardes (Ephesus, below) but it is now thought that his account may, in fact, be another version of the battle off the Keys of Cyprus (c.497), which took place after the attack on Sardes and the battle at Ephesus.
Plutarch, On the Malice of Herodotus, 24 (Moralia, 861b–d)

EPHESUS (c.498) – Ionian Revolt
At some stage (after the battle off Pamphylia if Plutarch's account is correct) the Greek and Ionian fleets were joined by five ships from Eretria in Euboea. Together they sailed to Ephesus whence they proceeded to march to Sardes and attack it. In the mêlée a building was set on fire and the flames spread rapidly through the dwellings of reed and thatch. On the arrival of Persian reinforcements the Ionians withdrew and marched off to rejoin their ships. The Persians caught up with them near the coast at Ephesus and inflicted a heavy defeat on them. Undeterred by this setback, the Ionians sailed to the Hellespont and gained control of Byzantium [*Istanbul*] and the surrounding towns. From there they launched a naval expedition, which won Caria over to their cause.
Herodotus, 5: 99–102

SALAMIS (CYPRUS) (c.497) ⎱ Ionian
KEYS OF CYPRUS (c.497) ⎰ Revolt
The news of the Ionian revolt stirred the Cyprian Greeks into action and they attacked the Phoenicians on the island. Onesilus, the Cyprian leader, sent urgent calls for help and the Ionians responded; so also, in opposite sense, did the Persians, who shipped a force across in a Phoenician fleet. There were battles on land and sea. On land, the Persians marched straight to Salamis [*Gazimağuza, formerly Famagusta*] on the east coast where they were met by the Cyprian army. But a considerable body of Greek troops serving with the Cyprians turned traitor, resulting in a resounding Persian victory. Many Cyprians were killed, including Onesilus.

Meanwhile the Phoenician fleet had sailed on round the headland known as the Keys of Cyprus (C. Cleides) [*C. Apostolos Andreas*] to engage the Ionians. On the sea, the Ionians fared much better, soundly defeating the Phoenician sailors. Unfortunately, in spite of this victory, by the beginning of 496 Cyprus was again in Persian hands.
Herodotus, 5: 110–113

MARSYAS R (497/6) – Ionian Revolt
When the Persians learnt that the Carians had thrown in their lot with the rebellious Ionians, they marched against Caria. The Carians got wind of this and massed at a place called White Pillars on the Marsyas [*Çine Çayi*], which was presumably close to the junction of that river with the Maeander [*Menderes*]. One of their leaders proposed that they should cross the Maeander and fight with the river in their rear, which would force them to remain at their posts and prevent them from fleeing. Instead, it was finally decided to make the Persians fight with the Maeander behind them on the grounds that if they fell back, they would be driven into the river. The Persians arrived, crossed the Maeander and encountered the Carians on the Marsyas. After a bitter struggle the Carians were eventually overwhelmed by weight of numbers. No fewer than 10,000 are said to have fallen by comparison with 2,000 Persians.
Herodotus, 5: 118–119

LABRA(U)NDA (496) – Ionian Revolt
The Carian survivors of the battle on the Marsyas (above) withdrew to the sanctuary of Zeus Stratios, a great grove of sacred plane trees near Labranda, and shut themselves up in it. While they were deliberating their next course of action, the Milesians and their allies came to offer help. The Persians attacked, and the ensuing battle resulted in a heavy defeat for the Carians and an even heavier one for the Milesians.
Herodotus, 5: 119–120

PEDASUS (496) – Ionian Revolt
After the battles at Labranda and the Marsyas river, a third encounter between the Carians and the Persians took place within the year. The Carians, learning of Persian plans to attack their towns, laid an ambush on the Pedasus road which ran from Labranda to Pedasus via Mylasa [*Milas*]. The Persians fell into the trap during a night march and were slaughtered. Three of their commanders were killed.
Herodotus, 5: 121

LADE ISL (494) – Ionian Revolt

In 494 the Persians assembled a fleet of 600 ships, notably Phoenician but with contingents from Cilicia, Cyprus and Egypt. They were intent on besieging Miletus, which they regarded as the centre of the revolt. The Ionians, for their part, decided to put all their resources into their navy. They assembled a fleet of 353 triremes from the various states and took up station near the small island of Lade, off Miletus on the Carian coast. The Ionian commander was a Phocaean, Dionysius by name, who inspired the men to work under him with great success. But he then proceeded to institute such a rigorous programme of training that the men refused to co-operate any longer. As a result, when the battle commenced, first the Samians and then the Lesbians took off and sailed for home, leaving the Persians to win the day. This defeat for the Ionians marked the twilight of their revolt. Nevertheless, their uprising had signally stretched the might of Persia, which they had gallantly withstood for six years.
Herodotus, 6: 7–15

SEPEIA (c.494) – Argive–Spartan Feud

This battle was the last in the long struggle for supremacy between Argos and her old rival Sparta, witnessed for example at Hysiae (669) and Thyreatis (545). It finally secured for Sparta the undisputed leadership of the Peloponnese. Cleomenes I of Sparta had been told by the Delphic oracle that he would take Argos. Inspired, he marched at the head of an army to the Argolid town of Sepeia near Tiryns, where the Argives took up a defensive position. Herodotus relates that another oracle had made the Argive generals apprehensive of treachery and trickery. To forestall any Spartan wiles, they adopted an unusual plan. They instructed their herald to listen to the orders issued by the Spartan herald and then to repeat them on the Argive side. Cleomenes soon realized what was happening. He instructed his men that when they heard the next call to breakfast, they were to pick up their arms and charge the enemy camp. Those of the Argives who were not killed while eating fled to a sacred wood nearby, which Cleomenes promptly fired with utter ruthlessness.
Herodotus, 6: 77–78

MALENE (493) – Ionian Revolt

Histiaeus, the tyrant of Miletus, gave up his job to do some services for the Persians. He was nevertheless suspected by his new masters and he

eventually fled and embraced the cause of the revolt. He collected a large force of Ionians and Aeolians and sailed the Aegean as a military adventurer. At Lesbos he ran short of supplies and crossed to the mainland to do some foraging in the Caicus valley [*Bakir Çayi*]. Unfortunately for him, the Persian general Harpagus was in the vicinity with a large force. Harpagus met Histiaeus as he came ashore and engaged him at Malene [near *Altinova*]. For a long while the two sides were well matched until the Persian cavalry arrived on the scene, totally upsetting the balance of forces. The Greeks fled and Histiaeus was captured and taken to Sardes, where he was impaled and decapitated.
Herodotus, 6: 28–29

HELORUS R (c.492) – Sicily: Internal Wars

Hippocrates, a tyrant of Gela in southern Sicily, had created an empire for himself by conquests in the island. He aimed to add Syracuse to his domain, to which end he attacked and defeated the Syracusans on the banks of the Helorus [*Tellaro*] about 20 miles from the city. But he was restrained by the intervention of Corinth and Corcyra from occupying the city.
Herodotus, 7: 154

MARATHON (490, September) – Persian War

In 490BC King Darius I of Persia launched a punitive expedition against Athens and Eretria (in Euboea) in reprisal for their part in the burning of Sardes a few years earlier (Ephesus, c.498). The expedition was under the joint command of Datis and Artaphernes. The fleet of 600 ships crossed the Aegean and sailed up the channel between Attica and Euboea to attack Eretria, where the inhabitants were overpowered and enslaved. The Persian force then crossed over the narrow waters to the Attic shore, where the plain of Marathon running down to the sea offered a perfect battleground for their troops and cavalry. (For some unstated reason the cavalry did not play a part in the battle.)

In Athens, the generals debated whether they should stay and defend their city or go out and face the enemy. It was the forcefulness and persistence of Miltiades which eventually persuaded them that they must fight. The Athenians hurried to the spot but, before leaving their city, they sent a champion runner called Pheidippides (Philippides) to Sparta to ask for help. He reached Sparta – a distance of about 140 miles from Athens – on the following day, only to find that the Spartans were engaged in a religious festival and could not leave until after the full moon. They arrived at Athens

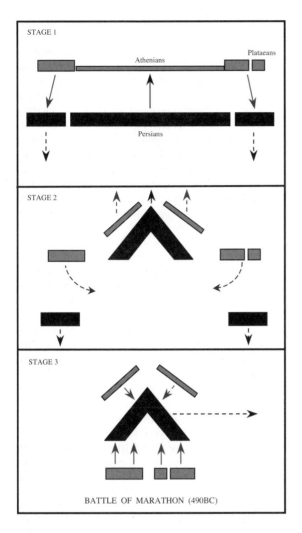

STAGE 1

Plataeans

Athenians

Persians

STAGE 2

STAGE 3

BATTLE OF MARATHON (490BC)

The Athenians were outnumbered, possibly by about two to one on modern estimates. To counter this disparity they extended their line to match the enemy's line by stretching and thinning their centre while keeping both wings at full strength. Callimachus was in command of the right wing, the traditional place of the polemarch; the Plataeans were on the extreme left of the line. At a given signal the whole line advanced at the double and engaged the enemy who, according to Herodotus, were not less than a mile away and who thought that the Greeks were quite mad to be charging like that without cavalry or archers in support. In the encounter the Persian centre got the better of the weak Greek centre and pushed it back. On both wings, however, the Greeks routed their opponents, who turned and fled, but the victors refrained from pursuing their more mobile, lightly clad enemy. Herodotus' Greek is unclear as to what happened next, signifying only that the Greek wings 'drew together'. Some authorities believe this to mean that they reformed and wheeled inwards to attack the enemy centre on the flanks; others hold that the two wings joined forces in the rear of the Persians (as shown in the battle plan). Whatever the manoeuvre, their attack was decisive. After a prolonged struggle the Persian survivors fled to their ships and were pursued and harassed as they tried to board. Seven of the ships were seized by the Greeks. After sailing away the Persians set course round the coast to Athens, hoping to find an undefended city. But the Athenians, in anticipation, moved swiftly and arrived there first. The Persians made no attempt to disembark but sailed away back to Asia.

Herodotus puts the number of Persians killed in the battle at a credible 6,400; the Greek losses amounted to 192. This disparity is attributable in large measure to the heavy armour of the Greek hoplites, who were pitted against an ill-protected foe. Contrary to the usual custom and as a mark of honour, the Greek dead were buried on the battlefield, where the mound which was raised over them is still visible. Their names were inscribed on stones, tribe by tribe. They included Callimachus.

The account of Herodotus leaves a host of riddles. Prominent among them is the whereabouts of the Persian cavalry, which the historian does not mention and which has been a matter of much debate. It is beyond the scope of this work to do more than mention the two main possibilities. If the Greek attack took place at dawn, the cavalry might have been caught unprepared while the horses were being watered in the marsh at the

on the third day after their departure – too late for the battle. The Athenians' only allies in the field supplementing their own force of about 9,000 hoplites were 1,000 soldiers from Plataea, with which Athens had an alliance and which she had assisted in the past.

At an assembly of the Athenian commanders, opinions were again divided. Half of the 10 generals (one for each tribe) were in favour of waiting until the Spartans arrived; the other half urged a showdown. In this impasse Miltiades again emerged as the man of the hour. An eleventh member of the gathering was the polemarch (war ruler) Callimachus, who was given the casting vote. Miltiades addressed him with such persuasion on the dire need to fight that Callimachus gave him his full support and voted for his plan of action.

north of the plain. It would have taken time to round them up, bridle them, and get them into line. They could have come into battle in the later stages but by then there was little that they could do. Alternatively, it is possible that the cavalry had been re-embarked with a small force of infantry in preparation for a rapid dash to Athens while the Athenians were otherwise engaged. There is some tenuous evidence in support of both of these theories but the balance appears to favour the first.

Although Marathon was the first battle of the Persian War, it had a decisive influence on the whole of the struggle to come by proving for the first time that the mighty Persian empire was not invincible. The boost to morale was enormous. What the Greeks had done once they could – and did – achieve again.

Herodotus, 6: 102–117; Cornelius Nepos, Miltiades, 4–5

THERMOPYLAE P (480, August) – Persian War

After Marathon, Darius wasted no time in planning a further expedition to subdue the Athenians but he died in 486 and was succeeded by his son Xerxes, who took over the lead. The expedition was to be a combined operation by land and sea on a scale larger than its predecessor of 490. On the other side of the Aegean the Athenians, thanks to the foresight of their great statesman Themistocles, had decided to become a sea power at the expense of their land force. They built 200 triremes, using the revenue from a recently discovered silver bed in the Laurion mining district to pay for them.

In 480 the Persian army crossed the Hellespont and marched down through Thrace, Macedonia and Thessaly while the fleet kept pace with it offshore. The Greeks under the supreme command of the Spartan king Leonidas decided to hold the pass of Thermopylae while their fleet took up station off Artemisium on the north coast of Euboea. In July, the Persian army arrived at Thermopylae and their navy lay off the Magnesian coast running north from Cape Sepias.

Thermopylae was a narrow pass in Locris with mountains on one side and a slope to the sea on the other. At its narrowest the track was only wide enough for one cart. A stone wall had been built across it as a defence many years before, and this the Greeks repaired. The army which arrived to defend the pass against Xerxes consisted of an advance guard of 300 Spartan hoplites and 4,900 men from other cities. Their leader was Leonidas

in person. The Persian hordes arrived soon afterwards, but for four days there were no hostilities; Xerxes did nothing in the full expectation that the Greeks would lose heart and withdraw. On the fifth day he ordered the Medes to charge the Greeks and the battle went on all day with terrible losses on the Persian side. The Medes were then replaced by the crack King's Immortals, but in another day of fierce fighting they fared no better. At that point a local man, Ephialtes, told Xerxes about a track which went over the hills and could be used to take the Greeks in the rear. At dusk a body of soldiers under Hydarnes was sent out with Ephialtes as guide, and by morning they were overlooking the Greeks in the pass. When Leonidas realized that death was inevitable, he dismissed all his troops with the exception of his 300 Spartans, for whom retreat would spell dishonour, and the 400 Thebans, who were suspected of having Persian sympathies and were retained as 'hostages'. The 700 Thespians also stayed, having refused to abandon the Spartans. It has been suggested that Leonidas did not in fact send the other troops away but ordered them *back*, outside the pass, where they would be in a position to attack an outflanking assailant and protect his own rear. If he really did so, the strategy failed.

In the morning, when Xerxes renewed his frontal assault, Leonidas and his band advanced beyond the wall into the open. At this point the Thebans walked away and surrendered to the enemy, saying that they had been coerced into joining Leonidas. (They were branded by the Persians for their pains.) Meanwhile Leonidas and the gallant Spartans and Thespians fought with the utmost valour, accounting for large numbers of the Persians. In the course of this fighting Leonidas fell and many others with him. The remainder managed to recover his body with great difficulty, but still they fought on until the troops with Hydarnes approached. They then withdrew behind the wall and took up a position in a tight body on a hillock where they fought to the last man. Their deeds have become a byword in the annals of history. Herodotus gives the number of Persian losses as 20,000, a figure which Xerxes tried to conceal by ordering the secret burial in camouflaged trenches of all but 1,000 corpses.

Diodorus preserves a strangely different 'endgame' to this epic, in which Leonidas and the Spartans are said to have made a nocturnal assault upon the Persian camp. They roamed through it all night in search of Xerxes, slaughtering the enemy until they themselves eventually succumbed at dawn. Herodotus knows nothing of all this, and he was the principal recorder of the era and a man of the century, with access to contemporary accounts.

Herodotus, 7: 201–228; Diodorus, 11: 6(3)–10

ARTEMISIUM PR (480, August) – Persian War

In the maritime events which paralleled the action at Thermopylae the weather was the Greeks' greatest ally. A great storm brewed up and destroyed, it is said, at least 400 of the Persian ships, which lay along the Magnesian coast. They were so numerous that most of them could not be beached and were lying vulnerably at anchor. After the storm had passed, the surviving Persian ships, still plentiful, sailed southward round Cape Sepias into the straits at the northern end of Euboea and anchored off Aphetae. Here they saw a small Greek force across the water at Artemisium on the northern coast of Euboea. In fact, the Greek fleet consisted of 271 triremes under the overall command of the Spartan Eurybiades. Themistocles commanded the Athenian contingent of 127 triremes. The Persians decided that it might be unwise to attack at once in case the Greeks made a run for it. Instead, the Persians detached a squadron of 200 ships to sail down the eastern (Aegean) side of Euboea and come up the Euripus (the straits on the western side between Euboea and the mainland), taking the Greeks in the rear. The Greeks had warning of this and were prepared to attack the Persian squadron as it came up the Euripus. As it did not appear, they decided to attack the main Persian force across the water. In view of their numerical inferiority, the Greeks formed themselves into a defensive circle, bows outward, and when they were attacked they succeeded in capturing 30 of the enemy ships before nightfall. That night there was another violent storm – another blessing for the Greeks because it destroyed the entire enemy squadron which was rounding Euboea. It is said that it forced every ship onto the rocks of the Hollows of Euboea, a particularly dangerous stretch of coast. On the following day the Greeks received a reinforcement of 53 ships from Athens. In celebration of these two events the Greeks again put to sea and attacked some Cilician ships, which they destroyed. These activities did not prevent the Persians from making one more attempt to repair their pride. On the third day they sailed forth and adopted a crescent formation with the aim of surrounding the enemy. In

the engagement the Greeks suffered heavily but the Persian losses were even greater. The final outcome was indecisive and the two sides withdrew.

Herodotus, 8: 6–18; Diodorus, 11: 12–13

SALAMIS ISL (480, September 28) – Persian War

The annihilation of the Spartan force at the pass of Thermopylae in 480 opened the way southward for the Persian army and prompted a general Greek withdrawal to the Isthmus. Athens was evacuated and the women and children were sent to Troezen, to the island of Salamis, and some to Aegina for safety. At the Isthmus, the only feasible place for a defensive stand, the Spartans were already barricading themselves into the Peloponnese behind walls. The Athenian navy retreated southward from Artemisium around the Attic coast and up the Saronic Gulf to the island of Salamis. Meanwhile the Persian army advanced through Boeotia and Attica, sacking Athens *en route*, while their navy followed in the wake of the Athenian fleet.

The island of Salamis lies at the northern end of the Saronic Gulf and is separated from Attica on its east by a channel which at its narrowest is only about a mile wide. At the southern, wider, end of this channel the narrow Cynosura promontory, about a mile long, projects eastwards from Salamis toward Attica. The entrance to the channel so formed is further obstructed by a small isle, Psyttalea, in the middle of the entrance.

Athens had become a naval power, thanks to the foresight of Themistocles. In the present emergency the Athenians had taken to their ships and any defeat of Athens must be at sea. But where should they stage the fight? At Salamis in the strait? Or in the open waters of the Saronic Gulf

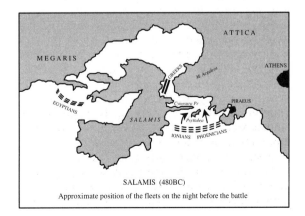

SALAMIS (480BC)
Approximate position of the fleets on the night before the battle

off the Isthmus, which they would be helping to defend? The Spartans put their interests first and opted for the latter course. Themistocles emphasized the disadvantages, notably that of fighting a numerically superior force in open waters. After much heated debate Themistocles, with threats of an Athenian withdrawal and a little trickery, won the day. By that time the Greek dilemma had anyway been resolved by the Persians. Xerxes had responded to a bogus message to the effect that the Greeks were intending to slip away and he had ordered his fleet to move forward and to block all the openings. The Phoenicians took up station between Attica and Psyttalea, the Ionians between Psyttalea and Salamis. It is also probable that the Egyptians took up station on the west side of the island between Salamis and Megaris, as Diodorus records. The Greek fleet was drawn up in the straits in the lea of the Cynosura promontory. Herodotus gives the complement as 378 ships on two occasions (although he itemizes the contingents to a total of 366); Aeschylus quotes the figure of 310. The Spartan Eurybiades was in overall command; Themistocles commanded the Athenian contingent, which numbered half of the total. During the night the Phoenicians and Ionians advanced into the channel between Salamis and the mainland so that by dawn they were in a position to attack. When it came, the Greeks' first move was to back water with the intention of luring the enemy further into the narrows. When the Greeks were almost aground they reversed direction and launched themselves at the enemy. The first ship to attack rammed an enemy vessel and became locked with it, disrupting the enemy lines. Then the Greeks moved in and started shearing their opponents' oars until the waters were choked with stationary hulls or capsized craft. As the leading enemy ships turned tail, they fell foul of those which were following them. There was no room for manoeuvre and the Persian numbers became an embarrassment to them. The chaos lasted all day, by the end of which the Persian armada was either crippled or destroyed. It was generally agreed that the Aeginetans provided the most distinguished contribution to the victory. When the enemy rout began, the Aeginetans were lying in wait for them, presumably in the Bay of Ambelakia, and took a heavy toll. Diodorus reports that more than 200 Persian ships were sunk or destroyed against a loss of 40 Greek vessels.

At the height of the struggle Aristides, who had been watching from Salamis, took a small force of hoplites across to the island of Psyttalea. He had

noted Persian soldiers, who had been landed there previously to save or kill shipwrecked sailors as the case demanded. Aristides destroyed the whole detachment.

An amusing incident concerns Queen Artemisia of Halicarnassus who was chased by an Athenian ship and found her escape blocked by some of her own ships. She made a quick decision and rammed one of her own ships, sinking it. This led the Athenians to believe that her ship must be a Greek one; conversely, Xerxes complimented her on sinking an enemy vessel.

Salamis was not decisive to the outcome of the campaign because the Persian land forces were still undefeated and indeed unchallenged. The sequel on land was fought the following year at Plataea (479). But Xerxes had seen enough and returned to Asia.

It is worth noting that Aeschylus was an eyewitness of the battle, possibly even a combatant, and that his *Persae* was first acted only eight years later.

*Herodotus, **8**: 43–95; Diodorus, **11**: 16–19; Aeschylus, Persae, 338ff.*

HIMERA (480) – Sicily: First Punic Invasion

While Greece was being attacked by Persia from the east, the Carthaginians were preparing an attack from the west – on the Greek colonies in Sicily. The synchrony of these two onslaughts was no mere coincidence but the result of an agreement between the two powers concerned. The excuse for an invasion of Sicily was provided by an appeal for help to the Carthaginians from the tyrant of Himera, who had been expelled by Theron, the tyrant of Acragas. The Carthaginians promptly sent a huge force, allegedly 300,000 men under Hamilcar, who set up two camps outside the north-coast town of Himera. One camp was for the navy, on the coastal side of the town, the other in the hills to the west. Theron sent for help to Gelon, tyrant of Syracuse, who arrived with speed from the east and set up his camp on the east bank of the Himera [*Imera*] river nearby.

Hamilcar sent a despatch to the people of Selinus (a dependency of Carthage on the south-west side of the island), asking them to send him some cavalrymen at his sea camp. The reply fell into the hands of Gelon who decided to make use of it. He sent some men of his own to the enemy's sea camp and, once inside, they started to burn all the enemy's ships. At the same time a prearranged signal was sent to Gelon's camp on receipt of which he promptly sallied out in battle order and, skirting to the south of the city, attacked the enemy's land camp. The battle was long and furious but in the end the Syracusans triumphed, heartened by the sight of the flames rising from the burning ships. It is said that no less than 150,000 of the Carthaginians were slain and the rest captured, but these numbers are quite unrealistic.

As for the fate of Hamilcar, accounts vary. According to Diodorus he was slain while making a sacrifice at the altar of Poseidon. Herodotus, in a more colourful account, reports that he sacrificed himself by leaping into the flames.

Diodorus, 11: 20–22; Herodotus, 7: 165–167

PLATAEA (479, August) – Persian War

After his defeat at Salamis (480) Xerxes returned to Asia, leaving his general Mardonius to withdraw to Thessaly with the bulk of the Persian land forces. Mardonius was aware of dissension between the Athenians and the Peloponnesians. The latter were still intent on fortifying the Isthmus and selfishly protecting themselves behind their wall at the expense of their allies. Accordingly, Mardonius made an attempt (the first of several) to detach the Athenians with seductive offers, which the Athenians rejected. Eventually the Lacedaemonians, under threats of Athenian acceptance of Persian terms, saw the obvious: they too would be doomed if they persisted in their isolationism. Yet they procrastinated for several days before despatching a force of 5,000 Spartans (each with seven helots in attendance). These were joined by 5,000 *perioikoi* and several thousand other Peloponnesian troops; also by 8,000 Athenians who emerged from the island of Salamis. The whole force was commanded by the Spartan Pausanias. In the meantime Mardonius had descended from Thessaly to Attica. When he heard of the Spartans' belated action, he completed the sack of Athens and withdrew to Boeotia where he took up a position on the river Asopus [*Assopos*] just north of Plataea. When the Greeks arrived on the scene, they assumed a position on the slopes of Mount Cithaeron. The subsequent actions are really two separate battles, among the most complex in Greek history. Throughout, the movements and positions of the Greeks were largely influenced by two factors, their total lack of cavalry and the need for water.

In the first engagement the Persian cavalry under Masistius attacked the Greeks at their most vulnerable point. This was held by the Megarians, who were soon hard pressed. The Athenians rallied to their assistance, and in the ensuing fighting Masistius was unhorsed and killed by a spear-thrust to his eye. After a final onslaught the cavalry withdrew, bewailing their loss. The Greeks then decided to move to lower ground where there was a spring. By this time additional reinforcements had brought their numbers up to around 40,000 hoplites with a similar number of auxiliaries. In their new position the opposing armies faced each other for some days, neither side making a move. The only action occurred when Mardonius sent his cavalry to the pass over Cithaeron, where it destroyed a large baggage train with food for the Greeks. After a further lull Mardonius launched a cavalry attack in which the Greeks were continually harassed with missiles. In addition, the spring became choked. Short of food and water, Pausanias decided to retreat at night to a piece of higher ground called the Island. But matters did not go according to plan. Some of the Greek contingents moved off but made straight for the environs of Plataea, removed from any subsequent action. Then, one of the Spartan commanders, Amompharetus by name, refused to dishonour his country by retreating. The night was wasted in attempts to persuade him. Near dawn, Pausanias reluctantly decided to abandon Amompharetus, hoping he would follow when he realized the earnest truth – which he did. The Athenians, for their part, refused to move until they saw the Spartans do likewise. When they did move, they took a different route. With the arrival of dawn, the Persians spotted Pausanias with the Spartans and Tegeates (the Athenians were out of sight). The Persian cavalry chased them, and Mardonius gave the order for a general advance. Pausanias sent a distress call to the Athenians, but on their way to help they were attacked by the Boeotians, who were fighting on the Persian side. It was a fierce onslaught, in which 300 of the Boeotians were killed before the rest were eventually overcome, and it pinned the Athenians down. The Spartans and Tegeates had to fight alone against the Persians. They broke furiously through a barricade of wicker shields protecting the archers and then forced the enemy back. The mere sight of other Persians retreating unnerved their colleagues. Artabazus with a force of 40,000 Persians turned his force about and fled toward the Hellespont without even entering the fray. But the main Persian body fought well until Mardonius fell. After that the battle was decided. There remained only the attack on the camp and the pursuit of the fugitives. At the camp, the Persians defending the palisade succeeded in keeping the

Spartans out, but matters changed when the Athenians finally arrived. After a long struggle the Greeks breached the defences, poured through the gap and massacred the terrified enemy. Herodotus would have us believe that only one in a hundred of this immense force survived the battle and the subsequent sack of their camp. The total Greek losses were said to be 1,360, which included 91 Spartans, 52 Athenians and 16 Tegeates.

The account of Herodotus contains some incidents and details which seem intended to boost the Athenian contribution at the expense of the Lacedaemonians. In the final decisive encounter the Spartans and Tegeates carried it all until near the very end. In Diodorus' compressed account, details are sparse and many of the intermediate activities are unmentioned. A picture of the complex chain of events fails to emerge.

Herodotus, 9: 19–70; Plutarch, Aristides, 11–19; Diodorus, 11: 30–32

MYCALE (479, August) – Persian War

At the time of the Greek victory at Plataea, another liberating battle was about to take place across the seas. The Greek fleet under Leotychides was at Delos when a message was received from the Samians, begging help against their Persian masters. Leotychides responded and sailed for Samos where the Persian fleet was anchored. Learning of their approach, the Persians for some unknown reason sent (or perhaps had already sent) their Phoenician contingent home. They themselves sailed to the mountainous promontory of Mycale [*Samsun*] on the mainland where they had a strong military force estimated at 60,000 men under the command of Tigranes. Here they beached their ships and built a rampart around them. Undeterred, the Greeks followed them, beached their ships and took up their positions confronting the enemy line. Once they had managed to burst through the line of enemy shields, a mass attack won the day. The balance was tipped by the Ionians, who deserted their Persian masters and actually attacked them. Most of the enemy, including Tigranes, were cut down either in battle or in the rout, but the Greeks also suffered heavy losses. The remnants of the Persian force retreated to Sardes.

Herodotus, 9: 90–104; Diodorus, 11: 34–36

EION (476) – Persian War

After the expulsion of the Persians from Greek soil, Sparta became half-hearted about any continuation of activities. One result of her withdrawal was the formation of the confederacy of Delos, a league of maritime cities, states and islands in and around the Aegean under the leadership of Athens. Its main objects were the protection of the liberated territories and the liberation of their brothers in Asia who were still under Persian domination. The conduct of the war was entrusted to Cimon, son of Miltiades. One of his first acts was to capture Eion, the port of Amphipolis and the most important Persian stronghold west of the Hellespont. This was defended by a gallant commander, Boges (Butes). Cimon began by defeating the Persians in a pitched battle and shutting them up in the town, after which he cut off all their supplies. The unyielding Boges, faced with starvation, would not give in but built a large pyre and, after killing his wife, family and entourage, he threw the bodies into the flames and then leapt in himself.

Herodotus, 7: 107; Plutarch, Cimon, 7

CUMAE (474) – Etruscan Expansion

Etruscan designs against the Greek colonies of southern Italy received a check at an earlier battle at Cumae (524) and again at Aricia (506). But although the land route might have been closed, the sea was still open. The Etruscans availed themselves of it and sent a fleet against Cumae, which appealed for help to Hieron, the tyrant of Syracuse. Hieron, recognizing the risks, responded by sending a fleet of triremes. The Etruscans suffered a severe defeat which put an end to their threat to the colonies of Magna Graecia.

Diodorus, 11: 51

TEGEA (c.473) – Spartan Aggression

In the years immediately succeeding the Persian invasions of Greece, the aspirations of Sparta were confined to the Peloponnese. Her old rival Argos, having recovered from her defeat at Sepeia (494), entered into an alliance with the Arcadian town of Tegea. Together they were defeated by Sparta outside the Tegeate walls.

Herodotus, 9: 35; Pausanias, 3: 11(7)

ACRAGAS (472) – Sicily: Internal Wars

Theron, the ruler of Acragas [*Agrigento*], died in 472 and was succeeded by his son, Thrasydaeus. But whereas the father had been a relatively benign despot, liked by his people, the son behaved like a true tyrant. When Hieron of Syracuse heard that Thrasydaeus was raising an army to attack his city, he gathered together a formidable force and was the first to strike, marching on Acragas. In a

fierce battle the Syracusans were victorious, losing some 2,000 men as compared with their opponents' loss of more than double that number. Thrasydaeus was expelled and fled to Megara in Greece, where he was condemned to death.
Diodorus, 11: 53(1–5)

DIPAEA (*c.*471) – Spartan Aggression
After the Spartan victory at Tegea (*c.*473) over Argos and the Tegeates all the Arcadian cities (except Mantinea) banded together against Sparta. The Spartans inflicted a crushing defeat on them at Dipaea.
Herodotus, 9: 35; Pausanias, 3: 11(7)

EURYMEDON R (*c.*468) – Persian War
The end of the Persian War in Greece did not signal the end of Graeco-Persian hostilities, but in the next phase the Greeks were on the offensive. Initially they were under the leadership of the Spartan Pausanias, but when he fell into disfavour the Athenians took over the command. This passed in due course to Cimon, son of Miltiades. His greatest achievement – and the climax of the campaign – was his double victory at the Eurymedon [*Köprü Çayi*], a major river in Asia Minor which flows southwards into the Mediterranean. Here he came upon the Persian navy and army. Their commander was not keen to fight because a further 80 Phoenician ships were on their way from Cyprus. Cimon, on the other hand, was determined to attack before these reinforcements arrived. He put to sea and bore down against the enemy navy, defeating it and sinking about 200 Phoenician ships. When the Persian army moved down to the shore against him, he landed his already exhausted hoplites with misgivings. After a fierce struggle, the Athenians forced their adversaries back with much slaughter and captured their camp. The Greek victory put Persia completely out of action in the Aegean. It was half a century before the Great King troubled Greece again.

Diodorus' account of this battle is more fanciful and far-fetched than the others, describing the Athenians dressed up and masquerading as Persians in a grand charade. It detracts from Cimon's huge success.
Thucydides, 1: 100(1); Diodorus, 11: 61; Plutarch, Cimon, 12(4)–13(2)

SYEDRA (*c.*468) – Persian War
At the time of the battle of the Eurymedon (above) 80 Phoenician ships were on their way to join the Persian fleet. Cimon learnt that they had put in to Syedra [near *Alanya*] on the Cilician coast. To complete his conquest, he sailed there and caught the enemy off guard before they had even heard of the fate of the main fleet at Eurymedon. He attacked and destroyed all the ships and most of the crews.
Plutarch, Cimon, 13(3–4)

PAPREMIS (459, summer) – Egyptian Revolt
In 465 Xerxes, king of Persia, was murdered, throwing the Persian court into disorder. The Egyptians seized the opportunity to rebel from the Persian yoke under the leadership of a Libyan by the name of Inaros, who invited the Athenians to assist him in overthrowing their old enemy. At that time a fleet of 200 Athenian and allied galleys was operating around Cyprus. They abandoned their campaign, crossed over to Egypt and joined up with the Egyptian army, which was encamped close to the Nile. In a furious battle at Papremis in the Nile delta they routed a Persian force under Achaemenes and then sailed up the Nile to Memphis, where they blockaded the retreating Persians. However, some historians hold that the Athenians arrived after the battle. The venture was ultimately a disaster, the Egyptians and their allies being defeated at Memphis by a relieving Persian force. According to Thucydides few of the Athenians lived to return to their homeland.
Herodotus, 3: 12; Diodorus, 11: 71 and 74(1–4); Thucydides, 1: 104

HALIEIS (459) – 'First Peloponnesian War'
In 459 the Megarians had a dispute with Corinth as a result of which they left the Peloponnesian league and placed themselves under Athenian protection. This move, which was highly advantageous to Athens, was equally an offence to Corinth and also to Sparta as the leader of the league. Hostilities broke out and continued sporadically over the next 15 years in what has been called the 'First Peloponnesian War'. In the first recorded incident the Athenians sent out a fleet which made a landing at Halieis [*Portochelion*], an Argolid town on the Gulf of Argolis. They were opposed by some Corinthian and Epidaurian troops who, according to Diodorus, were defeated. But the opposite result is reported by Thucydides, who lived during those times and must have had a more intimate knowledge of the events.
Thucydides, 1: 105(1); Diodorus, 11: 78(1–2)

CECRYPHALEA ISL (459) – 'First Peloponnesian War'

A naval action between Athenian and Peloponnesian fleets took place off the island of Cecryphalea [*Angistrion*] in the Saronic Gulf. The Athenians were the victors.

Thucydides, 1: 105(1); Diodorus, 11: 78(2)

AEGINA ISL (459) – 'First Peloponnesian War'

At this point, the island of Aegina in the Saronic Gulf became involved in the struggle. A great naval battle was fought off the island between Aeginetans and Athenians with their respective allies. The Athenians were victorious and captured 70 ships. They then set foot on the island and started to besiege the town.

Thucydides, 1: 105(2); Diodorus, 11: 78(3–4)

MEGARA (458) – 'First Peloponnesian War'

To relieve the Athenian siege of Aegina (above) the Corinthians walked into Megaris, the territory which joins the Peloponnese to the Greek mainland at Attica. They expected that the Athenians would be forced to withdraw from the one to protect the other, but expectation was not matched by actuality. The resourceful Athenians raised a force from the young and old in their city and marched to Megara under the command of Myronides. An indecisive action was fought but the Athenians immediately erected a trophy. Some days later the Corinthians, spurred on by the taunts of their old folk, sallied forth to put up their trophy, claiming that it had been their victory, whereupon the Athenians came out against them, overwhelmed them and then engaged and defeated the rest of their force.

Diodorus attributes these hostilities to a border dispute between Corinth and Megara in which the Megarians enlisted the help of the Athenians. This historian, also, mentions two battles but he says that the Athenians were the victors in both, although the first victory was gained only after a long hard fight. He adds that the battles were fought at Cimolia, the plain in which the city of Megara is situated.

Thucydides, 1: 105(2)–106; Diodorus, 11: 79(1–4)

TANAGRA (457, spring) – 'First Peloponnesian War'

When the Phocians started a campaign against Doris, the Spartans went to the assistance of the Dorians with a total force approaching 12,000 men commanded by Nicomedes. Having achieved their object, they realized that their return journey presented considerable difficulties because the Athenians controlled both of the main routes, one through the Megarid and the other by sea. Instead they marched eastwards in the direction of Athens whereupon the Athenians sent out an army 14,000 strong to meet them. The rival armies met at Tanagra in Boeotia, close to the Attic border, where in a hard-fought battle the Spartans and their allies won. They then proceeded home through the Megarid.

Thucydides, 1: 107–108(2); Diodorus, 11: 80(1–2)

OENOPHYTA (457) – 'First Peloponnesian War'

Two months after the battle of Tanagra (above) the Athenians again marched into Boeotia, under the command of Myronides. A decisive battle was fought against the Boeotians at Oenophyta [*Inophyta*] in which the Athenians triumphed. This gave them mastery of the whole of Boeotia and Phocis.

Thucydides, 1: 108(2–3); Diodorus, 11: 83(1)

SICYON (453) – 'First Peloponnesian War'

In another offensive expedition the Athenians under Tolmides sailed round the Peloponnese, burnt the Spartan dockyards, captured Corinthian Chalcis and finally landed in Sicyon in northern Argolis, north-west of Corinth. They defeated the Sicyonians in battle but were unable to take the city by assault. Shortly afterwards a second expedition, led by Pericles himself, met with a similar result. The Sicyonians were again forced back behind their walls but withstood a siege.

Thucydides, 1: 108(5) and 111(2); Diodorus, 11: 88(1–2)

MOTYUM (451, winter) – Sicily: Internal Wars

Diodorus Siculus records a Sicilian battle which happened in the neighbourhood of a place called Motyum (unknown), in the south of the island. The leader of the Siceli, a man called Ducetius, formed a union of the Sicel towns, seized others and laid siege to Motyum, which was held by a garrison from Acragas. When a joint force of Acragantini and Syracusans went to the help of the beleaguered garrison, Ducetius engaged them in battle with success and drove both parties out of their camps. As winter was setting in, they did not resume the struggle until the summer, when Nomae (below) became the scene of retribution.

Diodorus, 11: 91(1)

NOMAE (451, summer) – Sicily: Internal Wars
At the start of the summer following their defeat at Motyum (above) a strong force of Syracusans set out against Ducetius, who was encamped near Nomae, a place now unknown. After a fierce struggle the Syracusans overpowered the Sicels, who deserted their leader. He boldly repaired to Syracuse and took refuge at the altar in the market-place. The Syracusans magnanimously spared him and sent him to Corinth, ordering him to stay there. He did not obey for long and was the cause of further strife (Himera R, 446).
Diodorus, 11: 91(3–4)

SALAMIS (CYPRUS) (449) – Resumption of Persian War
As a result of the recent hostilities at home the Persian problem had been relegated to the back of the Athenian mind. Now, with a truce in force between Athens and the Peloponnese, the Athenians felt able to resume their war against Persia and to carry it into the enemy's camp. In 450 they sent an allied expedition comprising a total of 200 ships under the command of Cimon to Cyprus. Sixty of these ships were detached and sent to Egypt to help a local king who was defying the Persians. The rest began by laying siege to the Cypriot town of Citium [*Larnaca*]. Cimon's death during this blockade – and a shortage of food – caused it to be lifted. But before sailing for home, the fleet arrived at Salamis [*Gazimağuza*, formerly *Famagusta*] and gained a double victory against a combined Phoenician and Cilician fleet under Artabazus and against the enemy's land force commanded by Megabyzus. Despite this victory, the Athenians came to realize that they would not be in a position to wage wars abroad in addition to looking after their interests at home. At the instigation primarily of Pericles, they entered into negotiations with Persia which resulted in the 'Peace of Callias'.
Thucydides, 1: 112; Diodorus, 12: 3

CORONEA (447) – 'First Peloponnesian War'
As a result of the battle of Oenophyta (457) Boeotia came under the control of the Athenians. Ten years later a number of Boeotian towns, including Orchomenus and Chaeronea, were seized by Boeotian exiles. The Athenians under the command of Tolmides marched against them with 1,000 hoplites reinforced with contingents from their allies. They captured Chaeronea and left a garrison behind. On their return journey they were attacked near Coronea by exiles from Orchome-nus and others of a like mind and were defeated. Tolmides was killed and many of the hoplites were taken prisoner. The Athenians were forced to make a treaty relinquishing Boeotia in exchange for the return of their captured soldiers.
Thucydides, 1: 113; Diodorus, 12: 6

HIMERA R (446) – Sicily: Internal Wars
Following his defeat at Nomae (451) Ducetius, the leader of the Sicels, was allowed by the Syracusans to go free providing that he stayed in Corinth. He failed to comply and returned to Sicily with some colonists, claiming that the gods had told him to found a city in the island. This upset the inhabitants of Acragas [*Agrigento*] who had been allied with Syracuse against Ducetius in the past. They considered that they ought to have been consulted before Ducetius was freed. The Acragantini therefore declared war on Syracuse whereupon the other cities took sides, some with one faction and some with the other. The opposing factions pitched camps at the Himera River [*Salso*], which should not be confused with the Himera [*Imera*] in the north of the island. In the ensuing battle the Syracusans triumphed, after which a peace treaty was concluded. Ducetius, the cause of all this trouble, appears to have taken no part in the proceedings.
Diodorus, 12: 8

TRAGIA ISL (440) – Samian Revolt
In 446/5 a thirty years' truce was concluded between the Athenians and the Peloponnesians and their respective allies. In the sixth year of this truce war broke out between Samos, a member of the Athenian confederacy, and Miletus. At the request of the Milesians the Athenians intervened, and after setting up a democracy in Samos they left a garrison and returned home. However, some disaffected Samians had fled to the mainland where they raised a force of mercenaries with which they returned to Samos. There they attacked the democratic leaders and handed the Athenian garrison and officials over to the Persians. This goaded the Athenians into sailing against Samos with a fleet of 60 ships. Sixteen of these were deployed to other parts but the remaining 44, under the command of Pericles, fought with a Samian fleet of 70 ships off the Ionian island of Tragia [*Agathonission*]. In spite of their numerical inferiority the Athenians were victorious. Pericles then besieged the town of Samos by land and sea.
Thucydides, 1: 115(2)–116(1); Plutarch, Pericles, 25

SAMOS ISL (439) – Samian Revolt

After his victory off Tragia (above) Pericles seized the harbour of Samos and blockaded the town. At about this time he was reinforced with 40 ships from Athens and a further 25 from Chios and Lesbos. With 60 ships from this enlarged fleet he made a hurried departure, allegedly to intercept a Phoenician fleet which was on its way to help the Samians. Nothing more seems to have been heard of the Phoenicians or of any battle. What did happen was that during Pericles' absence the Samians, under Melissus, made a surprise sortie against the Athenian camp and, putting out to sea, defeated the ships that were launched against them. They gained a transient command of the sea. It lasted for about two weeks until the return of Pericles when they found themselves blockaded once more. After about nine months the city surrendered.

Thucydides, 1: 116(2)–117; Diodorus, 12: 27(4)–28(2); Plutarch, Pericles, 26

LEUCIMME PR (435, spring) – Corcyraean War

Spartan alarm at the growth of Athenian power was the real underlying cause of the great Peloponnesian War. This was triggered by three separate disputes, the first of which concerned Epidamnus [*Durazzo, Durrës*] on the Illyrian coast. In this city the democratic party threw out the aristocrats, who had aligned themselves with foreign enemies and had started attacking their own city. Epidamnus was a Corcyraean colony and so the democrats appealed to Corcyra [*Corfu*] for help, which was refused. However, Epidamnus had been founded by a Corinthian and so the democrats turned next to the mother city, a bitter enemy of Corcyra, which sent out a force by land to help them. At this news the Corcyraeans despatched a fleet, and when the Epidamnians refused to yield to their demands, they started to blockade the city with their 40 ships. The Corinthians responded by sending out a fleet of 68 ships, 30 of their own and the rest from various allies. The Corcyraeans sent an embassy to Corinth with demands; Corinth retorted with counter-demands. In the end, none of the proposals was accepted, and the Corinthians sent a declaration of war followed by a fleet of 75 ships with 2,000 hoplites on board. They had reached the promontory of Actium [*La Punta*] on the Acarnanian coast when the Corcyraeans put out to sea against them with a fleet of 80 ships. The Corcyraeans sank 15 of the enemy ships and won the battle decisively, gaining complete control of the seas in that area. Epidamnus surrendered to the besiegers on the same day as the battle. After the battle the Corcyraeans put up a trophy on the promontory of Leucimme at the southern end of their island. They then slew all their prisoners except the Corinthians, who remained in captivity.

Thucydides, 1: 29; Diodorus, 12: 30(2–5) and 31(2)

SYBOTA ISLS (433) – Corcyraean War

After their defeat by the Corcyraeans (above) the Corinthians returned home to lick their wounds and to throw themselves body and soul into an intensive programme of shipbuilding and training. Corcyra [*Corfu*] was alarmed and sought to join the Athenian league for protection whereupon the Corinthians asked for a hearing to put their view. A healthy Corcyraean navy suited the Athenians' own best interests and so they made a defensive alliance with Corcyra and sent 10 ships. These were only to be called upon in the event of an aggressive attack by Corinth with a view to landing on Corcyraean territory. Meanwhile, a Corinthian and allied fleet of 150 ships set sail for Corcyra under the command of Xenoclides. They anchored in a harbour on the mainland opposite Corcyra. When the Corcyraeans heard of this, they manned 110 ships (in addition to the 10 Athenian ships) and made a camp on one of the Sybota islands, which lie between the Epirote mainland and the southern tip of Corcyra. Both parties carried in their ships a number of hoplites, archers and javelin throwers with the result that when the two fleets sallied out and engaged, the battle was, as Thucydides says, more like a battle on land than sea. When ship collided with ship, disengagement was difficult owing to their numbers and close formation, and so the hoplites fought a pitched battle on the stationary decks. A Corcyraean squadron of 20 ships on the right of their line got the upper hand over their opposite numbers and drove them back to the land, where the Corcyraeans disembarked and set fire to the enemy camp. On their left, by contrast, the Corcyraeans were faring badly and the Athenians, who had so far refrained from joining in, began to support them and were eventually fighting the Corinthians openly. Nevertheless, the Corinthians managed to drive them to the land and were, on balance, the victors although both sides claimed the victory. The Corinthians had taken about 1,000 prisoners and had sunk around 70 enemy ships; the Corcyraeans had destroyed about 30.

As the Thirty Years' Peace between Athens and the Peloponnese was in force, the active engagement of the Athenians in an act of aggression against Corinthian ships was regarded in Corinth as a cause for war. It was one of the precipitating factors which led to the outbreak of the great Peloponnesian conflagration.
Thucydides, 1: 45–55; Diodorus, 12: 33

POTIDAEA (432) – Revolt of Potidaea
Potidaea was a town at the base of and guarding the Chalcidic peninsula of Pallene [*Kassandra*], the westernmost of the three 'fingers' of land which project southward into the Thracian Sea. It was a Corinthian colony and yet an ally of the Athenians, against whom Corinth wanted revenge for the happenings at Leucimme Pr (435) and Sybota (433). Athens feared that Potidaea might be induced to revolt by the combined influence of Corinth and of Perdiccas, the king of Macedonia, who had turned against the Athenians when they espoused his brothers. To protect their own interests, the Athenians required the Potidaeans to raze their city walls on the south side, facing the peninsula. They offered no protection against a land attack but would impede activities from the sea. The Athenians also stipulated the exile of the Corinthian magistrates. The Potidaeans refused and revolted from Athens, after receiving a promise from Sparta that she would invade Attica if the Athenians attacked Potidaea. Perdiccas stirred up the cauldron by organizing a general revolt in the region. Athens had anyway been on the point of sending 30 ships with 1,000 hoplites to Macedonia. These were subsequently reinforced from Athens by a further 40 ships with 2,000 hoplites under the command of Callias. At the same time the Corinthians sent their general Aristeus with 2,000 soldiers by land to reinforce Potidaea. Aristeus planned to take possession of the isthmus and await the Athenians. The other allies of the Spartans would stay outside the isthmus and would be in a position to take the Athenians in the rear when they arrived from Macedonia. However, when the Athenians did arrive, they had with them 600 Macedonian cavalry. This force was sent inland behind Potidaea, where it effectively neutralized the opposition and prevented any reinforcement of the troops on the isthmus from that quarter. The Athenian infantry proceeded to the isthmus and engaged the enemy. In the confrontation, the wing of picked troops commanded by Aristeus routed its opposite numbers and pursued them. Elsewhere the outcome was different; the Potidaeans and Peloponnesians were defeated and fled behind their fortifications. This presented the victorious Aristeus and his wing with the problem of how to rejoin the rest of his force in the town. He chose the 'safest' but still difficult route along the breakwater under heavy fire, which accounted for some more of his men. The Potidaean and allied casualties amounted in all to around 300; the Athenians lost only half that number but it included their general Callias. After the battle, Potidaea remained under siege by the Athenians until the winter of 430/29, when it surrendered.
Thucydides, 1: 56–63; Diodorus, 12: 34

SPARTOLUS (429, summer) – Peloponnesian War
In the summer after the fall of Potidaea the Athenians marched against the Chalcidians in Thrace with 2,000 hoplites and 200 cavalry under the command of their general Xenophon. They marched up to Spartolus in Bottiaea, hoping for an easy surrender with the help of a pro-Athenian faction within the town. But an opposing party sought help from Olynthus and was rewarded with a force of hoplites and other troops. This force sallied out and engaged the Athenians just outside the city. The Chalcidian hoplites and their auxiliaries were defeated by the Athenians and withdrew into the city; but the cavalry and light troops of the two sides fared in opposite sense, the Chalcidians winning. After this indecisive encounter some peltasts from Olynthus arrived to reinforce the Chalcidians. Encouraged by this support, the Chalcidians launched a fresh attack on the Athenians, who fell back. When the Athenians re-formed and charged, their enemy gave way only to return to the charge as the Athenians retired. In these to-and-fro tactics the Chalcidians were supported by frequent charges on the part of their cavalry, which resulted in a wholesale Athenian rout and the loss of 430 men with all their generals.
Thucydides, 2: 79

STRATUS (429, summer) – Peloponnesian War
The cities of the Ambracian and Chaonian regions of Epirus persuaded the Spartans to send troops and a fleet to Acarnania. The aim was to gain control of the area and to detach it from the Athenian alliance. The Ambraciots were colonists of Corinth, and so Corinth, Sicyon and other neighbouring towns were ready to assist by providing ships. The army, under the command of

Cnemus, consisted of 1,000 Peloponnesian hoplites with more than 2,000 allied troops from different tribes and peoples. With this force Cnemus crossed over from the Peloponnese and set out on foot. Arriving near Stratus in Acarnania, he intended to try to win over the city by negotiation, but his aim was foiled by the tempestuousness of the Chaonians. In its advance the army had marched in three divisions which were well apart and sometimes out of sight of each other. On arrival at the projected camp site the hot-headed Chaonians, who were well out in front, rushed straight forward to the attack on their own. When the Stratians realized that only a part of the force was advancing, they set up many small ambushes around the city and made a concerted attack on the Chaonians, who panicked and fled. After nightfall Cnemus retreated and his army dispersed.

Thucydides, 2: 81–82

CHALCIS (429, summer) – Peloponnesian War

The Corinthian and allied fleet which should have supported Cnemus during his Acarnanian advance to Stratus (above) fell foul of the Athenian admiral Phormio. He was based at Naupactus [*Lepanto*] and was guarding the waters leading into the Gulf of Corinth with 20 ships. As the Corinthians with their 47 ships sailed westwards along the Peloponnesian coast, they saw the Athenians keeping pace with them along the opposite shore. The Corinthian ships were a convoy of transports with supplies for the Acarnanian campaign. They were not prepared for a battle and did not envisage being attacked by a force less than half their size. But when they tried to cross the gulf at dawn, the Athenians sailed out against them from Chalcis and engaged them in mid-stream. The Corinthians adopted a radial formation, lining their ships up with the prows outwards in a great circle and with five of their best vessels in the centre in reserve. All the light craft were also in the middle for their protection. The Athenians formed up in line astern and sailed closely round the enemy circle as if about to ram, thereby squeezing them into an ever decreasing area. Phormio was waiting for the wind to blow up as was usual in that area at that time of day. When it did, the Corinthians, tightly packed and with no space left for manoeuvre, were in serious trouble. At the height of their confusion Phormio gave the signal to attack. The enemy put up no resistance but fled whenever they could disentangle themselves. The Athenians sank every enemy ship that they encountered in the fight and pursued and captured 12 more in flight.

Thucydides, 2: 83–84

NAUPACTUS (429, summer) – Peloponnesian War

After rebuilding and refurbishing their fleet following their defeat off Chalcis (above), the Corinthians and their allies sailed with 77 ships along the Peloponnesian coast to Rhium [*Rion*] at the entrance to the Gulf of Corinth. The Athenian admiral Phormio kept pace with them along the opposite coast to Antirrhium [*Antirrion*], which is just across the waters from Rhium. He still had only the original 20 ships that had fought at Chalcis because reinforcements had been delayed. The two fleets stayed put for several days within sight of each other. The Peloponnesians were the first to move. Seeing that Phormio would not venture into the narrow waters of the gulf, they would lure him by feigning an attack on his base at Naupactus [*Lepanto*]. At dawn they sailed along their coast with their fastest vessels in the lead, ready to cut Phormio's escape when they turned to attack him. Phormio was obliged to accept the bait against his will because he had left Naupactus undefended. He hurriedly embarked and was sailing along his shore when the enemy suddenly turned across the gulf and bore down on him. The 11 leading ships in the Athenian line slipped out of the net and managed to reach open water. The others were forced back onto the shore and immobilized, although a few were rescued by soldiers on shore who waded into the sea and fought it out on the decks. Meanwhile, the eleven Athenian ships which had escaped were pursued by the cream of the Peloponnesian fleet, the fastest 20. All but one of the Athenians managed to retain their lead and to reach Naupactus, where they turned and waited for their pursuers. The next arrival rowing toward Naupactus was their own eleventh member, hotly pursued by an enemy vessel. A merchantman was moored in its way. In a deft manoeuvre the Athenian ship suddenly rowed round the merchantman in a tight circle and rammed its pursuer amidships, sinking it. The Peloponnesians following on behind in an exultant mood were taken completely aback and were uncertain what to do. The Athenians solved their dilemma for them by falling on them like a pack of wolves and forcing them to flee. The Athenians captured six ships and regained the ships in tow which had been taken from them earlier.

Thucydides, 2: 86 and 90–92

MYTILENE (428) – Peloponnesian War
Mytilene [*Mytilini*] and most of the other towns on
the island of Lesbos staged a revolt from Athens
with the connivance of Sparta. The Athenians sent
40 triremes under the command of Cleippides and
hoped to catch the Mytilenians off guard while
they were celebrating a festival in honour of the
Malean Apollo. The Mytilenians got wind of this
and reinforced their walls instead of feasting.
When the fleet arrived, the Athenian commander
granted the islanders a temporary armistice while
they sent a delegation to Athens (and a furtive one
to Sparta). The mission to Athens failed to achieve
anything and so the Mytilenians marched out in
full force against the Athenian camp. In the
ensuing fight, they got the better of the Athenians
but did not feel strong enough to follow it up until
they received some help from outside. The help
never arrived. In the following year, the Athenians
besieged the town and the Mytilenians were forced
by starvation to capitulate.
Thucydides, 3: 3–5

CORCYRA ISL (427) – Peloponnesian War
A revolution broke out in Corcyra [*Corfu*]. It
began when Corcyraeans who had been taken
prisoner by the Corinthians were allowed to return
home on 'bail'. They had undertaken to win over
Corcyra from the Athenian alliance and the ruling
democratic party to the Corinthian cause. The
people of Corcyra thought otherwise. This resulted in several days of bitter street fighting in which
the ruling party was ousted and then the tables
were again turned. During a lull, 12 Athenian
ships arrived from Naupactus under the command
of Nicostratus, whose aim was to secure a settlement. Little or no progress had been made when
53 Peloponnesian ships arrived under the command of Alcidas. The Corcyraeans were at their
wits' end. They immediately prepared 60 ships and
sailed straight against the enemy, ignoring the
advice of the Athenians to let them move in first.
The Corcyraeans were so disorganized that the
result was scarcely in doubt. Two of their ships
deserted; the crews of the remainder were fighting
each other. The Peloponnesians, sizing up the
situation, detailed 20 ships to meet the Corcyraeans and the rest of the fleet to take on the
Athenians. Predictably, the Corcyraeans ran into
trouble and 13 of their ships were captured; the
remainder escaped. The Athenians, on their part,
were greatly outnumbered and did not risk an
attack on more than one enemy wing. The Peloponnesians then formed up in a circle and the

Athenians rowed around them, as they had done
so successfully at Naupactus (429). When the
enemy ships which had been chasing the Corcyraeans saw this, they came up in support of their
main body. The Athenians were forced to make a
withdrawal but did so in their own time to give the
remaining Corcyraeans time to complete their
escape. Surprisingly, the Peloponnesians did not
follow up their victory. The next day they sailed
away. The same evening they heard that a further
60 Athenian ships were on their way, news which
caused them to expedite their passage southwards.
Thucydides, 3: 75–78

TANAGRA (426, summer) – Peloponnesian War
During the summer the Athenians sent Nicias with
a force of 60 ships and 2,000 hoplites to subdue the
island of Melos, which had refused to join the
Athenian alliance. The expedition was fruitless.
They then sailed to the Attic town of Oropus and
marched across the Boeotian border to Tanagra.
There, as a result of prearranged signals, they met
an Athenian army from Athens under the command of Hipponicus and Eurymedon. The next
day a force from Tanagra came out against them.
In the ensuing battle the Athenians were victorious, after which the army returned to Athens and
Nicias marched back to his ships.
Thucydides, 3: 91

AEGITIUM (426, summer) – Peloponnesian
War
During the summer the Athenian general
Demosthenes had been sailing round the Peloponnese with a fleet of 30 ships. He then attacked
the island of Leucas off the coast of Acarnania – to
the great satisfaction of the Acarnanians, from
whom he received considerable reinforcements.
The Messenians among his troops persuaded him
that with such a large force it would be a better
idea to attack Aetolia, which constituted a threat
to Naupactus. These Messenian expatriates,
themselves living in Naupactus, pointed out that
as the Aetolians lived in widely scattered and
unfortified villages, their defeat would not be a
difficult matter. This plan suited Demosthenes'
ambitions as well as the self-interest of the
Messenians, who had been subjected to continual
harassment by their Aetolian neighbours.
Demosthenes therefore sailed along the coast to
West Locris and set out next day to invade Aetolia. The Aetolians, however, had forewarning of
this and came out in force with contingents from
every tribe in the area, near and far. The

Messenians continued to insist that there was no cause for alarm, and so Demosthenes pushed on without waiting for promised Locrian reinforcements. He marched against Aegitium and took it, while the inhabitants escaped and made for the hills above the town. At this point the Aetolian army arrived and attacked the Athenians from the high ground, running down from the hills on all sides to throw their javelins. They then fell back when the Athenians advanced, only to launch another onslaught. The battle progressed to and fro in this way for some time until the captain of the Athenian archers was killed. This was enough for his men, who dispersed. Many were killed in the rout, having been overtaken by the swift and lightly armed Aetolians. The main body of the army got lost and rushed into the forest, which the Aetolians promptly proceeded to fire. Among the survivors was Demosthenes, who refused to sail home with the others but remained behind at Naupactus rather than face the Athenians in disgrace.
Thucydides, 3: 97–98

MYLAE (426, summer) – Peloponnesian War
Syracuse and Leontini were at war. The Athenians had received an appeal for help from the Leontinians and had responded by sending a fleet of 20 ships. Ostensibly they acted because of their friendship and kinship, but their real aim, as Thucydides points out, was to prevent the Peloponnesians from obtaining corn from the west. The Athenians were also interested in spying out the land with a view to a possible future conquest of the whole island.

The following summer the Athenian fleet, commanded by Laches, set out for Mylae [*Milazzo*], which belonged to Messana. The garrison of Mylae consisted of two battalions of Messanians, who set an ambush for the Athenians. The ambush failed and the Messanians were defeated with heavy losses. The Athenians then compelled the town to surrender, after which they also obtained the surrender of Messana without a fight.
Thucydides, 3: 90

INESSA (426/5, winter) – Peloponnesian War
In the winter after their attack on Mylae [*Milazzo*] the Athenians and their allies marched against the town of Inessa (also called Aetna), which was garrisoned by Syracusans. The attackers failed to take the place and were forced to withdraw. As they did so, the Syracusans came

out and attacked and routed them, killing many of them.
Thucydides, 3: 103

OLPAE (426/5, winter) – Peloponnesian War
In Epirus the people of Ambracia [*Arta*], north of the Ambracian Gulf, marched with 3,000 hoplites into the territory of Amphilochian Argos on the east side of the gulf. They seized the fort of Olpae near the coast. The invasion had been agreed beforehand with the Spartan commander Eurylochus who, when he heard that it was in progress, set off to join the invaders and reached Olpae unmolested. On the other side, the Acarnanians, allies of Athens, sent a division of their army to the relief of Argos and invited Demosthenes to come and lead it. A message for help was also sent to 20 Athenian ships which were cruising off the Peloponnese under the command of Aristotle. Soon afterwards these ships sailed into the gulf, carrying Demosthenes with some hoplites and archers. They joined up with the Acarnanians and encamped near Olpae. Neither side made a move for several days but on the sixth day they drew up in battle order. The army of Demosthenes was greatly outnumbered and outflanked by the Peloponnesians. Demosthenes' ploy to deal with this situation was to place 400 hoplites and light troops in a well-hidden ambush. When the two armies engaged, the Peloponnesians on the left outflanked the enemy and were beginning to encircle the Athenian right as Demosthenes had envisaged. At that point the troops in ambush broke cover and attacked the enemy wing in the rear. The defeat of that wing was complete and Eurylochus himself was killed. Meanwhile the Peloponnesian right wing had defeated its opposite numbers and pursued them in their flight. But when they returned from the chase not knowing the outcome of the battle, they were immediately set upon and many were killed. The next day the Peloponnesian Menedaius, who had succeeded Eurylochus as commander, found himself virtually cut off both by land and sea. He was emphatically refused a truce under which he could retreat, but the wily Demosthenes came to a secret agreement with him allowing the Peloponnesians to sneak away furtively without the Ambraciots. This seemed certain to sow distrust of the Peloponnesians among their allies.
Thucydides, 3: 107–108

IDOMENE (426/5, winter) – Peloponnesian War
After the battle at Olpae (above), news reached

Demosthenes that an army from Ambracia [*Arta*] was marching south in response to an early message from Olpae for help. The Ambraciots knew nothing of the subsequent battle. Demosthenes planned an ambush and sent out an advance party while he followed later. The Ambraciots' route would take them by Idomene, the name given to two prominent hills between which there was a pass, now known as the pass of *Macrinoros*. During the night Demosthenes' advance party took possession of the southern hill unobtrusively. When the Ambraciots arrived, they reached the smaller, northern, hill first and decided to camp on it. At nightfall Demosthenes himself set out, taking half his army to the pass and sending the rest into the mountains behind. He then fell upon the enemy while they were still asleep. Most of them were killed where they lay; the rest were routed. The escapers headed for the mountains and into the arms of the second contingent. Thucydides does not report the number of dead because, as he says, in proportion to the size of the city the figures would not be believed.
Thucydides, 3: 110 and 112

STRAITS OF MESSINA (425) –
Peloponnesian War
In Sicily, the Syracusans had been equipping their fleet, which was now ready and was sent to guard Messana [*Messina*] against attacks from Rhegium [*Reggio*] on the other side of the *Straits of Messina* (ancient Siculum Fretum). At that time the Athenians were occupied elsewhere and their ships in the straits were reduced in numbers. The Syracusans saw this as a chance to try their fortunes in a naval engagement to see if they could gain superiority in the area. As it happened, the opportunity was forced on them when they had to escort one of their boats across. With more than 30 ships they came up against 16 Athenian and 8 Rhegian ships, which defeated them and sank one of their ships.
Thucydides, 4: 25(1–2)

NAXOS (425) – Sicily: Internal Wars
During a brief absence of the Athenian fleet on other business, the Messanians launched an attack in force on the neighbouring Chalcidian colony of Naxos [near *Taormina*] and forced the inhabitants inside their walls. While the Messanians were laying waste the surrounding country, many Sicels descended from the mountains to help the Naxians. Encouraged by this, the Naxians made a sortie from the town and fell upon the Messanians,

routing them. More than a thousand of the enemy were killed in the rout and many more were slaughtered later as they worked their way homeward.
Thucydides, 4: 25(7–9)

MESSANA (425) – Peloponnesian War
Immediately after the battle at Naxos (above) the inhabitants of Leontini [*Lentini*], backed by the Athenians, took advantage of the Messanians' weakness and attacked Messana [*Messina*]. However, the garrison made a sortie and routed the Leontinians, killing many of them. When the Athenians, who had anchored in the harbour, saw the rout, they disembarked and chased the Messanians back into their city. The Athenians put up a trophy in recognition of their part in the encounter but, on balance, the Messanians seem to have got the better of it.
Thucydides, 4: 25(10–11)

PYLOS (425, summer) – Peloponnesian War
The Athenian general Demosthenes had a plan. He wanted to establish a base in the western Peloponnese. Consequently, when the Athenians sent out a fleet of 40 ships bound for Sicily under generals Sophocles and Eurymedon, Demosthenes sailed with it and was told to use the fleet at his discretion. When they were off Messenia, Demosthenes asked the commanders to put in at

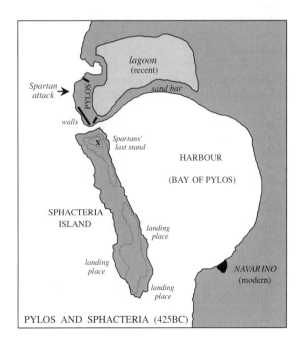

PYLOS AND SPHACTERIA (425BC)

Pylos [*Pylos*, formerly *Navarino*]. They objected, wanting to get on with their own commission. By chance a storm blew up and they were forced to shelter at Pylos. Demosthenes immediately proposed fortifying the place, or rather the relatively small areas which were not naturally protected, and the soldiers eventually built a wall in a few days to relieve their boredom. The fleet then departed on its way leaving Demosthenes with five ships. At that time the Peloponnesians had just invaded Attica for the fifth time. When they heard about the capture of Pylos, they hurried home and the Spartans marched to Pylos to relieve it. They also sent for their 60 ships in Corcyra. Likewise Demosthenes sent a message to Eurymedon asking him to return with his fleet.

Pylos is a rocky promontory which projects southwards across the northern end of a large bay on the south-west coast of Messenia. This natural barrier is continued by a narrow island called Sphacteria [*Sfaktiria*], which is nearly 3 miles long and which stretches from near the southern end of Pylos across the greater part of the mouth of the bay. The only entrances to the bay are a narrow channel between Pylos and Sphacteria and a wider one between Sphacteria and the mainland at the southern end of the bay. The Spartan plan was to deny the Athenians access to the harbour by blocking the entrances with ships. Furthermore, in case the Athenians landed on the uninhabited island of Sphacteria, the Spartans ferried some hoplites across to it. On Pylos, Demosthenes mustered his men, mostly sailors, and armed them as best he could. He posted most of them behind the wall and facing the land to repel any attack from that quarter. He himself with 60 hoplites descended to some rocky ground outside the fortifications and facing the open sea, below the point where their wall was weakest. When the Spartans came in to the attack, it was the assault from the sea that provided the most determined action. The Spartan admiral Thrasymelidas made his attack precisely where Demosthenes had expected, sending in a few ships at a time to try to secure a foothold on the shore. They failed. Their general Brasidas was outstanding in his daring, shouting to his men to break their ships up on the shore as long as they forced a landing. Still they failed; the Athenians did not yield an inch. The attacks continued into the next day. On the following day the Athenian fleet arrived, amounting to 50 ships by virtue of some reinforcements. The Spartan ships were all in the harbour and the entrances had not been blocked. As the Spartans did not come

out, the Athenians sailed in by both entrances and fell on the enemy line, disabling a number of ships and ramming those which had been driven ashore or had not been manned. After a bitter struggle the action was broken off. The Athenians then started sailing round the island of Sphacteria. The 420 Spartan hoplites commanded by Epitadas on the island were trapped. This so horrified Sparta that it was decided to conclude a truce pending an agreement to end the war. The truce, however, broke down as a result of some alleged infringements, and hostilities were resumed in the battle for Sphacteria (below).
Thucydides, 4: 8–15 and 23

SPHACTERIA ISL (425) – Peloponnesian War
The Spartan defeat in the naval encounter in the Bay of Pylos (above) left 420 Spartan hoplites commanded by Epitadas trapped on the uninhabited island of Sphacteria [*Sfaktiria*]. The Athenians immediately started sailing round the place in a regular guard duty, assuming that the victims would be subdued within a few days. Unfortunately for the Athenians, the necessities of life were smuggled in to the island by various means, even by divers under water, prolonging the siege (which eventually lasted for 72 days). The Athenians became restive and blamed their statesman Cleon, who in his turn blamed Nicias, the general in charge whom Cleon detested. Cleon high-handedly claimed that if he was in charge he would subdue the Spartans within 20 days, a boast which to his horror was accepted by Nicias. With no means of escape from his self-inflicted task, Cleon asked that Demosthenes, who was already at Pylos, should share the command with him, and he set sail with a force of archers and peltasts. On his arrival the two generals landed all their hoplites (about 800) on Sphacteria just before dawn and overran the first Spartan post, killing all the surprised and sleepy soldiers. The rest of the Athenian army, including the archers and peltasts, then landed and were posted in groups of around 200 on all the highest points of ground surrounding the Spartan main body. When the Spartans moved forward to attack, they were met by a barrage of spears, arrows and stones from the front and both flanks and could not get to grips with their lightly armed adversaries. After a lengthy period of this long-range fighting the Spartans became exhausted and fell back to a fort at the northernmost point of the island, behind which steep cliffs fell away to the sea. There the conflict became a stalemate until the commander of the Messenian

detachment serving with the Athenians offered to take a few men and climb round the cliffs to the unprotected rear of the enemy. When he and his men suddenly appeared behind them, the Spartans knew that they were beaten and agreed to surrender. Of the original 420 Spartan hoplites, 292 were captured, the rest having been killed. The Athenian losses were light.
Thucydides, 4: 26–39

SOLYGIA (425, summer) – Peloponnesian War
Shortly after the events at Pylos and Sphacteria, the Athenians launched an expedition against Corinthian territory. The force, under the command of Nicias, consisted of 80 ships with 2,000 Athenian hoplites, cavalry and various allied contingents. They landed by night undetected, on a beach which was overlooked by the Solygian hill and on which was the village of Solygia, a few miles south-west of Cenchreae [*Kecrees*]. The Corinthians under their general Lycophron came up to resist. They attacked the Athenian right wing, where most of the activity took place and where the battle seesawed for a long time. In the end the Corinthians were routed and withdrew to the hill, having lost their general. On seeing the arrival of reinforcements for their opponents, the Athenians beat a hasty retreat to their ships and sailed away. The Corinthian losses were 212; the Athenian dead numbered rather less than 50.
Thucydides, 4: 42–44

CYTHERA ISL (424, summer) – Peloponnesian War
In the summer, after their assault on Solygia (above) the Athenians made an expedition against Cythera [*Kithira*], an island off the southern end of Laconia. The population was composed of Lacedaemonians of the *perioikoi* and the island was of great strategic value to the mother state. The Athenian force consisted of 60 ships with 2,000 hoplites and some allied contingents under the command of Nicias and two other generals. They proceeded on foot to the city of Cythera, where all the inhabitants were drawn up to oppose them. In the ensuing battle the people of Cythera held their ground at first, but they were eventually routed and fled into the city. They agreed to submit to Athens in exchange for certain guarantees.
Thucydides, 4: 53–54

DELIUM (424, winter) – Peloponnesian War
This battle was the outcome of a plot which was hatched by some Boeotians in conjunction with the Athenian generals Demosthenes and Hippocrates. Their object was to overthrow the Boeotian regime in favour of a democracy. As part of this plan, the Athenians were to seize Delium [*Dilessi*], about 4 miles from Tanagra. Hippocrates achieved this and proceeded to fortify the place. Meanwhile the Boeotians were rallying from all parts to Tanagra. Pagondas, their supreme commander, led them out and took up a position on the far side of a hill from the Athenians. The Boeotian force consisted of 7,000 hoplites, more than 10,000 light troops and 1,000 cavalry. The Thebans were on the right wing and were massed 25 deep. The Athenian army was largely composed of hoplites, similar in number to their adversaries, with some cavalry. The engagement was started by the Boeotians, who crested the intervening hill and charged down on the foe. The extreme wings of the two armies, largely consisting of cavalry, failed to contact each other because both sides were held up by water courses. More centrally, the Boeotian right got the better of the opposing Athenians, forcing them back remorselessly. Their left, on the other hand, was badly mauled by the Athenians until Pagondas sent two squadrons of cavalry round the hill. The sudden appearance of these reinforcements created panic among the hitherto successful Athenians so that the whole army fled, pursued by the enemy. The Athenians lost nearly 1,000 of their hoplites, a very high percentage, which included their general Hippocrates; the Boeotians lost about 500. The Boeotians immediately besieged and recaptured Delium, using a flame-thrower.
Thucydides, 4: 90–96

SCIONE (423) – Peloponnesian War
Scione [near *Lutra*] was a town on the Chalcidic peninsula of Pallene [*Kassandra*]. In 423 it revolted from Athens and gave its allegiance to the Spartan general Brasidas, who had been campaigning in those regions. The timing was unfortunate because the Spartans and the Athenians were in the middle of negotiating an armistice for one year. The Athenians insisted that the revolt took place after the armistice had been agreed and was therefore governed by it; Brasidas, on the other hand, claimed that the armistice was not in force at the time and that the change of allegiance was therefore valid. (In fact it took place two days after the agreement.) Shortly afterwards the neighbouring town of Mende [*Kalandra*] in Pallene followed suit. Brasidas was temporarily absent in Macedonia at the time and so the Athenians sent 50 ships with

1,000 hoplites under Nicias and Nicostratus to occupy both cities. Mende did not in the end prove a difficult conquest as the inhabitants were divided. Some of them attacked and routed the Peloponnesians and then opened the gates to the Athenians. At Scione, on the other hand, the inhabitants and the Peloponnesians marched out and took up a strong position on a hill in front of the city. The Athenians made a direct assault on this vital position and drove the opposing forces from it, after which they were in a position to build blockading walls and to besiege the place.
Thucydides, 4: 122 and 130–131

LAODOCIUM (423, winter) – Local Dispute

Throughout the winter, Athens and Sparta observed an armistice which was in force for one year until the Pythian games. In this period of relative calm, the Arcadians of Tegea and Mantinea were involved in a local dispute. Such quarrels were common between them and were usually concerned with the water courses which tended to flood the territory of one or the other. On this occasion they fought a battle at a place called Laodocium (unidentified), the result of which was indecisive. Each side routed one wing of the opposition; both sides claimed a victory. Nightfall brought an end to the hostilities.
Thucydides, 4: 134

AMPHIPOLIS (422) – Peloponnesian War

At the end of a one year's armistice between Athens and Sparta, the Athenian general Cleon sailed out against various Thracian towns and arrived opposite Amphipolis, where he played a waiting game. Brasidas, the Spartan general in command at Amphipolis, had expected him and had taken up a defensive position on high ground with an excellent view across the river Strymon. He had a total force of around 5,000, which he divided between the city and his camp. Meanwhile the Athenians were becoming restless doing nothing and so Cleon, seeing no sign of activity on the walls, moved forward to a hill to reconnoitre. This prompted Brasidas to leave his camp and enter the city. Cleon was unwilling to risk a battle until he had received some reinforcements which he was expecting. He began a leisurely withdrawal, with the left wing in the lead, and himself took charge of the right wing, which he wheeled with its unshielded flank exposed to the enemy. At this point Brasidas saw his chance and suddenly charged out through the gates with 150 hoplites. He fell upon the disorganized Athenians, routing

their centre. The rest of the Spartan troops charged out of the city by another gate and bore down on the enemy from the other side. The Athenian left wing broke and fled. The right wing stood its ground but Cleon himself had no intention of doing so. He took to flight and was overtaken and killed. His hoplites, braver than their leader, formed up on a hill and resisted several attacks until they were surrounded and subjected to a shower of weapons, whereupon they too joined the others in flight. The brave Brasidas was wounded in the fight and died shortly afterwards in the city, to which he had been carried. The Athenian losses were about 600; their opponents lost only seven.
Thucydides, 5: 6–11

MANTINEA (418) – Peloponnesian War

War broke out between Epidaurus and Argos. Epidaurus was an ally of Sparta, and so the whole Spartan army under King Agis II marched against Argos. The two large armies with their respective allies became ranged against each other in the plain of Argos. Just as the engagement was about to begin the Argive commanders stepped forward and made proposals to King Agis for a truce, which was granted. The men on both sides were bitterly resentful of their commanders' high-handed actions, both sides maintaining that they had never had a better chance of winning. Shortly afterwards the Tegeates sent an urgent appeal to the Spartans for help against Mantinean aggression. If it was not forthcoming, they said, they would transfer their allegiance to Argos. This galvanized the Spartans into sending their entire force to Tegea, while collecting their Arcadian allies *en route* and sending to other states for reinforcements. The Spartans and their allies then invaded the territory of Mantinea. At this, the Argives, who had been joined by 1,000 Athenians and who supported Mantinea, took up an almost impregnable position in the hills. Agis was persuaded to withdraw, and he adopted a cunning plan. He began to divert the water courses from Tegea over Mantinean territory, hoping that this would bring the Argives down to fight. The ruse succeeded. The Argives descended into the plain and the next day they formed up in battle array without any enemy in sight. At that time the Spartans were returning from their aquatic operations, and they suddenly found themselves confronted with an army in battle order.

Thucydides deduces that the Spartans, excluding 600 Sciritae, numbered around 4,000, but he

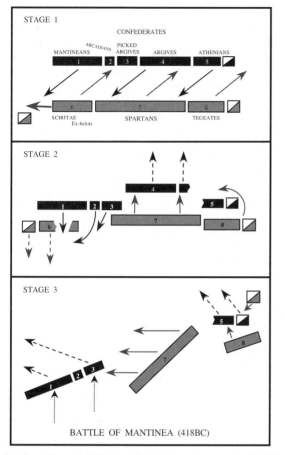

STAGE 1

CONFEDERATES

MANTINEANS — ARCADIANS — PICKED ARGIVES — ARGIVES — ATHENIANS

SCIRITAE — Ex-helots — SPARTANS — TEGEATES

STAGE 2

STAGE 3

BATTLE OF MANTINEA (418BC)

Based on a diagram in J. Hackett (ed.), *Warfare in the Ancient World, 1989*

left wing becomes exposed to encirclement by the opponent's extended right wing. To counteract this trend, Agis ordered the entire left wing – Sciritae and ex-helots – to move further to the left and he commanded two polemarchs on the right wing to move their regiments across to fill the gap. They refused to do this at such short notice. When the opposing armies closed, the Mantineans with their allies on the right swept into the hiatus in the Spartan ranks, surrounded the enemy troops in this area and forced them back as far as their transport line. In the centre and on the other wing matters were very different. King Agis and his special troops in the Spartan centre launched a furious attack upon the enemy centre and drove it into headlong flight, leaving the Athenians on the enemy left wing isolated. At the same time the Spartans and Tegeates on the right, who already outflanked the Athenians, started to encircle them. The Athenians only avoided complete destruction because Agis, having put the enemy centre to flight, wheeled his men to the assistance of his routed left wing. This was still being attacked by the Mantineans who, when they saw that the rest of their army had been defeated, turned and fled at sight of the approaching Spartans. Many Mantineans were killed in the pursuit. Agis' move relieved the pressure on the Athenians and gave them time to escape. On the Argive side, 1,100 were killed; it is said that the Spartan losses were about 300.

Thucydides, 5: 64–74

SYRACUSE: OLYMPIEIUM (415, winter) –
Peloponnesian War   Map 15

In the midsummer of 415 the Athenians launched a magnificent naval expedition bound for Sicily with the averred aim of helping the Leontines. The covert objective was to gain control of the whole island. The total fleet with allied ships amounted to 134 triremes with 5,100 hoplites and many light-armed troops. The commanders were Nicias (an ironical appointment in view of the fact that he had opposed the expedition from the start), Alcibiades and Lamachus. When they landed, Lamachus voted for sailing straight for Syracuse and fighting it out. The others disagreed, and they wasted time visiting Catana, Naxos and other places in search of support. At this point Alcibiades was recalled to Athens to stand trial in connexion with religious scandals. By the beginning of winter Nicias and Lamachus were ready to make a move but the Syracusans also were preparing for an attack. The generals therefore

admits that he finds it impossible to give accurate numbers for either side. The Spartan army appeared, he says, to be the larger. It is now thought likely that his figure of 4,000 was a considerable underestimate. In the deployment, Agis and the Spartans were in the centre. The Sciritae were on the left wing, and next to them were veteran ex-helots who had fought with Brasidas in Thrace. Between them and the centre was another contingent of freed helots. On the right were the Tegeates and other Arcadian allies with a few Spartans on the extreme wing. On the Argive side, the Mantineans held the right wing, the Athenians the left. As the armies approached each other, the right wings of both sides became unduly extended. In those days this was an almost automatic movement occasioned by the desire of each man to protect his right side behind his neighbour's shield, causing him to move to the right. As a result the

adopted a deceitful plan by sending a double agent to tell the Syracusans where and when they would be able to defeat the invaders. When the Syracusans acted on this information and set out with their entire army, the Athenians sailed up the coast and landed unmolested near the Olympieium within a mile of the Great Harbour. Next day the two sides took up positions for battle. The Athenians drew up half of their forces eight deep in advance; the other half was deployed in a hollow square (with the non-combatants in the centre) as a flexible reserve. The Syracusans drew up their entire line of hoplites 16 deep. When the armies came to close quarters, both sides stood firm for some time in spite of a thunderstorm which disconcerted the Syracusans. As Thucydides puts it, each Syracusan was fighting for his life on that day and his liberty thereafter, while the Athenians fought to conquer a country that was not their own. It was the Argives, on the Athenian right, who first forced the opposing wing back, after which the Athenians broke through the enemy centre. Cut in two, the Syracusan army took to flight. Casualties were about 260 on the Syracusan side; the Athenians and their allies lost approximately 50.
Thucydides, 6: 67–71; Plutarch, Nicias, 16

SYRACUSE: EPIPOLAE (414, spring) –
Peloponnesian War   Map 15
The Athenians sailed from their base at Catana and landed their whole force near Syracuse on the north side. From there the distance was rather more than half a mile to the heights of Epipolae, a plateau to the west of Syracuse which slopes down to the city from its summit at Euryelus. The army went straight up the slope at the double and occupied it unmolested. When the Syracusans realized what had happened, they set off up the slope with nearly 3 miles of climb from where they stood. Their defeat occasions little surprise, their leader Diomilus being killed with about 300 of his men.
Thucydides, 6: 97; Plutarch, Nicias, 17

SYRACUSE: SYCE (414, spring) –
Peloponnesian War   Map 15
After the battle for control of the heights of Epipolae (above), the Athenians moved down the east slope in the direction of the city to a place called Syce in the middle of the plateau, where they built a fort called the Circle. Their intention was to circumvallate the city by building walls out across the plateau on either side of the Circle and

continuing them down to the north and south shores. While they were at work on the Circle the Syracusans came out with some cavalry detachments, which succeeded in hampering the operation by making repeated guerilla attacks. The Athenians had originally landed in Sicily without any cavalry, but 250 cavalrymen had been sent out from Athens in response to an urgent request and a further 400 had been provided by allies. This force, accompanied by a division of hoplites, eventually charged the Syracusan cavalry and routed them.

The Syracusans next attempted to halt the Athenians' progress by building a counter-wall out from the city in the direction of the Circle. With this they aimed to cut the Athenians' line of fortification between the Circle and the southern edge of Epipolae. The Athenians bided their time until they saw a moment when the enemy fortifications were poorly guarded. They then attacked with 300 hoplites and destroyed the enemy's works with the loss of only a few men.
Thucydides, 6: 98

SYRACUSE: LYSIMELEIA (414) –
Peloponnesian War   Map 15
The Athenians continued their circumvallation of the city by starting to build a double wall from the southern edge of Epipolae across the flat ground by the marsh of Lysimeleia to the Great Harbour. The Syracusans tried to prevent this project by creating a second counter-wall consisting of a ditch and palisade extending from their city wall through the middle of the marsh, which would make it impossible for the Athenians to build right down to the sea. At that time the Athenians were still fortifying the cliffs at the edge of Epipolae. At dawn the whole army descended into the plain and captured the entire ditch and palisade. When fighting broke out, the Athenians sent the Syracusans flying to left and right and they would have scored a great success but for the disastrous loss of their best general, Lamachus. He, with a few others, had crossed a ditch to help his right wing and had become isolated and was killed.
Thucydides, 6: 101

SYRACUSE: EPIPOLAE (414) –
Peloponnesian War   Map 15
The Syracusans were now in despair and saw no hope of preventing a siege. They had already appealed to the Corinthians and the Spartans for military assistance and a commander, and the Spartans had appointed their general Gylippus to

undertake the task. He crossed to Sicily with two Spartan and two Corinthian ships, followed almost immediately by a Corinthian fleet of 14 ships. They arrived none too soon as the Athenian fortifications were nearing completion. The Athenians had made the great mistake of failing to press on earlier to complete their north wall, on which they were now working, from the Circle to the sea. As a result of this omission the enemy could still enter the city from the north bay. Under Gylippus' direction the Syracusans started building a third counter-wall, running from the northern suburb of Tycha toward the heights of Epipolae so that it would intercept the Athenian wall. While this was in progress Gylippus repeatedly lined up his army in front of the Athenian workings, and the enemy confronted him with their force. The first encounter between the adversaries took place in the space between the ends of the walls. This was too cramped for Gylippus' cavalry to manoeuvre, and his troops were defeated. In the second confrontation Nicias took the initiative because the Syracusans' wall almost reached his own unfinished fortifications. On this occasion Gylippus posted his cavalry on the Athenian flank in open ground beyond the walls. When his cavalry charged, they routed the enemy wing, after which the rest of the Athenian army gave way before Gylippus' hoplites and was driven back behind its fortifications. The Syracusans completed their wall the following night, finally preventing the Athenians from investing the city.
Thucydides, 7: 5–6

SYRACUSE: PLEMMYRIUM (413) –

Peloponnesian War   Map 15
The Spartan general Gylippus commanding the Syracusans had been touring the various cities of Sicily soliciting reinforcements. He returned to Syracuse with his recruits and encouraged the Syracusans to try their fortune in a sea battle. When the fleet was ready, Gylippus led out all his infantry by night with the intention of attacking the three Athenian-held forts on Plemmyrium. This was a headland which projected northward to form the southern jaw of the mouth of the Great Harbour. The Athenians had fortified it and had a mooring at its base. The citadel was on the northern promontory which formed the opposite jaw. While Gylippus was marching to the forts, the 35 Syracusan triremes stationed in the harbour were sailing up against the Athenians, while another 45 from the smaller harbour, which was

on the seaside of the city, were sailing round to threaten Plemmyrium from the open sea. The Athenians manned 60 ships. They sent 25 into the Great Harbour and 35 to the harbour mouth to deal with the 'outsiders'. Meanwhile the Athenians in Plemmyrium were distracted by the naval battle and were taken off guard by Gylippus, who attacked in the early morning and seized all three forts. The Syracusans did not fare so well at sea. The 'outsiders' forced the Athenians back and then entered the harbour but in an undisciplined manner. Without any order they presented an easy prey to the Athenians, who proceeded to worst both them and the hitherto successful 'insiders'. They sank 11 Syracusan ships and lost 3 of their own. Against that, the loss of the forts was a major disaster because they were used as depots and were full of stores of every kind. In addition, they had provided protection for incoming convoys. In the opinion of Thucydides, this loss was the principal cause of the impending deterioration of the Athenian army.
Thucydides, 7: 22–24

ERINEUS (413) – Peloponnesian War

For a long time the Peloponnesians had maintained a fleet of 25 ships opposite the Athenian squadron at Naupactus [*Lepanto*] in the Gulf of Corinth. Its purpose was to prevent the Athenians from attacking merchant convoys destined for the enemy in Sicily. The Peloponnesians had now prepared themselves for battle and had included a few extra ships to even the numbers. They were anchored off Erineus, a bare 12 miles east of Naupactus on the opposite shore, under the command of the Corinthian Polyanthes. The Athenians took the initiative and sailed out with 33 ships under Diphilus. The Corinthians bided their time before accepting the challenge and launching out into a battle which proved to be utterly indecisive. They had widened and strengthened the bows of their ships for greater efficacy in ramming head on. As a result, seven of the Athenian ships were put out of action, but three of their own were sunk. Both sides put up trophies!
Thucydides, 7: 34

SYRACUSE: HARBOUR (413) –

Peloponnesian War   Map 15
By this time virtually the whole of Sicily, except Acragas [*Agrigento*], had joined the Syracusans and supplied them with troops. On the Athenian side, Demosthenes and Eurymedon were on their

way, also with considerable reinforcements. In the meantime the Syracusans had modified their ships, shortening and strengthening their prows in the same way as the Corinthians had just done (Erineus, above). They were now keen to make a combined land and sea attack before the arrival of the Athenian reinforcements. On the first day of engagement nothing much was achieved. The two armies confronted each other around the walls but did not go into action. On the water, the Athenians put out 75 ships against the Syracusans' 80 but they did no more than spar. On the following day there were no hostilities, but on the third day the Syracusans again went into action by land and sea. Once again the two sides did no more than spar with each other until late in the day, when the Syracusans sent a message to the city officials asking them to bring the market to the harbour with provisions for sale. When the Syracusans backed water to the jetty, they gave the impression that they were retiring from the confrontation. Instead, after a quick meal, they again manned their ships and caught the Athenians unaware and in confusion. When the Athenians rallied and charged the enemy, they were met head on by the reinforced prows of the Syracusan vessels. Even more damage was done by a lot of small Syracusan boats which slipped under the Athenian oars so that missiles could be hurled at the sailors at point-blank range. When the Athenians fled to their anchorage, seven of their ships had been sunk and many had been disabled.
Thucydides, 7: 37–41

SYRACUSE: EPIPOLAE (413) –

Peloponnesian War   Map 15
Demosthenes and Eurymedon arrived with about 73 ships from Athens with 5,000 hoplites and large numbers of slingers, archers and javelin throwers, as well as stores. Demosthenes now took over from the hesitant and indecisive Nicias as the motive power. His aim was to capture the enemy camp on the heights of Epipolae, whence it would be easy also to take the Syracusans' single counter-wall. He and his force set out at midnight and approached Epipolae by a roundabout route from the far side via Euryelus, the summit. They captured the Syracusans' fort and routed the defenders before heading for the counter-wall. Meanwhile Gylippus and the Syracusans with their allies came up to join the battle. Initially all went well for the Athenians who forced the enemy back. They were intent on charging through the whole enemy army while they had the impetus.

However, the Boeotian allies of Gylippus stood up to them, charged and routed them. From that moment the Athenians fell into disorder and chaos. They were scattered and, in the darkness, it was impossible to identify friend from foe. By calling out the password to everyone they met, they soon gave it to the enemy with predictable result. The Syracusans, being still in a compact body, did not have these difficulties. Many of the Athenians and their allies were killed but the number is not reported.
Thucydides, 7: 43–44

SYRACUSE: HARBOUR (413) –

Peloponnesian War   Map 15
The Syracusans had received further reinforcements while the Athenian situation was getting worse every day. They prepared to sail away, but this was prevented by an eclipse of the moon. The soothsayer said that willy-nilly they would have to wait for thrice nine days. The Syracusans were determined to force a naval battle and sailed out with 76 ships. The Athenians opposed them with 86 vessels. Eurymedon, commanding the Athenian right wing, detached his ships and made a wide encircling sweep. The enemy, however, defeated the Athenian centre and then attended to Eurymedon, whom they caught in a narrow bay. He was killed and all his ships were destroyed, after which the rest of the fleet was forced ashore. Gylippus, seeing this, took part of his army to the shore to destroy the crews as they landed. Fortunately for the Athenians, their Etruscan allies also saw this and charged, driving Gylippus' vanguard into the marsh of Lysimeleia. More Syracusans and allies appeared but the Athenians drove them back after a successful engagement. They managed to rescue many of their ships but 18 were captured.
Thucydides, 7: 52–53

SYRACUSE: HARBOUR (413) –

Peloponnesian War   Map 15
The Syracusans were now determined to capture the whole of the huge Athenian force and put an end to their campaign. To this end they blocked up the mouth of the Great Harbour with a line of ships broadside on, barring any escape. The Athenians decided to put everything they had got into a sea battle and managed to man about 110 ships, with large numbers of archers and javelin throwers on board. Demosthenes and his colleagues embarked and sailed straight for the barrier blocking the mouth. The Syracusans and

their allies had already put out with about 75 ships under Gylippus and Pythen. Part of their fleet guarded the barrier; the others were stationed all round the harbour perimeter ready to attack the enemy from all sides. With a total number of almost 200 ships in the harbour, the ensuing action filled the whole arena. Never before, as Thucydides says, had so many ships fought in such a confined space. It was not a matter of ramming the enemy but of colliding with him and being bumped into at the same time. Consequently, much of the fighting was hand to hand on the decks, amid a bedlam of shouting which made orders inaudible. The action continued for a long while in this vein, but eventually Athenian resistance was broken and they were forced back to the shore. Their ships were abandoned wherever they beached and the crews fled to their camp. In spite of their defeat the Athenians still had more serviceable ships than the enemy, but the crews were so demoralized that any attempt to make a break-out by sea was out of the question. Two days after the disaster the whole Athenian and allied force started to make its way inland, subjected to continual harassment. Nicias and Demosthenes and their respective parties got separated and both surrendered. The two generals were ultimately executed. The Athenian expeditionary force had been destroyed *in toto*.
Thucydides, 7: 59–71; Plutarch, Nicias, *25*

SPIRAEUM (412) – Peloponnesian War
Taking advantage of the overwhelming defeat of Athens at Syracuse, the Lesbians, Chians and Erythraeans were all preparing to revolt. In this they were aided by the Spartans, who decided to sail first to Chios. Sparta and her allies had 39 ships in the Gulf of Corinth. Twenty-one of these were dragged across the Isthmus and set sail for Chios under the command of Alcamenes. Their departure was noted by the Athenians, who tailed them with a fleet of 37 ships and drove them into the harbour of Spiraeum at the southern end of Corinthia (not Piraeum, in the north of Corinthia, as corrupted in some manuscripts). The Athenians then attacked from their ships and from the shore, killing Alcamenes and disabling most of the enemy vessels. Later in the year the Peloponnesian ships, which had been repaired, broke out of the harbour. They defeated the Athenians who had been blockading them and captured four of their ships.
Thucydides, 8: 10 and 20(1)

CARDAMYLE (412)
BOLISSUS (412)
PHANAE PR (412)
LEUCONIUM (412)
} – Peloponnesian War

Among other islands and towns in the Aegean, Chios had revolted from Athens. The Athenian admirals, Leon and Diomedon, landed some hoplites at Cardamyle [*Kardamila*] and at Bolissus [*Volissos*] in Chios and defeated all the Chians who opposed them, inflicting heavy casualties. From Thucydides' account it seems clear that these landings resulted in only one battle, presumably in the north of the island where the landings took place about 12 miles apart. The Athenians then defeated the Chians a second time, at Phanae Promontory [*C. Masticho*], and in a third battle at Leuconium. After this last defeat the Chians decided that they had suffered enough and would give up resisting. They allowed the Athenians to ravage their land unmolested. There were now some among the Chians who realized that they had overestimated the Athenians' decline, and the thought of restoring their status quo began to enter their minds.
Thucydides, 8: 24(2–3)

MILETUS (412, summer) – Peloponnesian War
At the end of the summer a fresh fleet of 48 ships arrived in the Aegean from Athens carrying a total of 3,500 Athenian, Argive and allied hoplites. They landed at Miletus in Ionia, where the inhabitants came out with 800 hoplites reinforced by some Peloponnesians and mercenaries in the pay of the Persian satrap Tissaphernes, who was present in person with his cavalry. Like the Lacedaemonians, the Persians were taking advantage of Athenian weakness for their own ends. In the encounter, the Argives were headstrong and rushed out first to be defeated by the Milesians with the loss of 300 men. The Athenians, by contrast, worsted the rest of the army apart from the Milesians, who had taken no further part. One noteworthy opponent of the Athenians was Alcibiades, who had abandoned Athens in favour of Sparta and who fought in this battle with Tissaphernes. He reversed his allegiance again at a later date.
Thucydides, 8: 25

SYME ISL (411, January) – Peloponnesian War
In supporting the Peloponnesians, the Persians were taking advantage of the Athenian debilitation caused by their disastrous Sicilian campaign. In the winter of 411 the Spartans equipped 27 ships for Pharnabazus, who wanted a fleet for operation

in the Hellespont. When this fleet, commanded by Antisthenes, put in at Caunus [*Dalyan*] in Caria, he asked for a convoy along the coast. In response to this request, the Spartan commander Astyochus put out with a fleet from Miletus after which he heard that 20 Athenian ships under Charminus were keeping a watch for the same Peloponnesian fleet in the region of the island of Syme [*Simi*]. He therefore made directly for that island. In poor visibility, followed by darkness, his fleet became scattered with the result that the Athenians' first sight of him was in fact only a glimpse of his left wing. The Athenians proceeded against him with less than their full force, believing that these were the ships from Caunus that they had been waiting for. They started the fight well, sinking three ships and crippling others, until they suddenly found themselves confronted – indeed surrounded – by the rest of Astyochus' fleet, whereupon they took to flight after losing six ships.
*Thucydides, **8**: 41–42*

RHODES (411, winter) – Peloponnesian War
In the year 412 the Peloponnesians persuaded the Rhodians to revolt from Athens. At the beginning of the next year, the admirals Leon and Diomedon in command of the Athenian fleet in the Aegean proceeded to attack Rhodes, where they found the Peloponnesian fleet drawn up on the shore. They made a landing and defeated the Rhodians who opposed them, and then they retired. Although the deed has not been specifically reported, it is inconceivable that they failed to put the enemy ships out of action.
*Thucydides, **8**: 55(1)*

CHIOS ISL (411, spring) – Peloponnesian War
In 412 the Chians were among the first to revolt from Athens, but although they had been repeatedly promised help by the Peloponnesians, it never seemed to come. Their land had been ravaged and they were blockaded and cut off from the sea as a result of the Athenian victories (Cardamyle *et al.*, 412). Help eventually arrived in the person of a Spartan called Leon with 12 ships. The Chians then sailed out with 36 ships in an attempt to break the blockade. In a hard fight against the Athenian fleet of 32 ships they fared rather better than the enemy. The fighting was eventually abandoned owing to the lateness of the hour but the outcome, combined with the withdrawal of 24 Athenian ships for service elsewhere, gave the Chians some control of their seas.
*Thucydides, **8**: 61*

LAMPSACUS (411, April) – Peloponnesian War
Athens had lost practically everything in western Asia, but the northern and Hellespontine confederacy was still intact. The revolt of two of the Hellespontine towns was therefore a matter of great concern. Immediately after the naval battle off Chios (above), Abydus revolted from Athens and Lampsacus [*Lapseki*] followed suit two days later. Strombichides, who had been blockading Chios, immediately set out to quell them with 24 Athenian ships and some hoplites. At Lampsacus the people came out to oppose him but he defeated them and took the town. He was unsuccessful at Abydus.
*Thucydides, **8**: 62*

ERETRIA (411, September) – Peloponnesian War
The appearance of a squadron of Lacedaemonian ships off the island of Salamis caused considerable concern at Athens for the safety of the Piraeus. But the ships proceeded on their way round Cape Sunium and up the eastern coast of Attica to anchor at Oropus [*Skála Oropoú*], far too close to Euboea for the Athenians' liking. They were utterly dependent on Euboea for all their supplies, which they could no longer bring in by land past the Spartan-occupied and fortified fortress of Decelea [*Dekélia*]. To deal with the emergency they sent Thymochares with 36 ships manned by half-trained crews to Eretria in Euboea, where they were forced to fight immediately. Agesandridas, the Lacedaemonian commander, put out against them with his 42 ships and defeated them utterly almost from the start. He captured 22 Athenian ships and, soon afterwards, caused the whole of Euboea to revolt.
*Thucydides, **8**: 95*

CYNOSSEMA PR (411, winter) – Peloponnesian War
At the invitation of Pharnabazus, Mindarus and the Peloponnesian fleet in the Aegean put out from Miletus bound for the Hellespont. The Athenians were at Eresus [*Skála Eressu*] on the west coast of Lesbos waiting for him, but he gave them the slip by sailing up the mainland coast to the east of the island. As soon as the Athenians heard that Mindarus had reached his destination at Abydus, on the Asian side of the Hellespont, they hurried after him. The Peloponnesians came out to confront them in the straits. The Athenians under Thrasybulus and Thrasyllus lined up along the

European shore; the Peloponnesians faced them on the Asian side. Each side extended its line along its respective shoreline, but the Athenians were outnumbered by 86 enemy ships to their 76. Realizing that the Peloponnesians might try to outflank them and deny them an escape to the sea, they extended their right wing. This weakened their centre so badly that it was forced back onto the shore by the enemy, who chased the Athenians on land. In their hour of victory, however, the Peloponnesians became over-confident and disorganized. All along their line their ships started scattering in a disorderly pursuit of individual targets. Seeing this, Thrasybulus on the Athenian right wing immediately turned about and attacked them. He routed them, after which he turned his attention to the previously victorious enemy centre. In their disorganized state they proved easy prey, fleeing without offering any resistance. On the Athenian left, Thrasyllus was having a battle of his own against the Syracusans. The left wing had become extended beyond the promontory of Cynossema [*Kilitbahir*] and was out of sight of the rest of the battle. After a hard fight the Syracusans started to give way to Thrasyllus but, when they realized that the rest of the fleet had been defeated, they disintegrated altogether.

The account preserved by Diodorus is florid but sketchy. He makes no mention of the tactics or of the part played by the promontory of Cynossema. *Thucydides, 8: 104–105; Diodorus, 13: 39–40*

ABYDUS (411, early winter) – Peloponnesian War
The Spartan admiral Dorieus, in command of a small Peloponnesian fleet of 13 or 14 ships, sailed to the Hellespont to join Mindarus. He was attacked in the straits by an Athenian fleet and, seeing how numerous they were, he put in to the shore. When Mindarus heard what was happening, he put out from Abydus [*Nara*] with his entire fleet of 84 ships to rescue Dorieus. The Athenians confronted him and they fought long and hard, with no consistent advantage either way, until Alcibiades was sighted heading for the Hellespont with 18 or 20 Athenian ships. As soon as he had run up his pennant and identified himself, the Lacedaemonians turned and fled. They put into the shore near Abydus where Pharnabazus was encamped with his army. An Athenian attempt to follow the enemy and to tow their ships away was partly staved off by the Persians, but the Athenians did succeed in capturing 10 ships (Xenophon says 30).

Diodorus, 13: 45–46; Xenophon, Hellenica, 1: 1(4–8); Plutarch, Alcibiades, 27(1–3)

CYZICUS (410) – Peloponnesian War
In the spring the Spartan admiral Mindarus, with the help of Pharnabazus, had besieged and taken Cyzicus at the base of the Arctonnesus peninsula in the Propontis. The Athenians set sail with a fleet of 86 ships and made for Cyzicus. They disembarked their soldiers in Cyzican territory and divided the naval force into three squadrons under Alcibiades, Theramenes and Thrasybulus respectively. Alcibiades and his 20 ships sailed well ahead of the others and, according to plan, decoyed the Lacedaemonians out to battle with 60 to 80 ships. The other two squadrons then cut off the enemy's retreat. Mindarus landed where he could and the fight continued on land, Mindarus himself being slain. In Xenophon's account, Alcibiades in the lead caught the Lacedaemonians exercising well offshore and sailed in to cut them off. But the two reports of the battle agree that the entire Lacedaemonian fleet was either captured or destroyed. Cyzicus was occupied. After these events Sparta made peace overtures to Athens but these were rejected – mistakenly, as the next few years were to show.
Diodorus, 13: 49(2)–51; Xenophon, Hellenica, 1: 1(11–18); Plutarch, Alcibiades, 28

EPHESUS (409) – Peloponnesian War
Thrasyllus (or Thrasybulus according to one source) had been sent out to the Aegean war zone by the Athenians with 30 ships and a force of hoplites. He put in at Ephesus and landed the hoplites on one side of the city at the harbour called Coressus; the cavalry and the rest of the infantry he disembarked on the other side near the marsh (which is still in existence). When the inhabitants of the city came out to fight, they attacked the hoplites first, routing them and killing 100. Then they turned their attention to the other lot, routing them too and killing 300. It appears that the 'inhabitants' were not alone in their spirited defence. The Oxyrhynchus historian says that the Ephesian forces were commanded by Timarchus and Possicrates and that they included hoplites. Xenophon mentions an allied supporting force under Tissaphernes.
Diodorus, 13: 64(1); Xenophon, Hellenica, 1: 2(7–10); Hellenica Oxyrhynchia (Cairo)

CERATA MS (409) – Peloponnesian War
While Athens was heavily engaged abroad, the

Megarians seized the city of Nisaea which was the port of Megara but which had been captured by the Athenians. The Athenians sent Leotrophides and Timarchus against them with 1,000 infantry and 400 cavalry. The Megarians went out to meet them and drew up for battle near the twin peaks called Cerata ('The Horns') which are on the boundary between Megaris and Attica. Although the Athenians were greatly outnumbered by the enemy, they routed them and slew many of them. In contrast, some Spartans who were fighting with the Megarians retreated in good order with only about 20 casualties (the figure quoted in both sources) because the Athenians confined their bile to the Megarians with whom they were particularly furious.
Diodorus, 13: 65(1–2); Hellenica Oxyrhynchia, I.1 (Florence); Strabo, 9: 1, 11

HIMERA (409) – Sicily: Second Punic Invasion
In 409 the Carthaginians invaded Sicily for the second time. On this occasion they were commanded by Hannibal, the grandson of the Hamilcar who had led the first invasion. They began by laying siege to the city of Selinus and sacking it. Then they turned their attention to Himera, which Hannibal was determined to raze as a private revenge for the defeat and death of his grandfather (Himera, 480). He set up siege-engines and started to batter and undermine the walls, but the inhabitants decided that they would not suffer the same fate as the Selinuntians without a fight. They had received help from the Syracusans and other allies to the tune of 4,000 men under the command of Diocles the Syracusan. With these and their own men, totalling about 10,000, they made an unexpected sortie and threw the barbarians into disorder. The barbarians fled toward their camps on the hills, pursued by the Himeraeans who, according to accounts, killed several thousand of them. Hannibal then brought down more troops from the camps and put the Himeraeans to flight, killing about 3,000 of them. At this point 25 triremes which had been sent by the Sicilian Greeks arrived, and half of the Himeraeans were evacuated in them. Before the ships could return for the remainder, the city had fallen and was razed to the ground. Hannibal returned to Carthage with his booty, having wreaked his revenge.
Diodorus, 13: 59(4)–60

MOTYE (409) – Sicilian War of Hermocrates
Hermocrates the Syracusan had served as a general during the ill-fated Athenian expedition of 415–413. He was subsequently exiled by his political opponents but returned to Sicily in 409 enriched with gifts of Persian money from Pharnabazus. He used this to build some ships and raised an army of 6,000 warriors, intent on waging war against the Carthaginian bases in Sicily. He started by laying waste the territory of Motye [*Mozia*], a town on an islet close to Lilybaeum [*Marsala*], and defeating in battle all those who came out against him. Many were slain; the rest were forced back within their walls.
Diodorus, 13: 63(4)

PANORMUS (409) – Sicilian War of Hermocrates
After attacking Motye (above), Hermocrates proceeded to do the same at Panormus [*Palermo*]. He ravaged the territory, and when the inhabitants came out to fight him, he killed about 500 of them and shut the rest up in their city.
Diodorus, 13: 63(4)

CHALCEDON (408, spring) – Peloponnesian War
Chalcedon (*Kadiköy*) is on the Asian shore of the Propontis almost opposite Byzantium. In 409/8 it revolted from Athens. After the battle of Cyzicus (410), Theramenes was allotted a fleet with which to besiege the defecting city. He was joined by Alcibiades and Thrasyllus, and between them they built a stockade around the city extending from the Propontis on the south side to the Bosphorus on the north. Hippocrates, the Spartan governor, led his forces plus the citizens out of the city and attacked the Athenians. A fierce battle ensued in which Hippocrates was killed and many of his men either fell or took refuge. Theramenes subsequently came to an agreement with the Chalcedonians that he would spare the city on payment of their tribute with arrears. According to Xenophon, Pharnabazus also appeared on the scene with a relief army but was forced to withdraw.
Diodorus, 13: 66(1–2); Xenophon, Hellenica, 1: 3(4–7); Plutarch, Alcibiades, 30(1)

BYZANTIUM (408, winter) – Peloponnesian War
Following the recapture of Chalcedon (408), Alcibiades proceeded to Byzantium which had also revolted from Athens. When he had surrounded the city with a wall to lay siege to it, some officials offered to surrender the city on the understanding that it would not be sacked.

Alcibiades rejected the proposal, after which he spread the rumour that he had been called away to Ionia on urgent business. He sailed off with his fleet ostentatiously in broad daylight but returned stealthily during that night. After disembarking his infantry, he took up a position close to the city walls, while the fleet proceeded to the harbour and forced its way in with much noise. This brought the garrison of Peloponnesians, Boeotians and Megarians down to the harbour, where they routed the ships' crews and forced them back on board. Meanwhile, Alcibiades and the infantry had been admitted quietly into the city by sympathizers. When the enemy forces returned from the harbour and realized the truth, they formed up in line and engaged in a fierce battle with the Athenians. In the encounter, Alcibiades on one wing and Theramenes on the other were both victorious. The city had been handed over to Alcibiades on condition that there should be no reprisals against the Byzantines. The pledge was kept and no one was killed or exiled.
Plutarch, Alcibiades, *31*

GAURIUM (407) – Peloponnesian War

Alcibiades returned to Athens for the first time since his defection to the Spartans and subsequent return to the Athenian fold. In the meantime he had won a brilliant victory for Athens at Cyzicus (410). He was fêted and, moreover, was made – or indeed ordered to be – commander-in-chief of all the Athenian forces and armaments. His first action was to sail with 100 ships to the island of Andros, which had revolted. He seized the stronghold of Gaurium [*Gavrion*]. When the Andrians and the Peloponnesian garrison came out to fight, they were defeated and forced back behind their walls.
Diodorus, **13**: *69(4); Xenophon*, Hellenica, *1: 4(22)*

NOTIUM (406, spring) – Peloponnesian War

The successor to the Spartan admiral Mindarus was a man of great ability by the name of Lysander. When Alcibiades learnt that this new man was equipping his fleet at Ephesus, he sailed up to the harbour with all his ships but failed to elicit any response. He then moored most of his ships at Notium, at the north end of the bay, and left them in charge of his deputy Antiochus, ordering him not to get involved in any battles while he himself was away. In the descriptions of subsequent events there are differences between the accounts of the Oxyrhynchus historian and Diodorus, on the one hand, and Xenophon followed by Plutarch on the other. The events can be construed as follows. Against his orders Antiochus put to sea with 10 ships. He concealed eight of them in an ambush and sailed across the harbour in front of Lysander's nose. Lysander decided that this was his chance while Alcibiades was away. He put out to sea with his whole fleet, attacked and sank the leading enemy ship with Antiochus on board, and chased the rest homewards. This forced the Athenian fleet to appear in support. However, they were caught unprepared and trickled out individually as and when they were manned and were not in any battle order. In the ensuing fight they were easily defeated by Lysander and lost 22 ships. When Alcibiades heard news of this, he returned in haste and, manning every available trireme, he sailed out and challenged the enemy to battle. But Lysander once again declined.
Hellenica Oxyrhynchia, *IV; Diodorus*, **13**: *71; Xenophon*, Hellenica, *1: 5(11–14); Plutarch*, Alcibiades, *35(4–6)* and Lysander, *5(1–2)*

MYTILENE (406) – Peloponnesian War

The battle of Notium (above) threw the Athenian commander-in-chief Alcibiades into disgrace. He was replaced by the admiral Conon. On the Peloponnesian side, Lysander gave way to Callicratidas at the end of his term of office. It was not long before these newcomers clashed in an encounter at Mytilene on Lesbos. The two extant accounts of this battle differ in some respects. According to Diodorus, when Conon put to sea with 70 ships, he was seen and followed by Callicratidas with 170 ships. Conon decided to lure them on with the object of attacking their vanguard off Mytilene, to which he could repair if he was overcome. At the crucial moment his ships turned on the leading Peloponnesians, damaging some and throwing them into disorder. The enemy ships in the centre started to back water and wait for the rest of the fleet to catch up. But the Athenians on the left wing were over-zealous and, having routed the opposing ships, pursued them until they themselves were surrounded by the main body and driven ashore. Meanwhile Conon proceeded with 40 ships into the harbour at Mytilene and tried to block its entrance. After a long and bitter struggle the Peloponnesians forced their way in and drove the Athenians into the city, which Callicratidas then proceeded to invest.

In Xenophon's account, the two fleets reached the harbour at the same time, which forced Conon to fight at the entrance to the harbour. He lost 30 ships in the engagement and hauled the rest to safety in the lea of the fortifications.

Diodorus, 13: 77–79; Xenophon, Hellenica, 1: 6(15–18)

ARGINUSAE ISLS (406, August) –
Peloponnesian War

In response to their naval reverses at Notium and Mytilene in 406 the Athenians equipped 60 more ships and sent them to Samos. The generals on the spot had assembled a further 80 vessels, while the Samians provided another 10. With these 150 ships, under the command of Thrasyllus, they put out to sea and called in at the Arginusae islands, a group of small islands between the coast of Asia Minor and the southern point of Lesbos. They were intent on raising the siege of the Lesbian city of Mytilene, which had been invested by the Peloponnesians after their naval victory (Mytilene, above). When Callicratidas, the Lacedaemonian admiral, heard about this, he put to sea with 140 ships from Mytilene and confronted them.

There are two versions of the dispositions of the fleets. Diodorus maintains that Thrasyllus extended his line to include the chain of islands, with the ships filling the gaps between them. Callicratidas could not match this length of line and he divided his forces into two fleets, one on each wing. In command of the right wing, Callicratidas himself did considerable damage to a number of enemy ships until he rammed the trireme of Pericles, son of the statesman, and could not extricate his bow. The Athenians sprang onto his ship and put everybody on board to the sword. As soon as it was known that the admiral had been defeated and killed, the Peloponnesians on the right wing gave way and turned to flight. Those on the left wing, however, continued to fight stoutly for as long as they could. They were the Boeotians and Euboeans, who had revolted from Athens and were afraid of the consequences if they were captured. The losses were high: 25 Athenian ships, and 77 on the Peloponnesian side.

In Xenophon's version the Athenian ships were deployed in depth in two lines in order to prevent the Spartans with their superior seamanship from breaking through and then turning to attack from the rear. Such a disposition in depth was so unusual that it gives credence to Xenophon's account. This is further enhanced by his detailed description of the positions of the various commanders in the lines. Xenophon has practically nothing to say about the battle itself except that

Callicratidas fell overboard and was drowned. On casualty figures he is in agreement with Diodorus.

Immediately after the battle a great storm blew up, as a result of which the Athenian generals failed to stop and pick up their dead. This caused a furore with repercussions in Athens where six of the generals were tried and executed.

Diodorus, 13: 97–99; Xenophon, Hellenica, 1: 6(26–34)

ERYX (406) – Sicily: Third Punic Invasion

Carthage had resolved to gain control of the whole of Greek Sicily and had prepared another expedition, even greater than its predecessors, and again under the command of Hannibal (see Himera, 409). They despatched an advance fleet of 40 triremes. The Syracusans promptly appeared with a similar number of ships. Off Eryx [*Erice*] in the north west of the island a battle took place in which the Syracusans destroyed 15 Carthaginian ships. Hostilities were brought to an end by darkness, after which the rest of the invaders fled to the open sea. When word of this reached Carthage, Hannibal set out to sea with a task force of 50 ships, followed by the transports with all the armaments. This time they got through (below).

Diodorus, 13: 80(5–7)

ACRAGAS (406) – Sicily: Third Punic Invasion

When the Carthaginians invaded Sicily for the third time, they marched straight for Acragas [*Agrigento*]. The Acragantini rejected an offer of terms, and so a siege began. The Syracusans were eager to help the Acragantini. They collected their forces under a general Daphnaeus and set off toward Acragas, adding to their force with people from other towns as they went along until they numbered more than 30,000 foot with 5,000 cavalry. They were met by Himilco's Iberians and Campanians and more than 40,000 other troops. In the long battle which followed, the Syracusans won the day and killed more than 6,000 of the enemy; the rest fled to the larger of their two camps. The Syracusans would have crushed them completely but for the intervention of Daphnaeus, who restrained them in case Himilco appeared with another army. When the Syracusans arrived at the smaller of the two Carthaginian camps, they found it deserted and made it their quarters. Sadly, their victory made no significant difference to the end result. The large enemy camp was too well fortified to be attacked, and Acragas ultimately fell after a siege of eight months.

Diodorus, 13: 86(4)–87(2)

AEGOSPOTAMI R (405, summer) –
Peloponnesian War

The Spartan admiral Lysander sailed to the Hellespont with the primary aim of intercepting the merchant vessels from the Pontus Euxinus [*Black Sea*], notably those carrying corn to Athens, while at the same time dealing with renegade cities. He laid siege to the rich city of Lampsacus [*Lapseki*], an Athenian ally, at the northern end of the straits on the Asian shore. The Athenians with a fleet of 180 ships under Conon followed him to the Hellespont but, as Lampsacus had fallen by then, they put in at Sestus for provisions and then proceeded up the European shore to the creek of Aegospotami, closer to Lampsacus. They were determined to force Lysander to fight. At dawn Lysander manned his ships but told his men not to put to sea. The Athenians sailed up to the mouth of Lampsacus harbour, but when battle was not offered they returned to their base at Aegospotami. Lysander then sent some fast ships after them to spy on their activities and report back. He kept all his men on board until he had heard the report. For four days the same things happened. The Athenians presented themselves in battle order but the Peloponnesians would not come out to fight. At this point Alcibiades came to talk to the Athenian generals. He had retired to one of his two Thracian castles overlooking the Hellespont and had watched events. He now told the generals that they were in a bad position, moored on an open shore with no harbour and no city for supplies; the enemy had all these things and everything he needed. He advised the Athenians to move their anchorage to Sestus, but they told him to go back to his castle. The fifth day started like its predecessors. The Athenians sailed out and had to retire again, but the spy-ships had received special instructions. As soon as the spies saw that the Athenians had disembarked and were scattered far and wide in search of food, they started to return to Lampsacus and, when halfway across, signalled back to their base with a shield. Lysander immediately ordered the whole fleet out at full speed with the hoplites on board. Conon tried to recall his men but to no avail; they were too scattered. He himself got away in his ship, with seven others which had been fully manned and with the state trireme *Paralus*, the showpiece of the fleet. Lysander captured all the rest of the ships and most of the crews. This, then, amounted to the loss of the entire Athenian fleet, a disaster which brought Athens to submission and an end to the Peloponnesian War. The terms of the Peace were drawn up and imposed in 404.

Diodorus reports a different sequence of events on the day of the battle. He says that Philocles, the Athenian general of the day, had tired of Lysander's defensive attitude and set out against the enemy with 30 triremes after ordering the others to man their ships and follow. Lysander put to sea with all his ships and pursued Philocles back to his base, where the rest of the Athenian ships were caught unprepared and in confusion. This version undermines the brilliant simplicity of Lysander's strategy. Why would he put out against Philocles when he had consistently refused to fight each morning?
Xenophon, Hellenica, *2: 1(18–28); Diodorus, **13**: 105–106(7); Plutarch, Lysander, 9(4)–11*

SYRACUSE: NEAPOLIS (404) –
Revolt against Dionysius   Map 15
The Syracusans revolted against their tyrant, Dionysius I, and besieged him by pitching a camp on the heights of Epipolae overlooking the city. This blocked his route to the interior. Reinforcements did, however, get through to 'the Island' (Ortygia), where the citadel was situated. Twelve hundred Campanian cavalry, lured by promises, forced their way in, and 300 mercenaries arrived by sea. Encouraged by this, Dionysius led his forces out against the Syracusans and routed them without difficulty in the region of the southern suburb of Neapolis. In a show of benevolence the tyrant stopped his men from killing the fugitives and he buried the enemy's dead. The Syracusans replied that he deserved the same favour; may the gods allow them to see it granted!
*Diodorus, **14**: 8(6)–9(7)*

ACHARNAE (403) – Athenian Civil War
Athens was in the hands of the Thirty Tyrants, who lived up to their name with a vengeance, exiling citizens daily and putting others to death. The Thebans disapproved and offered hospitality to the exiles whether forced or voluntary. Their leader was an Athenian called Thrasybulus, in compulsory exile. In 404, with clandestine help from the Thebans, these exiles seized a stronghold in Attica called Phyle [*Fyli*] which was only 12 miles from Athens and was a good base for military excursions. In the following year the Thirty, realising that the number of exiles joining Thrasybulus was growing apace, gathered some troops and pitched camp near Acharnae [*Acharna*]. Thrasybulus responded by leading 1,200 of his

associates out of Phyle and delivering a strong and unexpected attack against his opponents by night. Many of them were killed, and the rest fled in terror back to Athens.
Diodorus, 14: 32(6)–33(1)

MUNYCHIA (403) – Athenian Civil War

Immediately after the battle at Acharnae (above), Thrasybulus and his band of exiles set out for the Piraeus and seized the hill of Munychia. The Thirty Tyrants went out against them with the Spartan garrison and the cavalry under the command of Critias. In the encounter Thrasybulus and his men filled the steep road near the summit. Their hoplites were in front, backed by the peltasts and javelin throwers, and behind them were the slingers. Their opponents blocked the road lower down. They had the advantage of numbers, perhaps five to one over their adversaries, but the exiles had the advantage of height. When the tyrants' men started to move uphill, they were doubtless met by a shower of missiles from above, after which the exiles' hoplites ran down and engaged them, killing Critias and about 70 of his men. The exiles' victory ended the reign of the Thirty Tyrants, who were deposed.
Xenophon, Hellenica, 2: 4(10–19); Diodorus, 14: 33(2–3)

CUNAXA (401, summer) – Rebellion of Cyrus

When Darius II of Persia died, he was succeeded by his eldest son Artaxerxes but Cyrus, the second son, plotted to seize the throne. He relied largely on an army of about 13,000 Greek mercenaries, who assembled at Sardes and marched to Babylonia under the leadership of Cyrus himself. *En route* they were joined by some reinforcements at Issus: 700 Spartan hoplites and 400 Greek mercenaries who had deserted from the service of the Persian general Abrocomas. Artaxerxes did not expect that his brother's army would ever reach Babylonia, but when Cyrus crossed the border the king decided that he must put a stop to the advance. The two armies met near the village of Cunaxa about 45 miles north of Babylon. There is considerable disagreement between sources in regard to the strength of the two armies, but all the estimates are unbelievably high. That Cyrus' party was greatly outnumbered by the king's men is the only certainty. On Cyrus' side, he himself was in the centre with hand-picked Persian troops and a squadron of cavalry; his oriental troops under Ariaeus were on the left and the Greeks were on the right under the command of Clearchus. The Greek line extended to the river Euphrates. On the king's side, the king himself was in the centre with a strong bodyguard. In front of his battle line he stationed a large number of scythed chariots, with a heavy concentration on his left opposite the Greeks. Just before the battle commenced, Cyrus rode up to Clearchus and asked him to move to the left and to position his men opposite the king and the enemy centre. The precise meaning of this request has aroused much speculation among modern historians. According to Xenophon, the Persians were so superior in number that their line – even their centre – extended beyond Cyrus' left. The debate, however, is rendered academic by the refusal of Clearchus to execute the proposed manoeuvre for fear that, in moving away from the Euphrates, he might be outflanked. Instead, as the rival armies approached each other, the Greeks surged forward and put the barbarians opposite them to flight. Xenophon records that they turned and fled even before they came within range of an arrow, and that only one Greek was lost in this part of the battle. The Greeks then followed up their victory, pursuing the enemy for a considerable distance. This was a fatal mistake. They should have wheeled left and attacked the enemy centre in the flank. In the meantime, on the other flank, the greatly extended Persian right wheeled round and attacked the troops of Ariaeus in the rear.

In the centre, Cyrus made a wild dash with his 600 horse against the 6,000 who surrounded Artaxerxes. His charge broke up the enemy contingent. The only eye-witness account of the subsequent events is that of Ctesias, Artaxerxes' physician, who was with him and treated him. According to Ctesias, Cyrus was attacking the enemy centre with some success when he caught sight of his brother. Cyrus threw his spear, wounding his brother in the chest and causing him to fall from his horse. The king rose to his feet and was taken to a hill nearby. Cyrus, surrounded by the enemy, was accepted as the new king until the turban which indicated his identity fell off his head. At this point a young Persian, unaware of Cyrus' identity, smote him near the eye with a javelin. He fell from his horse and was killed.

The death of Cyrus left the Greeks leaderless. They refused to surrender and had no alternative option but to try to make their way back to Greece. Their trials and tribulations – and ultimate success – are related in the *Anabasis* of Xenophon, the man who emerged as their leader.
Xenophon, Anabasis, 1: 8; Ctesias, cit. Plutarch, Artaxerxes, 11

CATANA (397) – First Punic War of Sicily
The Carthaginian Himilco wanted to extend his control of western Sicily to the whole of the island. His next objective was Syracuse. On the other side of the coin Dionysius, the tyrant of Syracuse, aimed to conquer the Carthaginian-controlled part of Sicily; his pressing need was to protect Syracuse. Himilco sent his admiral Magon with his whole fleet along the coast to the region of Naxos, on the east coast near Tauromenium [*Taormina*]. He arrived there himself with the army at the same time. At that point they had to part company owing to a recent eruption of Aetna. The land forces could not follow the coast and were forced to make a detour inland. Himilco was concerned lest the Sicilian Greeks should attack Magon at sea when he was devoid of land protection by the army. This in fact is what happened. Dionysius, appreciating the situation, hurried northward to Catana [*Catania*] on the coast south of Aetna and sent his brother Leptines with their whole fleet of about 180 ships to engage the enemy's 500 vessels. Leptines failed to keep the close order that Dionysius had adjured and advanced with his 30 best vessels way out in front. When Magon's ships surrounded him, the vessels became entangled and the antagonists boarded each other's ships and fought hand to hand. Leptines was driven off. The rest of his ships, arriving later and observing no order, were easily overcome. The Carthaginians pursued the disordered enemy and destroyed more than 100 of their ships. After a brief rest at Catana, Himilco's next stop was at Syracuse where 250 of his warships sailed into the Great Harbour accompanied by innumerable merchantmen, said to be in excess of 3,000.
*Diodorus, **14**: 59–60*

SYRACUSE (397) – First Punic War of Sicily
During the siege of Syracuse which followed the battle at Catana (above) there was just one recorded incident of armed hostility. The Syracusans, seeing a merchantman approaching laden with corn, sailed out against it with five ships, seized it and brought it in. The Carthaginians put out with 40 ships whereupon the Syracusans manned all of theirs. In the encounter the Syracusans captured the enemy flag-ship and destroyed 24 other vessels. They then pursued the fleeing ships back to their anchorage and challenged the Carthaginians to battle, but there was no response.
*Diodorus, **14**: 64(1–3)*

SYRACUSE (397) – First Punic War of Sicily
In his dealings with Himilco and the Carthaginians, Dionysius the tyrant of Syracuse had a great ally in the plague. It struck the enemy with extreme virulence, killing them by the thousand. This was the tyrant's opportunity. He manned 80 ships and ordered his admirals to attack the enemy's ships at dawn while he himself, profiting from a moonless night, made a detour and appeared at the enemy's camp unannounced at daybreak. He then sent a thousand mercenaries supported by cavalry against a part of the enemy camp, with instructions to the cavalry to withdraw as soon as blows were exchanged, leaving the mercenaries to their fate. These particular mercenaries were the biggest trouble-makers in the army and a thorn in the tyrant's flesh. When they had been disposed of in this ruthless manner, Dionysius attacked both the camp and the forts. At the same time the whole Syracusan fleet attacked the naval station so that the enemy did not know where to go or what to defend. Many of their ships were rammed while the Syracusan people joined in, boarding the ships and killing the crews. Dionysius himself, finding 40 ships drawn up on the beach and others close by at anchor, set fire to them. A strong wind fanning the flames completed the destruction. Now that the Carthaginians had been defeated both on land and sea, Himilco had perforce to enter into negotiations with Dionysius. For reasons of his own Dionysius connived at the escape of Himilco and his remaining Carthaginians, but the allies and mercenaries were left behind to their fate.
*Diodorus, **14**: 72–73*

DASCYLIUM (396, autumn) – Campaign of Agesilaus
In 396 king Agesilaus of Sparta led an army into Asia Minor. His avowed aim was to liberate the Asiatic Greeks from Persian domination and possibly even to unseat the Great King himself. His immediate opponent was the satrap Tissaphernes. Agesilaus prepared for a campaign in Caria, openly informing all the towns on his planned route of his future needs. Tissaphernes responded by taking his whole infantry across the river Maeander [*Menderes*] into Caria, whereupon Agesilaus promptly marched in the opposite direction into Phrygia. With the opposition lured elsewhere, his march was largely uneventful apart from the huge quantities of booty gained and one martial incident near Dascylium [*Ergili*]. Agesilaus' cavalry had ridden ahead to the top of a hill to reconnoitre, only to meet the cavalry of Pharnabazus who had done the same

thing from the other side. The Persians charged and killed a number of the Greeks with their javelins, causing the rest to flee. At this point Agesilaus came up with his hoplites who forced the Persians to withdraw.
Xenophon, Hellenica, 3: 4(13–14)

SARDES (395, spring) – Campaign of Agesilaus

In the spring, Agesilaus proclaimed that he was going to march into the heart of the country in Lydia. Tissaphernes, having been tricked once before (Dascylium, above), was convinced that Agesilaus really would invade Caria this time and he again stationed his cavalry in the plain of the Maeander [*Menderes*]. But this time Agesilaus meant what he said; he marched straight towards Sardes. There are considerable differences between the accounts by Xenophon and Diodorus of subsequent events, but Diodorus is in broad agreement with a third source, the Oxyrhynchus historian. The following outline is taken from Diodorus. Tissaphernes collected 10,000 cavalry and 50,000 infantry and stalked Agesilaus. When Agesilaus drew near to Sardes, he marched back approximately five miles and sent a Spartan called Xenocles with 1,400 men by night into a dense wood to set an ambush. At daybreak Agesilaus resumed his march forward with the barbarians advancing on him and harassing his rearguard. When he was well clear of the site of the ambush, he suddenly turned to face the Persians and gave Xenocles the signal to attack. The Persians, finding that they were caught between two forces, turned and fled. Agesilaus slew more than 6,000 of them in the pursuit and then captured and pillaged their camp. His own casualties were put at 600 by the Oxyrhynchus historian. When the Persian king heard about the battle, he was so enraged at the reverses to his cause that he ordered the decapitation of Tissaphernes.
Diodorus, 14: 80(1–4); Xenophon, Hellenica, 3: 4(21–24); Hellenica Oxyrhynchia, XI

DASCYLIUM (395, autumn) – Campaign of Agesilaus

This encounter was little more than a skirmish. During his second campaign in Phrygia, Agesilaus ravaged the lands all around Dascylium [near *Ergili*]. Here Pharnabazus resided in his palace, surrounded by well-kept parks with an abundance of wild animals and fish. The Greeks became so unaccustomed to any interference or molestation that they got into the habit of foraging as if they were on a picnic. On one occasion, however,

Pharnabazus himself appeared with two scythed chariots and about 400 cavalry. The scattered Greeks, about 700 in number, ran to close up in a body, which the Persians charged. About 100 of the Greeks were killed; the rest fled to rejoin Agesilaus.
Xenophon, Hellenica, 4: 1(15–19)

CAUE (395, autumn) – Campaign of Agesilaus

A few days after the above skirmish at Dascylium the Greeks heard that Pharnabazus was camping about 20 miles away at the village of Caue. Herippidas, a Spartan commander, asked Agesilaus for 2,000 hoplites, 2,000 peltasts and a cavalry force. By nightfall less than half of the detachments had reported. Herippidas, unwilling to call off his great moment, set off with the forces at his disposal and fell upon Pharnabazus' camp at dawn. The outposts were killed and the main body took to flight. The camp was captured together with large quantities of valuables, baggage and baggage animals.
Xenophon, Hellenica, 4: 1(20–24)

HALIARTUS (395) – Boeotian War

A trifling dispute between Phocis and Opuntian Locris brought war to Boeotia. The Phocians looked to Sparta for support; the Locrians appealed to the Thebans, who in turn sought help from their old enemy Athens. The Spartans were delighted to have a pretext for attacking Thebes and they made the first move with a double invasion of Boeotia. King Pausanias advanced from Sparta, and Lysander approached from Phocis on the other side. They had arranged to meet at Haliartus [*Aliartos*] but Lysander arrived there first and, not content to remain inactive, he attacked the town. News of this reached the Thebans, who came to the rescue with hoplites and cavalry, while those in the town suddenly sallied forth. A battle was fought close to the walls. Lysander was killed and his soldiers fled to the mountains with the Thebans in hot pursuit. A thousand of the fugitives were killed in the pursuit and more than 200 of the pursuers were slain.

Pausanias arrived with his army soon afterwards, but so did an Athenian army with Thrasybulus in command. Pausanias decided against incurring the high risk of a defeat and swallowed his Spartan pride by asking for a burial truce. This was granted on condition that the Spartans left the country.
Xenophon, Hellenica, 3: 5(17–20); Diodorus, 14: 81(1–3); Plutarch, Lysander, 28

NARYX (395) – Corinthian War

A general hatred of Lacedaemonia had built up throughout Greece. The Spartan rule was harsh. Moreover, the Spartans had been greedy in failing to reward any of their allies during the Peloponnesian war. Thebes and Athens, Corinth and Argos all joined in an alliance against them, which was soon increased by the addition of other states. Ismenias, the Theban leader of the Boeotians, gathered soldiers from recruited allies and took the field against the Phocians, who were under the protection of Sparta. While he was occupying quarters in Naryx in Locris, the Phocians came against him under the leadership of Alcisthenes the Laconian. In the ensuing battle Ismenias and the Boeotians were the victors. They pursued the enemy until nightfall and slew nearly 1,000 of them, but they themselves had lost about half that number in the battle.
Diodorus, 14: 82(7–10)

NEMEA R (394, July) – Corinthian War

When the Spartans realized that the greatest cities of Greece were ganging up against them in a grand alliance, they gathered an army and set out to meet the enemy, who were also on the march. The Spartans invaded Corinthian territory and met the Corinthian army close to the dried-up bed of the river Nemea on the border between Sicyonia and Corinthia. According to Xenophon, the Spartan forces consisted of a total of 13,500 hoplites and about 600 cavalry. Diodorus puts the figure at 23,000, which is probably nearer the truth. The other side boasted 24,000 hoplites and about 1,500 cavalry. In the engagement, the Boeotians on the confederate right wing led the advance, inclining to the right at the same time so as to outflank the enemy's left wing. This brought about the rout of the Achaeans on the Spartan left wing, which was followed by the flight of all the other Spartan allies on the left and in the centre as the confederates opposite them drove forward. Events were similar in reverse on the other wing, where the Spartans likewise inclined to their right and became so extended that half of them were not in contact with any foe. When they drove back the Athenians on the enemy left wing, the extended Spartan right wheeled round and attacked the enemy in the flank and rear, killing many men. They then proceeded to attack the exposed flanks of the confederates who were returning from the pursuit of the defeated Spartan allies. Diodorus quotes 1,100 killed on the Spartan side and 2,800 of the confederates. In the light of these figures a report

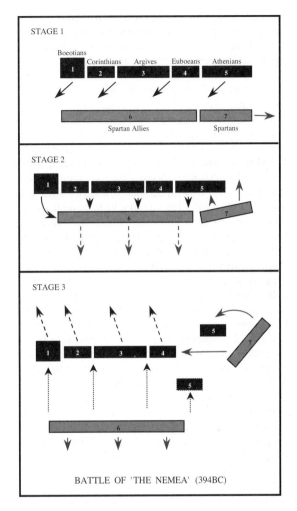

STAGE 1

Boeotians / Corinthians / Argives / Euboeans / Athenians
1 / 2 / 3 / 4 / 5

6 / 7

Spartan Allies / Spartans

STAGE 2

1 / 2 / 3 / 4 / 5

6 / 7

STAGE 3

5 / 7

1 / 2 / 3 / 4

5

6

BATTLE OF 'THE NEMEA' (394BC)

Based on a diagram in J. Hackett (ed.), *Warfare in the Ancient World*, 1989

to Agesilaus concerning a great battle (presumably 'the Nemea' as it is now generally called) is of interest. It recounts that the Spartans themselves had lost only eight men, although their allies had lost a certain number!
Xenophon, Hellenica, 4: 2(14–23); Diodorus, 14: 83(1–2)

NARTHACIUM M (394) – Campaign of Agesilaus

Agesilaus, king of Sparta, abandoned his Asian campaign and returned to Greece to help Sparta in the Corinthian War. During his passage through Thessaly he was harassed continually. When the Pharsalians hung on his flanks, he sent a force of 500 cavalry against them and led the charge himself. Polycharmus, in charge of the enemy cavalry, was killed and those of his men who were left on their feet fled to Mount Narthacium. Agesilaus was overjoyed that he had trounced Thessalian horsemen, who were renowned as the best in the land. He put up a trophy at the foot of the mount.

Xenophon, Hellenica, *4: 3(7–8); Plutarch*, Agesilaus, *16(5)*

CNIDUS (394, August) – Spartan–Persian War
The personality who loomed largest in connexion with the battle off Cnidus was the former Athenian admiral Conon. As commander-in-chief at Aegospotami (405), he was primarily responsible for the loss of the entire Greek navy, which heralded the end of the Peloponnesian war. He fled to Cyprus, and through the grace of influential Persian contacts he was appointed to the command of a Persian fleet. In midsummer of 394 Conon and Pharnabazus, as joint commanders of the king's fleet, appeared off Cnidus [*Knidus*] at the tip of the Cnidian Chersonese opposite the island of Cos. Pisander, the Spartan admiral, was in Cnidus. He sailed out against the king's fleet and, according to Xenophon, was greatly outnumbered by Conon's Greek contingent alone, against which he lined his ships. His allies deserted without a fight; Pisander himself died fighting in his ship. Conon had redeemed the disgrace of Aegospotami, inflicting a total victory over his hated enemy – Sparta.
Xenophon, Hellenica, *4: 3(10–12); Diodorus, 14: 83(4–7)*

CORONEA (394, August) – Corinthian War
After Mount Narthacium (394) Agesilaus' southward progress took him into Boeotia, where an enemy army was waiting to oppose him at Coronea. The two armies lined up opposite each other in the plain. The first move was made by the Thebans, who were on the confederate right wing and who charged the Orchomenians on Agesilaus' left and broke right through their line, routing them. In opposite sense, Agesilaus commanding the Spartan right routed all the contingents opposing him. The Argives did not even wait for the attack but fled to Mount Helicon. At this point the Thebans gave up pursuing their Orchomenian victims and returned to the battleground with the object of breaking through the lines and joining their allies on Mount Helicon. They were now in Agesilaus' rear. Agesilaus' easy option would have been to let the Thebans through and then attack them in the rear. Instead, he 'turned' his phalanx, probably by means of a 'countermarch' (p. 27), and then charged them at full tilt. They met head on, shield to shield, and fought ferociously with heavy losses on both sides. Those Thebans that did break through were pursued and attacked on the flanks. Agesilaus himself was wounded several times in the battle. Xenophon attributes the victory to his hero, Agesilaus, but the outcome was clearly inconclusive. Diodorus puts the casualties at 600 for the alliance and 350 for the Lacedaemonian side.
Xenophon, Hellenica, *4: 3(15–19); Plutarch*, Agesilaus, *18; Diodorus, 14: 84(1–2)*

ABACAENE (392) – Second Punic War of Sicily
The Carthaginian general Mago was in Sicily, presumably in command of the Phoenician-held territories. He launched an attack on the territory of Messana and then went into camp near Abacaene about 25 miles away. When Dionysius, tyrant of Syracuse, came up with his army, the forces drew up for battle. A sharp engagement ensued in which Dionysius was the victor. After losing more than 800 men the Carthaginians fled into the city.
Diodorus, 14: 90(3–4)

CORINTH: LONG WALLS (392) – Corinthian War
In a struggle between Sparta and a confederation of central Greek states, Corinth inevitably occupied a central position. In its midst there were quite a number of citizens who were favourable to Sparta and had been plotting against the government. They were unmasked and most were killed or exiled but some remained in the city. Two of these made contact with Praxitas, the commander of the Spartan garrison at Sicyon. They made arrangements to leave a gate open, by which Praxitas and his men gained access by night to the corridor between the Long Walls connecting the city with Lechaeum, the port of Corinth. He secured his position by building a stockade and digging a ditch from wall to wall. Two days later the Athenian general Iphicrates, who was in command in the city, came out with his mercenaries and the Corinthian inhabitants and Argive allies. The two sides lined up wall to wall, facing each other. Iphicrates, with numerical superiority, attacked at once and routed the Sicyonians in the enemy centre. He chased them down to the sea and killed many of them. Meanwhile, the Corinthian exiles on the Spartan right defeated the troops opposite them and forced them back almost to the

city wall. At the same time the Spartans attacked the Argives, routing them too. The net result was an undoubted Spartan victory and a lot of enemy corpses.
Xenophon, Hellenica, 4: 4(7–12); Diodorus, 14: 86(1–4)

PHLIUS (392) – Corinthian War
The Athenian general Iphicrates marched out of Corinth with his light-armed peltasts and invaded the territory of Phlius about 14 miles to the south-west. When the inhabitants came out against him, he slew more than 300 of them. After this, the Phliasians handed their city over to the Spartans for protection against further attacks from Corinth.
Xenophon, Hellenica, 4: 4(15); Diodorus, 14: 91(3)

SICYON (392) – Corinthian War
During the Corinthian war the Lacedaemonians made their headquarters at Sicyon, about 10 miles north-west of Corinth. After defeating the Phliasians (above), Iphicrates advanced against Sicyon where the inhabitants came out to fight in front of their walls. They were repulsed with a loss of about 500 men.
Diodorus, 14: 91(3)

RHEGIUM (391) – Sicilian Invasion of Italy
Having made himself ruler of all Greek Sicily, Dionysius I started to cast an eye across the water to Greek Italy, which he proceeded to invade. The primary object of his attention was Rhegium [*Reggio di Calabria*]. When the neighbouring states learnt of his presence, 60 ships set out from Croton to assist the Rhegians. Dionysius met them with 50 ships, and when they fled to the shore he started to tow their ships away. The Rhegians then appeared on the shore in force and maintained such a barrage of missiles from the land that Dionysius had to keep his distance. At this point a storm blew up, giving the Rhegians an opportunity to haul their ships up on land. Dionysius, on the other hand, lost seven ships and about 1,500 men, many of whom were cast ashore and taken prisoner. Dionysius himself eventually ended up in the harbour at Messana [*Messina*]. As winter was setting in, he abandoned hostilities and returned to Syracuse.
Diodorus, 14: 100

LAÜS (390) – Lucanian Expansion
At about this time the Lucanians were busily extending their power southwards into Bruttii.

When they overran the territory of Thurii, the Greek cities of Magna Graecia prepared to march to the assistance of the Thurians in accordance with the terms of their mutual agreement. But the Thurians were too impatient to wait for the arrival of their allies. They proceeded against the Lucanians on their own with their force of 14,000 infantry and 1,000 cavalry. The Lucanians withdrew into their own territory and were followed by the Thurians, who captured an outpost and became so over-confident that they resolved to besiege the prosperous city of Laüs at the mouth of the river Laüs [*Lao*]. Their route took them through a plain which was bordered by high hills and crags, upon the summits of which the Lucanians suddenly materialized with a force of 30,000 men and 4,000 horse. This host descended into the plain and overwhelmed the Greeks, of whom 10,000 were slain.
Diodorus, 14: 101–102(1)

LECHAEUM (390) – Corinthian War
The Athenian general Iphicrates is best known for his military reforms. He used mercenaries, whom he armed lightly as peltasts with equipment which he modified in the interest of increased mobility. They became a forerunner of the flying squad. It was with this force that Iphicrates earned the distinction of destroying half of a Spartan contingent in the following circumstances. Lechaeum, the port of Corinth, was in Spartan hands. In this town there were some Spartan soldiers from Amyclae [*Amykle*] who invariably went home on leave for the festival of Hyacinthia. In view of the warfare around Corinth, the Spartan garrison commander escorted these Amyclaean troops part way to Sicyon with a *mora* of hoplites (about 600) and some cavalry. The cavalry then proceeded as escort; the hoplites turned back. As they passed Corinth on the return journey, Iphicrates and his peltasts rushed out of Corinth and attacked them. The peltasts kept throwing their javelins and then withdrawing at speed, only to turn and throw again. The slow, heavy-armed hoplites could never make contact with them and could not cope with this form of warfare. One by one they were picked off until, according to Xenophon, about 250 had been killed. The engagement was one of the bitterest blows to Spartan pride.

Xenophon gives a full account of the action; the other sources only mention it.
Xenophon, Hellenica, 4: 5(11–17); Diodorus, 14: 91(2); Plutarch, Agesilaus, 22(2)

METHYMNA (389) – Revolt of Lesbos

It seemed to the Athenians that Spartan naval power was on the increase again, and so they despatched Thrasybulus with 40 ships to put things right. During this mission he sailed to Lesbos where all the cities except Mytilene were pro-Spartan. He assembled his own 400 hoplites and supplemented them with picked Mytilenaeans and with exiles from the other Lesbian cities, whom he led against Methymna [*Mithymna*]. The Spartan governor, Therimachus, went out to oppose the enemy with his marines plus the inhabitants of Methymna and the exiles from Mytilene. In the battle Therimachus himself was killed and many of his forces were cut down in the pursuit. As a result of the Athenian victory, a number of the cities were won over to the Athenian cause.

Xenophon, Hellenica, *4: 8(28–29), Diodorus, 14: 94(3–4)*

ELLEPORUS R (389) – Second Sicilian Invasion of Italy

Two years after his disaster at the *Straits of Messina* (391), Dionysius made a second expedition across the straits. When the Greeks of southern Italy learnt that he was on his way, they mustered their forces, in all about 25,000 infantry and 2,000 cavalry. They placed this army under the command of Croton [*Crotone*], the city which was most populated and had the largest number of Syracusan exiles. Heloris the Syracusan, a man who had been exiled by Dionysius, was appointed as their general. He led the entire army out toward Caulonia [*Monasterace*], which Dionysius had started to besiege. Heloris was encamped between Croton and Caulonia on the Elleporus (probably only a stream) when Dionysius heard of his approach, called off his siege and advanced to meet his adversary. As it happened, the tyrant had encamped only a few miles from Heloris when he heard of the Italiots' proximity. He got his army ready for combat and led it forward immediately. Heloris, by contrast, was unaware of the enemy presence. He was in the van of his army with only 500 troops, the remainder following at leisure. Though they put up a staunch fight, they were easily surrounded and massacred almost to a man, including Heloris himself. The rest of the army, arriving in scattered units, presented an easy prey. When they heard that their commander had been killed, they turned in flight and sought refuge on a hill to which 10,000 managed to escape. Unfortunately the hill was without water and Dionysius had surrounded it. The following day the Italiots

were suffering so badly that they surrendered. To their surprise and relief the tyrant allowed them all to go free, an act of apparent clemency which was completely at variance with his character and record. However, his motive was purely political, and the gesture paid good dividends in his desire to win over the individual communities.

Diodorus, 14: 103(4)–105

CREMASTE (388) – Command of Hellespont

Every merchant ship passing through the Bosphorus was subject to a toll for the benefit of Athenian coffers. The Spartans sent out Anaxibius to try to put a stop to this and to counteract the progressive inclination of the Hellespontine cities toward sympathy with Athens. Anaxibius started by seizing the merchantmen. The Athenian response was to send out Iphicrates with a force of about 1,200 peltasts, mostly men from his former force at Corinth (Lechaeum, 390). After a campaign of mutual raiding, Iphicrates heard that Anaxibius had gone away with most of his troops. Guessing that the other would return to Abydus with his men, Iphicrates crossed the straits by night and disembarked on Abydene territory after ordering the sea captains to sail straight on up the straits at dawn. He then went up into the mountains and laid an ambush. Anaxibius did return, marching without due care and attention. Iphicrates stayed in hiding until the enemy van was down in the plain of Cremaste with the rest of the army strung out in a long narrow line down the slope. Then he charged toward Anaxibius who, with a few others, died fighting. The rest fled and were pursued up to the city. About 250 were killed in the pursuit.

Xenophon, Hellenica, *4: 8(35–39)*

OLYNTHUS (382) – Olynthus Campaign

Olynthus, the largest town in Chalcidice, formed a Chalcidian league of common rights and peaceful purpose with the neighbouring communities. The idea grew and so did the league, which became more aggressively expansionist, threatening those who would not join. This led to calls for help to Sparta, a move which admirably suited that state to which the league in the north presented a threat. Teleutias, a brother of Agesilaus, was sent to wage war with 10,000 men, who were supplemented by sizeable contingents from the various allies. He halted about a mile and a half from Olynthus and lined up his men, taking command of the left wing himself and placing the Spartan and Theban cavalry on the right wing. When the enemy

emerged from the city and lined up, their cavalry charged the Spartan and Theban horsemen and routed them. The infantry next to the routed horse then began to give way. Complete disaster was avoided only by the Macedonian cavalry contingent, which charged at the city gates. Teleutias followed them up. This compelled the Olynthians to withdraw to their city as fast as they could in fear of being cut off from it. Xenophon calls this a victory for Teleutias, who set up a trophy, but in the absence of any casualty figures the outcome seems equivocal.
Xenophon, Hellenica, 5: 2(37–43)

OLYNTHUS (381) – Olynthus Campaign
In the continuing campaign against Olynthus Teleutias rode out one day against the city and ravaged the neighbouring territory. The Olynthian cavalry came out against him, crossed the intervening river and advanced. Teleutias ordered the peltasts to charge them, whereupon the cavalry calmly withdrew back over the river. When the peltasts crossed the river in pursuit, the Olynthian cavalry turned and charged. Teleutias, seeing this, led his hoplites to the rescue and ordered the peltasts to resume the pursuit, but they advanced too close to the walls and came under a hail of missiles, which forced them to retreat. At this moment the Olynthian cavalry charged out again, with peltasts in support and followed by Olynthian hoplites. Teleutias fell fighting, after which his whole army gave way and turned to flight. The enemy pursued them, killing many of them. Two more years elapsed before the Olynthians were forced to sue for peace and the Chalcidian league was dissolved. Olynthus was 'persuaded' to join the Lacedaemonian alliance.
Xenophon, Hellenica, 5: 3(3–6)

CITIUM (381) – Revolt of Evagoras
Evagoras of Cyprus, the king of Salamis [*Gazimağuza*, formerly *Famagusta*], adopted a policy of co-operation with Athens. Confrontation with Persia became inevitable sooner or later. Hostilities, once started, dragged on for 10 years until Evagoras forced a disastrous naval battle. Realizing that he was inferior in naval strength, he equipped 60 new ships and obtained a further 50 from his ally, King Hakori of Egypt. When the Persian fleet sailed past toward Citium [*Larnaca*], he fell upon them. Although the element of surprise and his orderly deployment gave him some initial success, this did not last. When the Persian admiral Glos restored order to his unsuspecting

fleet and counterattacked in force, Evagoras was routed and fled, losing many of his triremes.
Diodorus, 15: 3(4–6)

CABALA (379) – Third Punic War of Sicily
Dionysius I of Syracuse was ready for another war with Carthage. He only needed an excuse. He was aware that some of the cities which were controlled by the Carthaginians were not unwilling to revolt, and so he looked kindly on them and made alliances where these were acceptable. The Carthaginians sent ambassadors to protest. When they were ignored, Sicily's Third Punic War was ignited. The Carthaginians formed an alliance with the Italiots of southern Italy, with whom Dionysius was at war. They hired a lot of mercenaries and shipped a large force across to Sicily under the command of Mago. A battle which Diodorus calls an important pitched battle was fought near Cabala. The place itself is unknown, as also are the details of the fight, but it was a great victory for Dionysius and the Syracusans, who allegedly slew more than 10,000 of the barbarians and captured at least 5,000 more. Mago was killed. The Carthaginians sued for peace but considered the terms offered by Dionysius to be totally unacceptable. Two-faced, they simulated agreement and asked for time to consult their government. The period of truce was then used by them for intensive military exercises and training in readiness for the next onslaught (below).
Diodorus, 15: 15(2–4)

CRONIUM (379) – Third Punic War of Sicily
At the end of the brief period of truce following the battle of Cabala, the Carthaginian forces and the Sicilian Greeks of Dionysius again faced each other in readiness for battle, at a place called Cronium near Panormus [*Palermo*]. This time the tables were turned and the Carthaginians won a clear victory. Leptines, the brother of Dionysius, was killed while fighting valiantly on one wing. When the other wing was also crushed, the rest of the Greeks took to flight. In the pursuit no prisoners were taken and the Sicilian Greek losses were put at 14,000.
Diodorus, 15: 16(2–3)

NAXOS ISL (376, September) – Athenian–Spartan Naval War
In 378 and 377 Sparta conducted two fruitless invasions of Boeotia. With their plans baulked, it occurred to the Spartans to build up a naval force with which to cut off the grain supplies to Attica

from the Black Sea, a result which would be equally damaging to Boeotia. A fleet of 60 ships under the Spartan admiral Pollis started operating off the southern points of Euboea and Attica, closing the shipping routes as intended. The Athenians countered this by sending out their navy under Chabrias. He sailed to Naxos, which had just deserted the Athenian confederacy, and placed the town under siege. Pollis arrived to help the Naxians, and the two fleets lined up for a battle which was waged in the sound between Naxos and Paros. Pollis had 65 triremes; Chabrias had 83. Pollis himself is said to have led the Spartan right wing with such gusto that he sank and killed the commander of the Athenian left and destroyed or routed many of his ships. When Chabrias saw this, he sent a squadron to the support of the beleaguered wing and saved the day. Diodorus says that he destroyed 24 of the enemy ships and captured a further 8 with the loss of 18 Athenian ships. However, less than 20 years after the event Demosthenes declared that Chabrias took 49 of the enemy ships and, furthermore, that he never lost a ship while he was in command.

Diodorus, 15: 34(4)–35(2); Demosthenes, 20: 77–78

ALYZIA (375) – Athenian–Spartan Naval War
The Spartans' naval ploy to starve Athens, which was frustrated by the battle of Naxos (above), was followed by plans to invade Boeotia by crossing the Gulf of Corinth. Athens responded to this threat, at the request of Thebes, by manning 60 ships and appointing Timotheus as commander. His brief was to sail round the Peloponnese in a show of strength. After doing this, he sailed straight on to Corcyra [*Corfu*]. The Spartans replied by sending out a fleet of 55 ships under their admiral Nicolochus. He encountered Timotheus off Alyzia [near *Mitikas*] on the west coast of Acarnania. The two fleets engaged immediately and the Spartans were defeated. Figures of the losses are not available.

Xenophon, Hellenica, 5: 4(64–65)

TEGYRA (375) – Precursor to Era of Theban Hegemony
While Athens was waging war against the Lacedaemonian confederacy by sea (Naxos, 376; Alyzia, 375), the Thebans were busy driving the Spartan garrisons out of the Boeotian cities. On one such expedition their brilliant general Pelopidas was returning to Thebes from Orchomenus with some cavalry and the Sacred Band (an élite

corps of paired comrades or lovers). Near Tegyra they met some Spartans from Orchomenus marching in the opposite direction as they returned to their base after an expedition. They were emerging from a narrow defile in the hills and numbered between 700 and 1,000 men according to various estimates, considerably outnumbering Pelopidas' own band of 300 infantry. The Spartan polemarchs Gorgoleon and Theopompus were in command and confident of victory. Pelopidas ordered his cavalry to charge and they went for the enemy's centre, while he himself followed up the attack at the same point with the Sacred Band. The two Spartan commanders were both stationed at this point and both were killed. The frightened Spartans then parted their ranks to allow the Thebans to pass through, but Pelopidas had no such intention. He proceeded to attack those formations which still held firm until the entire force fled. Great was the moral effect of this victory. Never before had the Spartans been beaten by a force inferior in numbers to their own.

Although the term 'Era of Theban Hegemony' is usually applied to the 10-year period between the battles of Leuctra (371, below) and Mantinea (362), Tegyra was the first in the chain of resounding Theban victories.

Plutarch, Pelopidas, 17

LEUCTRA (371, July) – Era of Theban Hegemony
For a hundred years Athens and Sparta had rivalled each other for the leadership of Hellas, but other contestants were entering the ring. One was Jason of Pherae, the despot of a united Thessaly; another was Thebes. These last two formed an alliance together. In this year (371) a Peace was ratified, and stipulated that all parties were to recall their garrisons from foreign towns. Athens acquiesced; Sparta did not. Instead of disbanding his army, King Cleombrotus marched against Thebes. When he reached Leuctra, on some hills on the southern aspect of a plain, he found that his way northward was barred by the Theban army. The enemy occupied a position on the opposing hills across the plain. Both sides descended to the level ground of the valley to fight. The sizes of the armies are not known, but it is certain that the Thebans were heavily outnumbered. The Spartans were deployed in a long line 12 deep with their allies on the left. On the Theban side, the commander Epaminondas exhibited an unusual deployment in association with revolutionary tactics, for which he became famous. He massed

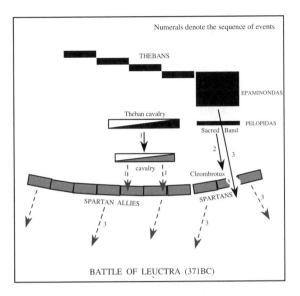

Numerals denote the sequence of events

THEBANS

EPAMINONDAS

Theban cavalry

PELOPIDAS

Sacred Band

cavalry

Cleombrotus

SPARTAN ALLIES

SPARTANS

BATTLE OF LEUCTRA (371BC)

his best men on the left in close formation about 50 deep, presenting an impenetrable phalanx. His weaker units he stationed on his right wing with instructions to withhold from the fighting. Both sides placed their cavalry out in front. The action began with a cavalry engagement, in which the Spartan horse were quickly worsted. When they turned to retreat, they fell foul of their own hoplites. In the meantime, Epaminondas had kept edging his phalanx to the left in an oblique formation, drawing the Spartan right under Cleombrotus away from the rest of his line. Cleombrotus attempted to change his formation to deal with this situation but Pelopidas with his Sacred Band of 300 seasoned troops charged him and caught him in mid-manoeuvre. Cleombrotus himself was killed. It was left to Epaminondas and the massive weight of his phalanx to complete the work and break through the enemy lines. Never before had the Spartans experienced such a defeat and rout.

There is no complete account of this famous battle. The clearest is Plutarch's. Xenophon and Diodorus are at variance in many respects and both of them make notable omissions.
Plutarch, Pelopidas, *20(1–3) and 23; Xenophon,* Hellenica, **6***: 4(8–15); Diodorus,* **15***: 53–56*

ORCHOMENUS (ARCADIA) (370) –
Arcadian League Feud
In 370 the Arcadians joined together to form a pan-Arcadian league, with the exceptions of Tegea, Orchomenus and Heraea. The Orchomenians had refused to join because of their hostility

to Mantinea. The Spartans, with whom Orchomenus was friendly, sent their general Polytropus with a force of 1,000 citizen hoplites and 500 refugees to Orchomenus to protect it. This did not deter the Mantineans, who marched against that city with 5,000 men under Lycomedes. According to Diodorus, a battle ensued outside the walls, in which Polytropus was killed and the Spartans were forced to withdraw. Xenophon adds that the Mantineans were forced to retreat at first but then turned on their pursuers, killing Polytropus and routing his men.
Xenophon, Hellenica, **6***: 5(13–14); Diodorus,* **15***: 62(1–2)*

CORINTH (369) – Second Theban Invasion of Peloponnese
In 369 the Thebans invaded the Peloponnese (for the second time) and joined up with their allies, the Arcadians, Argives and Boeotians. They were led by Epaminondas. The Athenians sent Chabrias with an army to Corinth against them. Earlier in the year Athens had formed an alliance with Sparta, and when the Spartans and their allies also arrived at Corinth, the combined force was said to number around 20,000. This did not stop the Thebans from forcing their way through the Isthmian defences and marching against various towns to the north and south of the Isthmus. On their way back, they assaulted Corinth itself. The Corinthians sallied out against them but were forced back within their walls and were too frightened to offer any further resistance. Chabrias, however, put up a stiff fight and succeeded in ejecting the enemy from the city. The Thebans then lined up in battle array outside the walls in preparation for a desperate assault. Chabrias advanced out in person with the Athenians and took up a position on some higher ground from which he and his men showered the enemy with missiles. A great many of the Thebans in the foremost ranks were killed and the others eventually took to flight and were pursued.
Xenophon, Hellenica, **7***: 1(18–19); Diodorus,* **15***: 69(1–4)*

MELEA ('TEARLESS BATTLE')
(368, summer)
Dionysius of Syracuse sent a force to the Peloponnese to help the Athenian–Spartan alliance in their fight against Thebes and her allies. These troops joined Archidamus and his Spartans and they set out on a campaign. They captured Caryae and had devastated the country round the district

of Parrhasia in Arcadia when the Argives and Arcadians came against them. Archidamus withdrew and camped in the hills above 'Melea'. (This was undoubtedly Malea in Arcadia, close to the Laconian border.) It so happened that the troops from Sicily had served their term abroad and were due to return home. They set out for Sparta but found their way barred by some Messenians who had blocked a narrow pass. Archidamus went to their assistance and had reached a branch road leading to Eutresia (a district adjacent to Maleatis) when the Arcadian and Argive armies appeared. At the junction of the roads to Eutresia and 'Melea', Archidamus drew up his troops and charged with such effect that the enemy fled and were cut down in great numbers by the cavalry. Diodorus puts their losses at an exorbitant 10,000. But however large the enemy death toll, the feature of the battle from which it derived its name was the absence of any Spartan casualties. Not a single man among them was killed.

Xenophon, Hellenica, 7: 1(28–32); Diodorus, 15: 72(3); Plutarch, Agesilaus, 33(3)

DREPANUM (368) – Fourth Punic War of Sicily
Dionysius I, tyrant of Syracuse, had amassed a large combined force reported to consist of 30,000 infantry, 3,000 horse and 300 triremes. His old enemy the Carthaginians, on the other hand, had been severely reduced by the plague, which gave him a good opportunity to strike. On some trumped-up pretext he invaded the Carthaginian-held territory in Sicily and captured several towns. Hearing that the Carthaginian dockyards had been destroyed by fire and anticipating no resistance, he sent only 130 of his triremes to the enemy naval base at Drepanum [Trapani], where they anchored in the harbour. The Carthaginians, however, manned 200 ships and sailed against the anchored fleet. The attack was such a complete surprise that the Carthaginians were able to tow most of Dionysius' fleet away. Soon afterwards the two sides agreed an armistice but a little later in the year Dionysius died.

Diodorus, 15: 73

LASION (365) – Elean–Arcadian War
For many years Elis and Arcadia had been disputing the possession of some territory which included the frontier stronghold of Lasion [near Kumanis]. At the time in question, the Arcadians were governing it but the Eleans seized some pretext to occupy it. The Arcadians mustered their army and marched against the place, where they encamped opposite the Elean army with its crack bands of 'Three Hundred' and 'Four Hundred'. During the night the Arcadians scaled the heights overlooking the Elean position, from which they descended on the enemy at dawn. The Eleans came out to meet them, but the numerical superiority of the enemy and his advantageous position ensured a smart Elean defeat.

Xenophon, Hellenica, 7: 4(12–13)

CROMNUS (365) – Elean–Arcadian War
After their defeat by the Arcadians at Lasion (above) the Eleans appealed to the Spartans for help. Archidamus responded by marching out with a citizen army from Sparta and capturing the Arcadian town of Cromnus, in which he left a garrison. After his departure the Arcadians built a double stockade around the place and besieged the Spartan garrison. Archidamus marched out again to lift the siege and noticed a hill which was crossed by the outer stockade. He sent a detachment round to it by a detour. When the Spartan peltasts in the lead saw the Arcadians outside the stockade, they charged down on them, but the enemy stood firm. A second charge was made but again the enemy held their ground or even advanced. Eventually Archidamus himself led his men up along the track in double file and encountered the Arcadians. The Spartans had little chance of success, marching up in column against an enemy who was drawn up in close order, shield to shield. In the fight, Archidamus was wounded almost immediately and there were many Spartan casualties among those in the lead. The Spartans had to retire. Later, the two sides lined up in battle formation on open ground but they agreed to call a truce and so the Spartans departed, leaving their garrison still in place and under siege. A later attempt to rescue it met with scant success.

Xenophon, Hellenica, 7: 4(20–25)

OLYMPIA (364) – Elean–Arcadian War
The Olympic Games were due to be held again, and the inhabitants of Pisa, a town close to Olympia, prepared to exercise their age-old rights as presidents. The Arcadians, who were still at loggerheads with the Eleans (Lasion, Cromnus, 365), joined the Pisatans in organizing the event. They also undertook the job of policing the precinct with the help of 2,000 hoplites from Argos and 400 Athenian cavalry. The games had already begun when the Eleans came marching down the road and reached the sacred precinct, the Altis. The Arcadians and their allies formed into line

along the river Cladaus, a stream which flowed past the Altis. The Eleans then formed up on the other side of the stream. It is uncertain which side struck first. Diodorus names the Pisatans and Arcadians as the aggressors, but Xenophon says that the Eleans charged across the stream and drove back the Arcadians first and then the Argives, pushing them into the precinct. The fighting was terminated by a hail of stones and missiles hurled from the neighbouring buildings and roofs. One missile killed the Elean commander, after which the troops retired to their camp.
Xenophon, Hellenica, *7: 4(28–31); Diodorus, **15**: 78(2–3)*

CYNOSCEPHALAE MS (364, July) – Era of Theban Hegemony

Alexander, the brutal tyrant of Pherae in Thessaly, was waging war on all around him. The Thessalians sent to Thebes, asking for help in the form of an army commanded by Pelopidas. The Boeotians agreed and gave Pelopidas 7,000 men. As he was leaving, there was a total eclipse of the sun (13 July), which was regarded as a sinister omen. This dismayed the Thebans. According to Plutarch, Pelopidas had to leave them behind and took with him only 300 cavalry from other cities, but he was joined at Pharsalus [*Farsala*] by a Thessalian contingent. Alexander came to meet him with a considerably larger force. The battle centred round the control of Cynoscephalae (Dogs' Heads) [*Chalkodonion*], a small range of hills rising in the middle of a plain. As both sides advanced toward the hills, Pelopidas ordered his cavalry to attack the enemy. They routed the enemy's horsemen and chased them over the plain, but in the meantime Alexander had occupied the heights. When the Thessalian cavalry tried to force their way up the steep slopes, they were beaten back. Pelopidas ordered them to attack the main body of enemy infantry on the plain while he himself charged up the slope and joined his infantry who were battling it out in the hills. He forced his way through to the front and led a furious charge. The enemy resisted one or two such assaults but then began to waver. At the same time the Thessalian cavalry, who had routed the infantry, were coming back up to help. Pelopidas had gained the summit when he caught sight of Alexander, the man who had thrown him into a prison some years before. All his hatred of the man rose within him and he charged his enemy, who retreated to the folds of his bodyguard. Hacking away in an attempt to get at him, Pelopidas was struck by javelins and killed.

While this was going on, the cavalry had launched another charge and this time they routed the enemy phalanx. The cavalry pursued the infantry for a considerable distance and cut down more than 3,000 of them, but no amount of enemy blood could compensate for the death of their beloved general.
Plutarch, Pelopidas, *31–32; Diodorus, **15**: 80*

MANTINEA (362) – Era of Theban Hegemony

In 362 the Theban general Epaminondas invaded the Peloponnese for the fourth time, at the head of the Boeotians and their allies from central Greece. The cause was a division within the Arcadian league. Tegea and Mantinea could not live happily side by side. Tegea gathered around itself a group of pro-Theban cities and appealed to Thebes for help, while Mantinea became the centre of an anti-Theban lobby which looked to Sparta and Athens for support. Epaminondas' aim was to bring the dissident elements back under Boeotian control. When he reached Tegea, he heard that the Spartans under Agesilaus were on the march. He immediately headed for Sparta in the expectation of finding it undefended, but a runner had tipped off Agesilaus who had promptly marched home again. Epaminondas now heard that the Mantineans had marched out to join the Spartans, and so he made a forced march to Mantinea expecting to find that city undefended. It was; but his arrival happened to coincide with the arrival of a force of 6,000 Athenians under Hegesileos, who drove him off smartly. The Spartans and Mantineans also turned up, bringing the strength of the anti-Theban party to more than 20,000 foot and 2,000 horse. Ranged against them under Epaminondas were the Thebans with the Tegeates and their Arcadian colleagues, and the Argives, amounting to 30,000 foot and 3,000 cavalry.

The battle took place in the plain, south of Mantinea, where the Spartans and their allies were lined up across the narrow end of the plain close to the city. The Mantineans were on the right wing with the Spartans next to them. The Athenians occupied the left wing; the remainder were in the centre. When Epaminondas marched out, he did not take up position opposite the enemy but led his men to the left toward the foot of the mountains as if he had no intention of fighting that day. He then lined them up, placing a solid mass of Boeotian hoplites in depth on the left wing. The rest, who were less important for his tactics, occupied the centre and right wing. His cavalry were stationed *en bloc* in front of the Theban phalanx, but he also

posted a body of horse and foot on some high ground on the far side of the Athenian left wing. Its purpose was to prevent the enemy left from wheeling round and attacking his phalanx in the flank. As Epaminondas' men were lined up along the base of the hills on the enemy's right, they advanced obliquely against the enemy with the strongest elements bearing the brunt. This was the tactic he had used so successfully at Leuctra (371). In the action, his cavalry routed their opposite numbers. The weight of the hoplites, which he was leading himself, then crashed through the enemy lines, putting the Spartans to flight. In this attack, he himself was killed, a disaster to the Thebans which stopped them from following up their victory. Elsewhere along the lines, there was little action. Both sides claimed victory and each put up a trophy, but history has unhesitatingly accorded the glory to the genius of Epaminondas.
Xenophon, Hellenica, *7: 5(21–27); Diodorus, 15: 84–87*

PEPARETHOS ISL (361) – Piratical Raid
After the defeat and repression of Alexander of Pherae by the Thebans (Cynoscephalae, 364), the tyrant became an ally of theirs. A few years later he sent some pirate ships against the Cyclades and then disembarked some mercenaries on the island of Peparethos [*Skopelos*] off Thessaly and besieged the city. The Athenians sent a force under Leosthenes, which Alexander attacked, taking it by surprise and defeating it. In addition, he captured five of their triremes and took 600 prisoners.
Diodorus, 15: 95(1–2)

METHONE (359) – Rise of Macedon
When Amyntas III of Macedon died, he was succeeded by his eldest son Alexander. A year later this son was assassinated by his brother-in-law, who seized the throne. He, in his turn, was disposed of by the second son of Amyntas, Perdiccas, who ruled until he was slain in battle by the Illyrians. The succession passed to the youngest brother, Philip, but there were other less rightful candidates who were the subjects of various intrigues. The Athenians supported a man called Argaeus and sent a force to Methone [*Methoni*], a Macedonian town north of Pydna [*Kitros*]. From here they sent Argaeus in the care of their mercenaries to Aegae, the old capital of Macedonia about 40 miles away, to press his claim. Nobody took any notice of him. On his way back to Methone, Philip was waiting for him with his soldiers and slew many of the mercenaries.

Argaeus dropped out of the running, leaving Philip II in power after his first engagement.
Diodorus, 16: 3(5–6)

HERACLEA LYNCESTIS (358) – Rise of Macedon
When Philip II of Macedon had come to power, the first task confronting him was to pacify or subdue the Illyrian and Paeonian tribes on his borders. Bardylis, the king of the Illyrians, had made frequent incursions into Macedonian territory and so Philip marched against him. The scene of the battle is not recorded by the ancient historians, but Beloch has placed it near *Monastir* [more recently *Bitola*], site of ancient Heraclea Lyncestis in Macedonia. It probably took place in the plain south of Lake Lychnitis [*Okhrida*]. Both sides mustered about 10,000 infantrymen and a few hundred horse. Bardylis formed his men into a square with his picked troops in the centre, while the flanks were weaker. Philip, noticing this, placed the élite of the Macedonians on his right wing under his command and made a determined assault on the left of the Illyrian square. At the same time, he instructed his cavalry to attack the barbarians' left wing in the flank and rear. For a long while the issue remained in doubt. Ultimately, the Illyrians succumbed to the combined attacks on all sides and took to flight, losing 7,000 killed. After this, they agreed to Philip's condition for peace that they should withdraw from all Macedonian cities.
Diodorus, 16: 4(3–7) and 8(1); Frontinus, Strategemata, 2: 3, 2; Beloch, Griechische Geschichte, 2nd edn, 3: 1,226, n.2.

SYRACUSE (357, summer) – Dion's Campaign
Map 15

In Syracuse the tyrannical excesses of Dionysius II offended Dion, who was both his brother-in-law and his son-in-law. Dion, with the help of Plato, attempted to reform the tyrant's way of thinking but without success. He was rewarded with banishment. Nine years later he collected a force of 800 mercenaries and made an expedition to Sicily, where he was joined by around 5,000 citizens. It happened that the tyrant was away at that time and so Dion was able to capture Syracuse with little difficulty. A week later Dionysius sailed into the harbour and entered the citadel. This had been built on a strip of land called Ortygia or simply 'the Island' between the harbour and the sea, and it was connected to the mainland by a narrow isthmus. Dion cut the citadel off by erecting a palisade across the isthmus. The tyrant attempted to come to terms with him and agreed to receive emissaries, but he promptly murdered them and ordered his mercenaries to attack the palisade. This action took the citizens by surprise and created panic. In an attempt to rally them, Dion charged into the midst of the enemy hacking at them and slaughtering them until he had been wounded several times. When he had been extricated from the mêlée by his own people, he managed to get on his horse and rode round the city rallying the Syracusans. He also ordered up a detachment of mercenaries who had been guarding another quarter of the city. When these arrived on the scene, fresh and full of energy, they routed the tyrant's men and drove them back inside the citadel. Of Dion's force 74 had been killed, but the enemy lost many more. Dion's efforts did not end as well as they had begun. He lost the confidence of the people and himself became despotic. In the end he was assassinated.

Plutarch, Dion, *29(6)–30; Diodorus,* **16:** *11(3)–12*

CHIOS ISL (357) – Social War

Mausolus succeeded to the position established by his father as the satrap or dynast of Caria. Not content with this, he wanted to expand his power to include the islands off the coast. In particular, he had his eye on Rhodes, Cos and Chios, which belonged to the Athenian alliance albeit with discontent. Mausolus fanned their smouldering grievances into a frank revolt from the alliance. The Athenians sent 60 ships to Chios under Chares and Chabrias, who found that the Chians had received reinforcements from Rhodes, Cos and Byzantium, and also from Mausolus. Chares, in charge of the land forces, advanced against the walls of Chios and was repelled by the enemy, who poured out of the gates from the city. Chabrias fared no better on the water. He met stiff opposition and he himself died fighting when his ship became the victim of a ram. The other ships were quickly extricated and escaped. This disastrous expedition was followed by an escalation of the war by the islanders, who proceeded to blockade Samos.

Diodorus, **16:** *7(3–4); Nepos,* Chabrias, *4*

EMBATA (356) – Social War

Following their defeat at Chios (above), the Athenians manned a further 60 ships and despatched the fleet to the troubled area under their generals Iphicrates and Timotheus to reinforce Chares. By then the rebellious islands had manned 100 ships, sacked the Athenian islands of Imbros and Lemnos, and blockaded Samos. The Athenian generals were all for besieging Byzantium until the enemy abandoned the attack on Samos and went to assist the Byzantines. Concerning the subsequent events the records are wanting. Nepos states that the Athenians set sail for Samos, but according to Diodorus, the opposing fleets met in the Hellespont. The actual site of the encounter is given by Polyaenus as Embata, which Stephanus calls Embaton and which he places in the territory of Erythrae, on the Ionian coast opposite Chios. When the fleets arrived in the straits off Embata, the weather was so stormy that the veterans, Iphicrates and Timotheus, said it would be folly to fight. Chares accused them of treason and proceeded alone to meet the enemy. He was defeated and lost many ships.

Diodorus, **16:** *21; Nepos,* Timotheus, *3; Polyaenus,* *3: 9, 29; Stephanus of Byzantium, s.v.* Ἔμβατον

DELPHI (356, summer) – Third Sacred War

After 10 years of hegemony the supremacy of Thebes had waned and her influence had become confined to the narrower field of Boeotia, Locris and Thessaly. Phocis had terminated her brief membership of the Boeotian alliance and represented an independent threat to her bigger neighbour. The Thebans trumped up a charge of sacrilege against Phocis before the outdated Amphictionic Council, resulting in a sentence of large fines with dire penalties against the accused. The Phocian citizen who took the lead in organizing resistance to this impost was a man called Philomelus. He hired some mercenaries and seized Delphi. He then sent envoys around the country, explaining that he was merely resuming Phocian rights that had been usurped. Sparta and Athens gave him support; Thebes prepared for war. Philomelus then fortified the shrine with a wall, raised 5,000 troops, and stood ready to join issue with any who disputed Phocian claims. The Locrians took the field and a battle was fought near the Phaedriades, the wall-like cliffs beneath Mount Parnassus which close the northern end of the glen in which Delphi was situated. Philomelus was the victor; the Locrians sustained heavy losses, some of them falling over the precipices or hurling themselves over the edge.

Diodorus, **16:** *28(1–3)*

NEON (354, autumn) – Third Sacred War

Their defeat at Delphi at the hands of the Phocians (above) caused the Locrians to seek help from the Thebans and their Amphictionic allies. Philomelus, the Phocian general, had foreseen the need for a bigger army and had assembled a considerable number of mercenaries, using the coffers at Delphi to offer high rates of pay. He advanced into Locrian territory and won a cavalry battle at an unknown site against the Locrians and Thebans. After this a Thessalian force arrived and was also defeated. The Phocians remained unvanquished until, at a place called Neon, they met up with a Theban army which far outnumbered their own. In a sharp battle the Phocians were defeated and Philomelus, who had been badly wounded, became cornered in a precipitous area. He decided to hurl himself over the edge.

Diodorus, 16: 31(3–5); Pausanias, 10: 2(2)

THE HERMEUM (353) – Third Sacred War

After the defeat and death of Philomelus at Neon (above), the Phocian cause was carried on by Onomarchus of Elataea. This general mustered troops and made as many allies as he could. He extended the power of Phocis far and wide with his military successes which, with his superior numbers, included two defeats of Philip of Macedon at places which are not recorded in the extant literature. After these events Philip went home, and Onomarchus marched into Boeotia. He defeated the Boeotians in a battle near the Temple of Hermes at Coronea, in which the Coronean citizens were killed to a man, while their mercenaries fled. Onomarchus subsequently captured the city.

Diodorus, 16: 35(3); Aristotle, Nicomachean Ethics, 3: 8(9), 1116b and scholiast

CROCIAN PLAIN (352) – Third Sacred War

Philip of Macedon had again descended into Thessaly, this time against the current tyrant of Pherae, Lycophron. When the tyrant summoned help from his Phocian allies, Onomarchus went to his assistance with 20,000 foot and 500 horse. Philip, with reinforcements from the Thessalian cavalry, came out against him with 20,000 foot and 3,000 horse. A bloody battle took place on the Crocian Plain, which bordered the western shore of the Pagasaean Gulf and is now the site of *Mikrothivai* airport. Philip was the victor by virtue of his superior cavalry. Many of the Phocians fled to the sea and tried to swim out to an Athenian fleet under Chares which 'happened to be sailing by'. Onomarchus was killed but the manner of his death is shrouded in conflicting reports. It is said that he was killed on the battlefield (Diodorus) or that he fled to the sea and was drowned (Philo Judaeus) or yet again that he was killed by his own

men (Pausanias). The casualty figures are more certain. Six thousand Phocians and mercenaries were slain; 3,000 were taken prisoner.

Diodorus, 16: 35(3–6) and 61(2); Pausanias, 10: 2(3); Philo Judaeus in Eusebius, Praeparatio Evangelica, 8: 14(33); Strabo, 9: 5,14; Stephanus of Byzantium, Κροχωτὸν πεδιον, s.v. Δημήτριον

ORCHOMENUS (352) ⎫
CEPHISUS R (352) ⎪
CORONEA (352) ⎬ – Third Sacred War
ABAE (352) ⎪
NARYX (352) ⎭

After the death of Onomarchus at or near the Crocian Plain (above), his brother Phayllus took command of the Phocian forces and revived the fortunes of his country. As he had immense funds obtained from the treasures of Delphi, he was well able to hire large numbers of mercenaries and even to entice cities to ally themselves with him. These advantages proved to be of no avail. With his forces he carried the war into Boeotia but, in spite of his numbers, he suffered a defeat with heavy losses near Orchomenus. This was only the first in a whole series of similar disasters. In a battle on the river Cephisus [*Kefissos*] 500 of his men were killed and 400 were taken prisoner. He was again defeated near Coronea in what seems to have been a minor engagement in that the Boeotians killed only 50 Phocians and took 130 prisoners. His fourth defeat occurred near Abae, where the Boeotians attacked his camp at night and inflicted heavy losses. He finally gained a victory at Naryx which at that time was being besieged. When the Boeotians went to the assistance of the city, Phayllus appeared and put the Boeotians to flight. He then stormed the city himself, took it and razed it.

Diodorus, 16: 37(5–6) and 38(4–5)

CHAERONEA (352/1) – Third Sacred War

When Phayllus, the Phocian commander, died, he was succeeded by his nephew Phalaecus, son of Onomarchus. This general was defeated soon afterwards by the Boeotians in a cavalry battle near Chaeronea, with the loss of a large number of his cavalrymen.

Diodorus, 16: 38(7)

ORNEAE (352/1) – Dispute over Megalopolis

The Spartans and the Megalopolitans had a dispute, as a result of which the Spartans under Archidamus overran the others' country. Argos, Sicyon and Messene turned out in force to assist

the Megalopolitans, while the Thebans sent them a detachment. Reinforcements for Sparta came from the Phocians. The Spartans and their allies captured the Argive city of Orneae, which was an ally of the Megalopolitans. When the Argives took the field against them, they defeated the Spartans killing more than 200 of them. The Thebans then appeared with an army said to be twice as large, in relation presumably to the Spartan force. A stubborn battle ensued, but Diodorus is unclear as to who precisely were the antagonists. We are told only that the outcome was in doubt and that the Argives and their allies withdrew.
Diodorus, 16: 39(1–5)

THELPUSA (352/1) – Dispute over Megalopolis

In a sequel to the battle at Orneae (above), the Thebans and their allies conquered the Spartans and Phocians near Thelpusa (sometimes recorded as Telphusa) in Arcadia and captured the Spartan commander Anaxander. A little later they won two other battles at places unrecorded.
Diodorus, 16: 39(6)

OLYNTHUS (348) – Rise of Macedon

Philip II of Macedon had considerably expanded his sway over the eastern seaboard of Greece. There were one or two pockets of resistance, notably the important Chalcidic city of Olynthus. Philip marched against it with a large army and defeated the Olynthians in two battles, shutting them up behind their walls. However, his persistent efforts to capture the place resulted in the loss of many of his men, and he eventually gained possession of the city through bribery and treachery.
Diodorus, 16: 53(2)

TAMYNAE (348, spring) – Revolt of Euboea

Philip of Macedon had set his sights on the island of Euboea and had been plotting to gain possession of it for some time. He stealthily took a force there and began installing some tyrants of his own. Plutarch, an Athens-orientated tyrant of Eretria, appealed to the Athenians who sent out an expedition under Phocion. This enterprising general found that the island was rotten with treachery and disaffection and that he had to resort to arms. He occupied a ridge above a deep defile which lay between himself and the plain around Tamynae. When the enemy advanced, Phocion was performing sacrifices and insisted on being undisturbed until he had finished, taking a long time over them. This may have been a ruse to draw the

enemy forward. Unfortunately, Plutarch, imagining cowardice on the part of his colleague, seized the initiative and charged the enemy with his mercenaries. This disordered attack met with a heavy repulse, which sent the attackers fleeing. Thus encouraged, the enemy charged forward to the palisade of Phocion's camp. By this time the sacrifices had been completed. The Athenians burst out and routed the leading attackers, cutting most of them down. Phocion then reformed his phalanx and made a furious attack on the rest of the enemy forces, scoring a complete victory.
Plutarch, Phocion, 12–13

HYAMPOLIS (347/6) – Third Sacred War

The Boeotians, after devastating Phocian territory in the region of Hyampolis (called Hya by Diodorus), proceeded to defeat their enemies in battle. Seventy Phocians were killed.
Diodorus, 16: 56(1)

CORONEA (347/6) – Third Sacred War

After the episode at Hyampolis (above), the Phocians and Boeotians again engaged, this time near Coronea. On this occasion the Boeotians were defeated with heavy losses. No further details are known. A year later an armistice terminated the Sacred War.
Diodorus, 16: 56(2)

HADRANUM (344) – Campaign of Timoleon

Greek Sicily was in the oppressive grip of Dionysius II, the tyrant of Syracuse. He had been expelled once but had managed a comeback. The Syracusans looked to Hicetas, ruler of Leontini [*Lentini*], for protection, but this double-dealing tyrant was no whit better than the other. He sided secretly with the Carthaginians, who appeared with a large fleet and bided their time. The Greek Sicilians appealed to Corinth, the founder of Syracuse, for help, which the Corinthians eagerly provided. They appointed Timoleon, a known tyrant-hater who had killed his own tyrannical brother, to lead the expedition. At that time in his mid-60s, he crossed the straits with a mere 700 mercenaries and landed at Tauromenium [*Taormina*], eluding the Carthaginian patrol ships, to find that Hicetas had defeated Dionysius and had seized control. The Sicilians as a whole were suspicious of another 'liberator' but the little town of Hadranum [*Adrano*] sent a message of welcome. Hearing about this, Hicetas proceeded there with 5,000 soldiers to put an end to Timoleon and his little force, which now totalled 1,200 men. When

Timoleon approached Hadranum on the second day of his march, he heard that Hicetas had arrived and was pitching his camp. Realizing that this was the best time to attack, he gave his men no time to rest but led them over the intervening 4 miles as fast as possible. Their onslaught completely surprised the enemy, who fled so quickly at sight of them that only 300 were killed and 600 taken prisoner.
Plutarch, Timoleon, *12; Diodorus,* **16:** *68(9–10)*

CRIMISUS R (339, June) – Campaign of Timoleon

In 339 the Carthaginians landed a huge force with a reputed 70,000 men under Hasdrubal and Hamilcar at Lilybaeum [*Marsala*] on the west coast of Sicily. They aimed to make a clean sweep of the island. Timoleon decided not to wait for them but to attack them on their own territory in the west. Under a temporary truce with Hicetas, the ruler of Leontini [*Lentini*], he obtained the service of the tyrant's troops who, when added to his own meagre few thousand, amounted to a total of no more than 12,000, of whom 1,000 mercenaries deserted. With this force Timoleon ascended a hill which was shrouded in morning mist. When the mist started to lift, he got his first view of the enemy hordes crossing the river Crimisus [*Fredolo*]. The chariots had already crossed, followed by a body of about 10,000 heavy infantry, including the crack formation of 2,500 Carthaginian citizens known as the Sacred Band. Timoleon realized that this was the time to attack, while the enemy was divided by the river. The cavalry went in first but were unable to penetrate the line of chariots, and so Timoleon advanced with the infantry. At first they were unable to make any impression on the heavily armoured enemy, but when they discarded their spears and drew their swords, their Greek skill with these weapons gave them the upper hand. At this point fortune lent a hand in the form of a violent thunderstorm with lightning, rain and hail. It came from behind the Greeks and drove into the faces of the enemy. The river overflowed its banks and the plain became a sea of rivulets. Above all there was mud. All this was to the disadvantage of the heavily armoured Carthaginians, who floundered around and, if they fell, could not get up again. When they turned to fly, some were washed away by the river, now a torrent, but many were despatched by the Greek light-armed troops who pursued them into the hills. It is said that 10,000 fell on the battlefield alone, of whom 3,000 were Carthaginians, and

that a further 15,000 were taken prisoner. The amount of valuable booty captured in the enemy camp was immense.
Plutarch, Timoleon, *25–29; Diodorus,* **16:** *77(4)–80*

DAMURIAS R (338) – Campaign of Timoleon

The temporary truce between Timoleon and the tyrant Hicetas was at an end after the battle at the Crimisus (above) and the defeat of their common Punic foe. They were back at each other's throats. When Timoleon was engaged in an expedition against Calauria, a town north of Syracuse, Hicetas raided Syracusan territory and did much damage. On his return, he marched right by Calauria to snub Timoleon, who had only a small force with him. Timoleon waited until the other had passed and then chased him with some cavalry and light-armed troops. On hearing about the pursuit, Hicetas crossed the river Damurias with its steep banks and waited on the far side. When Timoleon arrived, the sight of the enemy on the far bank provoked among his men such a display of rivalry and eagerness to get at them that Timoleon was forced to dictate the order of crossing. His men forced their way over and charged with such *élan* that the enemy troops fled leaving 1,000 dead behind them.
Plutarch, Timoleon, *31*

ABOLUS R (338) – Campaign of Timoleon

Shortly after his victory over Hicetas at the river Damurias (above), Timoleon captured the tyrant alive and had him executed. Next, he marched to Catana [*Catania*] against another of the tyrant rulers, Mamercus. Timoleon met him near the river Abolus (probably the Alabus [*Cantaro*]) and routed his army in a pitched battle, killing over 2,000 of his troops. Many of these were Carthaginian auxiliaries who had been supplied by Gisco. As a result, the Carthaginians sued for peace. Mamercus eventually took refuge with Hippo, the tyrant of Messana, but Timoleon blockaded that city and captured Hippo. Mamercus surrendered and was crucified by the Syracusans.
Plutarch, Timoleon, *34*

CHAERONEA (338, August) – Rise of Macedon

Philip of Macedon's aspiration was to be the master of the whole of Greece. He had some Greek allies but the Athenians with their dream of Greek liberty were the stumbling-block. The powerful oratory of Demosthenes ensured that there was no *rapprochement*. He even achieved the incredible,

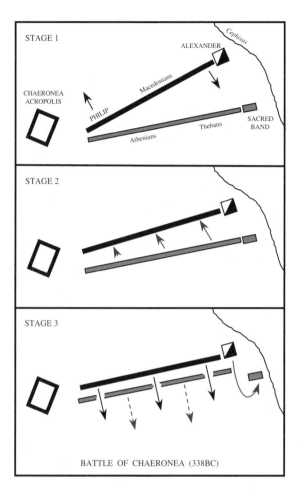

STAGE 1

CHAERONEA
ACROPOLIS

ALEXANDER

Cephisus

Macedonians

PHILIP

Athenians

Thebans

SACRED
BAND

STAGE 2

STAGE 3

BATTLE OF CHAERONEA (338BC)

an alliance between the two old rivals, Athens and Thebes, which together put an army in the field. After much politicking and manoeuvring, the Macedonian army of more than 30,000 infantry and 2,000 cavalry came face to face with the allied forces of approximately similar numbers at Chaeronea in Boeotia. There is only one account, brief and incomplete, of the battle as a whole. It has been necessary to reconstruct the tactics from scraps of information. The opposing lines extended from the city to the river Cephisus [*Kifissos*], a distance of about 2 miles. On the allied side, the Boeotians were under Theagenes and were headed by the Sacred Band of Thebans on the right wing bounded by the river; the Athenians under Chares occupied the left half of the line. On the other side, Philip placed his phalanx in the centre. The heavy cavalry under the command of his son, young Alexander, was placed on the left to oppose the dangerous Theban element. He himself took

charge of the Macedonian right wing. In the engagement Philip allowed the Macedonian right to fall gradually back, giving the enemy the impression that they were winning. But it is said that the Macedonians may also have been withdrawing deliberately onto higher ground so that their subsequent counterattack would catch the enemy at a disadvantage. When it came, the over-confident Athenians, now in some disorder, were overcome and fled to the hills. In the meantime, Alexander on the opposite flank had broken the Thebans. Moreover, the extension and subsequent disruption of the allied line had created gaps through which he charged and surrounded them. The captain of the Sacred Band of 300 was killed but its members refused to yield. Forty-six of them were taken alive (a statement based on the number of skeletons discovered); the rest stood their ground and died fighting to the end. Of the Athenians alone, 1,000 were killed and 2,000 captured. Among those who fled was the hoplite Demosthenes, whose flight evoked a tirade of sarcasm from Plutarch.

Diodorus, 16: 85(5)–86; Polyaenus, 4: 2, 2; Plutarch, Alexander, 12(3); Plutarch, Demosthenes, 20(2)

SHIPKA PASS (335, spring) – Alexander's First Campaign

Before Alexander embarked upon his great anabasis he undertook a campaign in Thrace and Illyria to subdue the threatening tribes who would be ready to attack and invade Macedonia as soon as his back was turned. Departing from Amphipolis, he headed northwards until he reached the Haemus range [*Stara Planina*], which he had to cross, probably by the pass which is now known as the *Shipka Pass*, 100 miles due east of *Sofia*. Here he met a large group of Thracians who had occupied the high ground and were intent on preventing his advance. They had a number of waggons, which they collected at the top of the pass with the object of sending them thundering down on the interlopers. Alexander's orders to his men were to open ranks and let the waggons through, if they had space to do so. If they could not move aside, they were to lie down flat on the ground in closely packed formation and interlock their shields over their bodies. In the event, Alexander's stratagem succeeded admirably. The waggons rattled and rolled over the shields and not a man was lost. In the subsequent assault on the Thracians, the archers were placed in front to meet any enemy attack, while the infantry followed up. Before the

troops could even get to close grips with the horde, the enemy fled, leaving some 1,500 dead in their wake.
Arrian, Anabasis, *1: 1(6–13)*

LYGINUS R (335) – Alexander's First Campaign
From the *Shipka Pass* (above), Alexander proceeded to cross the Haemus range and descend to the river Lyginus [*?Yantra*] in the territory of the Triballians. News of his approach had preceded him and Syrmus, the king, had sent the women and children to take refuge on an island called Peuce in the middle of the Danube, to which Syrmus and his court also repaired. But most of the male population retreated to the shelter of woods on the bank of the Lyginus until Alexander had moved further on. When Alexander heard about this, he retraced his steps and came upon the tribesmen as they were making camp. He ordered his archers and slingers to discharge their missiles into the woods and to drive the tribesmen out. When the enemy emerged to grapple with the light troops, Alexander sent the cavalry against them in two squadrons, one to either side, while the infantry attacked the centre. Once the fighting began at close range, the Triballians broke and fled. They lost 3,000 men against 50 on the Macedonian side.
Arrian, Anabasis, *1: 2*

ISTER R (335) – Alexander's First Campaign
Three days' march northward from the river Lyginus brought Alexander to the Ister [*Danube*] opposite the island of Peuce, on which Syrmus and some of the Triballians had taken refuge. A fleet of ships which Alexander had requisitioned from Byzantium was waiting for him. With these, he attempted a landing on the island, but circumstances were against him and he abandoned the idea and decided to cross the river instead. A force in excess of 10,000 Getae had already assembled on the far bank to resist any such move. During the night 4,000 of the Macedonian infantry and 1,500 cavalry were transported to the opposite shore in the ships, which were supplemented by numerous available native dugouts. The Getae reappeared at dawn as Alexander was advancing. The feat of the nocturnal crossing had already overawed them and the awe turned to fright at sight of the heavy infantry marching inexorably forward towards them. The first cavalry charge turned their fright into abject terror. They fled to their town, but had second thoughts and aban-

doned it in favour of the uninhabited hinterland. The town was razed to the ground.
Arrian, Anabasis, *1: 3–4(5)*

PELIUM (335) – Alexander's First Campaign
After subduing the Getae on the Ister (above), Alexander marched back southward over the *Shipka Pass* and then turned west toward Illyria. He made for the border fortress of Pelium, a stronghold used by the Illyrian chieftain Cleitus, who was in revolt. Alexander shut the people up in their town and was preparing to besiege it when a large force appeared under Glaucias, the chief of the Taulantians, who had allied himself with Cleitus. Pelium was surrounded by commanding heights, now occupied by Taulantians, who presented Alexander with a difficult problem. He only managed to withdraw his force by executing an ingenious tactic. He lined his men up and put them through a precise and complicated barrack-square drill routine in total silence. At the end of this ceremonial procedure with all its military precision Alexander formed his left into a wedge and advanced toward the enemy. They were so overawed by the spectacle they had witnessed that they abandoned their positions and retired to the town. They recovered sufficiently to descend and make an attack on the Macedonian rearguard as it was crossing the river, but a volley of missiles from every available weapon kept them at bay until the crossing had been effected. Three days later news was received that the forces of Cleitus and Glaucias, having seen the Macedonians off their premises, had camped carelessly without any precautions or guards. With a part of his force Alexander retraced his steps under cover of darkness and massacred the enemy in their sleep or in the course of fleeing, virtually annihilating them.
Arrian, Anabasis, *1: 5(5)–6*

THEBES (335, September) – Alexander's First Campaign
While Alexander was away in Illyria, Thebes revolted in an effort to throw off the Macedonian yoke. Alexander wasted no time in getting on the march and he arrived in Boeotia within a fortnight. He proceeded to Thebes and waited outside the walls, giving the Thebans time to change their minds and to submit. The Theban response was a major sortie, in which their cavalry together with a considerable supporting force of light infantry attacked the Macedonian outposts with missiles, causing a sizeable number of casualties. They were almost within striking distance of the main

Macedonian position when some archers and light infantry were ordered out to oppose them. The next day Alexander took up a position opposite the citadel of the Cadmea, which had been ringed with a double palisade. But still he made no move against the Thebans, hoping that they would come to terms with him. It was Alexander's general Perdiccas who began the assault, allegedly on his own initiative. He forced the outer palisade and burst through the breach but was seriously wounded before he had overcome the second palisade. Alexander ordered his archers and light-armed troops to the rescue. For a while the Thebans were contained but eventually they turned in fury on the Macedonians, who were forced to give ground and then take to flight. Alexander then launched an infantry attack against the Thebans, who were driven inside their city in such a panic that they failed to close the gates. The battle continued within the city until the Thebans broke and fled to the open country. Diodorus and Plutarch agree that the *coup de grâce* was administered by the Macedonian garrison in the Cadmea, which made a sortie and attacked the Thebans in the rear. The inhabitants who had not managed to effect an escape were butchered indiscriminately, after which the city was razed to the ground as a lesson to others.
Arrian, Anabasis, *1: 7(7)–8; Diodorus, 17: 11–13; Plutarch, Alexander, 11(4–6)*

GRANICUS R (334, May) – Alexander's Anabasis

Alexander crossed the Hellespont into Asia with a force generally estimated at 32,000 infantry and 5,100 cavalry. The Persians did not act in time to prevent the crossing but assembled their forces on the banks of the river Granicus [*Kocabas*]. Although a figure of 600,000 men has been quoted, Arrian's sober estimate is of 20,000 cavalry and a comparable number of mercenary foot soldiers. Their horsemen were, by all accounts, considerably superior in number to the Macedonian cavalry. King Darius himself was not present, and his forces were commanded by a number of satraps and generals. At their conference Memnon's was a lone voice against a fight. He advocated a scorched earth policy and an effort to carry the war into the invader's homeland. The others were jealous of his Greek origins and did not concur, with the result that the Persian forces took up position on the Granicus in the Adrastian plain. Their cavalry were deployed in breadth along the bank; behind them were the infantry,

who had little part to play in the battle until the late stages. The prospect confronting Alexander was daunting. The river was fast flowing and deep, while the far bank was high and slippery. Moreover, it was late in the day. Parmenio advocated a night attack but nothing, it is said, would deter Alexander from an immediate assault. The subsequent events are shrouded in uncertainty. With one exception the ancient sources proceed to describe a near-suicidal assault across the river. Diodorus is the dissenter. He alone refers to an easy, early-morning crossing of the river. Did Alexander move during the night and effect a dawn crossing at some ford further along the Granicus? This would be an obvious solution – unless the enemy anticipated it. According to Diodorus, they did not. But in any assessment of Diodorus' narrative versus the other historians, considerable weight must be attached to Arrian's account. His principal source on military matters was Ptolemy, son of Lagus, who fought with Alexander throughout the campaign. The following summary is based on Arrian's account.

The Persians outnumbered their foe in cavalry, in which they placed their hopes of victory. Their front consisted entirely of mounted troops on a broad front along the river bank. The infantry was posted behind the line on somewhat higher ground. Alexander placed his heavy infantry in the centre and the cavalry on both wings, Parmenio commanding the left side while he himself took charge of the right. The battle took place initially in the river and on the bank. At the outset, the Macedonian vanguard was repulsed from the bank with heavy losses. As the survivors were being pursued in the river Alexander, close behind them, led his men across on the right wing and threw the disorganized Persians into further disorder, establishing a bridgehead in the process. Meanwhile Macedonians were succeeding in crossing the river in increasing numbers. Alexander is heard of next in a ferocious assault on the Persian commanders, who were grouped together in front of their centre. In moving from his right wing to the centre, it is possible that Alexander was employing the same tactic that he used later (e.g. at Gaugamela) of making a pass at the wing in order to draw enemy forces away from the centre and to weaken it before he wheeled. Once he was in the centre of the fray, surrounded by the Persian 'top brass', the action became a series of duels which, with variations, form the greater part of the ancient accounts. In the process, Alexander received several thrusts, including a blow from a scimitar which split his helmet and just penetrated to the scalp. The eventual outcome was the death of several of the Persian commanders, among whom Arrian lists seven fatalities. This was too much for the Persian centre, which started to break, and when it failed to hold its ground both wings broke also with the loss of around 1,000 cavalrymen. With the cavalry battle at an end, the Macedonian infantry had little difficulty in routing the Persian foot who were by then totally unprotected. Finally, Alexander turned his attention to the Greek mercenaries who still remained firm on their high ground beyond the field. They asked for quarter but received none. Alexander himself led the charge against them and butchered them to a man, losing more of his own men in the process than in the previous fighting. Figures for the Persian losses range from 10,000 to 20,000 infantry and around 2,000 horse. These estimates are almost as incredible as the allegedly minute Macedonian losses, which have been variously put at a maximum of 30 infantrymen (minimum 9) and 120 cavalry of whom 25 were Companions killed in the first charge.

Arrian, Anabasis, *1: 12(8)–16; Diodorus, 17: 19–21; Plutarch, Alexander, 16; Justin, 11: 6(10–15)*

ISSUS (333, November) – Alexander's Anabasis Issus lay on the coast of Cilicia in the extreme north-east corner of the Mediterranean. It was surrounded landward by a great horseshoe of mountains which stretched from the Cilician coast round to the Syrian shore. Access through the mountains was by three passes: the Cilician Gates [*Gülek Boğazi*] from the north, the Amanian Gates [*Bahçe Pass*] from the north-east, and the Syrian Gates [*Beilan Pass*] from the south. Alexander advanced to Issus from the north through the Cilician Gates, at which he was virtually unopposed. The Great King, Darius III, was encamped at that time in the Assyrian plains east of the southern gate. His army was reputedly vast, variously estimated at an incredible 250,000 to 600,000 personnel, although these figures include camp followers and non-combatants of every description. When he heard that Alexander had advanced southwards from Issus through the Syrian Gates, the king was advised to stay where he was and fight it out in the plains where his cavalry and numbers would be to his advantage. But in a shrewd move he marched round through the Amanian Gates and encamped at Issus in Alexander's rear. Alexander turned round and retraced his steps to meet him, overjoyed at being

able to bring him to battle in a thoroughly confined space.

A river, the Pinarus, cut across the plain from hills to sea. The banks were steep and here Darius drew up his forces along the northern side. Initially he sent some cavalry and light infantry across the river to give protection during his deployments. In the centre he placed his Greek mercenary hoplites flanked with *Cardaces* (probably light-armed troops). On his left there were more *Cardaces*, extending to the base of the hills and following their contour round toward the south so that they faced Alexander's flank. The Persian right, along the shore, consisted of cavalry. The rest of the army was in the rear. As soon as Alexander's troops debouched from the narrow track onto the plain, he placed his heavy infantry in the centre and the Macedonian and Thessalian cavalry on the right under his command. On the left flank he had only some allied cavalry. This wing became seriously threatened when Darius withdrew the forces that he had sent across the river and detailed them to reinforce his right wing. It was vital to Alexander that his left wing should remain secure and not be outflanked, and so he transferred the Thessalian cavalry to that end of the line. A preliminary skirmish on his right convinced him that the enemy troops in the hillside on his flank presented no threat. They were easily dislodged and retreated further up the slopes. Alexander now advanced slowly. When he was within range of the enemy, he made a sudden charge through the stream against the Persian left, which collapsed. After routing that wing he made a determined dash straight for Darius. Several of the Persian commanders in Darius' entourage were killed, their deaths bearing witness to the ferocity of the attack and the proximity of Alexander to his principal target. In the meantime, however, things were going less well for the Macedonians in the centre, where the difficulty of negotiating the river bank caused considerable disorganization in their line. The Greek mercenaries serving with Darius saw their chance and made a furious onslaught. When Alexander observed his men hard pressed and in difficulties, he abandoned his attack on Darius and wheeled round to their assistance, attacking the enemy in the flank. This saved the day. A fierce cavalry battle also took place on the seashore, where the two sides were evenly matched until the Persians realized that Darius had taken to flight. Alexander's charge to the relief of his centre had given the king a respite in which he had transshipped from his chariot to a horse and had galloped into the hills. He had a sufficient lead over the pursuit to ensure a safe getaway.

The Persian casualties are recorded as a huge 110,000 by Arrian, Curtius, and Plutarch. Justin gives the same total with a breakdown of 61,000 foot, 10,000 horse and 40,000 captured. The disparity between these figures and the reported Macedonian losses of less than 500 men is eloquent.

Arrian, Anabasis, *2: 7–11; Curtius, 3: 8(27)–11; Diodorus, 17: 32(2)–34; Plutarch,* Alexander, *20; Justin, 11: 9(1–10)*

MEGALOPOLIS (331, autumn) – Greek Revolt

Alexander's absence in Asia provided the Greek city states with an excellent opportunity to rebel against the Macedonian yoke. The Peloponnese, in particular, was a hive of unrest. Agis III, the king of Sparta, induced the Achaeans, Eleans and Arcadians to join him, with the exception of Megalopolis. He raised an allied force of at least 20,000 foot and 2,000 horse, which he led out with the intention of attacking this recalcitrant city. The onus of subduing this rebellion rested with Antipater, Alexander's viceroy in Greece. After subduing an uprising in Thrace, he marched to the Peloponnese with a Macedonian and allied force of at least 40,000 men. The two armies engaged near Megalopolis in a battle about which little is known except that it took place in a restricted area. In consequence, the armies were unable to deploy fully and the Macedonian superiority in numbers may not have counted for much. In a long and fierce contest the Greek allies were eventually forced back with a loss of more than 5,300 of their number. The Macedonian losses are variously recorded as 3,500 (Diodorus) and 1,000 (Curtius). The details which are reported are largely concerned with the valiant fighting and heroic death of King Agis who, already wounded and unable to rise to his feet, still struggled to his knees and kept assailants at bay with a spear until he was killed by a lance.

Diodorus, 17: 62(6)–63; Curtius, 6: 1(1–16)

GAUGAMELA (331, October 1) – Alexander's Anabasis

After Issus (333) Alexander went southwards, capturing Tyre and Gaza and making an expedition into Egypt. On his return journey northwards he was told that Darius was encamped on the Tigris, to which he proceeded. Darius had moved from there but he had not gone far and was encamped with a considerably augmented army near Gaugamela. The conflict which was to take place there has been known in the past as the battle of Arbela [*Erbil*], this being the nearest town about 70 miles away. The little hamlet of Gaugamela near the river Bumodus or Boumelos [*Khazir*] was not considered worthy of significance. Thither Alexander marched to find that Darius had already prepared the battlefield by levelling the ground and clearing any obstacles which might make it unsuitable for chariots and cavalry.

The Persian army was said to number up to 1,000,000 foot soldiers, the lowest reported figure being 200,000. The true figure cannot be known, but it has been estimated that Alexander's cavalry was outnumbered about five to one. During the night before the battle Alexander lay working out his tactics and how best to offset the huge disparity in numbers. When he had formed his plan, he slept and had to be roused at daybreak. In the meantime, the Persian army which had lined up during the day retained its dispositions under arms all night for fear of a nocturnal attack. In their respective deployments next day the Persian line extended well beyond the Macedonian line on both wings. To counter this, Alexander placed cavalry on both wings and held them back in echelon formation to prevent them being outflanked. Another feature of his disposition was a large reserve formation of infantry in the rear. Their officers had been instructed to be ready to face about and meet any threat from behind. In the initial stages of the engagement, Alexander in command of his right kept edging further to his right until he was almost on the verge of the ground that had been cleared for the chariots. Darius ordered his mounted troops to encircle the Macedonian right. Alexander sent in another squadron; the Persians sent in more. In the bitter struggle which resulted, the Macedonian cavalry only just managed to hold off their attackers for long enough to give Alexander the chance he was waiting for. The repeated reinforcement of the Persian left with more and more squadrons depleted their front line until a gap appeared. Through this opening Alexander charged with the Companions and the heavy infantry in a wedge which made straight for Darius himself. The struggle in this part of the field was soon over and Darius fled. In the meantime, the Macedonians were in difficulties elsewhere. The Persian and Indian cavalry had burst right through a gap in the Macedonian front line and penetrated to the baggage in the rear. The reserve formation, acting on its instructions, faced about and drove them back again. At about the same time the Persian right launched an attack on the Macedonian left wing under Parmenio. Alexander, after driving Darius from the field, wheeled round and went to assist Parmenio but ran into the returning Persians and Indians. Here the heaviest fighting of the whole battle took place and about 60 of the Companions were killed. In the meantime, the Thessalian cavalry under Parmenio had worsted their attackers and the whole enemy line was in rout. Alexander pursued Darius as far as Arbela but found only his abandoned chariot and bow. Darius had made good his escape. Alexander's losses in the battle amounted to a few hundred men. On the Persian side the quoted figures range from 40,000 up to 300,000.

No mention has yet been made of the Persian scythed chariots upon which Darius set great store. They were launched in the earlier stages of the battle but proved to be a failure. Some got through to the Macedonian lines where the infantry parted ranks and allowed them to pass harmlessly through. Others that were made riderless by arrow or javelin became a menace to both sides and contributed nothing to a victory.

Alexander's triumph at Gaugamela is one of the truly decisive battles of history. It ended at a stroke the threat of Persian domination over all the peoples of the civilized world.
Arrian, Anabasis, 3: 8–15; Curtius, 4: 9(9–10) and 12–16; Diodorus, 17: 56–61; Plutarch, Alexander, 32–33

SUSIAN GATES (330, winter) – Alexander's Anabasis
Gaugamela, Babylon, the Tigris, Susa: such was Alexander's progress. From Susa his immediate objective was Persepolis, the capital city of the Persian empire, and he was in a hurry to get there before the Persian treasure was evacuated to safety. There were two routes: a long detour by the main road, and a direct track over the mountains through the pass known as the Susian or Persian Gates. Alexander split his forces. Parmenio was directed to take all the heavy-armed forces and the baggage by the road, while he himself set off with the rest into the hills. At the gates he came up against Ariobarzanes, the satrap, who had built defences across the pass and was reputed to be holding it with as many as 25,000 troops. When Alexander and his force approached, they were met by a barrage of missiles from above and huge boulders rolling down the hillside. They were

unable to get a hold on the rock face or to fight back at an enemy who was out of range. Even Alexander had to admit defeat by that route. The Macedonians had, however, taken a few prisoners, one of whom spoke their language and undertook to lead them by a difficult track which would bring them out on the far side of the enemy. Alexander had no choice but to accept the man's good faith. He told Craterus to stay behind at the bottom of the pass and to light many fires as if the whole force was encamped. He was to make a frontal assault up the defile as soon as he heard the hubbub above. Alexander then set off with the guide and a task force under cover of darkness. The distance to be covered was around 12 miles. Arrian's account makes the expedition sound like a cross-country jog, much of it executed at the double and achieved in one night. Curtius, on the other hand, gives a graphic description of the difficulties and dangers, of ravines to be circumvented and of snow-covered pitfalls. According to him, the trek took two nights and a day with a rest in the middle. When the party encountered a couple of outposts, the enemy either fled or were slaughtered. Apparently none of the fugitives had the presence of mind to warn the main body, and so Alexander's assault came as a complete surprise. He had also detached a part of his force to approach from a different direction, while at the same time the blare of a trumpet brought Craterus and his men into a frontal assault up the pass. Surrounded on all sides, the enemy had no means of escape and were massacred.
Arrian, Anabasis, 3: 18(1–9); Curtius, 5: 3(16)–4; Diodorus, 17: 68

JAXARTES R (328) – Alexander's Anabasis
After crossing the Caucasus, Alexander moved northward to Marakanda [*Samarkand*] and then turned east until he reached the river Jaxartes [*Syr-Darya*], which was wrongly identified as the Tanais. This was the most north-easterly point which he reached at the end of this leg of his expedition. By this river a party of Macedonians were foraging when they were attacked and slaughtered by a large group of tribesmen estimated to be about 30,000 in number. The enemy then withdrew to a high point in the hills, which was surrounded by steep cliffs on all sides. Alexander moved against this position but his men repeatedly failed to get a foothold on the precipitous slopes and were forced back by the missiles sent down on them from above. Alexander himself was wounded in the leg by an arrow. The

details of his subsequent success are not recorded but he eventually managed to take the place and inflict enormous losses on the natives. Many of them leapt over the edge of the cliffs and only 8,000 of the 30,000 are said to have escaped.
Arrian, Anabasis, *3: 30(7–11); Curtius, 7: 6(1–7)*

ALEXANDRIA ESCHATE (328) –
Alexander's Anabasis

It was on the river Jaxartes [*Syr-Darya*] that Alexander decided to found a city named after himself at this, the furthermost (eschate) point reached by his expedition on this leg of the journey. He spent three weeks fortifying the site of what is now *Leninabad*. During this time a horde of Asian Scythians arrived and occupied the opposite bank of the river. They made no move to leave but just stayed, watching and deriding the Macedonians. Alexander decided to move against them and crossed the river with his men in skin-floats. The archers and slingers were the first ashore, with instructions to keep the enemy at bay while the infantry landed. When the vanguard advanced, the Scythians rode around them in circles, discharging their missiles. A force of cavalry and light troops was sent against them. When these were nearly in contact with the enemy, Alexander ordered the three regiments of the Companions and the mounted javelin throwers to charge, while he followed up with the rest of the cavalry. This broke up the enemy's ring and turned them to flight. Around 1,000 were killed and many more perished in the pursuit.
Arrian, Anabasis, *4: 3(6)–4; Curtius, 7: 6(25–27) and 8(30)–9(16)*

HYDASPES R (326, July) – Alexander's
Anabasis

When Alexander reached the river Hydaspes [*Jhelum*], Porus, the king of the Pauravas, was waiting for him on the opposite bank with his army and his elephants. A direct crossing of the river was out of the question. Alexander sent a team back to the river Indus with instructions to dismantle the boats which he had left there and to bring them to the Hydaspes and reassemble them. In the meantime, he initiated activities aimed at confusing the enemy and keeping them guessing. He divided his men into groups and told them to keep moving up and down the river with an air of great purpose. Using this continual activity as a cover, he himself explored the area and discovered a likely place for a crossing, a wooded

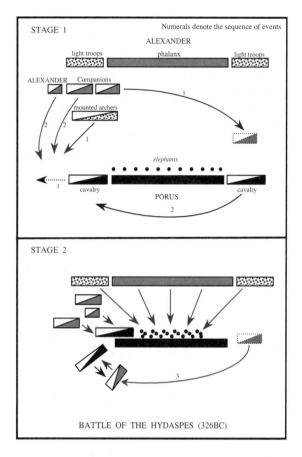

BATTLE OF THE HYDASPES (326BC)

promontory opposite an equally wooded island, where the crossing would be screened from view. It was about 18 miles from the main camp. On the chosen day, Alexander took with him the special squadron of the Companions and several other bodies of cavalry with which he detoured round to the crossing, leaving Craterus in charge of the main camp. The crossing was effected during darkness in the galleys and skin-floats which had previously been assembled on the spot. The invasion was reported to Porus, who sent his son to oppose it with a few thousand cavalry and some chariots. Alexander moved against them with his mounted archers and cavalry and put them to flight with a loss of about 400 men, including Porus' son. The chariots were useless. There had been heavy rain and they got stuck in the mud. In the meantime, Craterus had started crossing the river from the main camp as previously arranged. This put Porus in a dilemma. He decided to leave a small force with some elephants to oppose Craterus, while he marched against Alexander with his 30,000 infantry, 4,000 cavalry, and numerous chariots and elephants. He placed his elephants at intervals across his whole front, with the infantry in units behind the gaps between the animals. The cavalry were divided between the wings with a screen of chariots. Alexander knew that a direct assault against the Indian centre would be fraught with difficulty, as Porus had intended. He decided to concentrate his attack on the enemy's left wing. He sent his 1,000 strong force of mounted archers against that wing and followed them up himself with the Companions. As he had foreseen, the enemy withdrew all their cavalry from their right wing, allowing Alexander's cavalry on his left to follow them round and stay in their rear. This compelled the Indians to split their force and turn, disrupting their whole manoeuvre. At this point Alexander charged and drove the enemy left back onto the elephants. With both their wings disrupted, the Indians were becoming concentrated in their centre where the elephants started to have a field day. The Macedonian infantry who charged the centre suffered very badly, but as the scrum became more tightly packed, the Indians were unable to get out of the way of the wounded and maddened beasts. They were effectively pulped. Porus made one last ineffective elephant charge and then, wounded, retired from the field. Estimates of the Indian casualties range from 12,000 to 20,000, including Porus' two sons. The Macedonian losses were said to be 1,000 or less.

Arrian, Anabasis, *5: 8(4)–19; Curtius, 8: 13(5)–14; Diodorus, 17: 87–89(3); Plutarch, Alexander, 60–62(1)*

* * *

HELLENISTIC ERA

Alexander the Great died on 13 June 323, leaving no successor. The vacuum created by his death resulted in bitter infighting between his generals, who carved up the empire between them as his successors (diadochi). As a result, the military history of the period presents a tangled skein of disjointed episodes with lust for power as the principal connecting thread. Much of the ancient literature relating to the era has been lost. In consequence, the existing knowledge of a complex series of events has been pieced together from sources such as inscriptions, fragments and coins.

PLATAEA (323) – Lamian War
The death of Alexander the Great in June 323

prompted the Greeks to assert their liberty and establish their leadership of the states. They embarked on the construction of 240 ships and the levying of a mercenary force, and they also sent envoys to other cities and states to recruit support. An Athenian condottiere named Leosthenes raised several thousand mercenaries outside Athens. The Athenians sent him 7,000 more, but to join the army of Leosthenes near Thermopylae these reinforcements had to pass through Boeotia, which had a grudge against Athens. The Boeotians were at that time encamped near Plataea. Leosthenes took a part of his force into Boeotia and, after joining the Athenians, he lined his men up against the Boeotians. He defeated them in battle and then returned to Thermopylae where he planned to meet the Macedonian forces.
Diodorus, 18: 11(3–5)

THERMOPYLAE P (323, autumn) – Lamian War
On the death of Alexander, Macedon and the surrounding districts had been allotted to Antipater. His military strength was low because of the drainage of manpower occasioned by Alexander's campaign, the demobilized troops having not as yet returned home. When Antipater heard about the concerted action of the Greeks, he set out for Thessaly with the available force of 13,000 troops and his entire fleet of 110 triremes. The Thessalians, who had the best cavalry in the land, had been allies of Macedon but the Athenians had managed to seduce them. They deserted the Macedonians and rode off to join Leosthenes. The Greeks now far outnumbered the Macedonians, whom they defeated in battle near Thermopylae. Antipater was virtually trapped as he did not dare to attempt a northward journey home. He took refuge in Lamia just under 10 miles north of Thermopylae.
Diodorus, 18: 12(2–4)

LAMIA (322, spring) – Lamian War
After their defeat near Thermopylae (above), Antipater and his Macedonians took refuge in Lamia where they were besieged by Leosthenes and the Greeks. The siege was nearing success when Leosthenes was killed by a missile. Antiphilus was appointed to take over. In the meantime Leonnatus, who had been given control of Hellespontine Phrygia, came to the aid of Antipater. He crossed over to Europe and gathered a force of 20,000 infantry and 1,500 cavalry, which he led down through Thessaly. The Greeks

promptly abandoned the siege of Lamia and sent all their camp followers and baggage to Melitia 10 miles to the north, while they advanced to engage Leonnatus before he could join up with Antipater. Their force numbered 22,000 infantry and more than 3,500 cavalry, mostly Thessalian. In a fierce battle the Greeks proved superior both on horse and foot. Leonnatus was killed and the Macedonians withdrew from the plain and sought safety in some difficult high ground. Antipater came up and joined them on the following day but decided to avoid a further engagement. The battle was probably fought in the low ground of the Sperchius valley close to Lamia.

Diodorus, 18: 15(1–4); Plutarch, Phocion, 25(3)

RHAMNUS (322) – Lamian War
While the Greeks were defeating Antipater at Lamia, a man called Micion landed at Rhamnus in Attica with a large force of Macedonians and mercenaries. He was devastating the countryside in the neighbourhood when the Athenian general Phocion led an army against him. The Macedonians were utterly routed and Micion was killed.

Plutarch, Phocion, 25(1–2)

ABYDUS (322, ?March)
LICHADES ISLS (322) } – Lamian War
AMORGOS ISL (322, ?June)
There is no adequate account of the naval campaign which included at least two of these important battles, Abydus and Amorgos, and probably the third. The sole extant source is the account of Diodorus, which is condensed into 60 words and is, moreover, ambiguous concerning the number of battles involved. In recent years the campaign has been reconstructed by Walek, to whose exposition the reader is referred. His conclusions are summarized as follows. In 323 the Greeks embarked on the construction of 240 warships. Early in the following year they sent 170 ships under the command of Evetion to the Hellespont in an attempt to prevent Leonnatus from crossing to Europe to the aid of Antipater. They were engaged off Abydus by a Macedonian fleet of 240 ships under Cleitus, who defeated them. At the beginning of the campaign the Macedonians had a naval strength of 110 ships, which accompanied Antipater to Thessaly. However, they had access to reinforcements from many sources in Asia, which could explain their rapid change in fortune to a position of numerical superiority.

Later in the same year the fleets of Cleitus and Evetion again met in battle, off the Cycladean island of Amorgos. The Athenian fleet was annihilated in a decisive defeat which ended Athenian naval power for all time. The site of this battle is mentioned by Plutarch; the Parian Marble (an inscribed marble stele at Paros) gives the date.

Diodorus does not attach place names to either of these battles. He does, however, refer ambiguously to an action off the Echinades, which could be a third encounter. However, there are no known islands of that name in the Aegean region. The islands known as the Echinades are in the Ionic Sea and are clearly not the place referred to by Diodorus. If there was a third battle, it is most likely to have taken place in the Malian Gulf where a fleet of 110 Macedonian ships under Antipater was operating in conjunction with the land forces at Lamia. It is thought that a part of the original Athenian complement of 240 ships was sent to the Malian Gulf to block Antipater's fleet. After the battle off Abydus, Cleitus probably sailed to the gulf and destroyed the Athenian blockade off the Lichades islands in the mouth of the gulf. He then proceeded to Amorgos for the decisive battle.

Walek supports the view that corruption of the word 'Lichades' to 'Echinades' is the most probable explanation for the confusion.

Diodorus, 18: 15(8–9); T. Walek, Revue de Philologie, 48: 23–30, 1924; Plutarch, Demetrius, 11(3).

CRANNON (322, September) – Lamian War
Craterus crossed from Asia and arrived in Macedonia to reinforce Antipater. He set out with 6,000 infantry and *en route* enlisted 4,000 more, together with 1,000 Persian bowmen and slingers and 1,500 cavalry. This brought the combined forces up to 40,000 heavy infantry, 3,000 bowmen and 5,000 cavalry. They camped beside the river Peneus [*Pinios*] near Crannon in Thessaly. The Greeks who were encamped against them were much inferior in numbers, with only 25,000 infantry and 3,500 cavalry. In the battle the Greeks, to make up for their shortage in numbers, relied on the quality of their Thessalian cavalry and placed them out in front of the phalanx. Certainly, they were getting the better of it in the cavalry action. But when Antipater led his phalanx forward, matters took an opposite turn. By virtue of weight of numbers the Macedonians slaughtered the Greeks, who were forced to retreat to some higher ground. Here, they managed to repulse the enemy, and both sides disengaged. The losses were remarkably small: 500 on the Greek side and 130 Macedonians. Nevertheless, the Athenians decided to sue

for peace, which Antipater granted on condition that each city treated with him individually. This cunning move on his part disrupted the Greek alliance.

Diodorus, **18**: *16(4)–17(5); Plutarch,* Phocion, *26(1)*

HELLESPONT (321) – Wars of the Diadochi

Perdiccas, who was made regent of Alexander's kingdom, became anxious about Ptolemy's increasing power and decided to mount a campaign against him. But first he sent Eumenes to the Hellespont [*Dardanelles*] to prevent Antipater and Craterus from crossing into Asia or at the least to block their further progress. Eumenes was accompanied by two more commanders, Alcetas and Neoptolemus. Neoptolemus, however, was jealous of Eumenes. He made secret contact with Antigonus, the ruler of central and southern Asia Minor, and plotted against his own leader. When this was discovered, Eumenes forced him to fight and defeated him. The Macedonian soldiers of Neoptolemus then joined Eumenes, leaving Neoptolemus with only a few hundred horse with which to desert to Antipater. At this juncture Antipater and Craterus decided to split their forces. Antipater was to head south against Perdiccas; Craterus was to deal with Eumenes and then join Antipater. When Craterus and Eumenes confronted each other, each had 20,000 infantry but the phalanx of Craterus was superior, being largely composed of Macedonians of famed ability. Eumenes, on the other hand, pinned his fortune on his cavalry, of which he had 5,000 compared to his adversary's 2,000. Both sides stationed their cavalry on their wings. Craterus took command of his right wing himself while Neoptolemus had charge of the left. The action began when Craterus, in front of his picked troops, charged the enemy. According to Diodorus, his horse stumbled and threw its rider, who was trampled underfoot and killed. Plutarch says that Craterus was killed by the sword in hand-to-hand fighting. Whatever the cause, his death so encouraged the enemy that they charged from all sides and utterly defeated the opposing right wing, causing great slaughter. On the other wing, Neoptolemus was confronting Eumenes himself. The bitter feud between them ensured that the fight became a matter of single combat in a duel to the death. First they grappled on horseback until the horses moved away, leaving the riders to fall to the ground in locked embrace. Eumenes was the first to rise and he struck the other behind the knee,

preventing him from rising. Neoptolemus still managed to home two or three blows on Eumenes until the latter struck him in the neck and killed him. His death brought the residual fighting in the field to an end. Eumenes invited the defeated Macedonians to join him, a course to which they pledged themselves. But they deceived him and took themselves off by night to join Antipater.

Diodorus, **18**: *29–32*

CRETOPOLIS (319) – Wars of the Diadochi

In 320 Antigonus defeated Eumenes at an unknown site in Cappadocia. His next targets were Alcetas and Attalus, as they were big enough to make a bid for power. He set out from Cappadocia in the north of Asia Minor for Pisidia in the south, and covered the distance of about 290 miles to Cretopolis (precise location unknown) in seven days and nights. With more than 40,000 foot and 7,000 horse and some elephants, he got up close to Alcetas and occupied a ridge while the latter was still unaware of his presence. Alcetas, with only 16,000 foot and 900 horse, launched a cavalry attack on the enemy on the ridge. Antigonus responded by leading 6,000 cavalry in a furious charge against the opposing phalanx below the heights. Meanwhile the defenders on the ridge, who were greatly superior in number, routed the attacking force. Antigonus followed up this success by leading his whole army, including the elephants, down against the enemy infantry. Numbers told; the rout was complete. Alcetas managed to escape with his Pisidian friends and allies, but he was subsequently betrayed and killed by his own side. Attalus and many others were taken prisoner, but Antigonus came to terms with them and enlisted them into his army.

Diodorus, **18**: *44–45*

BOSPHORUS: I (318, summer) – Wars of the Diadochi

On the death of Antipater in 319, Polyperchon was appointed to assume the mantle of Macedonia. He tried to enlist the support of the Greek cities but ran foul of his predecessor's garrison at Munychia, where the commander fanned the flames by seizing the town of Piraeus. Polyperchon, who had given Cleitus the command of the fleet, sent the admiral out to the Hellespont to block the passage of forces which were being sent from Asia to Europe. Against him, Cassander (Antipater's son) sent Nicanor, the commander of the Munychian garrison, with his entire fleet of at least 100 vessels. These included the ships of Antigonus which Nicanor had taken over. A battle took place near Byzantium in which Cleitus was the victor, sinking 17 of the enemy ships and capturing at least 40. The rest escaped to Chalcedon [*Kadikoy*] across the water from Byzantium.

Diodorus, 18: 72(2–4)

BOSPHORUS: II (318, summer) – Wars of the Diadochi

After his victory on the Bosphorus (above), Cleitus did not allow for the resourcefulness of his opponents. Antigonus immediately collected auxiliary vessels from Byzantium and used them to transport light-armed troops by night to the opposite shore, where the enemy had encamped on land. Before dawn they fell on the enemy, who made for their ships in great disorder. At this point Nicanor, who had put to sea during the night, sailed in to the attack, ramming and damaging the enemy ships. In the end he captured all of them except for the flag. Cleitus put ashore and escaped, but he fell into the hands of some hostile soldiers and was killed.

Diodorus, 18: 72(5–9)

COPRATES R (317, July) – Wars of the Diadochi

Antigonus was determined to destroy Eumenes, who at that time was near Susa. When Eumenes heard of the other's approach through Babylonia, he marched to the river Pasitigris [*Karun*], which flowed from the mountains down into the Tigris. He encamped on the left (east) bank of the river. This placed the Pasitigris and the Coprates, a tributary running parallel with it, between himself and Susa to which Antigonus had advanced. When Antigonus reached the Coprates [*Dez*], he began to get his army across. Eumenes heard of this and crossed the Pasitigris into the 'no-man's land' between the rivers with 4,000 infantry and 1,300 horse. By then 3,000 of the enemy infantry had crossed the Coprates, together with 400 cavalry and some of the 6,000 soldiers who crossed sporadically when foraging. Eumenes took this lot by surprise and caused them to flee to the river. But most of their boats were grossly overladen with escaping humanity and sank, while soldiers who tried to swim were carried away and drowned. About 4,000 did not risk the water and were taken prisoner.

Diodorus, 19: 17–18

PARAETACENE (317, summer) – Wars of the Diadochi

After his victory at the Coprates (above), Eumenes moved to Persepolis where he heard the news that Antigonus had set out for Persia. He decided to go after his foe and to engage him in battle again. The two armies eventually came face to face in battle array in the land of the Paraetaceni. Antigonus had deployed his forces in the hills, from which he marched down obliquely with his right wing leading. He had 28,000 heavy infantry and 11,000 horse, together with some light infantry; Eumenes boasted a total force of 35,000 foot and 6,000 horse. On his left wing, which rested against the base of a hill, Eumenes placed a strong force of cavalry with protection from an arc of elephants in front. In the centre were the heavy infantry, including the veteran Silver Shields who had served with Alexander throughout his campaign. On the right, where Eumenes intended to take his stand, were his best cavalry units with elephants in

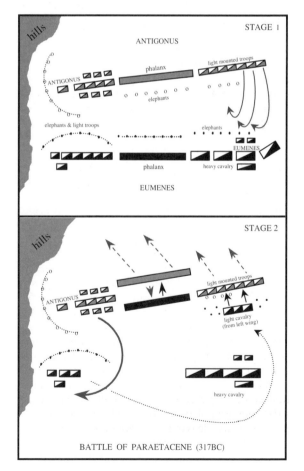

BATTLE OF PARAETACENE (317BC)

advance. Opposed to this wing on Antigonus' side were his lightest and most mobile cavalry. The phalanx was in the centre. The right wing was composed of cavalry with an arc of elephants protecting the flank. At the start of the action the light cavalry on Antigonus' left, who were opposed to Eumenes, began to harass the enemy with arrows without incurring any danger to themselves. They were dispersed by Eumenes, who made a flanking attack upon them with a squadron of light cavalry which he had ordered across from his left wing. Routed, Antigonus' skirmishers fled to the hills. While this had been going on, the phalanxes had engaged. In this quarter Eumenes was again victorious, by virtue of the valour and invincibility of the Silver Shields and in spite of their advanced age of 60–70 years or more. At this point, with everything seemingly against him, Antigonus pulled off a stroke which equalized the score. Noting that the advance of the enemy phalanx had detached it from their left flank, Antigonus charged through the gap and wheeled around the wing, attacking it in flank and rear. The attack was as successful as it was unexpected. Both sides started rallying their fugitives for a further encounter, but by an almost mutual consent arising from exhaustion they gave up and returned to their camps. Antigonus claimed the victory on a technicality, but he ignored the Pyrrhic element. He lost 3,700 foot killed and in excess of 4,000 wounded, in contrast to his opponent's loss of 540 infantry killed and around 1,000 injured.

Diodorus, 19: 26–31

GABENE (317/16, winter) – Wars of the Diadochi

After the battle in Paraetacene both armies went into winter quarters, Antigonus in Media and Eumenes in the district of Gabene in Persia. During the winter Antigonus decided to try to catch Eumenes off his guard while his enemy's troops were scattered around in their quarters. This involved a march across an uninhabited waterless desert to Gabene. Eumenes came to hear about this and, by a piece of subterfuge, managed to delay the other until he had assembled his own army. The total strength of Antigonus' force was 22,000 foot and 9,000 horse with 65 elephants. Against them, Eumenes boasted 36,700 foot soldiers, 6,000 cavalry and 114 elephants. Antigonus placed his infantry in the centre and his cavalry on the wings with the elephants out in advance across the whole line. He himself planned to fight on the

right with his son Demetrius. Seeing this deployment, Eumenes placed his best cavalry on his left, where he intended to oppose his rival in person, with a protecting arc of 60 elephants in front. On his right wing he drew up his weaker cavalry with orders to avoid giving battle. The infantry were placed in the centre with a line of elephants and light troops in front. The elephants were the first to advance and they raised up such a cloud of dust that the whole field became obscured. Taking advantage of this, Antigonus sent some cavalry to charge round the enemy's flank and capture his baggage train about half a mile in the rear. Meanwhile he himself joined battle with the opposing enemy wing, so successfully that a large number of the enemy cavalry took fright and deserted. Eumenes, heavily outnumbered as a result, took the rest of his cavalry round to the opposite wing. In the centre the Silver Shields put up a tremendous resistance with their usual valour, but as their left flank was exposed they were surrounded by enemy cavalry and forced to admit defeat. Eumenes' attempts to rally the infantry failed. The Macedonians, knowing that their wives and children in the baggage train were in enemy hands, refused to carry on and secretly negotiated with Antigonus. Seizing Eumenes, they handed him over to his rival, in whose army they then enlisted. Eumenes was executed.

Diodorus, 19: 39(6)–43; Plutarch, Eumenes, 16

APHRODISIAS (315) – Wars of the Diadochi

Seleucus was in Cyprus with his fleet when Polycleitus and one or two other generals sailed to join him for a conference on a plan of action. It was decided that Polycleitus should take 50 ships to the Peloponnese on an errand which proved, owing to a change in circumstances, to be unfounded. He turned round and made for Pamphylia where he ran along the coast eastwards to Aphrodisias in Cilicia. At that point he heard that Theodotus, the admiral of Antigonus, was some way behind him, sailing eastward from Patara in Lycia. Moreover, a land force under Perilaus was pacing Theodotus along the shore to protect him. In the light of this information Polycleitus disembarked his soldiers and concealed them somewhere along the enemy's route. He then anchored his ships out of sight behind a promontory. The enemy army was the first to fall into the ambush. Perilaus was captured and some of his soldiers were killed while others were taken prisoner. When the ships went to help their colleagues on shore, Polycleitus sailed up and routed them, capturing all the ships and many of

the crews. Theodotus himself was mortally wounded. After this resounding success Polycleitus sailed to Pelusium in the Nile delta, where Ptolemy honoured him as the author of an important victory.
Diodorus, 19: 64(4–7)

CAPRIMA (314) – Wars of the Diadochi

Cassander sent an expedition into Caria. In the previous year Ptolemaeus, the nephew and general of Antigonus, had conducted successful campaigns against Cassander's generals. Now Ptolemaeus was wintering in Caria, where he had divided his forces. A force of 8,000 infantry and 200 horse under Eupolemus was detached from Cassander's expeditionary force and sent to lie in wait for the enemy near Caprima, a place now unknown. However, the intended victim got wind of the plan. Gathering 8,300 foot and 600 horse from his wintering troops, he fell upon the enemy's camp at night and caught them asleep. Eupolemus was captured alive; the soldiers surrendered.
Diodorus, 19: 68(5–7)

GAZA (312) – Wars of the Diadochi

In 314 Antigonus was called away to the eastern part of his Asian province. He left his son, the 22-year-old Demetrius, with an army to keep guard in Syria. Ptolemy, urged on by Seleucus, took advantage of the situation and marched with 18,000 foot and 4,000 horse from Alexandria into Syria. He camped near Old Gaza, where Demetrius was waiting for him. Demetrius was urged by his friends not to engage so experienced a general and so large a force but he paid no heed and prepared for battle. He formed a strong left wing, where he himself intended to take part and with which he intended to decide the issue. It was composed entirely of cavalry with an advance guard of cavalry and a guard on the flank. In front of the whole wing he stationed 30 of his elephants interspersed with light-armed troops. Next to the wing he drew up his phalanx. On the right wing he placed more cavalry, who were told to refuse battle and hold themselves in reserve. When Ptolemy and Seleucus heard of the enemy dispositions, they strengthened their right wing to match Demetrius. On this wing they placed 3,000 of their best cavalry and, in front of them, the men who were in charge of spiked anti-elephant devices. With these dispositions an initial cavalry battle was a certainty. After it had raged for a considerable time with little advantage either way, Demetrius' elephants were urged forward to cre-

ate terror among the enemy. When they were arrested by the barrier of spikes, the enemy archers and javelin throwers started wounding the beasts and killing their riders. In the end all the beasts were captured. This scene created panic among Demetrius' cavalrymen, who turned to flight, leaving Demetrius with no alternative but to follow suit. As the fugitives were passing Gaza, many of them decided to abscond into the city. The crush trying to get in through the gates became so great that the gates could not be shut against the pursuing troops of Ptolemy, who forced their way inside with ease and captured the city. Demetrius lost 5,000 men killed; a further 8,000 were taken prisoner.
Diodorus, 19: 80(3)–84; Plutarch, *Demetrius*, 5

EURYMENAE (312) – Wars of the Diadochi

In Epirus, the death of King Aeacides resulted in the assumption of his brother, an unstable personality called Alcetas. This gentleman was hostile to Cassander. In consequence, Cassander's general in Acarnania, Lyciscus, took an army into Epirus in the hope of removing Alcetas. Alcetas sent his sons, Alexander and Teucer, to raise reinforcements while he took the field with his existing troops and waited for his sons to return. The Epirots, however, were frightened by the enemy's overwhelming numbers and deserted to them. Alcetas was taking refuge in Eurymenae in Epirus when his son Alexander arrived with a force and, in a violent battle, many of Lyciscus' troops were killed. Later, Deinias, another of Cassander's generals, arrived with reinforcements for the defeated army. This time Alexander and Teucer were defeated and fled with their father, while Lyciscus destroyed Eurymenae.
Diodorus, 19: 88

APOLLONIA (ILLYRIA) (312) – Wars of the Diadochi

Cassander, hearing of the defeat of his forces at the first battle of Eurymenae (above), marched into Epirus in person to help Lyciscus. Arriving to be told of the subsequent victory of his forces, he proceeded to Apollonia in Illyria where the people had revolted and driven out his garrisons. The citizens summoned help from their allies and drew up their forces before the walls. There was a hard battle in which the Apollonians had a considerable advantage in numbers, and Cassander was forced to flee.
Diodorus, 19: 89(1–2)

GALERIA (312) – Syracuse: Civil Strife

After the death of Timoleon, the great liberator, Sicily enjoyed a period of peace and liberty for 20 years. It was cut short abruptly in 317 when a ruthless dynast called Agathocles overthrew the oligarchs in Syracuse, killed or exiled all those who were against him, and seized control with absolute power. He proceeded to subjugate most of Sicily. Five years later Deinocrates, the leader of the Syracusan exiles, and his band were staying at a place called Galeria (or Galaria) at the invitation of the citizens. Deinocrates had with him over 3,000 foot soldiers and around 2,000 mounted men, who encamped outside the town. Agathocles promptly sent a force of 5,000 soldiers under Pasiphilus and Demophilus against them, and a battle ensued. The outcome was evenly balanced until one of the exiled leaders was slain, after which his wing was routed. Deinocrates himself was then also forced to withdraw, losing many men in the flight.

*Diodorus, **19**: 104(1–2)*

ECNOMUS M (311) – Punic War of Agathocles

The Carthaginians were disturbed by the threat posed to them in Sicily by Agathocles, whose forces were superior in number to their own. Reinforcements were sent out from Carthage with a determination to wage war with greater vigour. At that time the Carthaginians held the hill called Ecnomus [*M. Sole*] on the promontory of the same name [*Poggio di Sant' Angelo*]. Agathocles, having secured the city of Gela, occupied a stronghold called Phalarium, which was close to Ecnomus but separated from it by the river Himera [*Salso*]. Overt hostilities began when some Greeks started plundering on Carthaginian-held territory and enemy soldiers appeared to chase them off. Agathocles, foreseeing developments, placed some men in ambush beside the river. As the Carthaginians crossed the river in pursuit of their quarry, they were set upon. Agathocles decided that this was the time to make an all-out attack and he led his whole army against the enemy camp. There was a fierce battle for the moat and the ground around became littered with corpses. But when Hamilcar, son of Gisgo, saw that more and more Greeks were penetrating the camp, he brought up his Balearic slingers, numbering at least 1,000. These managed to reverse the tide and drive the Greeks out of the camp. Agathocles continued to press the attack at various points and with considerable success until, by chance, some reinforcements for the Carthaginians arrived by sea at the crucial moment and joined the fray. The Greeks were now being attacked on all sides and they fled, pursued by the enemy cavalry. About 500 of the Carthaginians fell in the battle, but the Greeks lost around 7,000. Exhausted fugitives who tried to quench their thirst at the salty river Himera (hence now called the *Salso*) added to the number of casualties.

*Diodorus, **19**: 108–109*

TUNES (310) – Punic War of Agathocles

Agathocles' defeat at Ecnomus (above) cost him much of Sicily. The people of the villages and towns showed their hatred for the tyrant by openly siding with the Carthaginians. He decided to turn the tables on the Carthaginians by invading Africa and carrying the war into their country. He manned 60 ships and after landing with his small army, he burnt his boats and proceeded to a place which Diodorus calls White Tunes (probably Tunes itself), which he captured. The Carthaginians, after recovering from the initial shock, marched against him with a force of citizen soldiers which has been variously estimated at 30,000 to 40,000 together with 1,000 cavalry and 2,000 chariots. An unknown general Hanno commanded the right wing composed of the élite Sacred Band of selected Carthaginian citizens; Bomilcar took the left wing. Against Bomilcar, Agathocles entrusted his right wing of 2,500 foot to his son, Agatharchus. He himself fought in front of the left wing with 1,000 hoplites, opposing the Sacred Band. In addition, he had 9,500 mixed soldiers and mercenaries and 500 archers and slingers. Noticing that his soldiers were frightened by the overwhelming odds against them, he is said to have released a number of owls which he had brought for the purpose. These settled on their shields and helmets and, being held sacred to Athena, were regarded as a good omen, restoring the men's courage. Hostilities began with a charge by the Punic charioteers in which some were shot down but most of the chariots were turned back against their own lines. A Punic cavalry charge was also withstood and achieved little. When the infantry engaged, a fierce struggle developed on the Sicilians' left wing, which was opposed by Hanno who fought a gallant fight in person. Although wounded many times, he refused to yield until he died of exhaustion. This disheartened the Carthaginians and correspondingly encouraged the Sicilians to fight the harder. Bomilcar started to withdraw with his wing, but he was pursued by Agathocles who converted an orderly retreat into a rout. The enemy fled towards

Carthage. Only the Sacred Band stood firm until, deserted, they could do no more. Estimates of the casualties vary greatly but all sources agree that the Carthaginians were the losers.

Diodorus, 20: 8(7) and 10(5)–13(1); Orosius, 4: 6(25); Justin, 22: 6(5–7)

SYRACUSE: EURYELUS (309)

– Punic War of Agathocles   Map 15
While Agathocles, the tyrant of Syracuse, was fighting the Carthaginians in Africa, Hamilcar, the Punic general in Sicily, was planning to storm Syracuse via Euryelus, the summit at the west end of Epipolae. The Syracusans, learning that Hamilcar intended to advance by night, sent out about 3,000 of their infantry and 400 cavalry to occupy Euryelus. When Hamilcar advanced after dark, he had with him not only his armed forces but baggage waggons, camp followers and riff-raff of all sorts. They got in each other's way in the narrow track leading to the top. The Syracusans saw their chance and charged down upon them from the higher ground, putting them to rout. Hamilcar himself resisted stoutly with a few others, but when they deserted him, he was taken captive. He was cruelly treated and was then beheaded. His head was sent to Agathocles in Africa as proof of the event.

Diodorus, 20: 29(2–11)

TUNES (309) – Punic War of Agathocles

Harmony within the Syracusan ranks in Africa was seriously disrupted by a drunken tiff in which Lyciscus, one of the generals, who had been invited to dinner by Agathocles, insulted his host's son Agatharchus. Agathocles ignored the insult but his enraged son killed the offender with a spear. The incident filled the troops with indignation and dissent. The Carthaginians, hearing about this, sent men to urge the Sicilians to desert to them. Agathocles restored order by means of one of his histrionic displays in which, appearing in civilian clothes, he threatened to kill himself if the men were displeased with him. They protested, implored and rallied round him *en masse*. Agathocles seized the moment. Changing hastily back into military garb, he led his men out against the Carthaginians. The enemy without, ignorant of the events within, assumed that these might be deserters. They were taken unaware and fled into their camp, losing many men in the process.

Diodorus, 20: 34

SYRACUSE (307) – Punic War of Agathocles

Agathocles' cause in Sicily had been going badly during his absence in Africa and so he set sail homewards, leaving his son in charge. He had not been home long before he heard of reverses suffered by his son and decided to return to Africa. He manned 17 warships but had to bide his time until he could give the slip to a force of 30 Carthaginian ships which were blockading the Syracusan harbour. It so happened that 18 ships, arriving from Etruria to reinforce him, managed to slip into the harbour undetected. Agathocles ordered them to remain in harbour until he had set out and drawn the Carthaginians out in pursuit. Then, when he saw the Etruscans following the Carthaginians out of the harbour, he turned and attacked the enemy from the front. The Carthaginians, caught between two fires, panicked and fled. Five of their ships were captured with their crews, and their commander killed himself when his flag-ship was on the point of being taken. By this victory the naval blockade of Syracuse was lifted, effectively ending the siege.

Diodorus, 20: 61(5–8)

ACRAGAS (307) – Sicily: Internal Wars

Encouraged by his naval victory off Syracuse (above), Agathocles sent his second-in-command, Leptines, against Acragas [*Agrigento*]. Xenodocus, the leader of the Acragantines, was a democrat and therefore an enemy of Agathocles. He had already been defeated once at an unknown site by the generals of Agathocles, with the result that the Acragantines were rebellious against Xenodocus to the great advantage of Leptines. At first Xenodocus refused to take the field at all. But when he was reproached with cowardice, he led out his troops which were numerically on a par with his opponents, although greatly inferior in morale and fitness. Leptines wasted no time in routing them and pursing them into their city, killing about 500 of them.

Diodorus, 20: 62(2–5)

SALAMIS (CYPRUS) (306) – Wars of the Diadochi

Antigonus embarked upon a campaign against the rival sea-power of Egypt. He ordered his son, Demetrius, to sail with an army to Cyprus and to prosecute the war against Ptolemy. Demetrius embarked 15,000 soldiers and landed them on the north coast of the island, whence he headed for Salamis [*Gazimağuza*, formerly *Famagusta*]. When he was within 5 miles of the place, Menelaus,

Ptolemy's brother and general, marched out to meet him with 12,000 foot and 800 horse. The battle was short-lived. Menelaus was routed and driven back into his city with the loss of 1,000 killed and 3,000 captives. Demetrius proceeded to besiege the city, using innovative siege-engines of various kinds for which he became noted.
Diodorus, 20: 47(1–3)

SALAMIS (CYPRUS) (306) – Wars of the Diadochi

When Ptolemy heard of the defeat of Menelaus by Demetrius at Salamis (above), he sailed from Egypt with a large force. He collected more ships at Paphos in Cyprus until he had at least 140 quinqueremes and quadriremes and over 200 transports with 10,000 infantrymen. He also directed Menelaus to send him the 60 ships in the harbour at Salamis. Demetrius likewise manned all his ships. He stationed 10 quinqueremes just outside the narrow harbour entrance to stop Menelaus from getting out and harassing his rear. He then moved out against the enemy with around 180 ships. With a strong left wing he overcame the enemy's right and finally routed it. Ptolemy also had strengthened his left wing, where he himself intended to fight, and he was able to rout the opposing ships. But when he turned to deal with the rest, he found that his right wing and part of the centre had disappeared, leaving Demetrius still in full cry. In a battle at the harbour entrance the 60 ships of Menelaus managed to overcome the 10 guard ships of Demetrius and to sail out, but they were too late. The defeat was overwhelming. Ptolemy fled with a squadron of eight ships, the sole survivors from his fleet, leaving behind more than 100 transports with 8,000 soldiers and all the supplies, arms and women. Antigonus was so elated at his son's victory that he assumed the title of king and accorded the same royal status to Demetrius.
Diodorus, 20: 49–52; Plutarch, Demetrius, 16

ELATEA (305) – Wars of the Diadochi

Cassander began a war against Athens in which he failed to capture his objective. When he and his Macedonians descended on Attica, a general called Olympiodorus sailed round to Aetolia and persuaded the Aetolians to give help. He drew the enemy into Phocis and defeated them in a battle at Elatea about which nothing further seems to be known.
Pausanias, 1: 26(3) and 10: 34(2)

TORGIUM (305) – Syracuse: Civil Strife

In Sicily Agathocles made peace with the Carthaginians but failed to come to terms with Deinocrates, the leader of the exiles, who enjoyed his position as head of a considerable party. A battle offered the only solution. Agathocles had with him a following of no more than 5,000 infantry and 800 horse, an insignificant force by comparison with the 25,000 foot and 3,000 horse mustered by his opponent. The armies encamped opposite each other near a place now unknown called Torgium where they lined up for battle. After a brief encounter, more than 2,000 of Deinocrates' troops deserted to the tyrant. This boosted the confidence of Agathocles' men and dismayed the enemy to such an extent that they broke into flight. Agathocles pursued them for a while and then sent them offers of peace. Most of the infantry, who had occupied a hill, came to terms with Agathocles and descended from their high point, whereupon Agathocles disarmed and surrounded them before shooting them all down.
Diodorus, 20: 89

IPSUS (301) – Wars of the Diadochi

The overriding aim of Antigonus was a reunification of Alexander's empire with himself at the top. His imperious attitude did not suit the other kings, who formed a coalition against him and his son Demetrius. Seleucus and Lysimachus brought Antigonus and Demetrius to battle near Ipsus in Phrygia. Plutarch records what little is known about the battle; Appian mentions the site of combat. The combatants were well matched with around 70,000 infantry and 10,000 cavalry on each side, but Seleucus was superior in elephant power, an element which was to play an important role. At the start of the battle Demetrius led his best cavalry in a charge against Seleucus' son, Antiochus. He routed him but got carried away and pressed the pursuit too far. Seleucus moved his elephants to block Demetrius and prevent him from rejoining his army. This left Antigonus' phalanx unprotected. Instead of charging the phalanx, Seleucus' infantry rode around it threateningly in the hope that the troops would change sides. A large band of them did in fact do so; the rest were routed and Antigonus was killed. Demetrius escaped with only 5,000 foot and 4,000 horse. The battle brought to an end the division of Alexander's empire as it had been. The territory formerly governed by Antigonus was carved up and new partitions took place.

Plutarch, Demetrius, 28–29; Appian, Syrian Wars, 55

MANTINEA (294) – Wars of the Diadochi

In 294 Demetrius entered Athens and assumed control. He immediately made plans for a conquest of Sparta. Meeting Archidamus, the king of Sparta, near Mantinea in Arcadia, he routed the Spartan forces and proceeded to invade Laconia.
Plutarch, Demetrius, 35(1)

SPARTA (294) – Wars of the Diadochi

After defeating the Spartans at Mantinea (above), Demetrius proceeded to Sparta and fought a pitched battle before the walls of the city. The absence of King Archidamus with his defeated army must have left the place with little defence because Demetrius, having killed 200 men and taken 500 prisoners, was on the point of capturing the city for the first time in its history. At that point, however, he received news that his cities in Asia had been seized by Lysimachus and that Ptolemy had overrun Cyprus. In consequence, Demetrius withdrew and Sparta was reprieved.
Plutarch, Demetrius, 35

EDESSA (286) – Wars of the Diadochi

Pyrrhus, firmly established in his native Epirus, invaded Macedonia and occupied much of it. A few years later Lysimachus marched against him and found him encamped at Edessa [*Vodena*]. Lysimachus attacked and by capturing the other's supplies inflicted considerable hardship on his troops. Pyrrhus was compelled to withdraw to his homeland.
Plutarch, Pyrrhus, 12(5–7)

CORUPEDIUM (281) – Wars of the Diadochi

The last two survivors among the former officers of Alexander the Great were Lysimachus and Seleucus Nicator, aged 74 and 77 respectively according to Justin. In 281, 42 years after the death of Alexander, these two old veterans met to fight for the mastery of their world. Lysimachus was killed in the battle. The site of the battle has been a source of confusion until recent times. Eusebius placed it in the plains of Corus (Corupedium), which an epigram suggested were in Phrygia. In a detailed study of the evidence, Keil concludes that the battle took place, not in Phrygia, but on the river Phrygius in Lydia. The Phrygius [*Kum Çay*], formerly the Hyllus, flowed into the river Hermon [*Gediz Nehri*] near Magnesia-ad-Sipylum [*Manisa*]. Furthermore, Keil is convinced that the plains of

Corus, quoted by Eusebius, and the plains of Cyrus in the region of Sardes, described by Strabo, were one and the same place.

The victory of Seleucus was short-lived. He himself was murdered by Ptolemy Ceraunus the following year. So ended the era of the diadochi.
Justin, 17: 1(7)–2(1); Orosius, 3: 23(58–62); Pausanias, 1: 10(5); Strabo, 13: 4, 5; Eusebius, Chronicle, cit. B.Keil, Revue de Philologie, 26: 257–262, 1902

HYBLAEUS R (*c.*280) – Sicily: Internal Wars

In Sicily most of the cities were ruled by their own tyrants. Hostilities broke out between Hicetas, the tyrant of Syracuse, and Phintias, his opposite number in Acragas [*Agrigento*]. When they met in battle near the River Hyblaeus, probably in the vicinity of Hybla Heraea, Hicetas was the victor.
Diodorus, 22: 2(1)

TERIAS R (280)

After his victory on the Hyblaeus (above), Hicetas was sufficiently emboldened to attack the Carthaginians. The battle took place near the river Terias in the region of Catane, where Hicetas was heavily defeated and lost many of his men.
Diodorus, 22: 2(1)

THERMOPYLAE P (279/8, winter) – Celtic Invasion

In the winter of 279/8 the Celts invaded the north of Greece and then split up into three groups, which went in different directions. The detachment under Brennus ravaged Macedonia and then proceeded southward toward Delphi. The ancient historians concur that Brennus had with him at least 160,000 infantry and horse, a grossly inflated figure. Modern estimates put the number of fighting men at a maximum of 20,000 to 30,000. This force reached Thermopylae, where the Gauls were met by a Greek defence force of about 30,000 men, with the largest contingent from Aetolia. The composition of the force has been itemized by Pausanias. A battle took place but the Gauls were inadequately armed and trained for an encounter against hoplites, particularly in an enclosed space. They were forced to withdraw, leaving behind many corpses buried in mud. It is said that the Greeks lost only 40 men. Brennus' response to his defeat was to send the larger part of his forces to ravage Aetolia with the object of drawing off the large Aetolian contingent in front of him. He then turned the pass by using the same route over the mountains as the Persians had used in 480. On this

occasion, the Greeks, warned of the manoeuvre did not wait to be outflanked and slaughtered. They dispersed to their homes.
Pausanias, 10: 20(3) and 21(2–4)

DELPHI (279/8, winter) – Celtic Invasion
When Brennus and his flying squad reached Delphi, they had a thoroughly sleepless night. The weather turned against them, bringing severe frost and snow. At sunrise the Greeks emerged from Delphi and made a frontal assault on the invaders. The native Phocians, however, knew the lie of the land. They worked their way round the skirts of Mount Parnassus until they were in the rear of the Gauls. The enemy were shot at with missiles from every angle. When Brennus was wounded and carried away fainting, the Gauls lost heart. They killed those of their number who were too weak to move, and they fled, being harassed at every step and prevented from foraging for food. It is said that about 6,000 of them were killed in battle and almost twice that number from other causes, but this total is probably more than their whole force. It is uncertain whether the Gauls ever got a foot inside Delphi, but the Temple at any rate was not violated.
Pausanias, 10: 23

LYSIMACHEIA (277) – Celtic Invasion
Of the three groups of Gauls who had invaded the north during the winter of 279/8, the division under Cerethrius overran Thrace and headed in the direction of the Propontis. It so happened that Antigonus Gonatas was encamped with his mercenaries in the vicinity of Lysimacheia at the base of the Thracian Chersonese [*Gallipoli Peninsula*]. When the Gauls turned up, he vacated his camp and concealed his men, leaving his ships beached as a bait. As he had expected, the Gauls fell for the deceit. Finding the camp empty, they plundered it and proceeded with their loot to attack the ships, only to find themselves trapped between the sea in front and Gonatas in their rear. The ensuing great victory launched Gonatas to fame.
Justin, 25: 1–2(7); Diogenes Laertius, 2: 141

SPARTA (272, spring)
Cleonymus, a Spartan of royal descent, possessed an autocratic disposition and had failed to endear himself to the people. This had created a chip on his shoulder and had given him a grudge against his fellow-citizens. Additionally, he had grievances against other members of the royal family. These sentiments led him to invite Pyrrhus to Sparta and

that adventurer arrived with 25,000 infantry, 200 horse and 24 elephants. As Plutarch remarks, it was clear from the scale of his army that Pyrrhus' intentions were not to conquer Sparta for Cleonymus but the Peloponnese for himself. Ignoring Cleonymus' request that he attack at once on the first evening, and despising the apparent weakness of the defence, Pyrrhus postponed hostilities until the morrow. During the night the Spartan citizens, women included, dug a large trench and placed waggons at each end, buried up to their axles, to impede the elephants. In the morning Pyrrhus led a frontal attack with his infantry but he failed to penetrate the Spartan line or to cross the ditch. His son Ptolemy then led a detachment of Gauls against the barricade of waggons. They had succeeded in freeing some of them when Acrotatus, the son of King Areus who was away in Crete, ran through the city with 300 men and managed to get round behind the Gauls. He drove them back with much slaughter. The assault was resumed on the following day and Pyrrhus himself was on the point of entering the city when his horse was wounded and threw him, giving the defenders time to rally and repel the enemy. The city was finally saved soon afterwards when a contingent of mercenaries sent by Gonatas arrived from Corinth, followed later by Areus, the king himself, who had just returned from Crete with 2,000 soldiers. Pyrrhus gave up the struggle and withdrew. According to Pausanias, Pyrrhus actually won at Sparta without a blow. This seems not to have been the case, but it might have been so if Pyrrhus had struck immediately on his arrival, as Cleonymus had requested.
Plutarch, Pyrrhus, 27–30(1); Pausanias, 1: 13(5)

ARGOS (272)
While Pyrrhus was at Sparta, a feud broke out at Argos. One party was supported by Antigonus Gonatas; the other party looked to Pyrrhus to join them. On his way he was delayed by Areus, who pursued him from Sparta and harassed him until Pyrrhus turned and counterattacked. By the time Pyrrhus reached Argos, Gonatas had forestalled him and was ensconced in an impregnable position on the heights, from which he refused to descend until it suited him. In the middle of the night the gates of the city were opened to Pyrrhus and he entered with his Gauls. But the gateway was too small for the elephants with their howdahs, which had to be removed. The bustle and hubbub roused the Argives, who sent for Gonatas. He arrived, as also did Areus, who had followed Pyrrhus and had

joined forces with the enemy. The resulting chaos and confusion in the narrow streets of the city, with elephants running amok and blocking the gates, has been well described by Plutarch but can fairly be left to the imagination. Pyrrhus himself, trying to hack a way out, was struck on the back of the neck by a tile thrown down from a housetop. Before he could recover his senses, a mercenary from the enemy camp clumsily hacked off his head. His army surrendered to Gonatas.
Plutarch, Pyrrhus, *30(1–2) and 31–34; Pausanias, 1: 13(6–7)*

ISTHMUS (265) – Chremonidean War
An Athenian statesman, Chremonides, introduced a decree whereby Athens joined the Peloponnesian coalition against Macedon. The subsequent war became known by his name. The move was engineered by Ptolemy II, who thus set the Greeks at war with Antigonus Gonatas. Gonatas had garrisons at Corinth and Megara, blocking land communication between Sparta and Athens. The connecting link between these cities was supposed to be an Egyptian fleet under the command of Patroclus, but he did not exert himself and would do no more than harass Gonatas. He made no attempt to land a Spartan force on Attic soil. Areus, king of Sparta, had more sense of commitment than the Egyptian, and he took the great risk of attempting a direct frontal assault by land against Gonatas' lines across the Isthmus. No details are available save that the operation was a failure and that Areus lost his life in the process. The contradictory statement of Pausanias to the effect that Areus ran short of supplies and withdrew his army is not regarded as factual.
Plutarch, Agis, *3(4); Pausanias, 3: 6(4–6)*

MEGALOPOLIS (263) – Local Feud
Megalopolis in Arcadia, the youngest city in Greece, was founded by Epaminondas after the battle of Leuctra (371) as a fence against Sparta. The hostility between the two cities was therefore innate. In 263 Acrotatus, the son of King Areus of Sparta, made another attack upon the rival city. It is thought possible that he may have been making a last weak effort to help Athens after the failure and death of his father at the Isthmus (265). If this was his objective, he never reached it. He encountered Aristodemus, the dictator of Megalopolis, who inflicted a heavy defeat and killed him in battle. It may be noted that Pausanias is confused about the Spartan royal lineage and ascribes

these events to the wrong Acrotatus, the grandfather of the leader involved.
Pausanias, 8: 27(11); Plutarch, Agis, *3(5)*

SARDES (262)
Eumenes I of Pergamum was an energetic leader who started building up an empire by winning over neighbouring towns from Antiochus I Soter, the son of Seleucus. In 262 he made a surprise attack upon Antiochus and inflicted a severe defeat on him under the walls of Sardes, Antiochus' capital.
Strabo, 13: 4, 2

ANDROS (246) </br> EPHESUS (c.246) </br> COS (c.246) – Third Syrian War
These three important naval battles ended Egyptian sea-power for ever at the hands of Antigonus Gonatas and the Rhodians. Information is sketchy and the dates have been widely disputed. Much of what is known or surmised has been derived largely from sources such as inscriptions and coins and by deduction from the recorded events of the time. The battle of Andros is mentioned by Trogus; Polyaenus gives a brief account of the engagement off Ephesus. By deduction, Tarn ascribes Andros to the spring of the year 246; Cos and Ephesus may also have taken place in that year, or possibly a year or so later. Tarn construes the course of events as follows. In the spring of 246, Antigonus Gonatas, aged about 73, personally led his fleet against an Egyptian fleet under Sophron and defeated him off Andros. Another Egyptian fleet under the Athenian exile Chremonides was defeated off Ephesus by the Rhodian admiral Agathostratus. Finally, Gonatas crossed the Aegean and, though heavily outnumbered, defeated the combined forces of Egypt in a decisive battle off Cos.

We are indebted to Polyaenus for some details of strategy in the action off Ephesus. He reports that Agathostratus, after lining up for battle, withdrew to his moorings as if in fear of a fight and then attacked the enemy by surprise as they were joyfully disembarking after their 'victory'.
W.W. Tarn, Antigonos Gonatas, *1913, pp. 378ff. and Appendix 12; Trogus,* Prologue 27; *Polyaenus, 5: 18*

ANCYRA (236) – 'War of the Brothers'
In 237, Seleucus II won two victories at unknown sites over his brother, Antiochus Hierax, who had sought to supplant him. Hierax then allied himself with the Galatians. When Seleucus invaded their

territory, he was utterly defeated by them in a battle near Ancyra [*Ankara*].
Trogus, Prologue 27

CHARES R (235) – Wars of the Achaean League
Initially the Achaean league was merely a handful of Achaean towns joined together in a confederacy. This state of affairs persisted until a Sicyonian statesman, Aratus, managed to get his non-Achaean home town incorporated in the league. Furthermore, he was appointed general of the league. With a fanatical hatred of tyrants he devoted his time to rooting them out whenever he could. He made many attempts against Aristippus at Argos but invariably failed to capture the city. On one occasion, having narrowly missed his objective, he withdrew his army and ravaged the surrounding territory. Aristippus came out and a fierce battle was fought at the river Chares. Most of Aratus' forces had gained the upper hand and had pursued the enemy for a considerable distance when Aratus, in a characteristically erratic fit of despair, withdrew to his camp, where he was upbraided by his indignant men. The enemy claimed the victory and put up a trophy. In shame, Aratus deployed his army next day, determined to fight again, but discretion prevailed when he saw that the enemy's forces had increased considerably in number.
Plutarch, Aratus, 28(1–3)

CLEONAE (235) – Wars of the Achaean League
When Aratus heard that Aristippus, the tyrant of Argos, was planning to attack Cleonae [*Kleonai*], he assembled his army and marched to the Corinthian town of Cenchreae [*Kecrees*], about 13 miles from Cleonae, in the hope that his departure would encourage the tyrant to proceed with his plans. The tyrant did, in fact, swallow the bait and set out from Argos with his forces. Aratus made a forced march by night with such speed that he entered Cleonae in the dark before the enemy appeared. At dawn the gates were thrown open and Aratus' army poured out and routed the surprised enemy. They were pursued as far as Mycenae, where the tyrant was overtaken and killed together with 1,500 of his men. It is said that Aratus did not lose a single man.
Plutarch, Aratus, 29(1–4)

PHYLACIA (233) – 'War of Demetrius'
Aratus, having defeated and disposed of one tyrant at Cleonae (above), turned his attention to another one, Lydiades of Megalopolis in Arcadia.

His plans proved superfluous because the tyrant underwent a conversion and decided to join the other side. Lydiades abdicated his power and incorporated Megalopolis into the Achaean league, of which he subsequently became general in alternation with Aratus. The conversion of Megalopolis to the Achaean cause was a blow to Demetrius II, the son and successor of Antigonus Gonatas, who sent an army to the Peloponnese. Bithys, the general, encountered Aratus and defeated him in a pitched battle at Phylacia near Tegea. Rumours were rife that Aratus had been captured or killed. However, a letter sent to Corinth ordering the Achaeans in the city to quit in view of Aratus' death was received by the man himself!
Plutarch, Aratus, 34(1–2)

MEDEON (231) – 'War of Demetrius'
Trouble arose on the north-west frontiers of Greece. The Aetolians invaded Acarnania and besieged the town of Medeon. The Acarnanians, traditionally friendly with Macedon, appealed to Demetrius II for help. This king was unable to assist them personally at the time, and he arranged for Agron to do so in his place. Agron was an Illyrian chieftain who had united the Illyrians and had gained for himself more power than any of the previous rulers. By night he sent out 100 boats with 5,000 Illyrians who advanced next morning against the enemy. The Aetolians drew up the bulk of their cavalry and their heavy infantry in front of their camp. They also quickly occupied some high ground in front of their line, where they stationed the rest of the cavalry and the light infantry. The Illyrians began hostilities by charging these troops, and with their superior numbers they dislodged them with ease, occupying the higher ground themselves. From this springboard they launched their second charge against the main Aetolian force in the plain. Their attack was supported by the citizens of the town, who made a sortie. The Aetolians were rapidly put to flight and many were killed or captured. All their baggage was seized. With their boats loaded with spoil, the Illyrians sailed for home.
Polybius, 2: 2–3

PHOENICE (230) – Illyrian Raids
King Agron of Illyria died a few days after the affair at Medeon (above) and was succeeded by his widow, Teuta. Her first actions were to condone piracy and to assemble a fleet and muster an army, which were given orders to treat all states alike as

enemies. They were adept at raiding and plundering unprotected seaboards. When they put in at Phoenice [*Finigi*] in Epirus, they encountered a group of Gauls who worked there and who readily helped them to capture the city. The Epirots, hearing about this, assembled their army and marched to the rescue. After pitching their camp opposite the town on the far side of the river, they tore up the planks of the bridge and developed a sense of false security. When the Illyrians noted the laxness of the Epirots, they sallied out, repaired the bridge, and crossed the river under cover of darkness. At daybreak, a battle commenced in which the Epirots were severely defeated, losing a large number of men either killed or captured. Not long afterwards the Illyrians were ordered home to deal with an emergency elsewhere, but their expedition had left its mark. Their success at Phoenice, the strongest city in Epirus, had put fear into the hearts of all the coastal Greeks.
Polybius, **2**: 5

CAICUS R (230) – Galatian Invasion
In a battle near the springs of the Caicus river [*Bakir Çayi*] King Attalus I secured a victory over the Tolistoagian Galatians. He recorded his thanks to Athena for this and other victories in a dedicatory inscription on a monument in Pergamum [*Bergama*].
M.M. Austin, The Hellenistic World, *1981, No. 197*

PERGAMUM (230) – Galatian Invasion
After their defeat at the Caicus valley (above), the Tolistoagii obtained reinforcements from the Tectosages and from Antiochus Hierax. They marched on Pergamum [*Bergama*] where Attalus I won a resounding victory near the temple of Aphrodite. This battle, which brought renown and a proclamation of kingship to Attalus I, is recorded in the dedicatory inscription of Attalus to Athena in Pergamum.
Strabo, **13**: 4, 2; *Trogus,* Prologue 27; *M.M. Austin,* The Hellenistic World, *1981, No. 197*

HELLESPONT (*c.* 229) ⎫ War against
COLOE L (*c.* 229) ⎬ – Antiochus
HARPASUS R (*c.* 229) ⎭ Hierax
These three battles, recorded in the dedicatory inscription of Attalus I to Athena in Pergamum, resulted in victories over Antiochus Hierax as he was driven from pillar to post. First he was expelled from the Hellespontine region of Phrygia.

Next he was forced out of Lydia after a defeat at Lake Coloe [*Marmara Gölü*] near Sardes. Third, he lost Caria in his defeat on the Harpasus [*Akçay*]. Friendless, within a couple of years he had lost his life as well.
M.M. Austin, The Hellenistic World, *1981, No. 197*

PAXOI ISLS (229, spring) – Illyrian Raids
The Illyrians were masters of piracy with an utter disregard for the nationality of their victims, who included Italian traders. This led to an increasing number of complaints to Rome, where the senate sent out two commissioners to Illyria to investigate. One of these officials spoke some words to Queen Teuta to which she took exception. She had him assassinated. The incident is noteworthy because it triggered the first Roman intervention in the Balkans.

Queen Teuta, in continuation of her warlike policies, fitted out a large fleet of galleys. Some of them were sent to Epidamnus [*Durrës*] where, taking the inhabitants by surprise, they all but captured the city. Rejoining the rest of the fleet, they proceeded to besiege Corcyra [*Corfu*], which appealed to the Achaeans and Aetolians for help. The two leagues manned 10 Achaean ships, which sailed for Corcyra and met the Illyrians off the Paxoi islands. The Illyrian tactics consisted of lashing their galleys together in groups of four and inviting a broadside attack from a ram. The Illyrians would then board the enemy craft in overwhelming numbers. In this way they captured four quadriremes and sank a quinquereme. The rest of the Achaean crews, overwhelmed by the enemy's success, set sail for home. The unfortunate Corcyreans had no alternative but to capitulate and to receive a garrison until the Romans arrived with offers of protection.
Polybius, **2**: 9–10

LYCAEUS M (227) – Cleomenean War
When Cleomenes III came to power in Sparta he wanted to stir up the people and make big changes. Reckoning that this would be more feasible in time of war, he engineered hostilities against the Achaean league. When Aratus led the Achaeans against the Eleans, who were not members of the league, Cleomenes went to the help of the defenders. Near Mount Lycaeus [*Likaon*] in Arcadia he fell upon the Achaeans, slaughtered and captured many of them and routed the whole army. As a postscript to this rout, rumours once more circulated to the effect that Aratus was dead, as had

happened at Phylacia (233). He made good use of them by launching a totally unexpected attack on the city of Mantinea, which he captured.
Plutarch, Cleomenes, *5(1) and* Aratus, *36(1–2); Polybius*, **2**: *51(3)*

LADOCEIA (227) – Cleomenean War

Continuing his campaign of unprovoked aggression, Cleomenes led an expedition into the territory of Megalopolis where he captured a fort called Leuctra. An Achaean force under Aratus came out to oppose him and a battle was fought at a site called Ladoceia, which was an open area in front of the city of Megalopolis. In the early stages of the encounter the Achaean light infantry drove the Spartans back to their camp. Aratus, however, in leading the pursuit with the main body of his troops, came to a deep ravine. He refused to allow his men to cross it and so he put a stop to the chase. Lydiades, the former tyrant of Megalopolis who had joined the Achaeans, was so infuriated by this that he took matters into his own hands and spurred his cavalry forward. Unfortunately, they became entangled and separated in a difficult area of terrain which was cluttered with vines, ditches and walls. When Cleomenes saw this, he sent in his light cavalry and archers. Lydiades was killed and his men fled as best they could. Encouraged by this, the Spartans rallied and fell upon the Achaeans, putting the entire army to flight.
Plutarch, Cleomenes, *6 and* Aratus, *36(3)–37; Polybius*, **2**: *51(3)*

ORCHOMENUS (ARCADIA) (227) – Cleomenean War

After suffering two defeats at the hands of Cleomenes, Aratus was on the point of resigning as the Achaean leader. However, he hung on for a little and was rewarded when he led his troops against Orchomenus in Arcadia, where he fought Megistonous, the stepfather of Cleomenes. He killed about 300 of the enemy and took Megistonous prisoner.
Plutarch, Aratus, *38(1)*

DYME (225) – Cleomenean War

The star of Cleomenes was in the ascendant while the fortunes of the Achaean league were on the wane. The Achaeans, under Aratus, came out in full force and pitched their camp at Dyme, near the shrine called the Hecatombaeum. Cleomenes arrived and thought it unwise to pitch camp between the city of Dyme, a founder member of

the Achaean league, and the enemy. Without waiting he forced the Achaeans to fight on the spot, routing their phalanx and winning a pitched battle while inflicting heavy losses.
Plutarch, Cleomenes, *14(2); Polybius*, **2**: *51(3)*

SELLASIA (222, July) – Cleomenean War

The Achaean league was in tatters, the constituent cities being captured by Cleomenes one after another. Aratus, the figurehead of the league, had only one course open, an appeal for help to the Macedonian ruler, Antigonus Doson, with whom he had been communicating furtively for some time. An agreement was reached and Antigonus marched south and entered the Peloponnese. The following summer he advanced into Laconia with a combined Macedonian and Achaean force of 28,000 infantry and 1,200 cavalry. Cleomenes had blocked all the passes except the one which he himself held with 20,000 men at Sellasia, about 8 miles north of Sparta. The road through the pass followed the river Oenous [*Inus*] between two hills, one called Evas on Cleomenes' left and the other named Olympus on the right. On Evas he posted the allied troops under his brother, Eucleidas, while he himself held Olympus with the Spartan phalanx and the mercenaries. The cavalry was posted by the river with a detachment of mercenaries. When Antigonus arrived, he saw the strength of the other's position and held off for several days while he explored the field. He could find no easy option. When he decided to fight, he placed his Macedonian infantry and the Illyrians against Evas with the Acarnanians and Cretans in support. Antigonus himself faced Olympus, with the mercenaries in front followed by a narrow phalanx of double the usual depth. His cavalry, with infantry support, opposed the enemy's. On the night before the battle Antigonus' Illyrians had moved forward to the foot of Evas and concealed themselves in a river bed. Just before the assault began next day Cleomenes saw no sign of the enemy Illyrians but was assured by one of his commanders that all was in order. (Plutarch recounts the story that this commander had been bribed by Antigonus beforehand to deny that anything was amiss.) The Illyrians began the assault by springing into view and attacking the hill. At this point Cleonymus' light-armed mercenaries noticed a gap in the enemy wing and launched a charge against the rear of the Illyrians. This move would have brought disaster to Antigonus but for the initiative of a young Megalopolitan cavalryman called Philopoemen, later to achieve fame, who rallied his colleagues and charged the Spartan cavalry. This diversion brought the Spartan light infantry back in defence, leaving Antigonus' right wing free to grapple with Eucleidas on Evas. In this, it was completely successful as a result of the Spartans' blunder in staying on the top of their hill instead of advancing down to meet their enemy on the slope. As it was, the Spartans could only withdraw downhill to their great disadvantage. On Olympus, the light troops of both sides engaged in a fierce struggle. But when Cleomenes saw that his brother had been routed off Evas and that his cavalry was having a bad time, he was afraid that he might be surrounded. He led out his whole force from behind his fortifications, and the two phalanxes engaged in a head-on charge. The battle seesawed for a while until a mass charge by Antigonus with his double phalanx in close order dislodged his opponent. The whole Spartan army took to its heels and fled. In contravention of Spartan tradition, Cleomenes escaped and fled the country to Egypt. Just after the battle Antigonus received news that he must return home immediately to deal with a local emergency. Had Cleomenes but known it, he would have been spared the utter defeat if he could have delayed the engagement for a few days.

Polybius, 2: 65–69; Plutarch, Cleomenes, *27(3)–28 and* Philopoemen, *6*

APOLLONIA (BABYLONIA) (220, winter) – Molon's Revolt

In 223 the Seleucid dominion acquired a new ruler, Antiochus III (the Great), in succession to his murdered brother, Seleucus III. Taking advantage of the youth of the new ruler, the governor of Media, Molon, rebelled. In a victory against a loyalist force on the Tigris, he also won Babylonia and the rest of Persia. Antiochus, hearing of this, gave up his designs against Syria in favour of bringing Molon to book. Assembling his army, he reached the Euphrates and proceeded to Antioch, which he reached in midwinter. Acting on the advice of a brilliant and experienced officer named Zeuxis, Antiochus crossed the Tigris and severed Molon's retreat to Media and his supplies. Advancing from there and marching for more than a week, he crossed Mount Oreicum and came to Apollonia where Molon was, in effect, cornered. Hearing of the king's approach, Molon made for the hilly part of the territory of Apollonia where his many slingers would be of great advantage. When the king arrived, the two armies

encamped 4 or 5 miles apart. The dispositions of the two forces have been detailed by Polybius but are largely irrelevant to the outcome because, as the armies closed, Molon's entire left wing went over to the king as soon as they saw him. On the right wing Molon himself, becoming completely surrounded, put an end to his life. All the other plotters escaped but they too subsequently killed themselves.

Polybius, 5: 51–54(4)

CAPHYAE (220) – Wars of the Achaean League

The Aetolians, noticing that the Achaeans had become idle and inactive, invaded Messenia and ravaged it. The Messenians appealed for help, and the Achaeans and their allies met and sent an ultimatum to the Aetolians to withdraw from Messenia and to keep off Achaean soil. The Aetolians decided that they had better conform for the time being, but the Achaeans did not trust them. Aratus, with a small force of 3,000 foot and 300 horse, shadowed Dorimachus and his Aetolians until Dorimachus decided to attack him while the other was low in numbers. The Achaeans had camped at Caphyae and on the approach of the Aetolians they lined up for battle in the plain with the river in their front. The Aetolians, avoiding a confrontation, marched towards some hills and were beginning to climb when Aratus sent out his cavalry and light troops to harass them. The Aetolian cavalry, who were still in the plain bringing up the rear, spurred forward to join their infantry in the foothills. Aratus took this to be a retreat and led his men forward at the double. In the meantime, the Aetolians had turned about and they fell on the Achaeans. As the Aetolians were superior in number and were charging from higher ground, they gained the upper hand and put the Achaeans to flight. Meanwhile the heavy-armed Achaeans, who had not yet entered the fray, were coming up to help. When they saw the flight of their comrades, they had no idea of what was going on and so they turned and joined the rout.

Polybius, 4: 11–12; Plutarch, Aratus, *47(2)*

PHAROS ISL (219) – Second Illyrian War

At the time of the First Illyrian War, Demetrius of Pharos was suspected by the Illyrians of duplicity. Afraid of their vengeance, he made contact with the Romans, who befriended him. Ten years later he had broken his treaty with them and was sacking Illyrian cities which were subject to Rome. In 219, Lucius Aemilius was despatched with an army to deal with the Illyrian problem. He captured the city of Dimale [*Krotina*] in a week, although the Illyrians had thought it to be impregnable. He then sailed to the island of Pharos [*Hvar*], off Illyria, to deal with Demetrius himself. The capital town, Pharos [*Starigrad*], was so strongly fortified and garrisoned that the consul resorted to a ruse. He sailed in at night with his whole force and disembarked most of it in secluded areas. The next day he sailed in himself with 20 ships to the town's harbour. Demetrius responded contemptuously with a sortie but found the fighting heavier than expected. Reinforcements were summoned from the town until, eventually, the whole garrison was taking part. At this point the concealed Roman force appeared on the scene and seized a hill between the town and the harbour. Demetrius broke off his attack in the harbour and directed his men toward the new threat on the hill. The Romans then charged down on them, while the first Roman force attacked them in the rear from the harbour. The Illyrians turned and fled. Demetrius made his way to a boat which he kept for the purpose and in which he escaped in the hours of darkness, eventually reaching the court of King Philip.

Polybius, 3: 18–19

ARISBA (218) – Gallic Uprising

When Attalus I was forced to wage war against the rebellious Achaeus, he imported a force of Gauls from Thrace. With their help he regained many of the Greek cities that had been won over by Achaeus. However, the Gauls in their turn ran out of control and started pillaging the towns in the region of the Hellespont, finally attacking Ilium. The inhabitants of Alexandria Troas raised the siege of Ilium and threw the Gauls out. The Gauls then seized Arisba, a few miles from Abydus, and began to harass the cities in that region. They were brought up short by Prusias, king of Bithynia, who led out an army and killed all the men in a pitched battle, afterwards slaying the women and children in their camp.

Polybius, 5: 111

RAPHIA (217) – Fourth Syrian War

After the battle of Ipsus (301), the territory of Syria was allocated to Seleucus. Ptolemy, however, had control of the southern part, to which the name Coele-Syria became restricted, and he refused to give it up. The boundary line between Seleucid and Ptolemaic Syria became a source of dispute which led to several wars. In 221 the reigning Seleucid, Antiochus III, was given

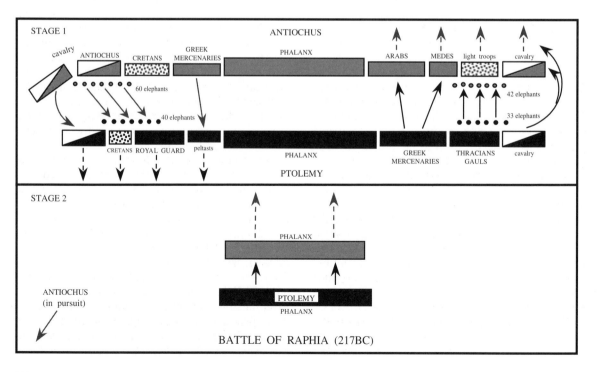

BATTLE OF RAPHIA (217BC)

grounds for recommencing hostilities, which developed into the Fourth Syrian War. After a few years spent in finishing other business, Antiochus marched south through Palestine with an army of 62,000 foot, 6,000 horse and 102 elephants. He passed Gaza and arrived at Raphia [*Rafah*]. Meanwhile, Ptolemy IV had departed eastwards from Alexandria and had also reached Raphia, the first city past the Egyptian border, with an army composed of 70,000 foot, 5,000 horse and 73 elephants. The two armies were encamped just over half a mile from each other. After several days of minor skirmishes the adversaries decided to fight it out. Their deployments have been given in detail by Polybius. In summary, each commander placed his phalanx in the centre and divided his cavalry between the wings, with various troops filling the gaps. Both sides positioned their elephants, approximately divided, in front of their wings. The two generals confronted each other, Ptolemy on his left wing, Antiochus on his right. The engagement commenced with a confrontation of the elephants, those of Antiochus being large Indian beasts while Ptolemy's were of the smaller African variety (according to Polybius).* In consequence, most of Ptolemy's animals declined to fight and headed back to their own lines where they caused some confusion. Meanwhile, Antiochus and his cavalry rode round the outside of his elephants and attacked the enemy cavalry, while on the inside of the elephants the Greek mercenaries attacked Ptolemy's peltasts. The whole of Ptolemy's left wing was forced back. On the opposite wing, exactly the same situation developed the other way round. Ptolemy's commander outflanked the enemy's cavalry and put it to flight, while the infantry routed their opposite numbers. This left the two phalanxes facing each other in naked isolation. At this point Antiochus made his great mistake. He was too busy pursuing the enemy's left wing to take note of events elsewhere. Ptolemy, by contrast, appeared in front of his phalanx and inspired his men. With lowered pikes the phalanx charged, and the enemy, failing in courage and support, soon turned and fled. Antiochus lost nearly 10,000 infantry killed and 4,000 taken prisoner in contrast to Ptolemy's losses of 1,500 foot and 700 horse. When he got home, Antiochus sued for peace and was granted a truce for one year.
*Polybius, 5: 79–86. *Recently confirmed: Peter Connolly, Greece and Rome at War, Greenhill, 1998, p. 75.*

LARISSUS R (209) – Wars of the Achaean League
The young Philopoemen, who had distinguished himself so well at Sellasia (222), was later appointed to lead the Achaean cavalry which became engaged in a battle against the Aetolians and Eleans. The encounter took place on the river Larissus, which formed the border between Achaea and Elis. Plutarch described it as a great battle, although almost nothing is known about it. It is, however, recorded that when the general in command of the Elean cavalry charged against Philopoemen personally, the latter coolly deflected the blow and killed his adversary. After seeing their leader fall, the Eleans lost heart and promptly fled.
Plutarch, Philopoemen, 7(6–7); Pausanias, 8: 49(7)

LABUS M (209) – Anabasis of Antiochus
Antiochus III earned his title of 'the Great' as a result of his anabasis of the eastern provinces. He started out from Media and, after crossing the Salt Desert, reached the Parthian capital of Hecatompylus. His next objective was an advance into Hyrcania, which involved crossing the pass over Mount Labus [*Elburz*]. The ascent to the pass covered nearly 35 miles, mostly rough going through a deep and rock-strewn gorge. The sides of the gorge were lined along the top by hordes of barbarians. Antiochus, forewarned, had detached groups of archers, slingers and javelin throwers under his general Diogenes. These he sent outside the defile to outflank the groups of barbarians and dislodge them from the higher ground, repeating the process as he advanced. On the eighth day Antiochus reached the top of the pass, where a whole mass of barbarians had congregated to oppose him. They fought fiercely against the phalanx and might have succeeded had they not been outflanked. But the light-armed troops had made a wide detour at night and occupied the heights in the rear of the enemy. This created panic and the barbarians took to flight. Antiochus then descended into Hyrcania, where he brought the Parthian king Arsaces to battle and forced him to sue for terms.
Polybius, 10: 29–31(4)

ARIUS R (208) – Anabasis of Antiochus
After dealing with the Parthians (above), Antiochus proceeded to Bactria against Euthydemus, a Greek who had seized control of the region. Antiochus heard that 10,000 of the usurper's

cavalry were guarding the ford over the river Arius [*Heri-Rud*]. He encamped a day's march away and advanced with his cavalry, light troops and 10,000 peltasts by night as he had heard that the enemy cavalry withdrew at dusk to their quarters. He had got most of his forces across the river before the Bactrian cavalry arrived on the scene. With 2,000 of his best cavalry the king faced the enemy while the rest of his forces drew themselves up in order. He repulsed the first enemy detachment but the second and third onslaughts got the better of him. At this point Panaetolus, in charge of the main forces, advanced and turned the Bactrians into headlong flight, killing many of them in the pursuit. As a result, Euthydemus withdrew from the area. In the battle, Antiochus received a blow in the mouth and lost several teeth.
Polybius, 10: 49

LAMIA (208) – Wars of the Achaean League
The Achaeans were being attacked on all sides. The Aetolians had crossed the intervening straits and were ravaging their land, while Machanidas, the tyrant of Sparta, was harassing them across their mutual border. In addition, King Attalus I of Pergamum, who supported the Aetolians, was believed to be on the point of crossing to Europe. The Achaeans appealed to Philip V of Macedon for help, and it suited him to descend into Greece in his own interests. The Aetolians, led by Pyrrhias, marched out and met him near Lamia. In addition to their own forces, the Aetolians had some of Attalus' troops as well as a thousand men sent from a Roman fleet. Philip fought two battles against Pyrrhias, winning both of them and forcing the Aetolians to shut themselves up in Lamia. A truce was subsequently arranged following the intervention of a combined deputation to Philip from Ptolemy, Athens, Rhodes and Chios. In truth, the real aim of these parties was to try to keep Philip out of Greek affairs.
Livy, 27: 30(1–2)

MANTINEA (207) – Wars of the Achaean League
Machanidas, the tyrant of Sparta, continually molested the Achaeans. He was eventually brought to book by Philopoemen at Mantinea, where the Achaean general had collected his forces. When Philopoemen heard that the enemy was advancing up the road from Tegea 10 miles to the south, he divided his forces into three parts and marched them out of the city. Running across the middle of the plain was a deep ditch along which

Philopoemen stationed his phalanx in several divisions. The Achaean cavalry were placed on the right wing. On the left were all the other forces, the light-armed troops, the heavy-armed cavalry, and all the mercenaries, with Philopoemen himself in charge of the mercenary cavalry. When Machanidas approached, he lined up his mercenaries facing the enemy and placed catapults at intervals in front. Philopoemen, realizing that Machanidas intended to shoot at his phalanx and throw it into disorder, wasted no time in opening the attack with his cavalry on the left. They were opposed by the enemy's opposite numbers. The light-armed troops went in to support their respective cavalries, and ultimately all the mercenaries of both sides on that wing became engaged. After a confused struggle the tyrant's mercenaries, who were superior in number, got the upper hand and routed the opposition, which fled back to the city. It was at this point that Machanidas made his great mistake. Instead of outflanking the enemy line, he pursued the routed forces with childish glee. Philopoemen remained calm. He allowed the tyrant's men to pass through in their pursuit and then wheeled the first section of his phalanx into the gap left by the enemy, outflanking their wing and cutting off the return of Machanidas and his men. The Spartan phalanx now acted on its own initiative in starting a charge which came to grief in the ditch. Under the impression that this would present little obstacle, the Spartans tried to clamber through it and presented an excellent target for Philopoemen's phalanx, which promptly countercharged with levelled spears. Most of the enemy who tried to cross died in the attempt. When the tyrant returned from the chase, he found himself cut off by the ditch with the only bridge in the hands of the enemy. He found a possible crossing place and urged his horse over, but Philopoemen was waiting for him on the other side and killed him.
Polybius, 11: 11–18; Pausanias, 8: 50(2)

SCOTITAS (201) – Wars of the Achaean League
The successor to Machanidas as tyrant of Sparta was the equally undesirable Nabis. Philopoemen, the general of the Achaeans, devolved a plan for amassing an Achaean force to oppose Nabis without the knowledge of the tyrant's secret police and spies. He sent letters to all the more distant towns telling them to collect all the men of military age and to proceed to the next town (named in the letter), where they were to hand in a similar letter. Philopoemen had calculated the time taken for

each of the human chains to reach the final destination, Tegea, so that he could arrange for them to arrive at the same time. In this way the men of Achaea converged on Tegea without knowing their ultimate destination or purpose. Having collected his army, Philopoemen sent his picked troops to make a raid on Laconia in order to draw out the tyrant's men. The Achaeans had been instructed that when they were attacked, they were to retire to Scotitas. In the meantime Philopoemen himself, with the main body of the troops, made a night march to Scotitas to set up an ambush. The subsequent events went entirely according to plan.

Scotitas was a district between Tegea and Sparta which, according to Pausanias, was a forest of oaks. A possible site has been noted by modern scholars.
Polybius, 16: 36–37; Pausanias, 3: 10(6)

CHIOS ISL (201, autumn)
In 202 the Rhodians declared war on Philip of Macedon. A year later, Philip's aggressive actions in the Aegean upset Attalus I of Pergamum, who began to wonder if he would be the next target and decided to ally himself with Rhodes. Action was not long delayed. Philip was besieging the town of Chios when Attalus and the Rhodians sailed up to blockade him. Philip had 53 decked warships and a large fleet of galleys and other ships. The allies had 65 decked ships and 3 triremes but fewer other craft. As Philip's siege had met with no success, he decided to make a quick run for the open sea and to trust to the unexpectedness of his move to effect an escape. As he sailed out of the harbour, Attalus came up and attacked Philip's right wing. Philip ordered that wing to face the enemy and fight. The Rhodians were further away. They arrived in time to attack the last of the Macedonian ships in the rear. The encounter then resolved itself into two separate battles: a fight close to the shore between Attalus and the Macedonian right, and a running fight between the Rhodians and the other enemy ships which were still proceeding toward the mainland. Attalus was gaining the upper hand over his Macedonian adversaries until he chased an enemy ship toward the shore and was cut off by the enemy from the open sea. He had no alternative but to beach his ships and effect an escape by land. Out at sea, superior Rhodian speed and seamanship prevailed. The Rhodians were adept at avoiding boarding contact with the Macedonians, who were valiant fighters on deck. Instead, the Rhodians concentrated on shearing oars and damaging ships. The Macedonians soon ran into

difficulties and eventually abandoned the scene altogether. The final outcome is best depicted by the human losses, the allies losing about 130 men between them as against 3,000 soldiers and 6,000 sailors on the Macedonian side. In spite of this disproportion Philip claimed the victory, but his action next day gave the lie to it when the allies again sailed against him and he declined the challenge.
Polybius, 16: 2–7

PANIUM (200 or 198) – Fifth Syrian War
Around the turn of the century Antiochus the Great invaded Coele-Syria for the second time. After an initial setback at the hands of a former Aetolian general called Scopas, who had transferred his services to Egypt, Antiochus met him again in a battle which is variously dated 200 or 198. The encounter took place near Panium [*Bāniyās*], where one of the sources of the Jordan springs from a cavern in the foothills of Mount Hermon. Here Antiochus destroyed the greater part of Scopas' army. We are indebted to Polybius for naming the site and telling us that the armies were lined up on level ground with Scopas' right wing resting on the hills. Polybius' passage is otherwise virtually confined to a diatribe against the errors and inconsistencies of the historian Zeno. He makes no attempt here to give an account of the battle, which remains obscure.
Polybius, 16: 18–19; Josephus, Jewish Antiquities, 12: 3, 3 (131–132); Stephanus of Byzantium, Πάνιον, s.v. Πανία

ATHACUS (200) – Second Macedonian War
Following the battle off Chios (201) Attalus of Pergamum and his Rhodian allies sought help from Rome against Philip of Macedon. The senate, which had its own reasons for distrusting and fearing Philip, sent him an ultimatum. This was rejected. The following year the Romans landed a force in Illyria under Sulpicius Galba, who proceeded eastwards into Macedonia. Philip marched westward to meet him. Neither side knew the whereabouts of the other, and so both sent out reconnaissance cavalry which eventually met and engaged in an indecisive skirmish. Philip himself then moved forward with 20,000 foot and 2,000 horse and fortified a hill near Athacus (unknown) about a mile from the Roman camp. On the third day Sulpicius led out his army. The king sent a detachment of Illyrians and Cretans with cavalry support to harass the Romans, who retaliated by opposing them with a force of similar size. The

Roman attack was stubborn and the enemy auxiliaries, lightly armed and accustomed only to hit-
and-run tactics, were taken aback by the static
hand-to-hand fighting and fled. On the next day
the two armies met in full force. The king had
previously posted some peltasts in ambush
between the camps, but they emerged too soon and
the Romans were the victors. The following day
the Romans again lined up and positioned some
elephants in front of their lines. The enemy
declined the challenge.
Livy, 31: 34(5)–36(6)

OTTOLOBUM (200) – Second Macedonian War

After the encounter at Athacus (above), Sulpicius
moved his camp to Ottolobum 8 miles from the
enemy to make it safer to forage. One day when
Philip saw the Romans widely dispersed while
foraging, he took his cavalry and Cretan auxiliaries and cut off their return to camp. He then
sent a part of his force against the foragers, among
whom they created much slaughter. Sulpicius, the
Roman consul, sent out his cavalry and then led
out the legions. The cavalry fared badly, particularly against the enemy troops blocking the way,
but when the Macedonians pursued the cavalry,
they got carried away by their zeal and ran into the
Roman cohorts. In their disorganized state, the
Macedonians suffered considerable slaughter and
they, in their turn, broke off and fled. The king
himself nearly succumbed, being thrown from his
horse and narrowly escaping being trodden
underfoot. The encounter cost the Macedonians
about 300 cavalry killed or captured. We know
nothing of the Roman losses.
Livy, 31: 36(5)–37

AOUS R (198) – Second Macedonian War

In 198 the Romans again crossed the Adriatic to
Epirus, with a fresh force under Titus Quinctius
Flamininus. He debated whether he should invade
Macedonia by the long circuitous route to the
north. The alternative was a direct but hazardous
route eastward through the enemy positions on the
river Aous [*Vijose*]. He decided to take it. When he
reached enemy-held territory near the river, he
vacillated for over a month until Philip submitted
proposals for peace. The consul's demands in
return were too stringent for Philip, who broke off
negotiations. War it was to be. The river Aous
flows through a narrow valley between two
mountains, both of which were fortified by the
Macedonians. One was occupied by light-armed

troops; the king's camp was pitched on the other.
Catapults and other engines of war were positioned on many of the crags. While Flamininus
was pondering over the difficulties, a shepherd was
brought to him who offered to lead him round the
enemy's dispositions by a track to a point which
overlooked the enemy. To avert the enemy's sus-
picions, Flamininus kept up his usual harassing
attacks for a couple of days and then sent out a
force of 4,000 picked infantry with 300 cavalry.
They were to proceed up the valley as far as the
horses could go, where the cavalry would stay put.
The infantry were to advance with the guide by
night, the moon at that time being full. On the
third day they reached their objective and sent up
the agreed smoke signal. The consul immediately
divided his force into three columns and sent one
up each side of the valley while he led the third up
the middle. The fighting was becoming fraught
with danger and difficulty for the Romans when a
shout and sounds of battle were heard from the
direction of the enemy's rear. This brought hostilities to an early end as the king's men scattered
and fled, if they could, hemmed in as they were in
front and behind. Unfortunately for the Romans,
pursuit was impossible in that terrain. The fleeing
king, when he realized this, stopped after a few
miles to collect stragglers. Surprisingly, the enemy
host reassembled with a loss of not more than
2,000 men.
*Livy, 32: 5(8)–6(4) and 10–12; Plutarch,
Flamininus, 3(4)–5(1)*

CYNOSCEPHALAE MS (197) – Second Macedonian War

In a new year of campaigning Philip descended
once more into Thessaly while Flamininus, collecting reinforcements *en route* (notably 6,000
Aetolians), marched up to the border. The king
and the general were soon to meet for the decisive
encounter. With well-matched forces of around
25,000 on each side, the two armies approached
the range of hills known as Cynoscephalae
[*Chalkodonion*] from different directions. As a
result, they encamped with hills between them so
that neither knew the position of the other. On the
following morning the whole area was shrouded in
dense mist which reduced the visibility to a low
level. Philip, impatient for action, immediately
sent out a task force to seize the summits of the
hills. Flamininus, a little more leisurely, also sent
out a reconnaissance squad, which met the
Macedonians in the pass. In the subsequent
skirmish the Romans came off worst and sent a

message for help. When reinforcements arrived, the tables were turned and the enemy retreated to the summit and asked their side for help. Philip sent a large reinforcement of cavalry and mercenaries which again turned the tables by driving the Romans from the ridge. At this point, both armies marched out in full force. Flamininus drew up his army at the foot of the hills and ordered the right half to stay put, with the elephants in front, while he himself led the left half against the enemy. Philip, on the other side of the pass, led his peltasts and part of his phalanx up the slope. His first move at the top of the pass was to occupy the summits on his left, which had been vacated by the Romans. On his right, however, his mercenaries reappeared in flight, hotly pursued by the Roman heavy-armed troops under Flamininus. Philip ordered the part of his phalanx which had reached the pass to double in depth, level their spears, and charge. The Romans had no chance of standing up to this weight of heavy armour charging down on them from above. They were being driven back and slaughtered. Flamininus decided that his only hope was a diversion by his right wing, of which he took command. With his elephants in front, he led the legions against the forces on the enemy left, who had only just completed the climb and were still in marching order. They were unoccupied and idly watching the battle. The approach of the elephants and the legions threw them into confusion so that they were utterly routed and hotly pursued. However, one Roman tribune on the right displayed a spark of initiative far beyond the call of mere pursuit. Having seen the enemy defeated in this part of the battle, he took a small force of twenty maniples and wheeled them round to attack the victorious Macedonian phalanx in the rear. A phalanx with spears around 20 feet long is a cumbersome instrument, incapable of any abrupt change in direction. In consequence, the tribune's action created havoc. The Macedonians, attacked from front and rear, raised their spears in token of surrender or dropped them and fled. The Romans lost about 700 killed in the battle, in contrast to the enemy losses of around 13,000 killed or captured. The result of the battle was a request by Philip for an armistice, and a peace was granted in 196 which effectively limited him to Macedonia.
*Polybius, **18**: 19–26; Livy, **33**: 6–10; Plutarch,* Flamininus, *7–8*

NEMEA R (197) – Wars of the Achaean League
In the year in which the battle of Cynoscephalae

had brought hostilities against Philip to an end in northern Greece, there was one further armed conflict with him further south, near Corinth. To Philip this city was a stronghold against the Greek cities and he had reinforced it to a total of 6,000 soldiers. With this force Androsthenes, the king's general, attacked the Achaeans and ravaged the surrounding territory. As Nicostratus, the Achaean leader, was at Sicyon with only 2,000 men, he was forced to stay put until he could obtain allies from the neighbouring states and arrange a secret place of assembly. This brought his strength up to more than 5,000 men. Androsthenes, in ignorance of this, had encamped on the river Nemea, a stream bordering the territories of Corinth and Sicyon. He sent out half his army with orders to lay waste all the surrounding countryside. Nicostratus seized the opportunity and sent out a detachment to block the pass leading to Corinthian territory, while with the bulk of his force he advanced upon the enemy camp in two columns from different directions. Androsthenes, taken completely by surprise, marched out with his depleted force and formed up by the river while recalling the foragers. The Macedonians put up a stout fight but the rest of the force, assembled in haste, did not stand up to the enemy but fled in disorder. The disciplined Macedonians managed to retire in a more orderly fashion until they also eventually took to flight. After the battle there was a great slaughter of the more distant foragers and of those who were still returning to camp. The enemy losses amounted *in toto* to 1,500 killed and 300 prisoners.
*Livy, **33**: 14–15*

ALABANDA (197)
In Asia, the Rhodians wanted to repossess the mainland district of Peraea in Caria which they had previously held. They sent out a mixed force of Achaean infantry and auxiliaries, amounting to 2,600 men, which was reinforced by a further 1,100 Achaeans. They set up camp at Alabanda [*Araphisar*]. The king's prefect, Dinocrates, recalled all the garrisons from towns in the region and collected a force similar in size to the enemy's. He marched to Alabanda and encamped close to them but on the opposite side of the river. When the two sides lined up for battle, the Achaeans crossed the river, followed by the auxiliaries, and confronted the enemy's left wing which consisted of 400 Agrianes. After a lengthy struggle the Achaeans managed to dislodge their opponents by weight of numbers. Up to that point the 500 Macedonians

on the enemy right flank had not yielded an inch, but when their left gave way, the phalanx was unable to turn to meet the thrust on their flank. They began to fall back, then threw away their arms and fled.

The Rhodian and Achaean victory was a wasted effort. If the victors had proceeded immediately to Stratonicea [*Eskihisar*], they would have gained it without a fight. Instead, they wasted time taking sundry forts and small towns, giving Dinocrates the opportunity to take refuge there and to reinforce the garrison with his surviving troops. When the Rhodians and Achaeans did get around to investing the city, the siege was unsuccessful.
Livy, 33: 18

SPARTA (195) – War against Nabis

Argos left the Achaean league and looked to Philip for help which he was not in a position to provide. Philip asked Nabis, usurper and tyrant of Sparta, to undertake the protection of Argos on his behalf. Nabis provided it by instituting a reign of terror. This prompted Flamininus to convene a conference of Greek delegates, at which war against the tyrant was agreed. By this, the Greeks meant war against Argos since Argos was the cause of it all. Flamininus retorted that he did not see the sense in going to war against the city which had appealed for help. He insisted on striking at the core of the problem, Sparta. When the Romans were marking out their camp in the vicinity of that city, they were attacked by the tyrant's auxiliary troops. This totally unexpected assault provoked some panic, but when the legions came up, the enemy was forced to retire to the city. On the following day Flamininus was marching along the river Eurotas when Nabis and his mercenaries suddenly burst out of the city through several gates and attacked the Roman rearguard of light infantry and cavalry. The tyrant had kept his men lined up in readiness within the walls against just such an opportunity. However, Appius Claudius in charge of the rearguard had also prepared his men for this sort of eventuality. He brought them round smartly and smote the enemy until they broke and fled. Later in the same year Flamininus besieged Nabis in Sparta and forced him to surrender, although Nabis was left in possession of the city.
Livy, 34: 28

GYTHEUM (192) – War against Nabis

Belligerent as ever, Nabis besieged Gytheum, a town and harbour in the south of Laconia. The Romans sent a fleet and garrison to defend the place but Philopoemen, the general of the Achaeans and arch-enemy of Nabis, became impatient at waiting for them and launched the ships of the Achaeans. At that time there was a famous old quadrireme which had been captured 80 years before and was in a state of extreme disrepair. Nothing daunted, Philopoemen ordered it to be launched as his flag-ship. In this hulk and in total ignorance of maritime matters, he led his fleet against the Spartan flotilla from Gytheum. At the first bump with another vessel the old ship disintegrated and the whole crew were taken prisoner. Philopoemen himself escaped in a light skiff. The rest of the fleet made off speedily as soon as their 'flag-ship' went down.
Livy, 35: 26; Plutarch, Philopoemen, 14(1–3)

PLEIAE (192) – War against Nabis

As a result of his lucky victory in the naval fiasco off Gytheum (above), Nabis considered that there was no further danger from the sea to his siege of that town. He decided to strengthen his land lines by withdrawing a third of his force from the siege and stationing it near Pleiae, where it would threaten the obvious approach route of a hostile army. The encampment consisted largely of huts made of reeds and thatched with leaves. Philopoemen determined to make a surprise attack on this camp with a new weapon – fire. He amassed a fleet of small craft into which he embarked a force of lightly armed soldiers. Landing them near Pleiae, he moved by night to the sleeping camp into which firebrands were thrown. Everything was destroyed and nearly everybody with it. Whether Philopoemen had heard of the similar attack in Africa by Scipio Africanus only 11 years previously is a matter for surmise.
Livy, 35: 27(1–9); Plutarch, Philopoemen, 14(4)

CAMP OF PYRRHUS (192) – War against Nabis

From Pleiae, Philopoemen proceeded northwards and threatened Sparta in order to lure Nabis, the tyrant of that city, away from the siege of Gytheum. It so happened that Gytheum had already fallen to Nabis, who marched after Philopoemen and encamped at an unidentified place called the Camp of Pyrrhus north of Sparta. Nabis was certain that his enemy would come that way, and events proved him right. The road was narrow, and Philopoemen's column was about 5 miles long with the cavalry and auxiliaries at the rear, where he expected an attack. He was caught

off balance when he found the enemy ahead confronting his van. His column was back to front for the occasion. His astuteness in coping with such situations has been well recorded, and in the present instance he managed to bring the Cretan auxiliaries and cavalry from the rear to the fore. He seized and fortified a cliff overlooking a stream from which both sides would have to get water. He also concealed a force of *caetrati* (shield bearers) in a secluded valley nearby. The following day the battle broke out on the banks of the stream between the cavalry and Cretan auxiliaries of both sides. The two sides were evenly balanced, but after a while the Achaeans were 'forced' to withdraw toward the ambush, as instructed. The enemy, chasing them through the defile, were suddenly confronted by the *caetrati,* fresh and full of vigour, and they fled without hesitation to their camp. Many never reached it. This was not the end of the slaughter. Philopoemen noticed that the fugitives scattered into the woods in all directions and he realized that sooner or later they would head back to Sparta. In so doing, they fell into the ambushes which he had set up in the hills around the city.
Livy, 35: 27(11)–29(7); Plutarch, Philopoemen, *14(5–7)*

THERMOPYLAE P (191) – War against Antiochus

The Aetolians considered that they had had a raw deal in the settlement that followed the Second Macedonian War. They aired their grudge by inviting Antiochus III to liberate Greece. In 192, the king landed in Thessaly with a force of around 10,000 men, but he received no help or warmth from the Greeks. When the Romans sent an expedition of 20,000 infantry with horse and elephants, which marched across Greece to Thessaly, Antiochus fell back on the pass of Thermopylae. He pitched his camp inside the pass, which he blocked with a stone wall, ditch and rampart. Then he sent 2,000 of the Aetolians to hold the heights overlooking the pass in order to prevent an outflanking movement such as that which defeated Leonidas in 480. When the Roman consul Acilius Glabrio arrived, he also encamped in the pass facing Antiochus. Noticing the Aetolians on the heights, he sent Marcus Cato and Lucius Valerius against them with 2,000 men each. Then he drew up his troops. The king had placed his phalanx in front of his rampart with a body of javelin throwers, archers and slingers on the lower slopes to his left. Initially, the phalanx easily withstood

the Romans, who were at the same time assailed with missiles from their right flank. Eventually the phalanx was forced to withdraw and to fall back behind the rampart. The manned barrier so formed might have proved impenetrable if Cato had not dislodged the Aetolians on the hill. But, having done so, he then descended onto the pass. The enemy did not wait to ascertain the size of his force but dropped their arms and fled. Pursuit was difficult owing to the terrain, the fortifications, and the presence of elephants, but the king lost virtually the whole of his army. The Romans suffered only about 200 casualties. After the battle Antiochus withdrew entirely from Greece and returned to Asia.

It may be noted that Appian, contrary to Livy, places the sea on Antiochus' left and quotes his dispositions as if he were facing eastwards in the battle. In fact, the Romans entered the pass from the west and the king escaped eastwards to Scarphea and thence to Chalcis.
Livy, 36: 15–19; Appian, Syrian Wars, *17–20; Plutarch,* Cato Major, *13–14*

CORYCUS PR (191) – War against Antiochus

The battle of Thermopylae (above) ended the war against Antiochus in Greece, but the Romans planned to extend it to Asia. They sent a fleet to the Aegean, where it was reinforced by Eumenes and a little later by the Rhodians. Polyxenidas, the king's admiral, was anxious to engage the Romans before the Rhodians could join them. The Romans and Eumenes had a combined strength of 105 decked ships and 50 open craft, with which they headed for Cape Corycus [*Koraka*]. Polyxenidas, who had been waiting for them nearby with 100 ships (Appian says 200) sailed out against them and deployed in a straight line with his right flank landward and his left in the open sea. In front of the Roman fleet were two Carthaginian ships which were fighting on the Roman side. They were engaged by three enemy ships. One of the Carthaginian vessels was attacked by two of the enemy and was easily captured; the other fled back to the fleet. This upset Gaius Livius, the Roman commander, who sailed his flag-ship between the two enemy victors and grappled and boarded both of them, capturing the pair. By then hostilities had broken out all along the line. The action of Livius had thrown the enemy's left wing into some confusion, and now Eumenes attacked their right wing. It was Polyxenidas on the right wing who began the flight. Realizing that the Romans were superior in the arts of grappling and hand-to-hand

fighting, he set sail and hurried away. The other wing soon followed suit. The Romans attempted to pursue them but their heavier, slower ships made it a profitless exercise. Nevertheless, the Romans had sunk 10 ships and captured 13 with their crews for the loss of only the one Carthaginian vessel.
Livy, 36: 44–45(4); Appian, Syrian Wars, *22*

PANORMUS (190) – War against Antiochus

The Roman commander, Livius, was away with his fleet at the Hellespont when the Rhodians sent him 36 ships under the command of Pausistratus to the naval base at Panormus near Ephesus. Antiochus' commander, Polyxenidas, himself a Rhodian who had been exiled for criminal activities, devised a scheme for getting his own back on his hated rival, Pausistratus. He offered to hand over the king's fleet in exchange for his freedom to return to Rhodes. In convincing Pausistratus of his good faith, Polyxenidas led the other to relax his vigilance. Then, by night, he landed some marines who were to create a disturbance on land behind the harbour of Panormus, while he himself sailed in and fell upon the unsuspecting Pausistratus at dawn. At first Pausistratus decided to fight it out on land but the approach of the marines forced him to change his mind. After a rapid re-embarkation he ordered his men to attempt to force a passage through the harbour entrance. Only seven ships escaped. They were vessels which were equipped with fire apparatus consisting of urns suspended on projecting poles and containing blazing material which could be poured onto an invader. Pausistratus' own ship was attacked by three enemy ships and sank, taking him with it.
Livy, 37: 10–11; Appian, Syrian Wars, *24*

PHOENICUS (190) – War against Antiochus

The Romans heard that an enemy fleet was being prepared in Cilicia. Gaius Livius was sent to intercept it and prevent it from joining up with Polyxenidas, Antiochus' commander, at Ephesus. He set sail for Patara with two quinqueremes and seven Rhodian quadriremes but was prevented by bad weather from putting in to the harbour. He proceeded to the more sheltered harbour of Phoenicus [*Finiki*] a couple of miles further on. The cliffs overlooking the harbour were soon crowded with the townspeople and with the king's garrison. Livius sent out some light-armed troops to harass the mob. When yet more people poured out of the town, he became apprehensive and sent his marines and seamen into the fight. They

suffered considerable casualties but eventually drove the throng back into the city, after which they abandoned the expedition.
Livy, 37: 16

PERGAMUM (190) – War against Antiochus

Seleucus, the son of Antiochus III, was ravaging the territory around Pergamum [*Bergama*] and was virtually imprisoning Eumenes' garrison within the city. Eumenes sailed to his naval base at Elaea, where he received 1,000 veteran Achaean infantry and 100 horse which had been sent to him by the Achaeans under the command of Diophanes. They were conducted into Pergamum by night and proceeded to observe the enemy's movements. Diophanes noted that the enemy, having met no opposition, had become contemptuous and ill disciplined. He tried to persuade the garrison commander to join him in a sally but the idea was rejected as folly. Undeterred, Diophanes marched his men out and stationed them quietly in front of the walls, facing an enemy of at least four times his strength. After a period of inactivity in which the enemy became careless and disorderly and started eating their lunch, Diophanes suddenly ordered a charge. The panic his men caused was out of all proportion to their numbers. The infantry slaughtered the scattered elements while many of the enemy were unable to mount or even catch their horses in time. On the following day the enemy arrived but with more caution. Diophanes marched his men out and the two sides faced each other all day uneventfully until, at sunset, the enemy packed up and started to leave the field. Diophanes waited motionlessly until they were just out of sight, when he charged their rear and drove them back to their camp. As a result of these exploits, Seleucus was forced to abandon his camp and to give up his activities against Pergamum.
Livy, 37: 20–21(3); Appian, Syrian Wars, *26*

SIDE (190, summer) – War against Antiochus

A Rhodian fleet under Eudamus was sent to intercept an enemy fleet which was reported to be on its way from Syria. In the bay of Pamphylia the Rhodians put in at the mouth of the Eurymedon [*Köprü Çayi*] where they heard that the enemy was close at hand off Side. On the next day both fleets moved out of harbour ready for battle. The Rhodian fleet consisted of 32 quadriremes and 4 triremes. The king's fleet, which was under the command of Hannibal, was rather bigger with 37 large ships, including 3 hepteremes and 4 hexer-

emes, as well as 10 triremes. As the fleets closed, the king's fleet was already in line abreast with Hannibal in command on the left, which stretched out to the open sea. The Rhodians came out in line astern and needed time to redeploy and extend their right wing out to sea. As a result, Eudamus on the right wing engaged Hannibal initially with only five ships. To offset this, matters were going well on the Rhodians' left where one of the king's hepteremes was sunk by a much smaller Rhodian vessel. It was not long before the enemy ships all along that wing were turning to flight. Meanwhile, Eudamus out in the open sea was being hard pressed by Hannibal, who enjoyed much greater numbers. Eudamus might well have been surrounded had he not raised a signal to rally assistance, bringing vessels to the flag which had already won their individual fights. It was now Hannibal's turn to feel the pinch and his wing began to withdraw. In the end, fewer than 20 of the enemy's ships escaped unscathed.
Livy, 37: 23–24

MYONNESUS PR (190) – War against Antiochus

The Roman fleet set out from its base in Samos in search of provisions. It had been heard that the people of Teos had made a generous offer of supplies to the enemy fleet, and so the Romans put in at Teos and started plundering the land. When Polyxenidas heard that the Romans were at Teos, not far from his base at Ephesus, he sailed with the king's fleet to the area and anchored in a secluded harbour on a small island called Macris opposite the promontory of Myonnesus [*C. Doğanbey*]. This promontory projects from the mainland south of Teos. While the Romans were anchored near Teos, a peasant reported that he had seen a fleet moored off the island of Macris for a couple of days. Consternation in the Roman camp led to a rapid embarkation, departure and deployment into line ready for any emergency. The Rhodians brought up the rear. The king's fleet was soon sighted, deploying into line abreast with its left wing so extended as to be capable of encircling the Romans. Eudamus, commander of the Rhodians, dealt with that situation by speedily moving from the rear to the extreme right wing, thus equalizing the lines. He then made straight for the flag-ship of Polyxenidas on the enemy left, after which both fleets became engaged along the whole line. The Romans under Aemilius Regillus had 80 ships, 22 being Rhodian; the enemy had 89 vessels, 5 of which were exceptionally large. However, the Roman inferiority in size and numbers was more than offset by their fire-carrying ships with blazing cauldrons suspended outboard at the ends of long poles. Nothing inspired so much terror in the enemy, who would not venture near them. In the action, the Romans broke through the enemy centre and then wheeled right to attack the rear of the king's left wing, which was already engaged with the Rhodians. The enemy right wing remained intact until the men saw Polyxenidas fleeing on the left, when they also took to flight. The enemy lost 42 ships captured or sunk (Appian says 29). In contrast, it is said that only two Roman ships were destroyed. As a result of this engagement Antiochus effectively lost control of the sea and became unable to defend his far-flung territories.
Livy, 37: 28–30; Appian, Syrian Wars, *27*

MAGNESIA-AD-SIPYLUM (190, December) – War against Antiochus

Having robbed Antiochus of any control at sea, the Romans were bent on completing the destruction with a victory on land. Although the king had a large force of 60,000 foot and 12,000 horse, he was apprehensive. He withdrew across the river Phrygius [*Kum Çay*] and established a strongly fortified encampment near Magnesia-ad-Sipylum [*Manisa*]. The consular army, with a total strength of about 30,000, advanced across the river and encamped about 2 to 3 miles away from the enemy. After several days of inaction in which the king refused to accept any challenge, the consul moved his camp nearer to the enemy and lined up for battle with his left wing against the river. The king accepted the challenge for fear of shame. The action started on the Roman right wing which was opposed by a mixed mass of light cavalry, preceded by scythed chariots and camels. Eumenes II, on the Roman right, took the initiative by sending his slingers and archers against the chariots, creating panic in the horses and disrupting the enemy wing. A charge by his cavalry followed and extended the disorder, which spread to include the whole of the flank. The Roman legions seized the opportunity to make a direct frontal attack on the enemy phalanx, which was in the centre of their line with elephants posted between the sections. In the meantime, Antiochus, who was in command of a large body of élite cavalry on the right wing, had noted that the enemy had thought it unnecessary to post any cavalry on their left, which was covered by the river. He executed the manoeuvre on which he had staked his chances by charging the infantry and outflanking them along the riverside and then driving them back to their camp. In this extended pursuit he threw away any chance of victory by failing to support his phalanx in its hour of need. It was driven back behind the rampart. Attalus, who was with his brother Eumenes on the Roman right, saw the situation on the opposite flank along the river. Being at that time unengaged, he charged across the field to the assistance of the camp guard and forced Antiochus back. The king, seeing that his whole army was giving way, fled. His reputed losses were 50,000 infantry and 3,000 cavalry against a loss on the Roman side of 350 men. After this total disaster Antiochus sent envoys to sue for peace.

Livy, 37: 37(6)–44(2); Appian, Syrian Wars, *30–36*

CUBALLUM (189) – Galatian Expedition
Although the Romans and their allies had conquered Antiochus the Great both on land and sea, they knew that there would be no peace in Asia until the Galatians had been subdued. These were a part of the Gallic horde which had invaded Macedonia with Brennus, some of whom had proceeded into Thrace and then, a little later, had crossed the Hellespont into Asia. Gnaeus Manlius Volso took over the Roman army (or at least part of it) after the battle of Magnesia and headed for the Galatian strongholds on Mounts Olympus [*Alis Daği*] and Magaba [*Elmadaği*], regrettably extorting money from most of the peaceful communities on his route. Manlius made his first contact with the enemy when he was encamped near the Galatian stronghold of Cuballum. His advance guards were suddenly attacked by enemy horsemen, who threw them into confusion and caused some casualties. The uproar brought out the Roman cavalry in a hurry and the Gauls were driven off with considerable losses.

Livy, 38: 18(5–6)

OLYMPUS M (189) – Galatian Expedition
Manlius Volso proceeded against the Tolostobogii who had fortified their position on the heights of Mount Olympus [*Alis Daği*] in the north of Galatia near the Bithynian border. He divided his force into three columns which started to climb up the only negotiable track. The Gauls decided to block their progress by sending around 4,000 men to occupy a hill which overlooked the road. Manlius had prepared for this sort of manoeuvre by equipping his men with a large number of missiles of various sorts. Accordingly, the Cretan archers,

slingers and javelin throwers were sent forward to discharge a barrage at the enemy horde. The enemy retaliated with their only missiles – stones. Moreover, they were inadequately protected and were fighting naked as was their wont. They made a disorderly retreat back to their camp, where they massed outside their rampart. There, the story was repeated, the Roman missiles driving the enemy back behind the ramparts. When the Romans burst into the camp, the Gauls took off and fled in all directions.

Livy, 38: 20–23; Appian, Syrian Wars, *42; Florus 1: 27(5–6)*

ANCYRA (189) – Galatian Expedition
When the consul returned from Mount Olympus (above) to his base at Ancyra [*Ankara*], some spokesmen from the Gallic tribe of Tectosages asked for a conference. They were given a date and place for a meeting but they failed to appear. On the second occasion negotiations could not be completed owing to the regrettable absence of the chieftain. A third appointment was made and they did appear – as an armed body of 1,000 horse charging down at full gallop. Manlius and the Romans, with an escort of only 500 horse, were forced to disperse and might well not have escaped at all but for an outpost of 600 cavalry which had been stationed near the camp to protect some foragers. The arrival on the scene of the outpost and the foragers turned the scales. These fresh reinforcements routed and pursued the Gauls, taking no prisoners. Few escaped.

Livy, 38: 25; Polybius, 21: 39

MAGABA M (189) – Galatian Expedition
Manlius Volso's assault on the headquarters of the Tectosagi on Mount Magaba [*Elmadaği*], 10 miles south of Ankara, was virtually a repeat performance of the attack on Mount Olympus, described above. The only significant difference was the state of mind of the enemy, who remembered the fate of their neighbours. The number of the enemy has been estimated at more than 60,000, of whom 8,000 are said to have been killed. After their defeat the Gauls sent envoys to ask for peace.

Livy, 38: 26–27; Appian, Syrian Wars, *42; Florus 1: 27(5–6)*

CYPSELA (188)
On his journey home from Galatia the consul Manlius Volso ran into trouble near Cypsela [*Ipsala*] in Thrace. He was marching down a long, narrow, wooded track when he was attacked by a

conglomerate of about 10,000 Thracian tribesmen. They waited until after his van had passed. Then, before the rearguard had come into view, they attacked and looted the baggage waggons in the middle of the column. When the troops from the van and rear rushed to the centre, a disorderly fight ensued and persisted until the Thracians withdrew at dusk. Both sides suffered heavy losses.
Livy, 38: 40(5)–41(3)

TEMPYRA (188)

After Cypsela (above), Manlius suffered a further attack from local tribes, in a pass near Tempyra in the south of Thrace. The situation was very different to Cypsela in that this pass was barren and totally devoid of hiding places. The Thrausi blatantly blocked the road with their numbers, enforcing an open battle. However, they failed to stand up to a Roman charge in close formation and were trapped and slaughtered in the defile of their own choice.
Livy, 38: 41(5–7)

EVANDER'S HILL (182) – Wars of the
Achaean League
The last exploit of Philopoemen, the general of the Achaeans, took place after a tyrannical Messenian called Dinocrates took Messene out of the Achaean confederacy. Philopoemen heard reports that the tyrant was heading for a village called Colonis (or Corone) with intent to take it. Although he himself was ailing at the time, he raised a body of horse from the young men of Megalopolis and set out to forestall the Messenian. According to Plutarch, he met Dinocrates at a place called Evander's Hill, possibly the Mount Eva near Messene referred to by Pausanias. Here he put Dinocrates to flight. The enemy rallied when they were joined by a body of about 500 men whose job it was to guard that area of the countryside. Philopoemen retreated with his men, bringing up the rear and turning to ward off any assailant. He got separated from his men and, on being thrown by his horse on rough ground, he suffered a head injury and was taken prisoner. Embassies for his release were answered by his death when he was made to drink hemlock. In revenge, Messene was captured by the Athenian confederacy in the same year.

Livy makes no mention of Evander's Hill or of anything suggestive of it. In his account, Philopoemen was riding through a dangerous valley on his way to Corone when he was taken by surprise by Dinocrates.

Plutarch, Philopoemen, 18(3–8); Livy, 39: 49(1–5); Pausanias, 4: 31(4)

CALLINICUS (171) – Third Macedonian War
The Romans drifted into another war against Macedon. For the third time they sent a force across the Adriatic, this time against King Perseus who had assumed the throne on the death of Philip V. The king had descended into Thessaly and had a permanent encampment at the foot of Mount Othrys, from which his men foraged throughout the surrounding lowlands. His forces amounted to nearly 40,000 infantry and 4,000 cavalry. The Romans under the consul P. Licinius Crassus marched from Epirus to Thessaly and encamped about 3 miles from Larissa [*Larisa*] above the river Peneus [*Pinios*]. Their total force was around 30,000 men. The initiative was taken by the Macedonians, who suddenly appeared in the offing with a large column of men while the Romans were conferring about their plans. The result was a skirmish in which neither side gained any advantage. For several days thereafter the Macedonians appeared at the same time of day. Each time, the Romans declined the challenge until one day Perseus arrived unexpectedly at dawn and drew up a battle line near a hill called Callinicus, less than half a mile from the Roman rampart. In consternation, the Romans arrayed their troops. The deployments of the two forces were broadly similar. Both sides placed their élite cavalry squadrons in the centre while on the wings cavalry were interspersed with light-armed troops. At the outset a vigorous charge by the enemy left wing threw the Roman right into confusion. Then the Macedonian centre forced the Romans back and routed them. Livy attempts to put a good Roman face on the events after that but the outcome was clearly a disaster. The Romans were only saved from almost total destruction when the Macedonians got scattered in pursuit and Perseus was advised not to follow up his victory any further. The Romans lost nearly 3,000 killed or captured in contrast to about 60 enemy casualties. After the battle Perseus made peace overtures but these were flatly rejected.
Livy, 42: 57–60(1); Plutarch, Aemilius Paulus, 9(2)

PHALANNA (171) – Third Macedonian War
The Romans, having reaped and gathered all the harvests around Crannon to the south of Larissa, moved to the fields of Phalanna [*Falanna*] north of the city. Perseus, learning that the enemy were

scattered and vulnerable, fell on them without warning with a small detachment. After seizing about 1,000 waggons and 600 men, he attacked a guard detachment consisting of about 800 Romans under a tribune, Lucius Pompeius. This officer withdrew his men to a hill where they were besieged with missiles and were completely surrounded but refused to surrender. The consul, on being told about this, proceeded to the assistance of the beleaguered men with his cavalry and light troops, followed by the legions. The enemy were routed, but when they tried to escape they ran into their own phalanx in a confined space and blocked its path. The phalanx had been summoned earlier by Perseus but it arrived too late. It has been said that 8,000 of the enemy were killed and nearly 3,000 taken prisoner against more than 4,000 dead on the Roman side. Although these figures seem to be inflated, the outcome dismayed Perseus to the extent that he decamped and withdrew into Macedonia.
Livy, 42: 65–66

USCANA (170) – Third Macedonian War
Gentius, the oppressive king of the Illyrians, was suspected of pro-Macedonian sympathies (which subsequently bloomed into a frank alliance with King Perseus of Macedon). The legate, Appius Claudius Cento, was sent against Gentius with 4,000 infantry, a force which he doubled by raising reinforcements from the allies. Uscana, an Illyrian town of around 10,000 inhabitants, sent secret messages to Appius to the effect that they wanted to betray the city to him. He fell for the bait and named a day. When his troops arrived within missile range of the apparently deserted city, the inhabitants sallied out *en masse*. The Romans, in unsuspecting disorder, failed to stand up to the charge and were slaughtered in flight. Barely 2,000 escaped back to the camp.
Livy, 43: 10

SCODRA (168) – Third Macedonian War
Gentius, the Illyrian king, who was now actively allied with Perseus, had withdrawn to his well-fortified town of Scodra [*Shkodër*]. The Roman praetor, L. Anicius Gallus, marched up to the walls of the town with his army in battle formation. If the inhabitants and militia had attempted to defend the place from the ramparts, they would almost certainly have succeeded in driving the Romans away. Instead, they sallied from the gate and were promptly routed. The Romans occupied the town where an abject and grovelling Gentius

was invited to dine with the praetor, after which he was placed under guard and then sent to Rome.
Livy, 44: 31

ELPEUS R (168) – Third Macedonian War
In 169, at the end of the campaigning season, Perseus fortified a strong position on the far bank of the dried-up river Elpeus, the course of which runs from Mount Olympus past Dium to the sea. In the following year the consul Aemilius Paulus advanced and took up a position on the opposite bank, facing the Macedonians. In his opinion the enemy's fortified bank presented an insuperable obstacle. The total width of the river bed between the banks was about a mile, and the bottom was rough and uneven. For two days engagements took place in the middle of this space between light-armed troops of the two sides. Heavy casualties occurred on both sides, particularly among the Romans. However, these were no ordinary battles for supremacy. They were engineered by the consul to divert the prying eyes of Perseus away from other happenings (see Pythium, below).
Livy, 44: 35(9–24)

PYTHIUM (168) – Third Macedonian War
When the consul Aemilius Paulus was encamped opposite Perseus on the Elpeus (above), a frontal assault across the river bed was out of the question. Somehow Paulus had to circumvent the enemy's position. He learnt that all the mountain passes were guarded with the sole exception of the Petra Pass, probably because the terrain was so inhospitable. He instigated a feint by dispatching Scipio Nasica with 8,000 men and 120 horse to Heracleum on the coast. After dark the force moved off in the opposite direction, skirting the south-west aspect of Mount Olympus and halting below Pythium, the sanctuary of Apollo on the west side of the mountain. Perseus, seeing Aemilius still in position opposite him, was unaware of Nasica's expedition until a deserter from that force told him the facts. Perseus immediately sent out 2,000 Macedonians with 10,000 mercenaries under the command of Milo to seize the passes. When this force encountered Nasica, there was a sharp conflict in which the enemy were put to a disgraceful flight. Nasica then led his men uneventfully through the Petra Pass and round the north of Olympus to the plain near Dium in the Macedonian rear. This forced Perseus to withdraw and he retired to the region of Pydna north of Dium.

The accounts of this expedition by Polybius,

Scipio Nasica and Livy are all lost. Happily, Plutarch has preserved their essence.
Plutarch, Aemilius Paulus, *15–16(3)*

PYDNA (168, summer) – Third Macedonian War
Aemilius Paulus marched from the river Elpeus to the plain near Pydna where he joined Scipio Nasica and encamped opposite Perseus. The battle began on the following day in the afternoon, a time chosen by Aemilius so that his men would not have to face the sun. It has been said that it was started by a trivial incident when a horse broke loose and was chased by some Romans toward the enemy position. The resulting skirmish escalated until the whole of the enemy force came out. It has also been suggested that Aemilius himself released the horse to trigger the action. The battle itself lasted less than one hour. The salient feature was the action in the centre of the field around the Macedonian phalanx. The Roman legions were unable to hold their ground and were forced back relentlessly until the consul noticed that, owing to some unevenness of the ground, there were gaps in the enemy phalanx. He immediately divided his men into small groups and sent them into the gaps to attack the enemy in their flanks. The Macedonians were unable to turn without getting their long pikes entangled with each other. When these were discarded, they had only short swords with which to fight, which were no match for the Roman arms. In consequence, the phalanx was gradually broken into segments which were attacked on all sides until the Macedonians fled. Perseus, with the cavalry, had already preceded them in flight. About 25,000 of the Macedonians were killed, rather more than half of the total force. It is said that only 80–100 Romans perished. The king later surrendered, bringing the war to an end.
Plutarch, Aemilius Paulus, *16(4)–22; Livy,* **44***: 40–42*

ORTHOSIA (167)
In Asia the inhabitants of Caunus [near *Dalyan*], a town in the Rhodian province of Peraea in south Caria, revolted from Rhodes. At the same time Mylasa and Alabanda had joined forces in seizing towns in the Rhodian province of Euromus. The Rhodians realized that if they lost all their possessions in the mainland in this way, they would be left with nothing but their infertile island, which could not support their people. Accordingly, they sent out armed forces which compelled the Caunians to submit and brought the inhabitants of

Mylasa and Alabanda to battle. These peoples were defeated in an engagement near Orthosia on the left bank of the river Meander [*Menderes*].
Livy, **45***: 25(11–13)*

BETH-HORON (166) – Maccabean Revolt
The Maccabean revolt had its origins in an attempt by Antiochus IV Epiphanes of Syria to force Hellenism upon the Jews. A priest named Mattathias rebelled and fled into the mountains with his family. He died soon afterwards, leaving one of his sons, Judas Maccabeus, as his successor. Judas collected a band of insurgents and, in a preliminary skirmish at an unknown place, the Samaritan general was killed. When Soron, the general in Coele-Syria, heard about the numbers that were joining Judas, he marched against him with a large army and met him at Beth-Horon [*Beit Ur*]. At sight of the enemy numbers Judas' men were reluctant to fight, but after much exhortation they engaged. When Soron himself was killed, the Syrians fled. About 800 of them were killed in the pursuit.
1. Maccabees, *3, 13–24; Josephus,* Jewish Antiquities, *12: 7, 1 (287–292)*

EMMAUS (166) – Maccabean Revolt
Before he went on a visit to Persia, Antiochus IV appointed a man called Lysias as his deputy and governor of the kingdom and ordered him to conquer Judaea and destroy the Jews. Lysias sent Gorgias against Judaea with a force of 40,000 infantry and 7,000 horse, which camped near Emmaus [*Amwas*]. From this force Gorgias detached 5,000 foot and 1,000 horse to make a surprise attack by night on Judas, who was camped not far away. Judas heard about this and turned the tables by surreptitiously leaving his camp and marching all night to Emmaus to attack the enemy camp. He had only 3,000 men with him but the element of surprise was sufficient to win him the battle and cause the enemy to flee. About 3,000 of them were slain in camp and during the pursuit.
1. Maccabees, *4, 1–15; Josephus,* Jewish Antiquities, *12: 7, 3–4 (298–311)*

BETH-ZUR (165) – Maccabean Revolt
In the year after the defeat of his forces at Emmaus (above), Lysias collected a larger army of 60,000 foot and 5,000 horse with which he encamped at the village of Beth-Zur [*Beit Sur*]. Judas went against him with only 10,000 men but they slew about 5,000 of the Syrian van, after which Lysias

withdrew to Antioch to collect an even greater force.

1. Maccabees, *4, 28–34; Josephus*, Jewish Antiquities, *12: 7, 5 (313–315)*

BATH-ZACHARIAS (162) – Maccabean Revolt

When Antiochus IV died in 163, his boy son Antiochus V Eupator raised a mighty army of 100,000 men with 20,000 horse and 32 elephants under Lysias and besieged Beth-Zur. When Judas encamped 9 miles away at Bath-Zacharias [*Beit Skaria*], Antiochus directed his army against him. Judas killed several hundred of the enemy, but the odds against him were too great and he decided to withdraw after his brother, Eleazar, had been crushed by an elephant.

1. Maccabees, *6, 28–47; Josephus*, Jewish Antiquities, *12: 9, 4 (367–375)*

CAPHARSALAMA (161) – Maccabean Revolt

Demetrius I of Syria had been held as a hostage in Rome and had seen his kingdom pass in his absence to Antiochus IV and V. He escaped in 162 and assumed the kingship after slaying the young Antiochus V and his regent Lysias. Pursuing the policy of his predecessors against the Jews, Demetrius sent a prince called Nicanor to treat with Judas openly but in reality to seize him. Judas, however, noted an ominous signal and, alerted to the plot, he fled. Nicanor then went against Judas with his army and a battle was fought near the village of Capharsalama. The author of *Maccabees*, a reliable historian, relates that 5,000 of Nicanor's men were killed, after which the rest fled to Jerusalem. The later source, Josephus, assigns the 5,000 casualties to Judas' band and declares Nicanor the winner and Judas the fugitive to Jerusalem, but there are inconsistencies which suggest corruption of the source. Jerusalem, for example, was in the hands of the Syrians – a most unlikely refuge for Judas.

1. Maccabees, *7, 31–32; Josephus*, Jewish Antiquities, *12: 10, 4 (402–405)*

ADASA (161) – Maccabean Revolt

After Capharsalama (above), Nicanor was reinforced with another Syrian army and encamped at Beth-Horon. Judas pitched his camp 4 miles away at Adasa [*Adaseh*] with no more than 3,000 men (Josephus says 1,000). Undeterred by the gross disparity of the forces, Judas engaged the enemy and slew many of them including Nicanor himself. After that, the Syrians gave up and fled. When Judas pursued them, the local inhabitants joined in the chase and helped to slaughter the fugitives until not one of the 9,000 remained alive.

1. Maccabees, *7, 39–46; Josephus*, Jewish Antiquities, *12: 10, 5 (408–411)*

BEREA (160) – Maccabean Revolt

When Demetrius I learnt of the defeat and death of Nicanor at Adasa, he sent Bacchides with 20,000 foot and 2,000 horse against Judas. The two sides met and faced each other at Berea [*Bireh*]. When the Jews saw the Syrian army, most of them lost heart and deserted Judas, leaving him with only 800 stalwarts who stood by their leader with a grim determination to sell themselves dearly. Judas had noticed that the strength of the enemy force lay in its right wing where Bacchides had positioned himself. Without hesitation he and his small band launched a desperate attack on that wing, breaking its ranks and putting them to flight. In the pursuit that followed, the enemy left wing seized the opportunity to attack the Jews in the rear and surround them. Many were killed on both sides, including Judas himself. His position as leader of the revolt was assumed by his brother Jonathan.

1. Maccabees, *9, 1–18; Josephus*, Jewish Antiquities, *12: 11, 1–2 (420–431)*

SPARTA (148) – Achaean War

The Achaeans picked a quarrel with the Lacedaemonians and assembled an expedition against Sparta under their general Damocritus. It was at this time that the propraetor Metellus arrived with an army in Macedonia. He requested a commission to look into Achaean affairs. The commission forbade the Achaeans to use arms against Sparta and told them to await the arrival of the peace commissioners. By the time Damocritus received these orders he had already marched on Sparta. The Spartans sallied out to defend their city but were soon overcome with the loss of about 1,000 of their number. Instead of capturing the city, as he could have done, Damocritus contented himself with looting the countryside. When he returned home, he was fined by the Achaeans for betraying their interests and was exiled.

Pausanias, 7: 13(1–2)

AZOTUS OR ASHDOD (147) – Maccabean Revolt

After the death of Judas Maccabeus at Berea (160), two of his brothers called Jonathan and Simon carried on his work through guerilla warfare against Bacchides, with whom they eventually came to terms. In 150, Alexander Balas, a pretended son of Antiochus IV, killed Demetrius I of Syria in battle at an unknown site and seized his kingdom. This inevitably brought him into conflict with the rightful heir, Demetrius' son and namesake. The situation proved advantageous to Jonathan when both sides wooed him with honours, each outbidding the other. It gave him an excellent opportunity to extend his dominion. In 147 he raised 10,000 men and was joined by Simon with whom he marched to Joppa [*Jaffa*]. The citizens refused to open the gates because a garrison had been installed by the governor of Coele-Syria, Apollonius Daus, who was hostile to Jonathan and had challenged him to battle. When Jonathan started to besiege the city, the citizens changed their minds and let him in. Apollonius then collected 8,000 foot and 3,000 horse and, appearing before Joppa, he proceeded to withdraw to Azotus in the hope of luring Jonathan into the plain. Apollonius was confident of victory by virtue of his cavalry on such suitable terrain. Jonathan marched out and followed the other to the plain near Azotus, where he was attacked in the rear by 1,000 cavalrymen whom Apollonius had left in ambush. Jonathan's men suffered the darts all day on their shields without making any attempt to retaliate. At the end of the day when the enemy's horses were tired and the darts had been used up, Simon and his force attacked the cavalry while Jonathan faced the infantry in front. The cavalry turned and fled, and when the infantry saw this they retreated to Azotus. Jonathan then set fire to the town, inflicting a total of nearly 8,000 casualties by sword and fire. This exploit gave him the valuable seaboard town of Joppa, which was to be succeeded in due course by further gains and expansion.

1. Maccabees, *10, 74–85; Josephus,* Jewish Antiquities, *13: 4, 3–4 (86–100)*

ALPHEUS R (146) – Achaean War
In 146 the general of the Achaeans was a man called Critolaus who was not only anti-Spartan but even more violently anti-Roman. He insulted the Roman ambassadors and brought their vengeance upon him in the form of an army, which defeated him and his forces alongside the river Alpheus [*Alfios*] in Elis. A Roman army was sent down by Metellus from Macedonia, but it may be doubted whether Metellus himself was in command, as Florus states, in view of his descent later in the year against Critolaus in central Greece (Scarphea, below). Florus also states, incorrectly, that the battle on the Alpheus ended the war at a single stroke.
Florus, 1: 32(2–3)

SCARPHEA (146) – Achaean War
Critolaus, the Achaean general, made an expedition against Heraclea in Malis which refused to join the Achaean league. This brought the Roman consul Metellus down on him from Macedonia. Critolaus was so petrified that he headed for refuge in Scarphea [near *Molos*] in Locris but he and his men were caught in flight by the forces of Metellus. A large number of them were killed and 1,000 were taken prisoner. Critolaus was never seen again.
Pausanias, 7: 15(2–3); Livy, epitome 52

CHAERONEA (146) – Achaean War
A force of 1,000 Arcadians who were connected with Critolaus' expedition (above) and who were marching to join him, had advanced as far as Elatea. After learning of the disaster at Scarphea, the Elateans ordered the Arcadians to leave their city. They were on their way back to the Peloponnese when Metellus met them at Chaeronea and massacred them.
Pausanias, 7: 15(3)

ISTHMUS (146) – Achaean War
Following the death of Critolaus, Diaeus was once again appointed general of the Achaeans. He assembled everyone of military age, the whole gathering amounting to 14,000 infantry and 600 horse. Of these, 4,000 men were detached and sent to garrison Megara to block a Roman advance, but as soon as the Romans drew near, they fled straight back to the Achaean camp at Corinth. The consul Lucius Mummius arrived on the scene and, after dismissing Metellus, assembled his army. This amounted to 23,000 foot and 3,500 horse with a few extras. After a cheeky sally by night, the Achaeans came out in force to fight in the neck of the Isthmus, but the cavalry fled at once without waiting for a charge. The infantry stood their ground until they were outflanked and put to flight, opening the way for Mummius, who sacked and burnt a virtually deserted city. It has been said that 20,000 were killed in the battle, but this figure exceeds the total Achaean numbers, many or most of whom seem to have fled.

The destruction of Corinth marks the end of Greek liberty. The Roman senate dissolved the

Achaean league and incorporated its constituent states into the new province of Macedon.

Pausanias, 7: 16(1–2); Florus, 1: 32(5); Livy, epitome 52

OENOPARAS R (145)

In 150, Alexander Balas, a pretender to the Seleucid kingdom, killed the king Demetrius I in battle at an unknown place and seized the kingdom. This brought the rightful successor, the future Demetrius II of Syria, from Crete with an army in search of vengeance. Ptolemy VI Philometor, also, waited in the wings for a chance to get his hands on the Seleucid kingdom. As Balas was his son-in-law, Ptolemy travelled to Syria with an army to assist him, only to discover a real or imaginary plot by Balas to kill him. He promptly removed his daughter from Balas' care and handed her to Demetrius, with whom he made a pact. He then persuaded the people of Antioch to accept Demetrius as their king. Balas, who was in Cilicia, returned to Syria with an army and confronted the forces of Ptolemy and Demetrius on the banks of the river Oenoparas [*Afrin*] near Antioch. The site has been named by Strabo. Balas was defeated and fled to Arabia where an Arabian prince cut off his head and sent it to Ptolemy. However, the recipient himself only survived the battle by a few days. He died from injuries received when his horse threw him in the battle. Demetrius alone survived and retained his rightful kingdom.

1. Maccabees, *11, 15–18; Josephus,* Jewish Antiquities, *13: 4, 8 (116–119); Strabo, 16: 2, 8; Livy,* epitome *52*

PART THREE

THE ROMAN WORLD

Chronological Table of Battles of The Roman World

BC	PLACE[1]	WAR OR EPISODE	VICTORS[2]	VANQUISHED[2]
502	Pometia		Latins	Romans
496	Regillus L		A. Postumius Albus Regillensis	Latini
495	Aricia		P. Servilius Priscus	Aurunci
482	Antium		Volsci	L. Aemilius Mamercus
482	Longula		L. Aemilius Mamercus	Volsci
480	Veii		(1) M. Fabius Vibulanus	Etruscans
			(2) Cn. Manlius Cincinnatus	
477	Cremera R		Veientes	Clan Fabii
477	Temple of Hope		C. Horatius Pulvillus $=$[3]	Etruscans $=$[3]
477	Colline Gate		C. Horatius Pulvillus $=$	Etruscans $=$
476	Janiculum		Sp. Servilius Structus	Etruscans
475	Veii		P. Valerius Publicola	Veientes and Sabini
468	Antium		T. Quinctius Capitolinus Barbatus	Antiates
465	Algidus M		(1) Q. Fabius Vibulanus	Aequi
			(2) T. Quinctius Capitolinus Barbatus	
458	Algidus M		L. Quinctius Cincinnatus	Aequi
455	Algidus M		T. Romilius Rocus Vaticanus	Aequi
449	Algidus M		L. Valerius Potitus	Volsci and Aequi
437	Fidenae		Mam. Aemilius Mamercus	Fidenates and Veientes
435	Nomentum		Q. Servilius Priscus Fidenas	Fidenates and Veientes
431	Algidus M		A. Postumius Tubertus	Volsci and Aequi
426	Fidenae		Mam. Aemilius Mamercus	Veientes and Fidenates
418	Algidus M		Aequi and Labici	(1) L. Sergius Fidenas
				(2) M. Papirius Mugilanus
418	Algidus M		Q. Servilius Priscus	Aequi and Labici
391	Gurasium		Romans	Volsci
390	Allia R	Gallic Invasion	Gauls (Brennus)	(1) Q. Servilius Fidenas
				(2) Q. Sulpicius Gallus
				(3) P. Cornelius Maluginensis

[1] *Abbreviations:* C – Cape; Isl(s) – Island(s); L – Lake; M(s) – Mountain(s); P – Pass; Pr – Promontory; R – River.

[2] *Praenomina:* A. – Aulus; Ap. – Appius; C. – Gaius; Cn. – Gnaeus; D. – Decimus; L. – Lucius; M. – Marcus; Mam. – Mamercus; M'. – Manius; P. – Publius; Q. – Quintus; Ser. – Servius; Sex. – Sextus; Sp. – Spurius; T. – Titus; Ti. – Tiberius.

[3] Equal symbols (=) after victor and vanquished denote an indecisive outcome.

* Battles so marked (between 219 and 146 BC) are described under *The Greek World*.

BC	PLACE	WAR OR EPISODE	VICTORS	VANQUISHED
390	Rome	Gallic Invasion	Gauls (Brennus)	? M. Furius Camillus
390	Veascium	Gallic Invasion	M. Furius Camillus	Gauls
389	Lanuvium		M. Furius Camillus	Volsci
389	Campus Martius		M. Furius Camillus	Volsci
389	Bola		M. Furius Camillus	Aequi
386	Satricum		M. Furius Camillus	Volsci, Latini and Hernici
382	Velitrae		(1) Sp. Papirius Crassus (2) L. Papirius Mugillanus	Veliterni
381	Satricum		M. Furius Camillus	Volsci and Praenestini
380	Allia R		T. Quinctius Cincinnatus	Praenestini
377	Satricum		(1) P. Valerius Potitus Publicola (2) L. Aemilius Mamercus	Latini and Volsci
362	Signia		Hernici	Genucius Aveninensis
362	Signia		Ap. Claudius Inregillensis	Hernici
361	Anio R	Gallic Invasion	(1) T. Quinctius Poenus Capitolinus Crispinus (2) T. Manlius Imperiosus Torquatus	Gauls
360	Colline Gate	Gallic Invasion	Q. Servilius Ahala	Gauls
358	Pedum	Gallic Invasion	C. Sulpicius Peticus	Gauls
357	Privernum		C. Marcius Rutulus	Privernates
346	Satricum		M. Valerius Maximus Corvus	Antiates and Volsci
343	Capua		Samnites	Campanians
343	Gaurus M	First Samnite War	M. Valerius Maximus Corvus	Samnites
343	Saticula	First Samnite War	A. Cornelius Cossus	Samnites
343	Suessula	First Samnite War	M. Valerius Maximus Corvus	Samnites
340	Veseris	Great Latin War	(1) T. Manlius Imperiosus Torquatus (2) P. Decius Mus	Samnites and Latini
340	Trifanum	Great Latin War	T. Manlius Imperiosus Torquatus	Numisius (Latini)
339	Fenectane Plains	Great Latin War	Q. Publilius Philo	Latini
338	Pedum	Great Latin War	L. Furius Camillus	Pedani
338	Astura R	Great Latin War	C. Maenius	Aricini *et al.*
338	Manduria	Tarentine Wars	Lucanians	Archidamus III of Sparta
331	Pandosia	Tarentine Wars	Lucanians	Alexander of Epirus
325	Imbrinium	Second Samnite War	Q. Fabius Maximus Rullianus	Samnites
321	Caudine Forks	Second Samnite War	Samnites (Gaius Pontius)	(1) T.Veturius Calvinus (2) Sp.Postumius Caudinus
316	Saticula	Second Samnite War	L. Aemilius Mamercus Privernas	Samnites
315	Saticula	Second Samnite War	(1) Q. Fabius Maximus Rullianus (2) Q. Aulius Cerretanus	Samnites
315	Lautulae	Second Samnite War	Samnites	Q. Fabius Maximus Rullianus
315	Tarracina	Second Samnite War	(1) Q. Fabius Maximus Rullianus (2) C. Fabius Ambustus	Samnites
314	Caudium	Second Samnite War	(1) C. Sulpicius Longus (2) M. Poetelius Libo	Samnites
311	Sutrium	Second Samnite War	Q. Aemilius Barbula	Etruscans
310	Sutrium	Second Samnite War	Q. Fabius Maximus Rullianus	Etruscans
310	Perusia	Second Samnite War	Q. Fabius Maximus Rullianus	Etruscans
310	Vadimonis L	Second Samnite War	Romans	Etruscans
310	Talium	Second Samnite War	? L. Papirius Cursor	Samnites

BC	PLACE	WAR OR EPISODE	VICTORS	VANQUISHED
308	Perusia	Second Samnite War	Q. Fabius Maximus Rullianus	Etruscans
308	Mevania	Second Samnite War	Q. Fabius Maximus Rullianus	Umbrians
307	Allifae	Second Samnite War	Q. Fabius Maximus Rullianus	Samnites
305	Tifernum	Second Samnite War	L. Postumius Megellus =	Samnites =
305	Bovianum	Second Samnite War	Ti. Minucius Augurinus	Samnites
305	Tifernum	Second Samnite War	(1) L. Postumius Megellus (2) Ti. Minucius Augurinus	Statius Gellius (Samnites)
302	Thuriae	Tarentine Wars	Romans	Cleonymus the Spartan
298	Bovianum	Third Samnite War	Cn. Fulvius Maximus Centumalus	Samnites
298	Volaterrae	Third Samnite War	L. Cornelius Scipio Barbatus	Etruscans
297	Tifernum	Third Samnite War	Q. Fabius Maximus Rullianus	Samnites
297	Beneventum	Third Samnite War	P. Decius Mus	Apulians
296	Volturnus R	Third Samnite War	L. Volumnius Flamma Violens	Staius Minatius (Samnites)
295	Camerinum	Third Samnite War	Samnites and Gauls	L. Cornelius Scipio Barbatus
295	Sentinum	Third Samnite War	(1) Q. Fabius Maximus Rullianus (2) P. Decius Mus	Samnites and Gellius Egnatius (Gauls)
295	Tifernus M	Third Samnite War	L. Volumnius Flamma Violens	Samnites
295	Caiatia	Third Samnite War	(1) Ap. Claudius Caecus (2) L. Volumnius Flamma Violens	Samnites
294	Luceria	Third Samnite War	M. Atilius Regulus	Samnites
293	Aquilonia	Third Samnite War	L. Papirius Cursor	Samnites
293	Herculaneum	Third Samnite War	Sp. Carvilius Maximus =	Samnites =
284	Arretium	Gallic Invasion	M'. Curius Dentatus	Senones
283	Vadimonis L	Gallic Invasion	P. Cornelius Dolabella	Boii and Etruscans
282	Populonia	Gallic Invasion	Romans	Boii and Etruscans
282	Tarentum, off	Tarentine War	Tarentini	L. Valerius
280	Heraclea	Tarentine (Pyrrhic) War	Pyrrhus	P. Valerius Laevinus
279	A(u)sculum Satrianum	Tarentine (Pyrrhic) War	Pyrrhus ? =	C. Fabricius Luscinus ? =
276	*Straits of Messina*	Tarentine (Pyrrhic) War	Carthaginians	Pyrrhus
275	Beneventum	Tarentine (Pyrrhic) War	M'. Curius Dentatus	Pyrrhus
274c.	Cyamosorus R	Mamertine War	Hiero II	Mamertines
265c.	Longanus R	Mamertine War	Hiero II	Mamertines
264	Messana	First Punic War	Ap. Claudius Caudex	Hiero II
264	Messana	First Punic War	Ap. Claudius Caudex	Carthaginians
262	Heraclea Minoa	First Punic War	Hanno	(1) L. Postumius Albinus (2) Q. Mamilius
262	Agrigentum	First Punic War	Romans	Hanno
260	Lipara	First Punic War	Boodes (Carthaginians)	Cn. Cornelius Scipio Asina
260	Cape of Italy, off	First Punic War	Romans	Hannibal
260	Mylae, off	First Punic War	C. Duilius	Carthaginians
260	Thermae Himerienses	First Punic War	Hamilcar	Roman Allies
258	Camarina	First Punic War	Carthaginians	A. Atilius Calatinus
257	Tyndaris, off	First Punic War	C. Atilius Regulus =	Hamilcar =
256	Ecnomus Pr, off	First Punic War	(1) M. Atilius Regulus (2) L. Manlius	Hamilcar
256	Adys	First Punic War	M. Atilius Regulus	Hasdrubal (son of Hanno)

143

BC	PLACE	WAR OR EPISODE	VICTORS	VANQUISHED
255	Bagradas R	First Punic War	Xanthippus (Carthaginians)	M. Atilius Regulus
255	Hermaeum C, off	First Punic War	(1) M. Aemilius Paulus	Carthaginians
			(2) Ser. Fulvius	
250	Panormus	First Punic War	L. Caecilius Metellus	Hasdrubal (son of Hanno)
249	Drepanum, off	First Punic War	Adherbal	P. Claudius Pulcher
245	Aegimurus Isl, off	First Punic War	Romans	Carthaginians
241	Aegetes Isls, off	First Punic War	C. Lutatius Catulus	Hanno
225	Clusium	Gallic Invasion	Gauls	Romans
225	Telamon	Gallic Invasion	(1) C. Atilius Regularis	Gauls
			(2) L. Aemilius Papus	
222	Clastidium	Gallic Invasion	M. Claudius Marcellus	Gauls
222	Mediolanum	Gallic Invasion	Cn. Cornelius Scipio Calvus	Gauls
219	Pharos Isl*	Second Illyrian War	L. Aemilius Paulus	Demetrius of Pharos
218	Rhodanus R	Second Punic War	Hannibal	Gauls
218	Ticinus R	Second Punic War	Hannibal	P. Cornelius Scipio
218	Lilybaeum, off	Second Punic War	Romans	Carthaginians
218	Trebia R	Second Punic War	Hannibal	Ti. Sempronius Longus
218	Cissis	Second Punic War	Cn. Cornelius Scipio Calvus	Hanno
217	Iberus R	Second Punic War	Cn. Cornelius Scipio Calvus	Hasdrubal Barca
217	Trasimenus L	Second Punic War	Hannibal	C. Flaminius
217	Callicula M	Second Punic War	Hannibal	Q. Fabius Maximus Verrucosus Cunctator
216	Gerunium	Second Punic War	Hannibal	M. Minucius Rufus
216	Cannae	Second Punic War	Hannibal	C. Terentius Varro
216	Nola	Second Punic War	M. Claudius Marcellus	Hannibal
215	Grumentum	Second Punic War	Ti. Sempronius Longus	Hanno
215	Nola	Second Punic War	M. Claudius Marcellus	Hannibal
215	Carales	Second Punic War	T. Manlius Torquatus	Hasdrubal the Bald
215	Ibera	Second Punic War	(1) Cn. Cornelius Scipio Calvus	Hasdrubal Barca
			(2) P. Cornelius Scipio	
215	Iliturgi (Tarracon.)	Second Punic War	(1) Cn. Cornelius Scipio Calvus	Hasdrubal Barca, Mago and Hamilcar (son of Bomilcar)
			(2) P. Cornelius Scipio	
215	Intibili	Second Punic War	(1) Cn. Cornelius Scipio Calvus	Hasdrubal Barca, Mago and Hamilcar (son of Bomilcar)
			(2) P. Cornelius Scipio	
214	Beneventum	Second Punic War	Ti. Sempronius Gracchus	Hanno
214	Nola	Second Punic War	M. Claudius Marcellus	Hannibal
213	Iliturgi (Baetica)	Second Punic War	Cn. Cornelius Scipio Calvus	Carthaginians
213	Munda	Second Punic War	Cn. Cornelius Scipio Calvus	Carthaginians
213	Aurinx	Second Punic War	Cn. Cornelius Scipio Calvus	Carthaginians
212	Capua	Second Punic War	Capuans	(1) Ap. Claudius Pulcher (2) Q. Fulvius Flaccus
212	Capua	Second Punic War	Hannibal =	(1) Ap. Claudius Pulcher = (2) Q. Fulvius Flaccus
212	Herdonea	Second Punic War	Hannibal	Cn. Fulvius Flaccus
211	Himera R	Second Punic War	M. Claudius Marcellus	Hanno and Epicydes
211	Upper Baetis R	Second Punic War	Masinissa, Indibilis and Carthaginians	P. Cornelius Scipio
211	Ilorci	Second Punic War	Hasdrubal Barca, Mago and Hasdrubal (son of Gisgo)	Cn. Cornelius Scipio Calvus

BC	PLACE	WAR OR EPISODE	VICTORS	VANQUISHED
211	Capua	Second Punic War	(1) Ap. Claudius Pulcher	Campanians
			(2) Q. Fulvius Flaccus	Hannibal
211	Colline Gate	Second Punic War	Q. Fulvius Flaccus	Hannibal
211	Anio R	Second Punic War	Q. Fulvius Flaccus =	Hannibal =
210	Sapriportis, off	Second Punic War	Democrates and Nico Perco	D. Quinctius
210	Herdonea	Second Punic War	Hannibal	Cn. Fulvius Centumalus
210	Numistro	Second Punic War	M. Claudius Marcellus =	Hannibal =
209	New Carthage	Second Punic War	P. Cornelius Scipio Africanus	Mago
209	Canusium	Second Punic War	Hannibal	M. Claudius Marcellus
208	Petelia	Second Punic War	Carthaginians	Romans
208	Venusia	Second Punic War	Hannibal	(1) M. Claudius Marcellus
				(2) T. Quinctius Crispinus
208	Locri Epizephyrii	Second Punic War	Hannibal and Mago	L. Cincius Alimentus
208	Clupea, off	Second Punic War	M. Valerius Laevinus	Carthaginians
208	Baecula	Second Punic War	P. Cornelius Scipio Africanus	Hasdrubal Barca
207	Carmone	Second Punic War	P. Cornelius Scipio Africanus	Hasdrubal (son of Gisgo)
207	Grumentum	Second Punic War	C. Claudius Nero	Hannibal
207	Venusia	Second Punic War	C. Claudius Nero	Hannibal
207	Metaurus R	Second Punic War	(1) M. Livius Salinator	Hasdrubal Barca
			(2) C. Claudius Nero	
206	Ilipa	Second Punic War	P. Cornelius Scipio Africanus	Hasdrubal (son of Gisgo)
206	Astapa	Second Punic War	L. Marcius Septimus	Astapenses
206	Carteia, off	Second Punic War	C. Laelius	Adherbal
204	Salaeca	Second Punic War	P. Cornelius Scipio Africanus	Hanno (son of Hamilcar)
204	Croton	Second Punic War	Hannibal	P. Sempronius Tuditanus
203	Utica	Second Punic War	P. Cornelius Scipio Africanus	Hasdrubal (son of Gisgo) and Syphax
203	Great Plains	Second Punic War	P. Cornelius Scipio Africanus	Hasdrubal (son of Gisgo) and Syphax
203	Ampsaga R (Cirta)	Second Punic War	C. Laelius and Masinissa	Syphax
203	Utica, off	Second Punic War	P. Cornelius Scipio Africanus =	Carthaginians =
202	Zama	Second Punic War	P. Cornelius Scipio Africanus	Hannibal
201	Mutilum	Gallic Uprising	C. Ampius	Gauls (Boii)
200	Cremona	Gallic Uprising	L. Furius Purpurio	Gauls (Insubres) and Hamilcar
200	Athacus*	Second Macedonian War	P. Sulpicius Galba Maximus	Philip V (Macedonians)
200	Ottolobum*	Second Macedonian War	P. Sulpicius Galba Maximus	Philip V (Macedonians)
198	Aous R*	Second Macedonian War	T. Quinctius Flamininus	Philip V (Macedonians)
197	Cynoscephalae Ms*	Second Macedonian War	T. Quinctius Flamininus	Philip V (Macedonians)
197	Mincius R	Gallic Uprising	C. Cornelius Cethegus	Gauls
196	Comum	Gallic Uprising	M. Claudius Marcellus	Gauls (Insubres and Comenses)
195	Sparta*	War against Nabis	T. Quinctius Flamininus	Nabis (Spartans)
195	Turda	Spanish Wars	Q. Minucius Thermus	Budares and Baesadines (Spaniards)
195	Iliturgi (Tarracon.)	Spanish Wars	M. Helvius	Celtiberi
195	Emporiae	Spanish Wars	M. Porcius Cato	Spaniards
194	Mediolanum	Gallic Uprising	L. Valerius Flaccus	Gauls (Boii and Insubres)

BC	PLACE	WAR OR EPISODE	VICTORS	VANQUISHED
193	Mutina	Gallic Uprising	L. Cornelius Merula	Gauls (Boii)
193	Ilipa	Spanish Wars	P. Cornelius Scipio Nasica	Lusitani ·
193	Toletum	Spanish Wars	M. Fulvius Nobilior	Vaccaei, Vettones *et al.*
192	Pisae	Ligurian Wars	Q. Minucius Thermus	Ligures
191	Thermopylae P*	War against Antiochus	M'. Acilius Glabrio and M. Porcius Cato	Antiochus III
191	Corycus Pr*	War against Antiochus	C. Livius Salinator and Eumenes II	Polyxenidas
190	Panormus*	War against Antiochus	Polyxenidas	Pausistratus (Rhodians)
190	Phoenicus*	War against Antiochus	C. Livius Salinator	Phoenicus
190	Side, off*	War against Antiochus	Eudamus (Rhodians)	Hannibal
190	Myonnesus Pr, off*	War against Antiochus	L. Aemilius Regillus and Eudamus	Polyxenidas
190	Magnesia-ad-Sipylum*	War against Antiochus	Cn. Domitius Ahenobarbus and Eumenes II	Antiochus III
190	Lyco	Spanish Wars	Lusitani	L. Aemilius Paulus
189	Cuballum*	Galatian Expedition	Cn. Manlius Volso	Galatians
189	Olympus M*	Galatian Expedition	Cn. Manlius Volso	Galatians
189	Ancyra*	Galatian Expedition	Cn. Manlius Volso	Galatians
189	Magaba M*	Galatian Expedition	Cn. Manlius Volso	Galatians
188	Cypsela*		Cn. Manlius Volso	Thracians
188	Tempyra*		Cn. Manlius Volso	Thracians
186	Hasta	Spanish Wars	C. Atinius	Lusitani
186	Calagurris	Spanish Wars	L. Manlius Acidinus Fulvianus	Celtiberi
185	Toletum	Spanish Wars	Spaniards	(1) C. Calpurnius Piso (2) L. Quinctius Crispinus
185	Tagus R	Spanish Wars	(1) C. Calpurnius Piso (2) L. Quinctius Crispinus	Spaniards
181	Aebura	Spanish Wars	Q. Fulvius Flaccus	Celtiberi
181	Contrebia	Spanish Wars	Q. Fulvius Flaccus	Celtiberi
180	Manlian Pass	Spanish Wars	Q. Fulvius Flaccus	Celtiberi
179	Complega	Spanish Wars	Ti. Sempronius Gracchus	Celtiberi
179	Alce	Spanish Wars	Ti. Sempronius Gracchus	Celtiberi
179	Chaunus M	Spanish Wars	Ti. Sempronius Gracchus	Celtiberi
178	Timavus R	Istrian War	A. Manlius Volso	Istri
177	Scultenna R	Ligurian Wars	C. Claudius Pulcher	Ligures
176	Campi Macri	Ligurian Wars	Q. Petilius Spurinus	Ligures
173	Carystus	Ligurian Wars	M. Popilius Laenas	Ligures
171	Callinicus*	Third Macedonian War	Perseus (Macedonians)	P. Licinius Crassus
171	Phalanna*	Third Macedonian War	L. Pompeius	Perseus (Macedonians)
170	Uscana*	Third Macedonian War	Gentius (Illyrians)	Ap. Claudius Cento
168	Scodra*	Third Macedonian War	L. Anicius Gallus	Gentius (Illyrians)
168	Elpeus R*	Third Macedonian War	L. Aemilius Paulus	Perseus (Macedonians)
168	Pythium*	Third Macedonian War	P. Cornelius Scipio Nasica Corculum	Milo (Macedonians)
168	Pydna*	Third Macedonian War	L. Aemilius Paulus	Perseus (Macedonians)

BC	PLACE	WAR OR EPISODE	VICTORS	VANQUISHED
153	Numantia	Spanish Wars	Celtiberi	Q. Fulvius Nobilior
151	Cauca	Spanish Wars	L. Licinius Lucullus	Vaccaei
151	Intercatia	Spanish Wars	P. Cornelius Scipio Aemilianus	Vaccaean (single combat)
149	Nepheris	Third Punic War	Hasdrubal	M' (or M). Manilius
147	Carthage, off	Third Punic War	P. Cornelius Scipio Aemilianus	Carthaginians
147	Tribola	Viriathus' Uprising	Viriathus	M (or C). Vetilius
146	Alpheus R*	Achaean War	Romans	Critolaus (Achaeans)
146	Scarphea*	Achaean War	Q. Caecilius Metellus Macedonicus	Critolaus (Macedonians)
146	Chaeronea*	Achaean War	Q. Caecilius Metellus Macedonicus	Arcadians
146	Isthmus*	Achaean War	L. Mummius	Diaeus (Achaeans)
141	Termantia	Spanish Wars	Q. Pompeius =	Termestini =
140	Erisana	Viriathus' Uprising	Viriathus	Q. Fabius Maximus Servilianus
130	Leucae	Aristonicus' Uprising	Aristonicus	P. Licinius Crassus Dives Mucianus
130	Stratonicea	Aristonicus' Uprising	M. Perperna	Aristonicus
121	Vindalium	Conquest of Gallia Narb.	Cn. Domitius Ahenobarbus	Allobroges
121	Isara R	Conquest of Gallia Narb.	Q. Fabius Maximus Allobrogicus	Bituitus (Arverni and Allobroges)
113	Noreia	Invasion by Northmen	Cimbri	Cn. Papirius Carbo
109	Suthul	Jugurthine War	Jugurtha	A. Postumius Albinus
109	Muthul R	Jugurthine War	Q. Caecilius Metellus Numidicus	Jugurtha
106	Cirta	Jugurthine War	C. Marius	Jugurtha and Bocchus
105	Arausio	Invasion by Northmen	Cimbri and Teutones	(1) Cn. Manlius (2) Q. Servilius Caepio
103	Scirthaea	Second Servile War	L. Licinius Lucullus	Salvius (Tryphon)
102	Aquae Sextiae	Invasion by Northmen	C. Marius	Teutones and Ambrones
101	Vercellae	Invasion by Northmen	(1) C. Marius (2) Q. Lutatius Catulus	Cimbri
90	Aesernia	Social War	Vettius Scaton (Italians)	L. Julius Caesar
90	Aesernia	Social War	L. Cornelius Sulla Felix	Italians
90	Grumentum	Social War	Marcus Lamponius (Italians)	P. Licinius Crassus
90	Acerrae	Social War	L. Julius Caesar	C. Papius Mutilus (Italians)
90	Tolenus R: I	Social War	Vettius Scaton (Marsi)	P. Rutilius Lupus
90	Tolenus R: II	Social War	C. Marius	Vettius Scaton (Marsi)
90	Teanum Sidicinum	Social War	Marius Egnatius (Samnites)	L. Julius Caesar
90	Falernus M	Social War	Italians	Cn. Pompeius Strabo
90	Firmum	Social War	Cn. Pompeius Strabo	Lafrenius (Italians)
89	Asculum Picenum	Social War	Cn. Pompeius Strabo	Vidacilius (Picentes)
89	Fucinus L	Social War	Marsi	L. Porcius Cato
89	Nola	Social War	L. Cornelius Sulla Felix	L. Cluentius (Italians)
89	Canusium	Social War	Samnites	C. Cosconius
89	Teanus R	Social War	Q. Caecilius Metellus Pius	Poppaedius Silo (Marsi)
88	Esquiline Forum	First Civil War	(1) L. Cornelius Sulla Felix (2) Q. Pompeius	(1) C. Marius (2) P. Sulpicius Rufus
88	Amnias R	First Mithridatic War	(1) Neoptolemus (2) Archelaus	Nicomedes IV (Bithynia)
88	Protopachium	First Mithridatic War	Neoptolemus	M'. Aquilius

BC	PLACE	WAR OR EPISODE	VICTORS	VANQUISHED
86	Chaeronea	First Mithridatic War	L. Cornelius Sulla Felix	Archelaus
86	Orchomenus	First Mithridatic War	L. Cornelius Sulla Felix	Archelaus
85	Tenedos Isl	First Mithridatic War	L. Licinius Lucullus	Neoptolemus
83	Canusium	First Civil War	L. Cornelius Sulla Felix	C. Norbanus
83	Capua	First Civil War	L. Cornelius Sulla Felix	(1) C. Norbanus
				(2) L. Cornelius Scipio Asiaticus
82	Aesis R	First Civil War	Cn. Pompeius Magnus	Carinas
82	Sacriportus	First Civil War	L. Cornelius Sulla Felix	C. Marius
82	Clanis R	First Civil War	L. Cornelius Sulla Felix	Cn. Papirius Carbo
82	Saturnia	First Civil War	L. Cornelius Sulla Felix	Marians
82	Clusium	First Civil War	L. Cornelius Sulla Felix	Cn. Papirius Carbo
82	Spoletium	First Civil War	Cn. Pompeius Magnus	Carinas
82	Faventia	First Civil War	Q. Caecilius Metellus Pius	(1) Cn. Papirius Carbo
				(2) C. Norbanus
82	Placentia	First Civil War	M. Lucullus	Cn. Papirius Carbo's Forces
82	Clusium	First Civil War	Cn. Pompeius Magnus	Cn. Papirius Carbo's Forces
82	Colline Gate	First Civil War	L. Cornelius Sulla Felix	(1) Papirius Carbo's Generals
				(2) Telesinus (Samnites)
80	Baetis R	Sertorian War	Q. Sertorius	L. Fufidius
79	Ana R	Sertorian War	L. Hirtuleius	M. Domitius Calvinus
78	Segovia	Sertorian War	L. Hirtuleius	L. Manlius
77	Milvian Bridge	Lepidus' Revolt	Q. Lutatius Catulus	M. Aemilius Lepidus
76	Lauro	Sertorian War	Q. Sertorius	Cn. Pompeius Magnus
75	Italica	Sertorian War	Q. Caecilius Metellus Pius	L. Hirtuleius
75	Valentia	Sertorian War	Cn. Pompeius Magnus	(1) C. Herennius
				(2) M. Perperna Veiento
75	Sucro R	Sertorian War	Q. Sertorius	Cn. Pompeius Magnus
75	Turia R	Sertorian War	(1) Cn. Pompeius Magnus	Q. Sertorius
			(2) Q. Caecilius Metellus Pius	
75	Saguntum	Sertorian War	(1) Cn. Pompeius Magnus	(1) Q. Sertorius
			(2) Q. Caecilius Metellus Pius	(2) M. Perperna Veiento
74	Calagurris	Sertorian War	Q. Sertorius	Cn. Pompeius Magnus
74	Chalcedon	Third Mithridatic War	Mithridates VI (Pontus)	M. Aurelius Cotta
74	Rhyndacus R	Third Mithridatic War	L. Licinius Lucullus	Mithridates VI (Pontus)
74	Aesepus R	Third Mithridatic War	L. Licinius Lucullus	Mithridates VI (Pontus)
73	Lemnos Isl	Third Mithridatic War	L. Licinius Lucullus	M. Marius *et al.*
73	Vesuvius M	Third Servile War	Spartacus	(1) C. Claudius Glaber
				(2) P. Varenus
72	Cabira	Third Mithridatic War	L. Licinius Lucullus' Forces	Mithridates VI (Pontus)
72	Garganus M	Third Servile War	L. Gellius Publicola	Crixus (Spartacus)
71	Camalatrum	Third Servile War	M. Licinius Crassus Dives	Castus and Cannicus (Spartacus)
71	Cantenna M	Third Servile War	M. Licinius Crassus Dives	Spartacus
71	Petelia	Third Servile War	Spartacus	Crassus' Lieutenants
71	Silarus R	Third Servile War	M. Licinius Crassus Dives	Spartacus
69	Cydonia	Third Mithridatic War	Q. Caecilius Metellus Creticus	Lasthenes (Cretans)
69	Tigranocerta	Third Mithridatic War	L. Licinius Lucullus	Tigranes the Great (Armenia)

BC	PLACE	WAR OR EPISODE	VICTORS	VANQUISHED
68	Arsanias R	Third Mithridatic War	L. Licinius Lucullus	Tigranes the Great (Armenia)
68	Comana Pontica	Third Mithridatic War	C. Valerius Triarius	Mithridates VI (Pontus)
67	Zela	Third Mithridatic War	Mithridates VI (Pontus)	C. Valerius Triarius
67	Coracesium	War against Pirates	Cn. Pompeius Magnus	Pirates
66	Nicopolis	Third Mithridatic War	Cn. Pompeius Magnus	Mithridates VI (Pontus)
66	Cyrus R	Third Mithridatic War	Cn. Pompeius Magnus	Oroeses (Albania)
65	Abas R	Third Mithridatic War	Cn. Pompeius Magnus	Oroeses (Albania)
62	Pistoria	Catiline Conspiracy	M. Petreius	L. Sergius Catilina
61	Solonium	Gallic Uprising	(1) L. Marius (2) Ser. Sulpicius Galba	Gauls (Allobroges)
61	Admagetobriga	Germanic Incursion	Ariovistus (Suebi)	Gauls
58	Arar R	Gallic War	C. Julius Caesar	Tigurini (Helvetii)
58	Bibracte	Gallic War	C. Julius Caesar	Helvetii
58	*Plain of Alsace*	Gallic War	C. Julius Caesar	Ariovistus
57	Axona R	Gallic War	C. Julius Caesar	Belgae
57	Sabis R	Gallic War	C.Julius Caesar	Nervii (Belgae)
57	Octodurus	Gallic War	Ser. Sulpicius Galba	Seduni and Veragri
57	Jerusalem	Jewish Revolt	A. Gabinius	Alexander (son of Aristobulus)
56	*Morbihan Gulf*	Gallic War	D. Junius Brutus	Gauls (Veneti)
56	Sotium	Gallic War	P. Licinius Crassus	Sotiates
55	Tabor M	Jewish Revolt	A. Gabinius	Alexander (son of Aristobulus)
53	Carrhae	Parthian War	M. Licinius Crassus Dives	Surenas (Parthians)
52	Noviodunum	Gallic War	C. Julius Caesar	Vercingetorix (Gauls)
52	Gergovia	Gallic War	Vercingetorix (Gauls)	C. Julius Caesar
52	Lutetia Parisiorum	Gallic War	T. Labienus	Camulogenus (Gauls)
52	Alesia	Gallic War	C. Julius Caesar	Vercingetorix (Gauls)
51	Uxellodunum	Gallic War	C. Caninius Rebilus	Drappes and Lucterius
51	Antigonea	Parthian War	C. Cassius Longinus	Osaces (Parthians)
51	Amanus M		M. Tullius Cicero	Amanienses
49	Massilia	Second Civil War	D. Junius Brutus	L. Domitius Ahenobarbus
49	Sicoris R	Second Civil War	L. Afranius	C. Fabius
49	Ilerda	Second Civil War	C. Julius Caesar	(1) L. Afranius (2) M. Petreius
49	Utica	Second Civil War	C. Scribonius Curio	P. Attius Varus
49	Bagradas R	Second Civil War	Saburra (Numidians)	C. Scribonius Curio
48	Salonae	Second Civil War	A. Gabinius	M. Octavius
48	Dyrrhachium	Second Civil War	Cn. Pompeius Magnus	C. Julius Caesar
48	Pharsalus	Second Civil War	C. Julius Caesar	Cn. Pompeius Magnus
47	Salonae	Second Civil War	Dalmatians	M. Octavius
47	Tauris Isl	Second Civil War	P. Vatinius	M. Octavius
47	Alexandria	Alexandrian War	Euphranor	Alexandrians
47	Nilus R	Alexandrian War	C. Julius Caesar	Ptolemy XIII
47	Nicopolis	Revolt of Pharnaces	Pharnaces	Cn. Domitius Calvinus
47	Zela	Revolt of Pharnaces	C. Julius Caesar	Pharnaces
46	Hadrumentum	Second Civil War	Numidians	C. Julius Caesar
46	Ruspina	Second Civil War	T. Labienus	C. Julius Caesar
46	Thapsus	Second Civil War	C. Julius Caesar	Q. Caecilius Metellus Pius Scipio

BC	PLACE	WAR OR EPISODE	VICTORS	VANQUISHED
46	Hippo Regius	Second Civil War	P. Sittius	Q. Caecilius Metellus Pius Scipio
46	Carteia, off	Second Civil War	C. Didius	P. Attius Varus
45	Munda	Second Civil War	C. Julius Caesar	Cn. Pompeius Magnus (son)
43	Forum Gallorum: I	War of Mutina	M. Antonius	(1) C. Vibius Pansa Caetronianus (2) D. Carfulenus
43	Forum Gallorum: II	War of Mutina	A. Hirtius	M. Antonius
43	Mutina	War of Mutina	(1) C. Octavianus (2) A. Hirtius	M. Antonius
42	Laodicea	Campaign of Cassius	C. Cassius Longinus	P. Cornelius Dolabella
42	Myndus, off	Campaign of Cassius	C. Cassius Longinus	Alexander and Mnaseas (Rhodians)
42	Rhodes, off	Campaign of Cassius	C. Cassius Longinus	Rhodians
42	Scyllaeum Pr, off	War against Pompeius	Sex. Pompeius Magnus Pius	Q. Salvidienus Rufus
42	Philippi: I	Second Triumvirate	(1) M. Antonius (2) M. Junius Brutus	(1) C. Cassius Longinus (2) C. Octavianus
42	Philippi: II	Second Triumvirate	M. Antonius	M. Junius Brutus
39	Cilician Gates	Parthian War	P. Ventidius Bassus	Parthians
39	Amanus M	Parthian War	P. Ventidius Bassus	Phranapates (Parthians)
38	Gindarus	Parthian War	P. Ventidius Bassus	Pacorus (Parthians)
38	Cumae, off	War against Pompeius	Menecrates	Menodorus and Calvinius Sabinus
36	Mylae, off	War against Pompeius	M. Vipsanius Agrippa	Demochares (or Papias)
36	Tauromenium, off	War against Pompeius	Sex. Pompeius Magnus Pius	C. Octavianus
36	Naulochus, off	War against Pompeius	M. Vipsanius Agrippa	Sex. Pompeius Magnus Pius
36	Phraaspa	Parthian War	M. Antonius =	Phraates IV (Parthia) =
31	Actium Pr, off	War against Cleopatra	C. Octavianus	M. Antonius and Cleopatra VII

Battles of The Roman World

INTRODUCTION

From the days of the monarchy Rome aspired to be the controlling influence over the whole of Italy. Her expansion resulted in part from peaceful processes of amalgamation and alliance but notably from wars. The history of the Republic in the fifth and fourth centuries reads like a seemingly unending succession of revolts and reprisals, sieges and sorties, truces and trickeries. Many of the early engagements are known only from passing mentions. Those that have passed into recorded 'history' have done so with a varying admixture of legendary embellishment or fictitious material or both. How much is legend, fiction or fact is a question which has been – and still is – a matter of dispute. The problem has been discussed at more length in the section, Reliability of Data (p. 32).

Rome was not involved in any conflicts outside Italy for more than two centuries after the foundation of the Republic, although latterly the Tarentines invited a general and his army from Greece to fight their war with Rome for them. By the end of this time Rome controlled the whole of peninsular Italy. The scenario changed with the advent of the Punic Wars, which took Rome overseas with a vengeance.

* * * * * * *

POMETIA (502)[1]

Pometia (or Suessa Pometia), a Latin colony, threw off its allegiance to Rome and joined the Auruncans. The Romans promptly invaded Auruncan territory and smashed the natives in a blood bath. The following year they turned their whole attention to Pometia, which they attempted to reduce by assault and battery. In rage and desperation the occupants poured out of the town carrying firebrands, with which they set fire to the

siege-engines and created havoc. They inflicted heavy casualties on the enemy, nearly killing one of the two consuls, and they forced the Romans to withdraw and lick their wounds.

Pometia was situated close to the Pomptinae Paludes [*Pontine Marshes*], to which it gave its name, but the exact location is undefined.
Livy, 2: 16(8–9)

REGILLUS L (496)

The prospect of war with the Latins had been looming for some time and had reached inevitable proportions. Aulus Postumius, who had been granted dictatorial powers as the sole commander-in-chief, proceeded with a powerful army of around 24,000 men to Lake Regillus, about 15 miles south-east of Rome. There he met the Latin forces, which were said to be about 40,000 strong with 3,000 horse. It was said that the hated Tarquins were with the Latins, including the old Tarquinius Superbus in person and in his 90s. The Tarquin presence further inflamed the passions of the Romans, whose initial onslaught caused the Latins to give ground. A company of Roman exiles was sent to reinforce the Latin front and they managed to push the Romans back. At this point Postumius ordered his personal guard of picked cavalry to cut down every Roman soldier who was trying to save his skin. This had the desired effect. Attacked from front and rear the fleeing Romans turned and faced the enemy, whereupon the dictator's cavalry, fresh and vigorous, dismounted and joined the fight on foot. To urge his men to maximum effort, the dictator adopted the novel stratagem of seizing a standard and hurling it into the midst of the enemy ranks for his men to recover. No ploy was more calculated to spur a Roman soldier to frenzy. The Latins broke and fled, pursued and cut down by their opponents. According to Dionysius only 10,000 Latins returned to their homes; there are no figures for the Roman losses.

Lake Regillus exists no longer. Its most likely site is thought to have been the modern *Pantano*

---

[1] Bracketed figures in the subtitles are dates, all of which are BC.
[2] The word 'above' in brackets refers throughout to the immediately preceding entry.

Secco, a volcanic depression which was drained in the seventeenth century.

Livy, 2:19–20; Dionysius of Halicarnassus, Roman Antiquities, *6: 4–12; Florus 1: 5(1–4)*

ARICIA (495)

The Auruncans were the aggressors in a battle with the Romans under their consul Publius Servilius. The armies met near Aricia [*Ariccia*], about 15 miles south-east of Rome. Both sides encamped on nearby hills before advancing to the plain, where the Romans routed their adversaries.

Livy, 2: 26(4–6); Dionysius of Halicarnassus, Roman Antiquities, *6: 32(3)–33*

ANTIUM (482)

The Volscians decided to make war upon Rome. Learning of their intentions, the Romans sent the consul Lucius Aemilius at the head of an army against Antium [*Anzio*], where he encamped on a hill opposite the enemy. When the two sides descended to level ground to fight, the battle was fiercely contested with no advantage either way. Both sides stood firm until eventually the Volscians deceived their opponents by starting to give ground and retreat. The Romans, assuming that they were winning, followed in an undisciplined fashion, some of them stopping to strip the corpses and to plunder. When the Volscians saw this, they retired uphill as far as their camp and then faced about and stood firm. At this point their comrades who had been left behind in the camp rushed out and joined in the fight. The roles were now reversed. The Romans, fighting at a disadvantage, fled; the Volscians pursued, causing a heavy slaughter.

Dionysius of Halicarnassus, Roman Antiquities, *8: 83(3)–85(3)*

LONGULA (482)

On the night after their reverse at Antium (above)[2] the Roman consul Lucius Aemilius led his men away in silence, unnoticed by the enemy. The following afternoon he encamped on top of a hill near Longula, about 10 miles from Antium. When the Volscians heard of this move and were told that the enemy were few in number and had many wounded, they abandoned their celebrations and marched out, encamping opposite the Romans. They tried to pull down the palisades but were eventually repulsed by the Roman cavalry, who sallied out against them on foot, followed by the veteran *triarii*. In the following days the Volscians, who greatly outnumbered the Romans, repeatedly

challenged them to fight, but the challenge was declined by the consul. The situation was saved by the other consul, Caeso Fabius, who sent reinforcements to the besieged Lucius. These managed to enter the camp unperceived by the enemy. When the enemy next attacked the camp, the Romans pulled down the ramparts and fell upon them. The Volscians, fighting uphill, were hurled back with many losses and took to flight.

Dionysius of Halicarnassus, Roman Antiquities, *8: 85(4)–86*

VEII (480)

The Veientes were bent on war with Rome, which at this time was full of internal dissensions. The soldiers were disobeying orders, and in a recent campaign they had actually walked off the battlefield to make sure that their commander did not get the credit for a victory! With considerable misgivings the two consuls, Marcus Fabius and Gnaeus Manlius, marched against the Veientes and their Etruscan allies but hesitated to give battle. They were more afraid of the actions of their own troops than of the enemy. Day after day the Veientes taunted the Romans with cowardice until, as their consuls hoped, their soldiers became so incensed that they demanded to be led out to fight. Each man took an oath to win or die. In the battle the fighting was ferocious and its course seesawed with many changes of tide and fortune. It lasted from noon until sunset, both sides sustaining heavy losses. The consul Manlius was slain, as also was a former consul, Quintus Fabius. But the ultimate victory went to the Romans, whose foe abandoned their camp and withdrew during the night.

Livy, 2: 44(7)–47(9); Dionysius of Halicarnassus, Roman Antiquities, *9: 5–13(2)*

CREMERA R (477)

The Veientes, the most powerful community in Etruria, were a constant thorn in the Roman side, distracting her by continual acts of provocation and preventing her from giving her attention elsewhere. In view of this situation one of the Roman clans, the Fabii, offered to muster a small army from the midst of their family and to police the border with Veii. They built a fort on the banks of the Cremera [*Fosso della Valchetta*], a stream which flows into the Tiber about 5 miles north of Rome. In many raids and skirmishes they were successful, but the Veii eventually set a trap for them, luring them out into an ambush and then surrounding them. The Fabians gathered in a

wedge formation and managed to break out of the circle and gain some high ground but to no avail. The enemy sent a force round behind the hill and took them in the rear. There was only one Fabian survivor – a mere boy. Every man among the band was killed, said to be 306 in number.
Livy, 2: 49(8–50); Dionysius of Halicarnassus, Roman Antiquities, **9**: 19–21

TEMPLE OF HOPE (477)
After annihilating the Fabii at the River Cremera (above), the Etruscans pushed southward and occupied the Janiculan hill on the doorstep of Rome. The consul Gaius Horatius was immediately recalled from operations against the Volscians, and a battle was fought about 1 mile from the city, near the Temple of Hope. Livy describes the result as indecisive. Dionysius, on the other hand, refers to the enemy being overcome and thrown back.
Livy, 2: 51(2); Dionysius of Halicarnassus, Roman Antiquities, **9**: 24(4)

COLLINE GATE (477)
Almost immediately after the battle near the Temple of Hope a further encounter, even closer to the city, took place against the Etruscans at the Porta Collina. According to Livy the Roman troops won only a slight advantage. Nevertheless, it boosted their morale and staved off the immediate threat.
Livy, 2: 51(2); Dionysius of Halicarnassus, Roman Antiquities, **9**: 24(4)

JANICULUM (476)
The Etruscans' modest reverses at the Temple of Hope and the Colline Gate in the previous year did nothing to stop their marauding. One night they crossed the Tiber and attacked the camp of the consul Servilius. They were repelled with heavy losses and struggled back to the Janiculan hill, but Servilius followed them and set up camp at the base of it. The next day he rashly attempted to storm the enemy position on top of the hill, an encounter which would have been a complete disaster for Rome but for the timely arrival of his colleague Verginius. Caught between two fires, the enemy was badly mangled, a result which ended the current series of hostilities in the vicinity of Rome itself.
Livy, 2: 51(6–9)

VEII (475)
War broke out again with the Veientes, with whom the Sabines had joined forces. The consul Valerius was sent to Veii, 12 miles north of Rome, with an army reinforced with allied contingents. He made an immediate assault upon the Sabines who had assumed a position just outside the town walls. The attack took the enemy by complete surprise. Valerius gained possession of the gate and his men poured into the town and massacred the inhabitants. Thus both Veientes and Sabini, Rome's two most powerful foes, were defeated at one fell swoop.
Livy, 2: 53(1–3)

ANTIUM (468)
In operations against the Volscians there was a bitter struggle about 4 miles from Antium [*Anzio*]. The Romans were outnumbered and would have fallen back if the consul, Titus Quinctius, had not put fresh heart into his men by telling them – falsely – that their other wing was winning. Having gained the advantage, he did not dare to push forward too hard but withdrew to his camp. All was quiet for a day or two until the enemy, who had been reinforced, suddenly launched a night attack on the Roman camp. Livy reports that the consul, with presence of mind, took a body of men accompanied by trumpeters on horseback outside the defences and instructed them to move about and make a lot of noise. This deceived the enemy until dawn when the Romans, being rested and fresh, formed battle lines against the sleepless enemy. It was a bitter struggle, but the enemy eventually withdrew to higher ground where the battle continued to rage. After sustaining heavy losses the Romans eventually gained the summit and the enemy's camp. The Volscians fled and were pursued to Antium, which surrendered a few days later.
Dionysius of Halicarnassus, Roman Antiquities, **9**: 57–58; *Livy, 2: 64(5)–65*

ALGIDUS M (465)
The Aequians were causing trouble and so the consul Quintus Fabius marched against them and defeated them. A truce was granted but the enemy promptly broke it by making a raid into Latium. A campaign against them was begun and dragged on into its third year, by which time Quintus Fabius was again one of the consuls. He gave them a stern warning in the hope that his name as their previous victor would bring them to heel. When the Aequians paid no heed – apart from manhandling the Roman envoys – both consuls led their armies to Algidus [*Compatri*] against them. A fierce battle

ensued in which no quarter was given on either side. The Aequians were forced to retreat, still refusing to admit defeat. Instead, they made a sudden violent incursion across the border, which caused considerable alarm in Rome where it was magnified out of all proportion. The consul Titus Quinctius took the matter in hand, calmly pointing out that the enemy had already been defeated. He marched to the frontier but found no enemy on Roman soil. In the meantime, Fabius, knowing the route the enemy would take, had fallen upon them. They were so impeded by the plunder that they had amassed during their raid that they were scarcely able to move. Few of them escaped alive.
Livy, 3: 2(6)–3(8)

ALGIDUS M (458)

Once again the Aequians menaced Rome. They broke a truce, which had been made only the previous year, and fortified a position on Mount Algidus [*M. Compatri*] about 14 miles south-east of the city. The consul Minucius was sent out to attack them but he was too cautious or timid to leave the fortifications of his camp. The Aequians promptly walled him in with earthworks, which caused a state of panic in Rome. Tradition maintains that the Romans summoned their hero Lucius Quinctius Cincinnatus from his farm and appointed him dictator to deal with the emergency. He levied an army and ordered each man to collect and bring a dozen stakes. On Algidus, he deployed his men in a circle around the Aequian camp and got each man to dig a trench and fix his stake, thereby putting the besieger under siege with a continuous trench and palisade. As soon as Minucius realized that help was at hand, he attacked the enemy from the inside of their circle. This left the dictator free to complete the circumvallation before assaulting the enemy's outer defences. Attacked from both sides the Aequians surrendered and were made to pass under the yoke.
Livy, 3: 26–28

ALGIDUS M (455)

Alarming news reached Rome to the effect that Tusculum, 12 miles south-east of the city, had been attacked by the Aequians. The Tusculans had recently rendered good services to Rome, and so it was a matter of honour to give them assistance. Both consuls were sent out and they made contact with the enemy at their usual base on Mount Algidus. In the subsequent battle the Aequians were badly trounced and lost 7,000 men, according to Livy.

Dionysius gives a rather different and more elaborate account of an action which seems, however, to be the same one by virtue of the similarity of causation and circumstance. In his version, the encounter took place about 4 miles from Antium [*Anzio*] as the Aequians were returning home. They were encamped on top of a steep hill. Romilius, the Roman consul in charge, asked a seasoned veteran called Siccius, who had volunteered for service with a band of 800 older men, to climb straight up the hill and attack the enemy camp – an act of certain death. Siccius, who was something of a braggart, was goaded into acceptance but had different ideas. He led his men to the top by a circuitous sheltered track, captured the enemy camp, and then proceeded to descend and attack the main body of the enemy in the rear. According to this version the Roman success was entirely attributable to Siccius and his little band of seasoned veterans.
Livy, 3: 31(3–4); Dionysius of Halicarnassus, Roman Antiquities, 10: 43–47

ALGIDUS M (449)

Six years after their defeat of 455 (above), the Aequians joined forces with the Volscians on Mount Algidus [*M. Compatri*]. The consul Valerius, who was sent out to deal with them, trod cautiously. He set up camp about a mile from the enemy and doggedly refused to respond to their challenges to fight. The enemy accepted this as weakness and started pillaging the countryside in a disorderly way, giving Valerius the opportunity he had been waiting for to attack. The enemy garrison sallied out to meet him but were still in a disorderly state when the attack struck home. After a brisk struggle the consul ordered his cavalry to charge. Some of them broke clean through the enemy lines while others skirted round and cut off their retreat. Few escaped.
Livy, 3: 60–61(10); Dionysius of Halicarnassus, Roman Antiquities, 11: 47

FIDENAE (437)

In 437 Fidenae, a town 5 miles north of Rome, severed its allegiance to Rome and joined up with the Etruscans in Veii [*Isola Farnese*], 10 miles to the north-west. To add to this disloyalty the Fidenates murdered four Roman envoys. The Romans marched out against the Veientes and won a costly victory south of the river Anio [*Aniene*] on Roman territory, but it was enough to force the enemy to withdraw back across the river. They took up position before the walls of Fidenae.

To cope with the emergency the Romans appointed a dictator, Mamercus Aemilius, who camped a few miles south of the enemy and then marched out to give battle. The two armies faced each other in the space between their camps. The action was begun by the dictator, who ordered the cavalry to charge, followed by the infantry. In the ensuing mêlée the King of Veii, who stood out as a champion fighter, was killed. This so disheartened the Etruscans that they fled and were cut down by the Romans in pursuit.
Livy, 4: 17(6)–19

NOMENTUM (435)
Rome was plagued with a serious epidemic which brought her almost to a standstill. To make matters worse the men of Fidenae chose this moment to venture into Roman territory. The aggressors' allies, the Veientes, sent them reinforcements, and their combined armies advanced almost to the Colline Gate. To meet the emergency the senate appointed a dictator, Quintus Servilius, who promptly ordered a muster of every man who was in a fit state to bear arms. This caused the enemy to have second thoughts and they started to withdraw, but Servilius pursued them and inflicted a defeat on them near Nomentum [*Mentana*], 12 miles north-east of Rome. The enemy found refuge in Fidenae, where Servilius proceeded to undermine the walls with saps and capture the town.
Livy, 4: 21(6)–22(2)

ALGIDUS M (431)
The Volscians and Aequians were again intent on war and on a larger scale than before. They raised two large armies and took up separate positions on Mount Algidus [*M. Compatri*] about 14 miles south-east of Rome. The two Roman consuls in that year did not see eye to eye on anything and were continually bickering. In consequence, the senate appointed a dictator, Aulus Postumius Tubertus, to raise an army and to take supreme charge. Rome's allies were also told to levy troops. On Algidus, the Romans and their allies followed the enemy's precedent by setting up two encampments. Hostilities started with almost continuous skirmishing as the dictator encouraged his men to flex their muscles. It also proved to the enemy that they were unlikely to win in a straight fight. Instead, they resorted to a night attack on the consul's camp, as a result of which one of their own camps was largely deserted. The dictator, whose camp was unassailed, sent troops to storm it and captured it almost without a fight. The

dictator himself then took another body of men around the outside of the field and attacked the enemy's rear. The enemy were surrounded, but under the leadership of one heroic stalwart they rallied and made a brave stand. They were eventually forced to surrender and every man was sold into slavery.
Livy, 4: 26–29(4)

FIDENAE (426)
The Veientes were dissatisfied with some minor defeat which they inflicted on the Romans. They wanted more action and sought help from the neighbouring communities. The Fidenates alone favoured renewed hostilities and joined them; or rather the Veientes joined Fidenae, the town which they had decided to use as their joint base. Mamercus Aemilius, the dictator for this emergency, marched out from Rome and encamped a mile and a half south of Fidenae, where he was protected by hills on his right and the Tiber on his left. He then sent out a detachment to occupy a ridge in the enemy's rear, behind which his men would be screened. Next morning the Veientes took the field and Mamercus ordered his infantry out to oppose them at the double. After a tremendous clash the Veientes had begun to yield when suddenly a vast horde of creatures poured out of Fidenae waving firebrands. The Romans were temporarily nonplussed by this novel form of warfare but the dictator rallied them, telling his men either to seize the torches or to use their swords against the otherwise unarmed multitude. At this point, the detachment on the ridge was summoned by the dictator and suddenly appeared in the enemy's rear. The Veientes were surrounded and fled, mostly to the Tiber where many were cut down or drowned. The Fidenates managed to escape through their camp and into the town, but the pursuing Romans forced their way in too. After further fighting the occupants surrendered.
Livy, 4: 31(6)–33

ALGIDUS M (418)
At the beginning of the year a delegation from Tusculum reported to Rome that a new enemy, the town of Labici, had conspired with an Aequian force to raid their territory and was at that time encamped on Mount Algidus. War was declared on Labici, and an army was sent out under the leadership of two of the military tribunes, Lucius Sergius and Marcus Papirius. The trouble was that the tribunes could not agree on anything and were forced to come to an arrangement whereby they

assumed command in turn on alternate days. A divided command had caused defeats in the past and it did so again. When the enemy withdrew to their ramparts, feigning fear, the Romans incautiously followed them up and were caught off guard by an Aequian attack, which forced them in headlong flight down a gully. The remnants of the army on the field made for Tusculum.
Livy, 4: 45(5)–46(7)

ALGIDUS M (418)
The senate responded to the debacle on Algidus (above) by appointing a dictator, Quintus Servilius Priscus, who led a reserve army to Algidus and ordered the forces who had fled to Tusculum to join him. This time it was the enemy who were over-confident. One Roman cavalry charge followed by a massed infantry attack disorganized them so completely that they fled to their camp, which was assaulted by the Romans and captured with ease. The survivors took refuge in Labici, which the dictator proceeded to capture and sack.
Livy, 4: 46(8)–47(6)

GURASIUM (391)
Diodorus reports a bloody battle at Gurasium against the Volscians, many of whom were killed. The place is unknown and Livy does not mention the incident.
Diodorus, 14: 109(7)

ALLIA R (390, July 18) – Gallic Invasion
At this point in the early history of Rome a new foe appeared. There was a mass migration of Gallic tribes across the Alps and down through Italy as far as Rome itself. The Romans appeared to be unaware of the magnitude of this invasion or of its speed of advance. They did not even appoint a dictator. Their army of 40,000 foot, under a tribune or two, marched out and had covered a bare 11 miles before it encountered the Gauls at the confluence of the Allia and Tiber rivers. The ground around was swarming with the Gallic horde, reported to be about 70,000 in number. The tribunes extended their lines as far and as thinly as they dared, and some reserves were posted on high ground to one side. The Gallic chieftain, Brennus, attacked the reserves first to prevent them from descending on his flank when he turned his attention to the main Roman body. But this body did not wait. The reserves, driven from the hills, descended *en masse* to their colleagues in the plain, who were thrown into confusion. They fled in blind panic and were cut down as they fled. Men

on the wing nearest the river tried to get across and about half of them reached Veii. Those on the opposite wing made for Rome where survivors shut themselves up in the Citadel. The battle and the day have gone down as the blackest in early Roman history.

The date 390 is the conventional Varronian date for the battle of the Allia and the subsequent sack of Rome (below). The chronology of Polybius places these events in 387/6, which many authorities regard as nearer the truth.
Livy, 5: 37(6)–38; Diodorus, 14: 114–115(2); Plutarch, Camillus, 18(4)–19(1)

ROME (390) – Gallic Invasion
After their victory at the river Allia (above), the Gauls swept on to Rome, which was undefended apart from the fortress on the Capitol to which every man capable of fighting had repaired. The Gauls entered the open city without opposition and proceeded to sack it. The Livian version of events proceeds as follows. Matters were looking up in Veii by virtue of its reinforcement by soldiers who had fled there from the Allia and from Rome, in addition to volunteers from surrounding communities. All they lacked was a commander. The obvious choice was the veteran soldier, Camillus, who had once been dictator and who was living in voluntary exile in Ardea, 24 miles south of Rome. He was ready to act if the senate agreed. A messenger was therefore sent to the senate in the Citadel, which approved the request and appointed Camillus as dictator for the second time. Camillus had already, on his own initiative, rallied the Ardeans and destroyed a neighbouring Gallic camp while its occupants slept in the middle of the night. He now summoned the force from Veii to join him and marched on Rome, arriving just when the senate was bargaining with Brennus and had agreed to give him 1,000 lb. of gold in exchange for his departure. Camillus put a stop to that. The city, full of rubble, was no place for a major encounter but the Gauls were taken by surprise and were scattered. A second encounter was then fought later 8 miles to the east on the road to Gabii. The enemy army was annihilated. It was a decisive triumph for the Romans which, in conjunction with the subsequent rebuilding of the City which Camillus organized, earned for him the title of Second Founder of Rome.

Such is the tale – doubtless largely legend – perpetuated in tradition and told by Livy. A very different version is given by Diodorus in which Camillus does not feature in the City. The Gauls

are bought off with gold and take themselves away. However, the gold is recovered after a defeat of the Gauls by Camillus shortly afterwards (Veascium, 390). The truth of the matter probably rests with Polybius in his assertion that the Gauls negotiated a treaty with the Romans and returned home safely. Livy himself says as much in a later passage. Polybius points out that the Gauls had good reason to secure a quick settlement and a hasty departure because their own country had just been invaded.
Livy, 5: 49(4–5) and 10: 16(6); Plutarch, Camillus, 22–29; Diodorus, 14: 116; Polybius, 2:18(1–3)

VEASCIUM (390) – Gallic Invasion
In the account of Diodorus, the Gauls, on their way from Rome after sacking it, laid siege to the city of Veascium, a place now unknown. The dictator Camillus attacked them, killed most of them and regained possession of the gold which had been paid to the Gauls as the price for their departure from Rome. This is probably a legendary embellishment, which is at variance with the equally suspect Livian version (above). The engagement, if it occurred, suggests that Veascium might have been the place a few miles east of the City on the road to Gabii where Livy places a final encounter between Camillus and the Gauls.
Diodorus, 14: 117(5)

LANUVIUM (389)
The Volscians and Etruscans did not give Rome long to recover from the sack of the City. They saw their chance of eliminating her completely in her enfeebled state. To combat the threat, the veteran Camillus was again appointed dictator, this for the third time. He mustered every available able-bodied man and youth and set out to attack the Volscian camp near Lanuvium [*Lanuvio*], south of Mount Alban [*Colli Albani*]. The news that Camillus was in command in person caused such a panic among the Volscians that they blockaded themselves behind an impenetrable barricade of logs. Camillus ordered his men to fire the barricade. They burnt a way through it, entered the enemy camp and routed the occupants. They then pursued the fugitives and laid waste their territory until the Volscians at last surrendered – after 70 years of repeated warfare.

Diodorus and Plutarch give a different account of the defeat of the Volscians in a very different setting (Campus Martius, below). It seems virtually certain, however, that all three historians are referring to the same battle because they all refer to the appointment of Camillus as dictator for the third time, the use of incendiary tactics, and the total subjugation of the Volsci.
Livy, 6: 2

CAMPUS MARTIUS (389)
This engagement is clearly the same decisive battle against the Volscians as the one at Lanuvium (above) described by Livy, although in a very different guise and setting. According to Diodorus and Plutarch the Volscians descended on Rome, in contrast to the Romans marching against them. Vastly superior in numbers, they were opposed by a Roman force encamped on the Campus Martius (Diodorus) or Mount Marcius (Plutarch). A plea was sent to the City for help and Camillus, appointed dictator for the third time, enrolled every available man. With this relief force he marched out at night and took up a position in the enemy's rear. He then set fire to the enemy's camp, driving the Volscians out into the arms of the original force, which cut them down almost to a man.
Diodorus, 14: 117(1–3); Plutarch, Camillus, 34

BOLA (389)
After defeating the Volscians, Camillus proceeded against the Aequi and encountered their army near Bola, north-east of Mount Algidus [*M. Compatri*]. He took them by surprise and slew most of them, according to Diodorus, capturing both the enemy camp and the town in the process. From Bola he marched against the Etruscans at Sutrium [*Sutri*], where the enemy were so much off guard and disorganized that they surrendered virtually without a fight.
Livy, 6: 2(14); Diodorus, 14: 117(4)

SATRICUM (386)
News reached Rome that the people of Antium were under arms and were assembling Volscian forces at Satricum [*Conca*], combined with large numbers of Latini and Hernici. Camillus, accompanied by Publius Valerius, set out with an army to confront them. On seeing the huge scale of the opposition, composed of both old and new enemies, the Romans were dispirited and required much exhortation from Camillus who eventually – and in spite of his advanced age – charged the enemy in person. His men cheered and rushed forward as a whole, forcing back the Antiates, who were filled with panic at the mere sight of Camillus in the forefront. In their flight they were badly

hampered by their very numbers, many of them being cut down. The Latini and Hernici deserted and went home; the abandoned Antiates shut themselves up in Satricum. The next day the Romans took the town with the help of scaling ladders, and the Volscians surrendered.
Livy, 6: 7–8

VELITRAE (382)

A new enemy cropped up. The citizens of the colony of Velitrae [*Velletri*], on the south slope of the Alban hills, revolted against Rome in 383. This disloyalty went unpunished for so long that others were beginning to follow suit. In the following year the senate decided to act and the consular tribunes, Spurius and Lucius Papirius, led out the army. A successful battle was fought near Velitrae against the colonists, who had been reinforced with a comparable number of supporting troops from Praeneste [*Palestrina*]. The enemy fled in retreat to the town, but the tribunes refrained from attacking it in view of its status as a colony.
Livy, 6: 22(1–3)

SATRICUM (381)

The behaviour of the Praenestines in allying themselves with the rebellious colony of Velitrae (above) enraged the Romans, who declared war on them. Praeneste [*Palestrina*] promptly joined forces with the Volscians and attacked the Roman colony of Satricum [*Conca*], taking it by storm and maltreating their prisoners. This stung the Romans into electing Camillus as consular tribune for the sixth time and putting him in charge of the whole conduct of the war. He set out for Satricum with four legions totalling 16,000 men. The enemy, confident in their numerical superiority, were impatient and advanced almost up to the Roman rampart. This enraged the Romans so much that the second tribune, a brash young man called Lucius Furius, disregarded the prudence of Camillus and worked the men up to fever pitch. In the ensuing conflict the enemy at first gave way, retiring uphill toward their camp where they had left some strong cohorts. When the Romans broke ranks to pursue the 'fugitives' they suddenly found themselves exposed to attack from the higher ground. They turned and fled back to their camp. Camillus could contain himself no longer. Though infirm and far advanced in years, he was hoisted into his saddle, threw in the reserves, and imbued feelings of shame in his fugitives, who turned again to face the foe. The sight of Camillus in the front rank

had the usual beneficial effect. After a fierce struggle the enemy were finally routed.
Livy, 6: 22(4)–24; Plutarch, Camillus, 37

ALLIA R (380)

The citizens of Praeneste [*Palestrina*] were getting restless again. When they heard that the Romans had not recruited a new army and were bickering among themselves, they saw that this was their golden opportunity. They marched right up to the Colline Gate, which aroused so much panic in Rome that Titus Quinctius Cincinnatus was appointed dictator. On hearing this, the Praenestini retreated to the river Allia where they set up camp, congratulating themselves on the choice of a site which would be certain to inhibit the Romans by arousing gloomy memories of their disaster of 10 years before (Allia, 390). In the event the Romans launched a cavalry charge to disrupt the enemy ranks and followed this up with an attack on foot. The enemy could withstand neither. They turned and fled back to their town, shut themselves up in it and surrendered.
Livy, 6: 28–9

SATRICUM (377)

The Latins and the Volscians joined forces and camped near Satricum [*Conca*]. A Roman army was sent out against them under two of the military tribunes, Publius Valerius and Lucius Aemilius. They attacked the enemy at once and were gaining the upper hand when violent winds and a rainstorm brought the action to a standstill. The fighting was resumed next day, on which the enemy stood firm until a cavalry charge threw them into disorder. When the infantry followed this up, the enemy lines broke altogether and their troops scattered and fled into Satricum, being cut down by the cavalry as they went. That night the fugitives fled on from Satricum to Antium [*Anzio*], moving so speedily that the Romans were unable even to harass them.
Livy, 6: 32(4)

SIGNIA (362)

There had been defection among the Hernici for a few years, but as the Romans had been battling with internal problems, nothing had been done about it. Eventually they declared war and assigned the conduct of it to Lucius Genucius, who was the first of their recently introduced plebeian consuls to have such full responsibility. This matter of making plebeians and patricians alike eligible for such posts had caused a lot of misgiv-

ing. Consequently, it was with much bating of Roman breath that Lucius led out his army against the Hernici near the Roman colony of Signia [*Segni*] – and straight into an ambush. Lucius was killed; his army fled. When the news reached Rome, there was less dismay at the disaster than anger among the patricians over the ominous effects of appointing plebeian commanders.
Livy, 7: 6(7–9)

SIGNIA (362)
As a result of the debacle at Signia (above), Appius Claudius, who had opposed plebeian consuls, was nominated dictator and levied more troops. Before they could reach the Hernici a legate in the Roman camp near Signia, Gaius Sulpicius by name, had started to turn the tables. When the Hernici approached the stockade with over-confidence, he led a sortie which forced them back in disorder. At this point the dictator arrived and the two armies joined forces. The enemy likewise mobilized every available man. The two armies met in the middle of the two-mile long plain which separated their respective camps. At first the fighting was evenly balanced with no advantage either way. Repeated charges by the Roman cavalry failed to disrupt the enemy lines. Filled with bitter frustration, they dismounted and charged the enemy on foot. So furious was their onslaught that they would have crashed right through the lines if they had not come up against the enemy's special picked cohorts. The resulting clash was both bloody and evenly matched until the Romans, with a supreme effort, forced the enemy to give some ground. This concession was soon turned into a rout as the enemy took to their heels and fled back to their camp. It was by then too late in the day for an attack on the camp, which the Hernici abandoned during the night. As their column of fugitives passed the walls of Signia, the inhabitants came out and 'helped' them on their way. The casualties in the battle were heavy on both sides, the Romans losing a quarter of their men.
Livy, 7: 7–8

ANIO R (361) – Gallic Invasion
Nearly 30 years after the Roman disaster at the river Allia at the hands of the Gauls, another Gallic incursion took place. Livy confidently asserts that the intruders encamped at the third milestone along the Via Salaria on the far side of the bridge over the river Anio [*Aniene*]. Poenus, the dictator, met the challenge by marching forth with an immense army and camping opposite the Gauls

at the other end of the bridge, on the near bank of the river. After a number of futile skirmishes for possession of the bridge, a Gaul of gigantic proportions advanced onto it and bellowed to the bravest Roman to come out and fight him in single combat. The challenge was met with a prolonged silence until Titus Manlius, with the dictator's permission, stepped forward and confronted the Gaul. With his shield Manlius knocked up his opponent's shield and then, raising his sword, slipped in close to the Gaul and struck him in the belly with fatal result. He removed a torque from around the dead Gaul's neck, thenceforth earning for himself the nickname 'Torquatus'. The Gauls were so stunned by the defeat of their champion that they took themselves off to Tibur [*Tivoli*] and allied themselves with the Tiburtines.
Livy, 7: 9(6)–11(1)

COLLINE GATE (360) – Gallic Invasion
Tibur [*Tivoli*] was behind a lot of damaging raids in the region, in which considerable support was provided by the Gauls. To the Romans, the Gallic presence necessitated a dictator as commander-in-chief, and Quintus Servilius Ahala was appointed to the position. He ordered the consul to lead his army against Tibur and to pen the Tiburtines up in their own domain, while he himself mustered every man of military age to deal with the Gauls. A long and bloody battle was fought within sight of the Colline Gate with the result that the Gauls were eventually forced to retreat and then to flee. They headed for Tibur where the consul rounded them up and forced them inside.
Livy, 7: 11(3–7)

PEDUM (358) – Gallic Invasion
The Gauls returned to menace the Romans again, setting up camp near Pedum. Gaius Sulpicius was made dictator to cope with the emergency. With a thought for the Gauls' difficulties and steady deterioration through lack of supplies, he decided to prolong the war and instituted severe punishment for anyone who attacked the enemy without his permission. This enraged his men, who became outspoken and rebellious. A deputation approached the dictator to voice the general grievance, and he agreed to meet their wishes. The order was given for an engagement on the following day. In the meantime he gave orders for the pack-saddles to be taken off the mules, after which he armed the muleteers and told this body of almost 1,000 men to go up into the woods in the mountains above the camp by night. They were to

hide themselves until they received a given signal. Next morning he deployed his troops along the slower slopes at the edge of the plain so that the enemy would be forced to face the mountains behind him. When the Gauls realized that the Romans had lined up for battle, they rushed into the fray like mad creatures. At first they concentrated their attack against the Roman right until they were repulsed by a cavalry charge. Sulpicius now turned his attention to his left wing where an assault was brewing, and at the same time he gave the signal to the muleteers. When the Gauls heard the battle-cry coming from the heights and saw the 'cavalry' descending the hillside, they made for their camp in headlong flight, only to be confronted by the master of Horse, Marcus Valerius. They turned and fled to the mountains into the arms of the muleteers.
Livy, 7: 12(8–9) and 14(6)–15(8)

PRIVERNUM (357)

The recorded engagements during 357 have received no more than a passing mention with the exception of one, which did not resound to the credit of the Romans. The consul Gaius Marcius led a plundering army without provocation into the territory of Privernum [*Priverno*], where peace had reigned for many years. He let his men have their fill of loot. When the inhabitants camped behind strong entrenchments in front of their walls, the Romans drove them back into their town with a single charge and were intent on taking it and pillaging it. The sight of the scaling ladders led the citizens to surrender.
Livy, 7: 16(3–6)

SATRICUM (346)

News reached Rome that Volscian envoys from Antium [*Anzio*] were trying to stir up the Latin peoples. The consul Marcus Valerius Corvus was therefore ordered to attack the Volscians. He marched against Satricum [*Conca*] where he was confronted by the Antiates and other Volscians, who were defeated and fled to the shelter of the city. When the Romans brought up scaling ladders, the inhabitants gave themselves up to the number of about 4,000 soldiers.
Livy, 7: 27(5–8)

CAPUA (343)

The Samnites made an unprovoked attack upon the Sidicini, who were weak and helpless and who looked to the Campanians for assistance. The Samnites then shifted their aim and targeted the Campanians with their whole military might. First, they occupied Mount Tifata about 3 miles north of Capua. Then they descended to the plain between Tifata and Capua and fought the Campanians, who lost and were driven back within their walls after losing the best of their fighting force. The Campanians sent envoys to the Romans to beg for military assistance, an act which led to the First Samnite War (below).
Livy, 7: 29(4–7)

GAURUS M (343) – First Samnite War

Rome and Samnium had been at peace. Trouble broke out because the Samnites molested the Campanians (Capua, above), who appealed to the Romans for help. The senate refused to take up arms against the Samnites with whom it was already bound by treaty, but it sent envoys to intercede. The Samnites, however, were so uncompromising that the senate declared war. The consul Valerius led out an army against the Samnites and camped near Mount Gaurus, west of Neapolis [*Naples*]. The two antagonists were so well matched in numbers and determination that the battle raged for a considerable time in which neither side yielded. Eventually Valerius ordered an all-out onslaught with a cavalry attack on each wing, while the infantry made a final desperate push. Even this failed to shift the enemy at first but they finally showed signs of giving ground, which was soon turned into a rout. Many of them were slaughtered before nightfall put an end to further pursuit.
Livy, 7: 32(2) and 33

SATICULA (343) – First Samnite War

While Valerius was fighting the Samnites at Mount Gaurus in Campania, the other consul Cornelius was encamped with the second army near Saticula in Samnium. When he decided to move against the enemy, his route took him through densely wooded country in which there was a deep ravine. He rashly entered the ravine, oblivious to the presence of surrounding Samnites. Impending disaster was prevented by the initiative of a military tribune, Publius Decius, who pointed to a hill which rose above the wood and overlooked the enemy camp. He asked to be allowed to take about 3,000 men in an attempt to occupy the hill. Unnoticed by the enemy, he climbed to its base through the woodland and achieved his objective, attracting the attention of the enemy and allowing the consul to withdraw unmolested. Decius and his men stayed on the hill until it was nearly dark and then stole quietly down and made

their escape, picking their way through the sleeping enemy. On the following morning they returned to their own camp, where Decius immediately proposed to the consul that it would be an excellent time to mount an immediate attack on the unsuspecting enemy. The consul agreed and the army marched out. After taking a safer route than their previous one they caught the Samnites off guard, scattered far and wide and often unarmed. The enemy fled to their camp in terror and were butchered when the camp was taken. Although this can hardly be described as a proper battle, the engagement is of note on account of the magnitude of the Samnite losses. Livy puts the figure at 30,000 killed.
Livy, 7: 34–36

SUESSULA (343) – First Samnite War
After their defeat at the hands of the consul Valerius at Mount Gaurus (343) the Samnites mustered for another assault and encamped near Suessula. Appeals for help were sent by the Suessulani to Valerius, who marched immediately to the rescue, travelling light. He chose a site for his camp which was near the enemy, and although it was small it was adequate for his needs. When the Samnites formed up for battle, nobody came out to challenge them and so they advanced to the Roman camp. They were amazed by its small size and decided that it presented no threat to themselves. Clearly the Romans had nothing much in the way of stores and provisions and would soon be starving anyway. The Samnites therefore decided that they would attend to their own needs, and they scattered around the countryside in search of forage. When Valerius saw that the enemy had dispersed in this way he led out his men and captured their camp at the first assault. The cavalry were then sent out to round up and slaughter the foragers. The number slain is not reported but the capture of 170 military standards gives an indication of a sizeable massacre.
Livy, 7: 37(4–17)

VESERIS R (340) – Great Latin War
In 341, after the First Samnite War, the Romans renewed their previous treaty with the Samnites. This upset their more recent allies in Campania on whose behalf the war had been declared. The Campanians then sought allies among some of the Latin cities. They in turn had their own grievances against Rome, which were fanned into a quarrel and eventually an ultimatum. The Roman response was to send out an army under two consuls, who camped near Capua. They had been joined *en route* by an army of Samnites, who were faithful to the treaty of the previous year. The engagement took place at the foot of Vesuvius near a river – probably just a stream – called the Veseris.* The two sides were equally matched, but after a while the first line of the Roman left wing started to fall back. Decius Mus, the consul commanding that wing, 'devoted' himself by invoking the gods in a spiritual ritual, after which he mounted his horse and charged straight into the midst of the enemy horde. Eventually he succumbed to a rain of missiles but not before his example had inspired his men and brought confusion to the enemy right wing. Thus far the veterans had not seen any action on either side; both commanders had kept them in reserve. When the consul Titus Manlius ordered the rearmost line forward, the enemy assumed that they were the pick and they sent forward their own veterans. The enemy fought hard, but when they began to show signs of exhaustion Manlius gave the signal to his veterans to engage. This fresh army of seasoned and rested men broke up the enemy's formation, inflicting heavy slaughter. Scarcely a quarter of them were left alive.

According to Livy, some historians held that the Samnites did not in fact join the fray until they were certain of the outcome.
*Livy, 8: 8(19)–10; *W. Smith (ed.), A Dictionary of Greek and Roman Geography, 1873*; s.v. Veseris

TRIFANUM (340) – Great Latin War
Numisius, the Latin commander, raised another army from among the Latin and Volscian peoples, who were not told the truth about the disaster at Veseris (above). The consul Titus Manlius Torquatus, victor of Veseris, met this army near Trifanum in southern Latium. The two sides plunged straight into a battle which ended with a Roman victory. The enemy losses were so great that the Latins gave themselves up, followed by the Campanians. This would have ended the war but for the fact that the Latins were made to give up their territory as punishment for their disloyalty. The resentment so engendered ensured that hostilities did not in fact cease.
Livy, 8: 11(11–13)

FENECTANE PLAINS (339) – Great Latin War
The Latins took up arms again in resentment for the loss of their land after their defeat at Trifanum

(above). They were defeated by Quintus Publilius Philo on the Fenectane Plains, a place which is now unknown.
Livy, 8: 12(5)

PEDUM (338) – Great Latin War
While Publilius Philo was defeating the Latins on the Fenectane Plains (above), his colleague Tiberius Aemilius Mamercinus led his army against Pedum. When he heard that Publilius had been decreed a triumph, he abandoned his as yet unfinished campaign and returned to Rome to demand a triumph for himself! The senate was outraged. Pedum had to wait until the following year, when Lucius Furius Camillus successfully fought a very powerful army from Tibur which was allied with the Pedani. During the battle, which took place in the neighbourhood of Pedum, the occupants of the town suddenly sallied out. With part of his army Camillus drove them back inside and scaled the walls to capture the town, all in the same day. The capture of this town marked the beginning of the end of the Latin War. The consuls, with their morale at peak level, toured round the Latin cities capturing each in turn until they had subdued the whole of Latium and established their supremacy.
Livy, 8: 13(6–8)

ASTURA R (338) – Great Latin War
Some of the forces which were marching to the assistance of the Pedani before the battle of Pedum (above) never reached their destination. Camillus' consular colleague, Gaius Maenius, intercepted and routed forces from Aricia, Lanuvium and Velitrae near the Astura river, as they were joining up with Volscians from Antium.
Livy, 8: 13(4–5)

MANDURIA (338) – Tarentine Wars
In southernmost Italy, the prosperous people of Tarentum started engaging adventurers from mainland Greece to help them protect their interests. The first of these 'outsiders' was a Spartan king, Archidamus III, who perished in a battle against the Lucanians at Manduria. The details are unknown.
Plutarch, Agis, 3(2)

PANDOSIA (331) – Tarentine Wars
Seven years after the death of Archidamus at Manduria (above), the Tarentines engaged his brother-in-law, King Alexander of Epirus, in a similar role. In a series of engagements he routed

neighbouring armies and took several towns. His last engagement took place near the Bruttian city of Pandosia, where he took up a position on a triad of hills on each of which he built a camp. The two subsidiary camps were overwhelmed by a surprise attack by Lucanians. Alexander, however, managed to break out of his camp, accompanied by his entourage of Lucanian exiles, but it so happened that they had previously made an offer to the enemy to bargain him in exchange for their safe return home. He was killed with a javelin by one of them.
Livy, 8: 24

IMBRINIUM (325) – Second Samnite War
Peace with the Samnites broke down when, in 327 in an endeavour to extend their influence westward, they put a garrison into the Greek town of Neapolis [*Naples*]. Capua protested and the Romans besieged Neapolis. A dictator Lucius Papirius Cursor was appointed to manage the war against Samnium. He had to pay a visit to Rome connected with the auspices and adjured his master of Horse, Q. Fabius Maximus Rullianus, not to engage the enemy while he, the dictator, was away. However, Quintus Fabius learnt from scouts that everything seemed very quiet on the Samnite front, and so he marshalled his troops and marched on Imbrinium (now unknown), where he encountered the Samnites and became engaged in a pitched battle. This was an outstanding success for the Romans. After several charges the cavalry cut their way through, followed by the infantry. According to some estimates they slaughtered as many as 20,000 men.
Livy, 8: 30(1–7)

CAUDINE FORKS (321) – Second Samnite War
The disastrous confrontation between Romans and Samnites at the Caudine Forks cannot strictly be termed a battle because no sword was raised. It was a classic ambush, which brought unparalleled shame and disgrace to the Romans. The Forks were situated in Samnium between Capua and Beneventum but the exact site cannot be identified with certainty.

The Samnite chief, Gaius Pontius, camped with his army near Caudium [*Montesarchio*] after spreading rumours about that the Samnites were in Apulia besieging Luceria in strength. These rumours were reinforced by 'shepherds', who were likewise agents of deception. The Romans, who were encamped near Calatia in Campania, were

keen to go to the assistance of their staunch Lucerian allies. In view of the rumours of the Samnite whereabouts, the consuls Titus Veturius Calvinus and Spurius Postumius decided to take the shorter but more hazardous route through the Caudine Forks in Samnium. This feature consisted of a large grassy bowl surrounded by mountains on all sides. Access to the bowl was by a deep defile through the rocky hills to the west and a similar one to the east. The Romans gained the central plain by travelling the western gorge, but when they approached the eastern exit they found it blocked by felled trees and boulders. An attempt to retrace their steps was foiled by a similar blockage of the western approach. The enemy occupied the heads of the passes and the ridges all around. The Romans camped in the plain for the night, but the next day, as all attempts to break out were fruitless, they had no alternative but to capitulate. The Samnite chief dictated a treaty by guarantee, reinforced by hostages, and ordered the whole army from the consuls downwards to be sent under the yoke – the supreme disgrace and humiliation in the eyes of the Romans.
Livy, 9: 2–6(2)

SATICULA (316) – Second Samnite War
The Romans wriggled out of the Caudine Peace and the guarantees extracted from them after their humiliation at the Caudine Forks (above). Instead, they used the interlude to make a big increase in their armed forces to enable them to resume the Samnite War. They then besieged and took Luceria [*Lucera*], captured Satricum [*Conca*] through treachery, and attempted an assault on Saticula even though the Samnites were encamped nearby with a large army. When the inhabitants of Saticula made a sudden violent sortie, the Romans found themselves fighting on two fronts. The dictator Lucius Aemilius concentrated his efforts on driving the population back into their town before turning to face the Samnites. Victory was slow in coming but the Samnites were eventually forced back into their camp, from which they stole away under cover of darkness, leaving the Romans to proceed with the siege. In retaliation, the Samnites laid siege to a Roman town.
Livy, 9: 21; Diodorus, 19: 72(4)

SATICULA (315) – Second Samnite War
The siege of Saticula, commenced in 316, continued into the following year when reinforcements arrived from Rome under the new dictator, Quintus Fabius. The Samnites had returned with

reinforcements and were camped in the same place as in the previous year. They kept riding up to the ramparts on nuisance raids until the master of Horse, Quintus Aulius, mustered all his cavalry and charged at them full tilt. It is said that the master of Horse himself rode at the Samnite general with levelled spear and killed him outright, whereupon the general's brother dragged the Roman from his saddle and wreaked his revenge. The forces on both sides then dismounted and fought around the bodies. The Romans came off best and the Samnites abandoned Saticula once more.
Livy, 9: 22

LAUTULAE (315) – Second Samnite War
The accounts of this engagement are conflicting. It seems certain that a Roman army under the dictatorship of Quintus Fabius encountered the Samnites in the defile of Lautulae [*Passo di Portella*] near the coastal town of Tarracina [*Terracina*]. Livy describes the outcome of the encounter as indecisive when it was terminated by nightfall, but he admits that some sources called it a defeat. Diodorus, referring to the place as Laustolae, certainly talks of panic which spread through the whole army and led to flight. Aulius alone, he says, stood his ground and gained a hero's death. (According to Livy, Quintus Aulius, the master of Horse, had been killed earlier in the year at Saticula.)
Livy, 9: 23(1–5); Diodorus, 19: 72(6–7)

TARRACINA (315) – Second Samnite War
After his failure in the defile of Lautulae (above) near Tarracina the dictator, Quintus Fabius, rested his men for a few days in their camp and endeavoured to boost their morale. Meanwhile a relief army was sent out from Rome under Gaius Fabius, the master of Horse, who was to replace the dead Quintus Aulius. When Gaius Fabius was in the offing, but keeping deliberately out of sight, the dictator drew up his men and engaged the Samnites while Gaius Fabius, on receipt of an agreed signal, attacked the enemy in the rear. After a bitter struggle the Romans won a great victory and put the enemy to flight.

It seems that this encounter recorded by Livy is perhaps the same battle as the one placed near Tarracina by Diodorus who, however, assigns it to the following year. Diodorus' information is scanty but he records that more than 10,000 Samnites were killed in the pursuit.
Livy, 9: 23(6–17); Diodorus, 19: 76(1–2)

CAUDIUM (314) – Second Samnite War
Disturbances in Campania caused the Samnites to concentrate their forces in Caudium [*Montesarchio*], where they would be in a position to attack Capua if an opportunity occurred. The Roman consuls led a powerful army to the area and both sides camped opposite each other in the plain below the Caudine Forks. When they formed up for action, the consul Sulpicius took charge of the right wing which was very extended; the Samnites extended their left wing to match. The other consul, Poetelius, took command of the Roman left, which was stationed in close formation and was reinforced with auxiliary cohorts brought forward from the rear. With these forces Poetelius forced the enemy infantry back, whereupon the Samnite cavalry on the extreme right wheeled in to the attack. As they did so, the Roman cavalry charged them at full tilt, throwing everything into confusion and forcing the enemy to flee from this part of the field. On the other flank, the fortunes were reversed and the Samnites broke through the Roman lines. The Romans, however, regained their confidence when they saw that their troops in the rest of the field were victorious. They regained the lost ground and the Samnites gave up and fled.
Livy, 9: 27

SUTRIUM (311) – Second Samnite War
At this point in the Samnite War the Etruscans mobilized and intervened by attacking Sutrium [*Sutri*], which was allied with Rome. The consul Aemilius led an army to raise the siege. The Etruscan army, which was numerically superior, took the field ready for battle and the consul drew up his line not far away. There was no action until after midday when the Etruscans, impatient to settle matters, raised a shout and charged. The issue hung in the balance for a long while until the Roman second line was ordered to the front to relieve the exhausted first line. The Etruscans, who had no fresh reserves, fell where they fought. There was no rout or flight. The survivors were only saved by the advent of dusk, when the retreat was sounded.
Livy, **9**: 32

SUTRIUM (310) – Second Samnite War
As the Etruscans had resumed the siege of Sutrium [*Sutri*], the consul Quintus Fabius led an army to relieve it. At the foot of the mountains (the peak of Mount Ciminius is only 10 miles from Sutrium), he was confronted by the Etruscans drawn up for

battle in huge numbers. To gain some advantage against their numerical superiority he led his men up the lower slopes of the hills. The enemy rushed into battle brandishing their swords to be met by javelins and rocks, which threw them into disorder. They were unable to get to close quarters until the Romans did it for them by charging downhill and routing them. The fugitives were barred from their camp by the Roman cavalry and fled instead into the Ciminian Forest. Many thousands of them were killed.
Livy, **9**: 35

PERUSIA (310) – Second Samnite War
After his rout of the Etruscans near Sutrium (above), the consul Fabius decided to pursue them and to extend the sphere of activity northwards into central Etruria. He successfully eluded the Etruscan guards and took his army by the most direct route through the dense, dreaded and dangerous Ciminian forest to the plain on the far side. In the meantime the Etruscans had assembled a large army, and they camped in the plain not far from the Roman ramparts. But their enemy showed no sign of fighting. Eager for a battle, many of the Etruscans moved up to the Roman ramparts and decided to stay there until the enemy came out. Then in the small hours of the night the Romans were woken and drawn up within their defences. Shortly before dawn they burst out of the camp and attacked. Many of the Etruscans were killed while still asleep or only half-awake; the rest had no time to arm themselves. They were pursued as they fled to the woods or their camp, but the camp itself was taken later. It is stated that about 60,000 were killed or captured. In consequence, envoys from Perusia and other cities sought a treaty with the Romans. They were granted a truce for 30 years.

Livy holds that this battle was fought on the south side of the Ciminian forest near Sutrium [*Sutri*] but he notes that other historians place it on the north side near Perusia [*Perugia*]. Diodorus is one of them. His contention is supported by the movements of Fabius, who had come from Sutrium after the battle there earlier in the year and who aimed to carry hostilities northwards.
Livy, 9: 36(9)–37; Diodorus, 20: 35(1–3)

VADIMONIS L (310) – Second Samnite War
In continuation of the Etruscan take-over of what had started as a Samnite war, a fierce battle was fought near Lake Vadimo (the English form of the Latin name) [*Lago di Bassano*] in which neither

Romans nor Etruscans yielded an inch. As the front line fell, the next line took its place until the cavalry dismounted and advanced to the fore. Eventually the Etruscans began to break, after which their flight gathered momentum. Their camp was sacked. Livy goes so far as to say that on that day the power of the Etruscans was broken for the first time.
Livy, **9**: *39(4–11)*

TALIUM (310) – Second Samnite War
Diodorus reports a battle at a place called Talium, in which the Roman consuls defeated the Samnites. Talium is now unknown. On the following day, a second battle took place in which many of the Samnites were either killed or taken prisoner. One or other of these encounters may have been the overwhelming victory of the dictator Papirius Cursor in Samnite territory which Livy recounts without any reference to place. Livy does not, however, mention two battles.
Diodorus, **20**: *26(3–4); Livy,* **9**: *40(1–14)*

PERUSIA (308) – Second Samnite War
The Etruscans' military might was severally attenuated after their defeat near Lake Vadimo (310). The remnants were engaged by the consul Fabius near Perusia [*Perugia*], a city which had broken the recent 30-year truce granted after the earlier battle there (Perusia, 310). He won a clear victory and would have proceeded to take the town if the inhabitants had not surrendered it.
Livy, **9**: *40(18–21); Diodorus,* **20**: *35(4)*

MEVANIA (308) – Second Samnite War
As the Etruscans settled in peace, the Umbrians arose in revolt. The consul Fabius moved against them at Mevania [*Bevagna*] where they were gathered, and they launched forth into an unusual sort of battle. The enemy did not wait for a second but started rushing wildly over the Romans' earthworks while the consul was still entrenching his camp. When the consul had assembled his forces and let them off the leash, they seemed to be attacking men who were unarmed. The Romans wrenched the standards from the bearers' hands and dragged the bearers bodily to the consul, thereafter returning to the mêlée for a further grab. The methods were those of dragging, pushing and shoving, using shields rather than swords. In consequence, many more of the enemy were captured than killed; the rest surrendered.
Livy, **9**: *41(8–20)*

ALLIFAE (307) – Second Samnite War
In recognition of the successes of Quintus Fabius, the senate extended his command into the following year, in which he proceeded to defeat the Samnite army near Allifae [*Alife*] in no uncertain way. The enemy were routed and driven back to their camp, which was surrounded by the Romans before darkness fell. Early next morning the Samnites surrendered and all were sent under the yoke.
Livy, **9**: *42(6–7)*

TIFERNUM (305) ⎫
BOVIANUM (305) ⎬ – Second Samnite War
TIFERNUM (305) ⎭
The Samnites continued their warlike activities, carrying out raids in Campania. Accordingly the two consuls were sent out, both to Samnium but to different areas. Lucius Postumius made for Tifernum, a town now unknown in the region of Mount Tifernus [*Miletto*]. There he engaged the enemy who, according to some of Livy's sources, were definitely defeated. Others, however, maintained that the fighting was indecisive and that Postumius, feigning fright, led his troops by night into the mountains where he built a secure camp. The enemy followed him and camped nearby. Leaving a garrison in the camp, Postumius crept out with his legions and went to join his colleague Tiberius Minucius who was confronting another Samnite army near Bovianum [*Bojano*].

Minucius at Bovianum had been engaging the enemy in a long and indecisive battle when Postumius arrived and threw his fresh legions into the attack. The enemy were by then too exhausted to escape and they are said to have been completely annihilated. The Romans captured 21 standards.

After their combined success against the Samnites at Bovianum the consuls Postumius and Minucius marched to the camp which Postumius had left garrisoned in the region of Mount Tifernus. The Samnites in that area had camped 2 miles away. Both consuls attacked them and put them to flight, capturing 26 standards as well as the Samnite commander, Statius Gellius. Peace with Samnium was restored the following year.
Livy, **9**: *44(5–13); cf. Diodorus,* **20**: *90(3–4)*

THURIAE (302) – Tarentine Wars
An extension of the Samnite War into Apulia caused uneasiness among the Tarentines, who once again invited assistance from outside as at Manduria (338) and Pandosia (331). A Greek fleet under Cleonymus the Spartan landed and

captured the city of Thuriae (unknown) in the territory of the Sallentini in Calabria. A Roman army was sent against the Greeks, routed them and drove them back to their ships, but some said that Cleonymus had already departed without setting eyes on any Romans.
Livy, 10: 2(1–3)

BOVIANUM (298) – Third Samnite War

The Third Samnite War arose from a complaint to the consuls by the Lucanians against the Samnites, whom they accused of having invaded their territory. The Romans agreed to a treaty with Lucania and issued an order to the Samnites to withdraw from Lucanian territory. The Samnites were inflexible and so the senate called for war. The consul Gnaeus Fulvius marched out against the Samnites and fought a 'famous' battle near Bovianum [*Bojano*] in Samnium, but no details seem to be available.
Livy, 10: 12(1–3) and (9)

VOLATERRAE (298) – Third Samnite War

While the third war with the Samnites was getting under way, the Etruscans also were preparing for a resumption of hostilities in contravention of the existing truce. The consul Lucius Cornelius Scipio marched out against them and was confronted by his enemy near Volaterrae [*Volterra*]. The fight was a long and hard one, with heavy losses on both sides and no clear result either way by nightfall. In the morning when the Romans marched out there was no enemy to fight. The Etruscans had slunk away in the night, thereby conceding the victory.
Livy, 10: 12(1–6)

TIFERNUM (297) – Third Samnite War

The consuls for the year were Quintus Fabius Maximus (for the fourth time) and Publius Decius Mus (for the third time). They led their armies into Samnium by different routes. Fabius' scouts were quick to spot that the Samnites were drawn up in a remote valley near Tifernum with the object of ambushing and attacking the Romans from higher ground. Fabius brazenly led his men in square formation right up to the enemy's place of concealment. As their ruse was obviously no secret, the Samnites descended to level ground to fight a regular engagement. This proved to be evenly matched. Nowhere did the enemy give ground and so Fabius ordered the cavalry to charge. The Samnites resisted even this and stayed firm. As a precaution, Fabius had also adopted a stratagem.

He had withdrawn the veterans of the first legion from the battle and had asked them to take a circuitous route to the hills just behind the enemy and to climb up from the far side. At the sight of this party descending in their rear, the Samnites assumed or were led to believe that the second consul had arrived with a fresh army, while they themselves were in an exhausted state. The thought created panic and they fled far and wide. Twenty-three standards were captured and 3,400 of the enemy were killed.
Livy, 10: 14

BENEVENTUM (MALEVENTUM) (297) – Third Samnite War

While Quintus Fabius was engaging the Samnites near Tifernum, his colleague Publius Decius was camping near Maleventum (called Beneventum [*Benevento*] after 268) to prevent the Apulians from joining up with the Samnites. He drew them into battle and defeated them in an engagement which was more flight than fight. Only 2,000 Apulians were killed. Thereafter the two consuls joined forces and spent four months ravaging the land and destroying everything.
Livy, 10: 15(1–2)

VOLTURNUS R (296) – Third Samnite War

At a time when the entire Roman war machine was mainly directed against the Etruscans, the Samnites seized the opportunity to invade Campania and despoil the land. At that time the consul Volumnius was returning to Samnium and he changed his course to intercept the enemy who, he learnt, were encamped on the river Volturnus [*Volturno*]. He encamped just far enough from them to prevent them learning of his presence. The next morning he heard from spies that the enemy were leaving to return to Samnium and that they had so much booty that they were in complete disorder, each man fending for himself. What a heaven-sent opportunity! The consul charged the enemy's column and overpowered the men with little difficulty as most of them carried spoils in preference to arms. The camp was then assaulted with a predictable result. To add to the Samnites' turmoil, their prisoners broke loose. Moreover, the prisoners seized the Samnite general and led him, still mounted, to the Roman consul. A total of 6,000 Samnites were slain and 2,500 were taken prisoner. The Roman losses, probably minute, are not recorded; on the other hand, they did recover 7,400 prisoners and a vast amount of stolen loot.
Livy, 10: 20

CAMERINUM (295) – Third Samnite War

The armed forces of the Etruscans, Samnites, Umbrians and Gauls were combining into a massive force with the intention of finally subduing Rome. As a foretaste of things to come, a combined force of Samnites and Gauls arrived in the neighbourhood of Camerinum [*Camerino*] in Umbria (erroneously referred to as Clusium by Livy). Scipio, the commander of the Roman camp, was conscious of his numerical inferiority and led his men up a hill between his camp and the town. Through inadequate reconnaissance he was unaware that the enemy had already approached it from the other side. The legion was attacked and surrounded, incurring heavy losses or, as some authorities say, total destruction.
Livy, 10: 26(7–11); Polybius, 2:19(5)

SENTINUM (295) – Third Samnite War

A few days after Camerinum (above), the consuls, Quintus Fabius (for the fifth time) and Publius Decius (fourth time), led out all their forces and encountered the enemy near Sentinum in Umbria. The enemy decided to split their forces. The Samnites and Gauls were to engage the Romans while the Umbrians and Etruscans attacked the Roman camp. These plans were foiled by deserters who disclosed them to Fabius. He then sent messages to the commanders of two other Roman armies which had been stationed not far from Rome, asking them to move to Clusium and devastate Etruscan lands. This forced the Etruscans to withdraw from Sentinum. Fabius and Decius now tried to tempt the enemy into action. For two days the enemy declined the challenge, but on the third day both sides lined up and engaged. The two sides were well matched but progress on the two wings was very dissimilar. Fabius, on the Roman right, knew from long experience that both Samnites and Gauls tended to flag if the struggle dragged on. Faced with the Samnites, he deliberately prolonged the battle. When he was certain of their fatigue, he urged his men on, threw in all his reserves and ordered the cavalry to charge the enemy flank. This was too much for them and they fled back to camp. Matters were very different on the Roman left where Decius, younger and more strong-headed than Fabius, poured in all his resources from the start. He called on the cavalry to attack, but at the second charge they were carried on too far into the midst of the enemy infantry. Here they were met by a countercharge of chariots and waggons driven by armed Gauls, which terrified the Roman mounts. The cavalry were overthrown and the legionaries were trampled underfoot and run over by vehicles. When Decius saw the havoc, he 'devoted' himself as his father had done at Veseris (340) and galloped into the Gallic lines, throwing himself on their weapons. This had the desired effect. The Romans abandoned their flight and returned to the fight. At this point, reserves taken by Fabius from his rearmost line arrived in support. In the face of this renewed pressure, the tightly packed Gauls formed themselves into a defensive *testudo* ('tortoise' shell of overlapping shields). Fabius then detached the 500-strong Campanian cavalry squadron and ordered them to circle round and attack the Gauls in the rear. The cavalry were followed by the third legion, with instructions to make the most of the disarray and panic caused by the Campanians. Fabius then rode to the Samnite camp, to which the terrified horde was being driven, and after a short struggle the camp was taken. Enemy losses were 25,000 killed including the Samnite commander, Gellius Egnatius; 8,000 were taken prisoner. The army of Publius Decius lost 7,000 men; Fabius lost 1,700.
Livy, 10: 26(14)–29; Polybius, 2: 19(6)

TIFERNUS M (295) – Third Samnite War

While the great battle of Sentinum was in progress, the proconsul Lucius Volumnius was campaigning in Samnium where he forced a Samnite army up Mount Tifernus [*Miletto*] and then routed it and put it to flight.
Livy, 10: 30(7)

CAIATIA (295) – Third Samnite War

Despite the Roman victories at Sentinum and Mount Tifernus earlier in the year, there was still no peace in Samnium or Etruria. Some of the Samnite legions were pursued by Appius Claudius, others by Lucius Volumnius. The Samnites then came together and took up a position near Caiatia [*Caiazzo*], where Appius and Volumnius also joined forces. In the ensuing battle the Samnite losses were 16,300 killed and 2,700 captured; the Romans lost 2,700.
Livy, 10: 31(5–7)

LUCERIA (294) – Third Samnite War

In the words of Livy, there are still more Samnite wars to be recounted. When the Samnites were attacking Luceria [*Lucera*] in Apulia, the consul Marcus Atilius led his legions to the rescue. The Samnites fought so fiercely and so well that the Roman losses were much the greater. The

Romans, unaccustomed to reverses, became dispirited. Although the Samnites were the clear victors in the preliminary encounter, they too were lacking in martial zeal and wanted to retire without a further fight. Their difficulty lay in the fact that the only road led past the Roman camp. The Romans, however, were in a state of virtual mutiny. The consul tried hard with minimal success to put some life into his men. Eventually, when the Samnites started to approach down the road, the Romans reluctantly straggled out of their camp. Some sort of encounter was inevitable because each side thought that the other was determined to fight, although nothing was further from the truth. Both sides formed up in line, but nobody moved. Atilius then sent in a few squadrons of cavalry but for the most part they were unhorsed. The rest trampled on the Roman soldiers who had gone to their help. This was enough to start a rout which sent the entire Roman army heading for its camp. The consul took decisive action. He placed a cavalry guard on the gate and issued an order that anybody, Roman or Samnite, who made for the rampart should be treated as an enemy. The cavalry levelled their spears at their own side and drove the infantry back. Eventually the army turned to face the enemy, who had still refrained from pressing any attack. The exhortations of the consul were ultimately rewarded with success. His men developed some martial zest and drove the Samnites back to their pile of baggage in the road, where they formed a circle around it. This was rapidly dispelled by an onslaught of the Roman infantry from the front while the cavalry attacked the rear. The number of Samnites taken prisoner reached 7,800, and they were sent under the yoke; nearly 5,000 had been killed. However, the Romans too had suffered badly, with an overall loss of 7,800 men in the two days of conflicts.
Livy, 10: 35–36(15)

AQUILONIA (293) – Third Samnite War
The Samnites were well prepared for a showdown. They had held a levy of all those of military age and had told the whole army, numbering in excess of 36,000, to report at Aquilonia [*Lacedonia*]. The consuls left Rome separately and led their armies into Samnium, where Papirius arrived outside Aquilonia; Carvilius camped outside Cominium [*San Donato Val di Comino*] about 20 miles away. They arranged that when Papirius attacked, Carvilius would do likewise at Cominium to

prevent the Samnites there from sending relief to Aquilonia. Before taking the field Papirius ordered a legate, Spurius Nautius, to take the mules with three cohorts of allied troops by a hidden route to a hill in full view and to await a given signal. The encounter then commenced and was in the Romans' favour from the start. The Samnites were hard pressed and cut down right, left and centre. In the middle of the carnage a dense cloud of dust was seen coming over a hill, apparently raised by a great army. It was stirred up by Nautius and his cavalry of muleteers, who were trailing branches along the ground. A shout was raised that Cominium had fallen and that here was the other army coming to their support. As the *coup de grâce*, Papirius gave a prearranged signal to the cavalry to charge against the enemy with full force. This routed them, and they were pursued in every direction as they fled. The town was captured shortly afterwards. The Samnite losses on that day were 20,340 killed and 3,870 taken prisoner, with the capture of 97 standards. The Roman casualties are not recorded.
Livy, 10: 38–42

HERCULANEUM (293) – Third Samnite War
As a result of the battle of Aquilonia (above), there was no remaining Samnite army which was capable of a pitched battle. Attacks on Samnite cities were the only form of warfare left to the Romans. But at Herculaneum in Samnium (a place now unknown) the consul Carvilius had to fight a regular battle. The result was 'uncertain' and his losses were greater then the enemy's. However, he recouped by shutting the enemy inside their town, which he stormed and took.
Livy, 10: 45(8–11)

ARRETIUM (284) – Gallic Invasion
The Gauls had been checked at Sentinum (295) but not crushed. Ten years later they reinvaded Etruria and besieged Arretium [*Arezzo*]. A Roman relief force attacked the enemy before the walls, but it was defeated and the praetor was killed. Manius Curius Dentatus was appointed in his place. He sent a delegation to negotiate the return of prisoners, but the Gauls treacherously massacred the envoys. In reprisal, Curius Dentatus led a Roman force against the Senones, the Gallic tribe responsible, and defeated them in a pitched battle at an unspecified place in their own territory. He drove them from their homeland.
Polybius, 2: 19(7–11)

VADIMONIS L (283) – Gallic Invasion

When the Boii saw the expulsion of the Senones from their homeland after the battle at Arretium (above), they feared a similar fate for themselves. They mobilized their forces, called on the Etruscans for help and marched in the direction of Rome. Their progress was arrested some 50 miles short of the City by P. Cornelius Dolabella, who fought and defeated them near Lake Vadimo [*Lago di Bassano*]. The Etruscans were largely wiped out and only a few of the Boii escaped.
Polybius, 2: 20(1–3)

POPULONIA (282) – Gallic Invasion

In spite of their disaster at Lake Vadimo (above), the Boii and the Etruscans again joined forces in the next year and challenged the Romans. Again they suffered a total defeat. A modern historian cites Populonia, a town on the Etruscan coast, as the site of the battle but the evidence for this is unclear. After the battle, the Boii sued for peace. They remained on peaceful terms with Rome for nearly half a century.
Polybius, 2: 20(4–5)

TARENTUM (282) – Tarentine War

The Romans sent an admiral, Lucius Valerius, with a small fleet on some errand to the Gulf of Tarentum [*Taranto*]. On the supposition that the Tarentines were friendly, he anchored off their city. His move, however, caused bitter resentment. The Tarentines had been associating clandestinely with various enemies of Rome, and their guilt feelings aroused the suspicion that Valerius was sailing against them. They set sail and attacked him in his innocence and sank his flag-ship and many others. The Romans responded by sending envoys but the Tarentines merely mocked them, which goaded the Romans into a declaration of war.
Dio Cassius, 9: (5–6); Zonaras, 8, 2; Orosius, 4: 1(1); Livy, epitome 12

HERACLEA (280) – Tarentine (Pyrrhic) War

With a war impending between Rome and Tarentum, the Tarentines as usual resorted to military leadership from abroad. They invited Pyrrhus of Epirus to come and manage their affairs. Pyrrhus' voyage to Italy was beset by squalls and he eventually took to the water and struggled ashore like a damp squib. With what remained of his force he proceeded to Tarentum, where he heard that the consul Valerius Laevinus was advancing against him with a large army. Although his allies had not yet arrived, he marched out and pitched camp near the river Siris [*Sinni*] not far from Heraclea [*Policoro*] in Lucania only to find that the Romans were close by on the other side of the river. Laevinus was anxious to forestall the arrival of reinforcements for Pyrrhus, and he managed to cross the river despite the guard which Pyrrhus had stationed. Pyrrhus opposed him with a charge by his 3,000 mounted troops. When these forces started to give ground, he ordered his infantry to charge. The Romans in their turn gave ground and so the battle seesawed many times. Eventually the Romans were driven back by Pyrrhus' elephants which created panic in the Roman horses. As the enemy faltered, Pyrrhus launched a charge with his Thessalian cavalry, which routed them. According to one source quoted by Plutarch, the Romans lost nearly 15,000 men and Pyrrhus 13,000, but another of his sources quoted more modest figures of 7,000 and 4,000 respectively. Pyrrhus' victory was sufficiently impressive to win over other Greek cities as well as the Lucanians and Samnites to his side.
Plutarch, Pyrrhus, 16(3)–17; Zonaras, 8: 3; Orosius, 4: 1(8–15); Livy, epitome 13

ASCULUM SATRIANUM (279, spring) – Tarentine (Pyrrhic) War

Pyrrhus' second encounter with the Romans occurred in Apulia, which he had invaded. He attacked the Romans, under Gaius Fabricius, at the city of Asculum [*Ascoli Satriano*] but the terrain was unfavourable for both cavalry and elephants. The fighting was fierce and there were heavy losses before nightfall ended the hostilities. The next day Pyrrhus forced a fight on even terrain, which he occupied at first light. He launched a charge with his heavy infantry in close formation, forcing the Romans to oppose him with their swords against his pikes. After a long struggle the battle was turning in Pyrrhus' favour when the *coup de grâce* was administered by his elephants. Even the Romans could not stand up to their weight and unstoppability. Six thousand of the Romans were killed; Pyrrhus, however, lost rather more than half of that number.

Such is the account given by Plutarch, but other sources differ in many respects. Dionysius speaks of only one battle but he does tell us that the two armies were reasonably matched with Pyrrhus fielding 70,000 foot against a somewhat larger Roman force. Pyrrhus, on the other hand, was slightly superior in cavalry and had 19 elephants. Dionysius also lists the various nationals

comprising each army and details their battle order. However, he fails to follow up this information with a clear and orderly account of the battle as a whole or with any meaningful casualty figures. He maintains that Pyrrhus' elephants were stopped by Roman waggons equipped with jibs carrying fire-bearing grapnels, but Pyrrhus' light-armed troops disabled the waggons. Fighting was eventually brought to an end by sunset in an action which was thoroughly indecisive, a conclusion with which Livy agrees. Other sources, however, contend that the outcome was a defeat for Pyrrhus (Dio) or even a disaster (Orosius). The casualty figures given by Orosius were 5,000 for the Romans as against a massive 20,000 on Pyrrhus' side – a result which could hardly rate even as a 'Pyrrhic' victory!
Plutarch, Pyrrhus, *21(5–10); Dionysius of Halicarnassus*, Roman Antiquities, *20: 1–3; Zonaras*, **8**: *5; Orosius*, **4**: *1(19–23); Livy*, epitome *13*

STRAITS OF MESSINA (276) – Tarentine (Pyrrhic) War

After the battle of Asculum (above), Pyrrhus received a delegation inviting him to visit Sicily. He accepted, but his high hopes did not materialize and he returned to Italy under a cloud. While he was crossing the straits with 110 decked ships and many auxiliary vessels, the Carthaginians attacked him. At that time the Romans had no more than a few ships, and the Carthaginians provided the fleet against Pyrrhus under a treaty. They sank 70 of his ships and disabled many others.
Appian, Samnite History, *12(2); Plutarch*, Pyrrhus, *24(1)*

BENEVENTUM (275) – Tarentine (Pyrrhic) War

Pyrrhus entered into a third and final round against the Romans. One of their armies was encamped in Samnite territory under Manius Curius Dentatus; the other was in Lucania. Pyrrhus sent a part of his army into Lucania to engage that consul and prevent him from joining forces with his colleague. He himself took the main body against Curius, who was camped in the Arusine Plain near Beneventum [*Benevento*]. Pyrrhus was eager to get to grips with his opponent before the latter could receive reinforcements. Accordingly, he took his best troops and elephants on a roundabout night march to the enemy's camp. This took longer than he predicted and his descent from high ground was revealed to the enemy by the advent of dawn. Curius led out his troops,

routed Pyrrhus' advance guard and drove his main body onto the plain. On open ground Curius drove back one of the opposing wings but in another part of the front his men were overwhelmed by Pyrrhus' elephants. He then summoned up all the auxiliaries who had been left to guard the camp and threw them into the fray. They charged in, throwing their javelins at the elephants and forcing them to turn about and trample on their own troops. Casualty figures are lacking, Orosius alone putting Pyrrhus' dead at an incredible 33,000 out of a force of 80,000. But the victory indubitably belonged to the Romans. Dionysius of Halicarnassus points out that Pyrrhus was the greatest general of the day with a seasoned army that was three times larger than his adversary's. He attributes Pyrrhus' defeat in this battle to the fatigue occasioned by the heavy armour of the hoplites on a long, hilly, cross-country march.
Plutarch, Pyrrhus, *24(4)–25; Orosius*, **4**: *2(3–6); Dionysius of Halicarnassus*, Roman Antiquities, *20: 10–11; Livy*, epitome *14*

CYAMOSORUS R (c.274) – Mamertine War

In about 288 a band of discharged Campanian mercenaries who had been imported into Sicily in the service of Agathocles seized Messana [*Messina*] and imposed a rule of tyranny and terror on the surrounding countryside. They assumed the name of Mamertines. They harassed the neighbouring Carthaginians and Syracusans until, after a few years of such aggravation, a young Syracusan commander called Hiero (the future Hiero II of Syracuse) decided to kill two birds with one stone. He had come to the conclusion that his mercenaries were potentially mutinous trouble-makers. He therefore led them out against the Mamertines of Messana and, having pitched camp against the enemy near Centuripa [*Centuripe*], he drew up his men near the river Cyamosorus [upper *Simeto*]. The mercenaries were then ordered to advance and were left to their fate. The Syracusan infantry and cavalry under the personal command of Hiero were withheld and withdrew to Syracuse while the mercenaries were being butchered.
Polybius, **1**: *9(1–6)*

LONGANUS R (c.265) – Mamertine War

The battle of Cyamosorus (above) was aimed at ridding Hiero of his unreliable mercenaries rather more than the Mamertines, who had been allowed to win an easy victory. That they continued to be aggressive is no matter for surprise. Hiero therefore led out his troops and engaged the Mamer-

tines near the river Longanus [*Longano*] in the plain of Mylae [*Milazzo*], not far from Messana. He crushed them completely and captured their leaders. This seems likely to be the battle which Diodorus described as taking place on the river Loitanus (unknown). In the account of Diodorus, Hiero succeeded by an outflanking movement, sending a picked body of men round to the far side of a hill occupied by the enemy. After their defeat some of the Mamertines sought protection from Carthage while others turned to Rome, emphasizing that they, the Mamertines, were originally Campanians and therefore neighbours. The stage was being set for that great Punic–Roman struggle, the First Punic War.
Polybius, 1: 9(7–9); Diodorus, 22: 13(2–4)

MESSANA (264) – First Punic War
The year 264 marks the onset of the First Punic War, a struggle for control of Sicily between Rome and Carthage. The trigger was a disturbance in the city of Messana [*Messina*], where a band of discharged Campanian mercenaries, known as Mamertines, had taken control and had entrenched themselves. When they were defeated by Hiero II of Syracuse at the river Longanus (above), some of the Mamertines appealed to Carthage for help; others looked to Rome. While the Romans deliberated, a Punic commander, Hanno, took up residence in the citadel. But when the Mamertines heard that the Romans had eventually decided to send an expedition, they contrived to get Hanno to leave and then handed their city over to the Romans. The Carthaginians crucified Hanno and laid siege to Messana.

When the Carthaginians started to besiege Messana, Hiero of Syracuse decided to join forces with them in an attempt to rid Sicily of the Mamertines once and for all. He marched his forces out of Syracuse and advanced on Messana, setting up camp on the opposite side of the city to the Carthaginians. Meanwhile, the Roman consul, Appius Claudius, set sail and negotiated the dangerous crossing over the Phoenician-controlled straits by night. He made his way into the besieged city. This was, in fact, the first occasion on which the Romans transported an army by sea. As Appius was now surrounded on all sides by warring factions, a fight seemed inevitable. He decided to tackle the Syracusans first, led out his men and drew them up in battle order. Hiero followed suit. In the ensuing strenuous battle Appius got the better of his opponent and drove the whole army

back to its camp. That night Hiero disengaged and withdrew to Syracuse.
Polybius, 1: 11(9–15); Zonaras, 8: 9

MESSANA (264) – First Punic War
After the success of his drive against the Syracusans (above), Appius decided to tackle his other opponent, the Carthaginians, without delay. He led his troops out to battle at first light, and in the ensuing engagement he killed many of them. The rest were forced to retreat in disorder to neighbouring towns.
Polybius, 1: 12(1–4); Zonaras, 8: 9

HERACLEA MINOA (262) – First Punic War
The First Punic War commenced in earnest at Heraclea Minoa, which was a little under 20 miles up the coast to the north-west of Agrigentum [*Agrigento*]. The Carthaginians had concentrated all their troops and supplies in their base at Agrigentum under the leadership of Hannibal (one of many of that name). The Roman consuls, Lucius Postumius and Quintus Mamilius, seized the initiative and concentrated their entire force against Agrigentum, camping about a mile from the city and confining the enemy within the city walls. Their next move was to divide their forces and to set up a second camp on the other side of the city, which faced Heraclea. The ground between the camps was trenched, fortified and patrolled, and after five months the besieged were starving. In response to repeated pleas for help, the Carthaginians at home sent a powerful force to Sicily to join their other general, Hanno, whose base was at Heraclea. Hanno (not the same Hanno as at Messana in 264) then seized the initiative and was the clear winner in a cavalry engagement. He sent out his Numidian cavalry as an advance guard, with orders to lure out the Roman horse and then to fall back on their own lines. The Roman cavalry pursued them only to find themselves surrounded as the Numidians wheeled round and charged, killing many of them.
Polybius, 1: 19(1–4)

AGRIGENTUM (262) – First Punic War
After his success at Heraclea (above), Hanno moved his camp and occupied a hill only a little over a mile away from the Roman camp. But he failed to follow up his advantage and did nothing for two months until pressed by the desperate Hannibal in the besieged and starved city of Agrigentum (formerly Acragas) [*Agrigento*]. This

forced Hanno to risk a battle. The action, which took place between the camps, was long drawn-out, but the Romans eventually drove the Carthaginian mercenaries back onto their own supporting units and elephants, creating confusion which turned into a general rout. The greater part of their force was slaughtered on the field. Unfortunately, in the period of exhaustion after battle the Romans were off their guard. Hannibal seized the opportunity to extricate his force from the besieged city and withdraw unobserved. The statement of Zonaras that Hannibal's men were recognized and killed seems improbable in view of their number, estimated by Polybius to be in excess of 50,000.

Polybius, 1: 19(5–11); Zonaras, 8: 10

LIPARA (260) – First Punic War

The consul Gnaeus Cornelius Scipio was placed in command of a fleet destined for Sicily as soon as it had been fitted out. Scipio himself sailed ahead to Messana with the 17 ships which were ready. He was told that the Carthaginian-held town of Lipara [*Lipari*] on the nearby island of that name would be betrayed to him, but this was a ruse. After the unsuspecting Scipio had anchored off the town, Hannibal, the Carthaginian general in Panormus [*Palermo*], despatched a Carthaginian senator called Boödes with 20 ships to Lipara by night, trapping Scipio in the harbour. The subsequent fate of the Romans is in dispute. Polybius records that the crews fled inland and that Scipio surrendered himself and was taken to Hannibal with the captured ships. According to Zonaras, Scipio and the Roman tribunes were invited aboard the flag-ship to discuss terms but were then taken captive and sent to Carthage.

Polybius, 1: 21(4–8); Zonaras, 8: 10; Livy, epitome 17

CAPE OF ITALY (260) – First Punic War

A few days after Scipio's debacle at Lipara the main Roman fleet was sailing down the west coast of Italy to Sicily. When Hannibal heard about this, he headed towards them with his 50 ships in order to spy out their strength and dispositions. As he was rounding a promontory which Polybius refers to only as an unspecified Italian cape, he suddenly came upon the enemy. In the ensuing engagement, Hannibal lost most of his ships but managed against all hope to make his escape with the remainder.

Polybius, 1: 21(9–11)

MYLAE (260, summer) – First Punic War

When Gaius Duilius, the commander of the Roman army in Sicily, heard about the naval disaster at Lipara (260), he handed over his command and joined the fleet. Hearing that the Carthaginians were in the vicinity of Mylae [*Milazzo*], Duilius sailed out with his total force of 120 ships. The Carthaginians immediately put out to meet him with their 130 ships (Diodorus says 200) and, displaying complete confidence, they headed straight for the enemy. The Romans, however, had been aware that their ships were inferior to the Carthaginian vessels in speed and manoeuvrability. To compensate for this they had equipped their ships with 'ravens'. This device, which is described in detail by Polybius, consisted basically of a gangway 36 feet in length which was hinged to the prow of the ship and was carried normally in a vertical position. When an enemy ship was within range of the 'raven', it was lowered onto the enemy deck and held the ship fast. As a result of these tactics the Carthaginians did not meet with the expected success but with grappling gangways and boarding Romans in hand-to-hand fighting. They eventually turned and fled, losing 50 ships. This battle has been called the first victory of the Roman navy, but in fact the lesser known victory off the cape of Italy (above) preceded it.

Polybius, 1: 22–23; Zonaras, 8: 11; Diodorus, 23: 1; Livy, epitome 17

THERMAE HIMERIENSES (260) – First Punic War

It came to the attention of the Carthaginians that there was bickering between the Romans and their allies, who had encamped apart. The allies were near Thermae Himerienses [*Termini Imerese*] on the north coast of Sicily. Hamilcar, who had replaced Hannibal as Carthaginian commander, launched a surprise attack on the allies while they were striking camp and killed some 4,000 of them. (Diodorus puts the casualties at 6,000 Romans without specifying that they were allies.)

Polybius, 1: 24(3–4); Diodorus, 23: 9(4)

CAMARINA (258) – First Punic War

When the Romans set out to attack Camarina, the consul Atilius rashly led his men into a ravine where they were ambushed by the Carthaginians. They would have been utterly destroyed but for the courage and action of a military tribune, Marcus Calpurnius, who spotted that one of the surrounding hills had been left unoccupied by the

enemy by virtue of its steepness. Calpurnius asked for 300 men, with whom he seized the mound, thereby diverting all enemy attention upon himself and his band. The Carthaginians made a united assault upon them during the course of which the Roman army slipped out of the ravine. In the fierce battle on the hill all 300 Romans fell. Calpurnius, severely wounded, was left for dead among the corpses but he alone survived. When found alive by the enemy, his life was spared.
Zonaras, 8: 12; Livy, epitome *17; Orosius, 4: 8(1–3)*

TYNDARIS (257) – First Punic War

The two versions of this encounter differ markedly. According to Polybius, the Roman consul Gaius Atilius Regulus was anchored off Tyndaris when he saw the Carthaginian fleet sailing past him, presumably unaware of his presence in the lea of a promontory. He sailed out immediately with an advance guard of 10 of his fastest ships, ordering the rest to follow. When the Carthaginians saw the advance squadron way out in front, they turned and surrounded it and sank nine of the vessels. The consul's ship alone escaped by virtue of its speed. The subsequent arrival of the rest of the Roman fleet reversed the picture. The Romans took up formation and sank eight enemy ships while capturing another 10. Zonaras, on the other hand, says that it was the Carthaginians who were lying in wait below the height of Tyndaris. When the Romans saw them, they sent half their fleet round the promontory to lure the Carthaginians forth. On the arrival of the other half of the Roman fleet, the Carthaginian commander Hamilcar was routed and lost most of his ships. It will be noted that whichever version of the events is correct, the Romans were the victors.
Polybius, 1: 25(1–4); Zonaras, 8: 12

ECNOMUS PR (256) – First Punic War

The Romans, pleased with their Sicilian successes, made plans to extend their operations to the Carthaginian motherland by sailing to Africa. The Carthaginians, on the other hand, were aware of the vulnerability of their homeland and decided to have a trial of strength at sea. The Roman fleet, which is said to have consisted of 330 warships, sailed from Italy via Messana to Ecnomus [*Poggio di Sant' Angelo*] on the south Sicilian coast, which was to be their springboard for the crossing to Africa. The Carthaginians, with a fleet of similar size sailed round from western Sicily and anchored at Heraclea Minoa about 40 miles west of

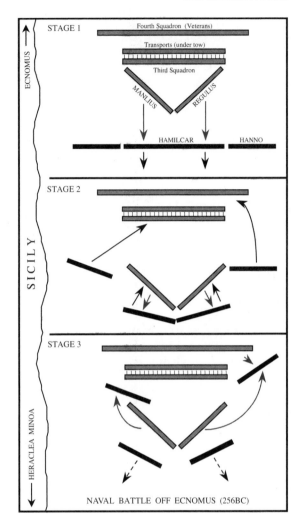

NAVAL BATTLE OFF ECNOMUS (256BC)

Ecnomus. The subsequent battle when the two fleets met has been fully described by Polybius. The Romans adopted a triangular formation which was led at the apex by the ships of the two consuls, Regulus and Manlius, while two other squadrons provided a strong base to the wedge. The Carthaginians under Hamilcar opposed this with a single line of ships abreast, reaching to the shore on their left and with an extended right wing under Hanno which could outflank the enemy. The action began when the Romans attacked the Carthaginian centre, which had orders to retire, luring the Romans in pursuit. In this way the leading Roman squadrons became separated from the slower ones at the back, which were towing and protecting the transport vessels. At this point Hamilcar ordered the Carthaginian centre to turn

and engage its pursuers. At the same time Hanno's right wing outflanked the Romans and attacked their veteran squadron in the rear, while the left wing engaged the squadron towing the transport vessels. There were thus three separate actions in progress and each was a well-matched contest in strength. The greater speed of the Carthaginian ships enabled them to draw rings round the enemy, but any ship which came within striking distance of a Roman vessel found itself grappled by a 'raven' (see Mylae, 260) and boarded. Ultimately, Hamilcar's squadron was routed by the leading Roman squadrons, leaving Regulus free to sail to the rescue of the veterans and transports at the rear. Here the Carthaginians now found themselves being attacked from the front and rear, and they withdrew. Manlius, likewise freed from his engagement, went to the assistance of the Romans who were penned in close to the shore by the Carthaginian left. Fear of the Roman 'ravens' had prevented the besiegers from closing in and destroying their quarry. Manlius, now joined by Regulus, surrounded the enemy and captured 50 of them. In the action as a whole 24 Roman ships were sunk; the Carthaginians lost more than 30 ships sunk and 64 captured complete with crews. After taking on victuals and effecting repairs the Roman fleet set out again for Africa.
Polybius, 1: 25(7)–28

ADYS (256) – First Punic War

When the Romans landed in Africa, they captured Clupea [*Kelibia*] and set about plundering the countryside. On one of these expeditions the consul Regulus reached the town of Adys and set about besieging it. The Carthaginians led out their troops from Carthage under the command of Hasdrubal (son of Hanno) together with Hamilcar, who had been urgently recalled from Sicily. They occupied some high ground which overlooked the Romans but they ignored the difficult nature of the terrain, which was totally unsuitable for their greatest asset, the cavalry and elephants. This decided the Romans to strike first, at dawn and from both sides of the hill. They were met by a vigorous charge by the Carthaginian mercenaries, who forced the first legion to turn about and run. But the mercenaries went too far and found themselves surrounded by the Roman division attacking the hill from the other side. This victory left the Romans free to maraud and sack the towns, in the process of which they seized Tunes. On the back of his success, Regulus opened negotiations with the Carthaginians, but his

conditions were so harsh that they were rejected outright.
Polybius, 1: 30(4–14)

BAGRADAS R (255, spring) – First Punic War

Dispirited but defiant, the Carthaginians trained a new army with recruited reinforcements from Greece. These included a veteran Lacedaemonian officer named Xanthippus, who rapidly assumed command and trained the army in the best Spartan traditions. Morale soared. He persuaded the Carthaginians to overcome their fears and to descend from the heights into the plains of the Bagradas [*Medjerda*] valley where the enemy was encamped and where, he assured his men, they would be invincible. Polybius quotes their roll as 12,000 infantry, 4,000 cavalry and 100 elephants. When the Romans pitched camp nearby, the Carthaginians accepted the challenge and gave Xanthippus full powers of command. He ordered the elephants to the front of the whole army and divided the cavalry between the wings. The Romans opposed the elephants with their light-armed troops in the front, covering a deep formation of legionaries behind them. Their cavalry, also, were on the wings. When Xanthippus gave the order, the elephants charged and trampled the front maniples underfoot. At the same time the Carthaginian cavalry, who were numerically much superior, routed their opposite numbers on both flanks and proceeded to attack the Roman rear, which became completely surrounded. A few men who managed to retreat were subsequently captured; they included the commander Regulus. Only about 2,000 Romans survived, mainly from the left wing which had not been confronted by the elephants. They had managed to rush their opposing Carthaginian mercenaries and drive them back to their camp. The sole Carthaginian losses were about 800 of these mercenaries.
Polybius, 1: 32–34; Zonaras, 8: 13; Appian, Punic Wars, 3; Livy, epitome 18

HERMAEUM C (255, summer) – First Punic War

Following the Roman disaster in the Bagradas valley (above), the citizens at home immediately fitted out a new fleet with a view to rescuing the remnants of their army in Africa. They are said to have launched 350 ships, which they sent out under Marcus Aemilius and Servius Fulvius. Near Cape Hermaeum [*Cape Bon*] this fleet encountered the patrolling Carthaginian fleet, on which it inflicted a severe defeat, capturing 114 ships

(Diodorus says 24) with their crews. It is said by Zonaras that at the height of the battle the Romans in Aspis (also known as Clupea) [*Kelibia*], who were the object of the rescue mission, sailed out and attacked the Carthaginians in the rear. After the battle, they joined the Roman fleet on its return journey to Italy. Unfortunately, they ran into an appalling storm off Camarina in Sicily and less than a quarter of their ships survived.
Polybius, 1: 36(5–12); Zonaras, 8: 14; Diodorus, 23: 18(1)

PANORMUS (250, June) – First Punic War
In 254 the Romans assaulted Panormus [*Palermo*] by land and sea and carried it. The ensuing four years were a period of stalemate. The defeat of Regulus (Bagradas, 255) had instilled into the Romans an abject terror of the enemy's elephants. Encouraged, Hasdrubal decided to recover Panormus and he marched out of Lilybaeum [*Marsala*] and camped on the border. The consul Lucius Caecilius Metellus made no response, hoping to lure the enemy closer. Attributing the Roman's inertia to fear, Hasdrubal pressed on and eventually, in the absence of any Roman move, he crossed the river in front of the town with his whole force including the elephants. Metellus then began to harass the beasts, ordering his light-armed troops to fire missiles at them from outside the wall and then to retreat to a prepared trench as the elephants charged. When the elephants began to attack the trench, they became targets for the archers on the walls. Before long the animals stampeded and turned on their own troops. At this point Metellus led out his force and charged the enemy flank, putting the whole army to headlong flight. Ten elephants were captured and the rest, totalling 120, were rounded up and later were transported to Rome. The victory restored the morale of the Roman troops.
Polybius, 1: 40; Zonaras, 8: 14; Diodorus, 23: 21

DREPANUM (249) – First Punic War
By the year 249 the Romans were in control of the whole of Sicily with the exception of Lilybaeum [*Marsala*] and Drepanum [*Trapani*] on the west coast. After investing Lilybaeum without success, they decided to launch an attack with their whole fleet on the Carthaginian base at Drepanum while maintaining the siege of Lilybaeum. Under the command of Publius Claudius Pulcher they put to sea at midnight unobserved by the enemy in Lilybaeum. When Adherbal, the Carthaginian commander at Drepanum, saw the fleet

approaching, he hastily mustered his crews and ordered them to get under way and follow his ship. He led them out of the harbour, clinging to the shore on the opposite side of the harbour to the one by which the Romans were entering. Pulcher saw what was happening too late; he was leading his fleet from behind! By the time he realized the truth, some of his ships were in the harbour while others were in the entrance or approaching it. He gave orders for the whole fleet to put out to sea – with devastating results. In the process of turning, ships fouled each other, oars were broken and confusion reigned. Eventually, as the ships cleared the harbour, they were brought into line abreast close to the shore. This position proved to be their undoing. The enemy ships, which were anyway the faster, could manoeuvre in the open sea as they pleased; the Romans could hardly move. When the Roman commander saw the carnage, he fled with some 30 other ships which could escape. The remaining 93 vessels were all captured with their crews, apart from the sailors who beached their ships and fled.
Polybius, 1: 49–51; Diodorus, 24: 1(5); Livy, epitome 19

AEGIMURUS ISL (245) – First Punic War
The chronicle of Florus reports a naval battle near Aegimurus [*Al Djamur*], a small island off the Bay of Carthage. A Carthaginian fleet sailing against Italy was engaged and defeated by a Roman fleet. Unfortunately, the Roman ships laden with booty were subsequently wrecked by a storm. This action appears to be otherwise unmentioned in the extant literature.
Florus, 1: 18(30–32)

AEGATES ISLS (241, summer) – First Punic War
The Romans had come to realize that they were making no progress on land, largely as a result of Hamilcar Barca's outstanding leadership of the Carthaginians since he had assumed the command in 247. They could only win the war by a victory at sea. In spite of their major defeat at Drepanum (249) and the loss of several fleets wrecked by storms, they decided to make one more attempt. A fleet of 200 quinqueremes was built through private enterprise and money. The ships were built to a design copied from a Carthaginian ship which had been so fast and manoeuvrable that it had been able to run the blockade at Lilybaeum on many occasions. This new fleet sailed for Sicily under the command of Gaius Lutatius and took

the enemy by surprise. The Punic fleet had sailed home to Carthage with no suspicion of impending trouble. As soon as the Carthaginians heard the news, they fitted out their ships and loaded them with provisions for their forces who were engaged with the Romans at Eryx [*Erice*]. Their commander Hanno planned to sail direct to Eryx to offload the stores and to take on some mercenary marines as well as Hasdrubal Barca himself, and then to engage the Romans. Lutatius anticipated his thoughts and sailed to the island of Aegusa [*Favignana*], the largest of the Aegates islands [*Egadi*] off north-west Sicily, from which he could bar the passage to Eryx of the enemy fleet, which was expected the next day. That day turned out to be rough with an unfavourable wind, but Lutatius in his agony of mind could not afford to let the enemy lighten their load and take on troops at Eryx. When they were sighted, he made his decision, put to sea and faced the enemy in line abreast. The respective conditions of the two fleets were now the antithesis of those which had pertained at Drepanum (249). The Romans were geared for fighting; the enemy ships were loaded with supplies and their men were raw recruits enlisted in emergency. The Carthaginians had rashly assumed that the Roman navy would not bother them again. In the event they were worsted all along the line from the very start. Fifty of their ships were sunk and 70 captured with crews. According to Polybius the Romans took nearly 10,000 prisoners in the battle. Polybius does not give the Roman losses, but Diodorus quotes 30 ships sunk and 50 badly damaged. The immediate effect of this battle was that the Carthaginians could no longer supply their troops in the field, and so they gave Hamilcar Barca, their commander in Sicily, the authority to act at his discretion. Left with no way of saving his troops, he prudently asked for negotiations, which brought this long and weary war to an end.

Polybius, 1: 59–61; Diodorus, 24: 11; Livy, epitome 19

CLUSIUM (225) – Gallic Invasion

Throughout the First Punic War the Gauls refrained from embarrassing the Romans with a second front. They had been completely crushed a bare 20 years beforehand, and it was not until some years after the Punic War that Gallic unrest recurred. The two largest tribes, the Insubres and the Boii, joined forces and enlisted support from other tribes, raising a total of 50,000 infantry and 20,000 cavalry. In 225 this force descended into the Po valley and advanced on Etruria. Help for the Romans was forthcoming on all sides in central and southern Italy. The forces in position for defence of the boundaries alone amounted, so it is said, to 130,000 infantry, with several times that number fit for service. When the invading Gauls reached Clusium [*Chiusi*], they heard that a Roman army was coming up behind them. They turned to face it and the two armies had almost made contact by sunset, when they camped for the night. After lighting their camp fires the Gauls withdrew by night in the direction of Faesulae [*Fiesoli*] to set up an ambush, leaving their cavalry at the camp. At daybreak the Romans spotted the cavalry and advanced against them, while the cavalry, following instructions, withdrew toward Faesulae with the Romans in pursuit. At the site of the ambush the Gauls sprang up and charged. In the ensuing fight the Romans were outnumbered and lost 6,000 men. The rest fled to a hill which the Gauls tried to seize but without success, and so they put a cavalry guard on it, determined to have another try next day. Meanwhile the consul Lucius Aemilius Papus, in charge of a second Roman army near the Adriatic, had heard of the invasion of Etruria and had hurried south, reaching the battlefield at the crucial moment. He camped near the enemy and lit camp fires. When the Gauls saw the flames, they realized the truth of the situation and decided to pull out before dawn and make for home.

This encounter has sometimes been referred to as the battle of Faesulae [*Fiesoli*], north of Florence. If this was the site, the ensuing battle at Telamon 90 miles south of Faesulae would be inexplicable if the Gauls were heading homeward as reported. It has been said that the Gauls withdrew from Clusium *in the direction of Faesulae* and set up an ambush in the space of one night. It seems probable to the present writer that the ambush was much closer to Clusium than Faesulae.

Polybius, 2: 25–26

TELAMON (225) – Gallic Invasion

After the battle of Clusium (above), the Gauls marched to the Etrurian coast and started northwards, pursued by Paulus and his legions. At the same time the consul Gaius Atilius Regularis, returning from Sardinia with his forces, had landed at Pisa and was marching south to Rome. When the Gauls were in the neighbourhood of Telamon [*Talamone*], Atilius learnt from some captured foragers of the proximity of the Gallic army and of the presence of Aemilius Papus with

his army in their rear. Atilius immediately led his cavalry to occupy a hill which was on the line of the Gauls' advance. When the Gauls realized that they were sandwiched between two armies, they deployed their forces back to back. On his arrival, the first action of Papus was to send his cavalry to support his colleague in the fight for the hill, to which the initial fighting was confined. The consul Atilius was killed in this action but his cavalry fought on and eventually won the coveted high ground. Meanwhile, the infantry of the three armies had begun to close. In the terrifying tumult that followed, the Roman javelin throwers had the first pick and executed much damage, particularly among the warriors of the Gasatae who preferred to fight naked. They cracked. Next, the Roman infantry advanced, but they were held by the other tribes who, although savagely mauled, stood their ground with great courage. The end was brought about by the Roman cavalry in a furious charge from the hill which had been captured earlier. The Gallic cavalry fled and the foot soldiers were cut to pieces. The Gallic losses have been given as 40,000 killed and at least 10,000 captured, including one of their kings. Another king took his own life. The Roman victory terminated the largest and last of the Gallic invasions, but the aftermath lingered on for a few more years.
Polybius, 2: 27–31(2)

CLASTIDIUM (222) – Gallic Invasion
Not content with their utter defeat of the Gauls, the Romans were determined to clear the Insubres out of the Po valley completely. In 223 the consul Gaius Flaminius crossed the Padus [*Po*] and defeated the Insubres at an unknown river. The following year the Gauls sued for peace but the new consuls, Marcus Claudius Marcellus and Gnaeus Cornelius, were uncompromising. They besieged the town of Acerrae; the Gauls responded by laying siege to Clastidium [*Casteggio*]. Claudius then set off with his cavalry to rescue the besieged, which caused the Gauls to raise the siege and to march out to meet him. Their force included some 10,000 Gasatae, who had joined their compatriots either for money or, according to Plutarch, to foment unrest. The Romans were greatly outnumbered and, to compensate for this, Marcellus extended his wings. When, as a result, the Gauls found themselves being encircled by the Roman cavalry, they gave way and were either cut down or put to flight. Never before in Roman history did so few cavalrymen inflict such a defeat upon so many foot and horse combined.

An account of a single hand-to-hand combat between Marcellus himself and the king of the Gauls is included in Plutarch's account. Marcellus despatched the Gaul with his spear, earning for himself the right to dedicate the *spolia opima* to Jupiter Feretrius. He was only the third person in Roman history to win the honour, the first traditionally being Romulus.
Polybius, 2: 34(1–9); Plutarch, Marcellus, 6(2)– 7(4); Livy, epitome 20

MEDIOLANUM (222) – Gallic Invasion
From Clastidium (above) the Gauls withdrew to Mediolanum [*Milan*], pursued by Gnaeus Cornelius who had meanwhile captured Acerrae. When Cornelius decided to head back to Acerrae, the Gauls in Mediolanum made a sortie and attacked the Roman rearguard, routing a part of it. The Roman vanguard was then ordered back to make a counterattack, as a result of which the Gauls broke up and fled to the mountains. Cornelius went on to capture Mediolanum, after which the Insubres submitted and were granted peace.
Polybius, 2: 34(10)–35(1)

PHAROS ISL (219) – Second Illyrian War
Described under *The Greek World*, p. 121.

RHODANUS R (218) – Second Punic War
While the Romans were involved with the Gallic invasion of 225–222, the Carthaginians were empire-building in Spain, accumulating resources and reaping considerable Iberian military manpower in the process. Another war with Rome was clearly in mind. In 221 Hannibal, the 25-year-old son of Hamilcar Barca, assumed the Punic command and turned the probability of war into a certainty. The spark which ignited the Second Punic War was an affair at Saguntum, the only city south of the Ebro which was not held by the Carthaginians. Hannibal threatened to attack the city, to which the Romans had promised protection. The Romans protested but Carthage upheld the actions of Hannibal, who proceeded to capture the place all the same after eight months of siege. The Punic government's refusal to surrender Hannibal at the request of the Romans led to a prompt declaration of war in 218. The Carthaginians had not been able to rebuild their navy, and so it appeared to the Romans that the war would be an 'away' match in Spain and Africa. Hannibal had other ideas. He planned to circumvent the enemy at sea and to invade their home by land.

In the spring of 218 Hannibal crossed the river

Iberus [*Ebro*] and started his march to northern Italy. With a force reputed to consist of 50,000 foot with 9,000 horse and 37 elephants he reached the Rhodanus [*Rhône*], where he encountered his first major opposition. The natives on the right bank were amenable and helped to build a fleet of canoes; but on the opposite bank a large force of barbarians assembled menacingly. To deal with this threat Hannibal sent a detachment upstream under the command of Hanno, son of Bomilcar. After about 25 miles they reached a convenient place for crossing the river on rafts. Having done so, they proceeded downstream and lit a smoke fire as a signal to Hannibal that they were across and close at hand. Hannibal immediately ordered his men to start ferrying themselves over, whereupon Hanno and his men appeared, set fire to the Gallic camp and took the horde completely by surprise. This gave Hannibal the opportunity to form up those who had landed and engage the enemy on the other flank. They promptly turned and fled.

In the meantime Publius Cornelius Scipio (father of Africanus Major) and his brother Gnaeus had set sail from Pisa with an army bound for Spain. Five days later Publius dropped anchor at the eastern end of the Rhône delta and was amazed to learn that Hannibal had already reached the river. Publius sent out a reconnaissance party of 300 horsemen, who met and clashed with 500 Numidians from Hannibal's camp on a similar errand. In a fierce skirmish, with heavy losses on both sides, the Numidians were defeated and fled. But when Scipio followed upstream with his whole army, he found that Hannibal had already marched off and eluded him.
Polybius, 3: 42–45; Livy, 21: 26(3–5) and 27–29

TICINUS R (218) – Second Punic War
Hannibal crossed the Alps in a fortnight and descended into the Po valley with a force reduced to half the size. He lost no time in augmenting it with recruits from the disaffected Gauls. In the meantime, Publius Cornelius Scipio, who had coincidentally arrived at the Rhône crossing three days after Hannibal had left, set sail homewards with a small detachment to Pisae [*Pisa*]. Taking command of the legions stationed in the area, he marched northwards to the Po valley, crossed the river and advanced westward to the river Ticinus, which flowed southwards from Lake Verbanus [*Maggiore*] into the Po. He crossed this river and took up station on the west bank 5 miles from Victumulae [*Vigerano*]. The Roman and Cartha-

ginian armies were now almost in contact, and the next morning both generals led out their cavalry and engaged. Scipio also took his javelin throwers, whom he placed in the van. On the other side, Hannibal put his heavy cavalry in front and kept his Numidian cavalry out on the wings. When the action began, the initial Carthaginian charge was so fast and furious that the Roman javelin throwers had no time to throw their missiles and were compelled to retreat through the ranks to the rear. The Roman cavalry managed to hold the enemy charge, inflicting heavy losses, until the Numidians outflanked them and fell upon them from the rear. The javelin throwers, now in the rear, were the first to succumb, being trampled underfoot. The Roman cavalry were then attacked from the rear as well as the front and they broke and fled. Scipio himself was severely wounded in the battle and owed his life to the intervention of his young son. This was only the first of a series of crushing defeats sustained by the Romans at the hands of Hannibal.
Polybius, 3: 65; Livy, 21: 45–46

LILYBAEUM (218) – Second Punic War
In the Sicilian arena, Carthage sent 20 quinqueremes with 1,000 soldiers to raid the coast. Seventeen of them reached the Lipara islands off northeast Sicily but three were swept off course into the Siculum Fretum [*Straits of Messina*]. Hiero II, the tyrant of Syracuse and a faithful ally of Rome, happened to be in Messana [*Messina*] and saw the ships. He sent out 12 warships which captured the three errant Carthaginian vessels and brought them into harbour. It was learnt from the captured crews that another squadron of 35 quinqueremes was on its way, with Lilybaeum [*Marsala*] as the primary objective. Hiero informed the Romans who issued a general alert. The Carthaginians intended to land just before dawn, but they were spotted in the moonlight and soon realized that they had been observed. They lay offshore, preparing for a battle. When the Romans sailed out against them, it became obvious that the Carthaginian ships carried few soldiers. Whereas the Romans strained to grapple and board, their opponents did their best to elude close contact. This did not prevent the Romans from surrounding seven of the enemy vessels, whereupon the rest fled. The Romans suffered damage to only one ship.
Livy, 21: 49–50

TREBIA R (218, December) – Second Punic War
After his defeat at the Ticinus (218) Scipio camped at Placentia [*Piacenza*]. Two days later Hannibal arrived and camped close by. For the Romans the situation was made the more alarming by a treacherous nocturnal attack by the Gauls serving in their army, who then defected to the Carthaginians. Scipio saw the danger of a mass swing of all the Gallic tribes to the enemy cause, and so he marched to the river Trebia [*Trebbia*] where the tribes were loyal allies. He was harassed by Hannibal's Numidian cavalry but managed to cross the river with most of his force and camped on the right (east) bank. Hannibal followed and pitched his camp a few miles away on the left bank. At this point the consul Titus Sempronius Longus, who had been recalled from Sicily, arrived with his legions after a march of 40 days. As Scipio had been severely wounded at the Ticinus, the enthusiastic and ambitious Longus assumed the command. He was itching for a battle, which Hannibal duly provided. At daybreak Hannibal ordered his Numidians to cross the river and to try to entice the Romans into action before they were fully prepared. Longus responded by sending out his cavalry, followed by 6,000 javelin-throwers and then the rest of the army consisting of 16,000 Roman infantry and 20,000 allies. In pursuit of the Numidians, they waded across the Trebia, which was swollen with the winter rains and icy cold. In consequence, they started the battle in a frozen, wet and hungry state, as Hannibal had intended. He then led out his own fresh and well-fed troops and drew up the infantry in a line 20,000 strong with the 10,000 horse divided between the two wings. The elephants he placed in front of the infantry's wings. Confronting this army were 16,000 Roman infantry and 20,000 allies with the 4,000 horse divided between the two wings. The action was started by the light-armed troops. The Carthaginians gained the upper hand in this, the Romans having already discharged most of their missiles against the Numidian cavalry. When these skirmishers had retired and the heavy infantry had engaged, the Carthaginian cavalry immediately attacked on both wings. The Roman cavalry, who were numerically inferior, fell back and exposed the infantry's flanks to attack. At this point the Romans were suddenly and unexpectedly charged from the rear. Hannibal had previously set up a trap and had sent his brother Mago with 1,000 horse and an equal number of foot to conceal themselves in a watercourse with high banks obscured by bramble. These forces now emerged

and created confusion in the Roman ranks. The wings, which were pressed from the front by the elephants and on their flanks by the light-armed troops, were forced back. The Roman centre, which had up till then resisted the enemy, now found itself pushed forward by its own forces in the rear and completely surrounded. This body of 10,000 men adopted their only means of escape by hacking a way through the Carthaginian line, after which they withdrew to Placentia.
Polybius, 3: 71–74; Livy, 21: 54–56

CISSIS (218) – Second Punic War
When Publius Scipio interrupted his journey to Spain at the Rhône delta (Rhodanus, 218) and returned to Italy to intercept Hannibal, he told his brother Gnaeus, who was with him, to take the forces on to Spain. There, Gnaeus developed a reputation for clement behaviour among the tribes, which gained him many allies and reinforcements. The commander responsible for the defence of Carthaginian interests in Spain north of the Ebro was Hanno (a common Punic name). Deciding that he must act before the entire region passed under Roman control, he confronted Scipio near Cissis [probably *Guissona*] and prepared for battle. Scipio accepted the challenge willingly, knowing that there was a second Carthaginian army to be reckoned with and preferring to fight the two armies separately. In the fight against Hanno, 6,000 of the enemy were killed and a further 2,000 were taken prisoner including the commander himself. The enemy camp proved to be a rich source of booty.
Livy, 21: 60(5–9); Polybius, 3: 76(5–6)

IBERUS R (217, summer) – Second Punic War
At the beginning of summer the Carthaginian admiral Hamilcar put out of New Carthage with a fleet of 40 decked ships and sailed northwards along the coast to the mouth of the Iberus [*Ebro*]. Hasdrubal, the commander in Spain, kept pace with him, marching his army along the shore. Gnaeus Scipio, hearing of this, manned 35 ships and appeared off the Iberus. When he learnt that the enemy fleet was anchored off the mouth of the river, he sailed in against it and caught the enemy totally unprepared. The Carthaginians scarcely put up any resistance but fell back on the shore, beaching their ships and leaping out to the protection afforded by the armed forces drawn up on the beach. The Romans sailed in boldly and towed away every ship which could be floated – 25 of them. As a result of this modest action the Romans

established their naval supremacy along the coast for the time being.
Polybius, 3: 95–96(6); Livy, 22: 19–20(1–3)

TRASIMENUS L (217, June 21) – Second Punic War

While matters were going well for the Romans in Spain, they suffered nothing but a series of major reverses nearer home. In the spring, Hannibal started marching south again, through Etruria. Characteristically, he chose to go through the marshes, a route which involved four days and three nights of marching and privation and which would be totally unexpected by the enemy. The Roman consul Gaius Flaminius had pitched camp at Arretium [*Arezzo*], close to Hannibal's route after he had emerged from the marshes. He was a vain and overconfident man, and Hannibal had heard as much. The Carthaginian decided to play on the other's weakness by ignoring Flaminius and advancing straight past him, ravaging the countryside as he went. This was too much for the Roman, who was lured into following his enemy into a trap. The road, little more than a narrow path, ran around the north shore of Lake Trasimenus [*Trasimene*]. The approach to the western end of the lake was a narrow defile, after which the ground levelled out into a small hill-locked valley. At the eastern end of this there was a mountainous barrier with sheer slopes, where Hannibal positioned himself with his veterans. He concealed his light-armed troops in the hills north of the lake; the cavalry he placed out of sight close to the western defile so that they could block it when the enemy was in the trap. Flaminius camped nearby for the night and led his men on a misty dawn through the defile into the valley. The Carthaginians fell on them out of the mist on all sides. A carnage resulted in which Flaminius was killed, while those in the rear were trapped between hills and lake. Many drowned attempting to swim to safety in full armour. Altogether about 15,000 perished and similar numbers were taken captive. Around 6,000 escaped temporarily into the mist but were rounded up later. Livy, however, says that around 10,000 men managed to find their way back to Rome. The Carthaginian losses amounted to about 1,500.
Polybius, 3: 83–84; Livy, 22: 4–7(1–5)

CALLICULA (ERIBIANUS) M (217) – Second Punic War

Hannibal's victory at Trasimene (above) opened the road to Rome, but for various reasons he decided to turn aside. He pillaged his way through all the territories on the Adriatic side of the Apennines down into Apulia, ravaging the land as he went. While this was going on, the Romans had appointed Quintus Fabius Maximus as dictator. Their military forces at that time consisted of four hastily conscripted legions together with their second army, which had been guarding the Adriatic approaches at the time of Trasimene. The dictator assumed command of the lot and camped near the Carthaginians. Hannibal immediately led out his army and confronted the Romans but he failed to elicit any response. Thereafter, Fabius employed the dogging and delaying tactics for which he became noted and which earned him the appellation of Cunctator. Wherever Hannibal went, Fabius shadowed him, constantly harassing but keeping his distance. In this way they passed through Samnium. Hannibal then descended through a pass near the mount called Callicula (Livy) or Eribianus (Polybius) into the Falernian Plain around Capua, the richest and most fertile area in the whole of Italy. He hoped that the sight of him plundering and devastating this beautiful region would entice his enemy to give battle. If Fabius refrained, it would at least show to all around that he, Hannibal, was the indisputable master who could do as he chose with impunity. This would encourage them to abandon their allegiance to Rome and join him. Fabius, as usual, stuck to his plan and moved along the ridges, resisting any temptation to descend and fight.

It occurred to Fabius that in due course Hannibal would want to leave the plain by the same route that he had come. There are but few routes out of the plain and Fabius had already blocked two of them with garrisons. Accordingly he sent 4,000 men up the pass by Mount Callicula and he himself camped on a hill overlooking it. It began to look as though the master of traps had himself been trapped. Hannibal, realising his position, developed a most ingenious plan. He got his men to collect as many dry faggots as they could and to round up 2,000 of the strongest oxen from the stock which they had captured. As soon as it was dark the oxen were driven up to the pass and the faggots were tied to their horns. The faggots were then set on fire and the beasts were driven hard up to the top of the hills. The Roman garrison in the pass, thinking that the enemy was escaping over the top, moved up to meet him. The apparitions that they encountered puzzled and terrified them into keeping their distance from the flaming monsters. Meanwhile, Hannibal led his army through the pass unopposed, while Fabius remained within his camp, also puzzled and fearing a trap.

The arrival of dawn found the Roman garrison still on top of the hill and in the company of the Carthaginians who had driven the beasts. There had been virtually no action during the confusion of the night, but now the two parties closed. The Carthaginians were heavily outnumbered and would have been wiped out but for the arrival of a Spanish detachment which had been sent back by Hannibal. In the ensuing engagement the Romans came off worst, losing 'a number' of men according to Livy; Polybius puts their losses at about a thousand.
Polybius, 3: 92–94(6); Livy, 22: 15–18(4)

GERUNIUM (216) – Second Punic War
Hannibal had by now amassed an immense quantity of plunder and provisions, and he settled on Gerunium as an ideal place for storage and for his winter quarters. He seized it and fortified his encampment in front of the town. The Romans camped nearby.

The cautious tactics of Fabius were scorned as cowardly by his deputy Marcus Minucius who, after a successful skirmish, became even more intolerably overconfident. Fabius, aware of this, offered him a choice between command of the army on alternate days or total command of half the army. Minucius accepted the division, and the two halves camped a mile or two apart. Hannibal, also, was aware of the schism and of Minucius' impulsiveness, and so he set a trap. Between his camp and that of Minucius was a small hill surrounded by rough ground and hollows. Hannibal sent out a contingent of 500 cavalry and 5,000 infantry by night with orders to conceal themselves in this terrain. Then at daybreak he sent a small party of light-armed troops to occupy the hill. When Minucius saw this, he sent out his light-armed troops followed by the cavalry. Hannibal sent reinforcements, and so Minucius engaged with his heavy infantry. Hannibal then appeared with his cavalry and the rest of his army. At this point the signal was given to the troops lying in ambush, who charged out from all directions. The result might have been a complete disaster if Fabius had not been watching the action and had not hastily brought his army up to the rescue. This put heart into the Romans who rallied and managed to withdraw to safety. As it was, they lost many of the light infantry and even more of the legionaries. The effects of his impetuosity and of his salvation by Fabius were salutary lessons to

Minucius, who was thereafter content to play second fiddle to his now revered superior.
Polybius, 3: 104–105; Livy, 22: 28–29; Plutarch, Fabius Maximus, 11–12

CANNAE (216, August 2) – Second Punic War
In the spring of 216 Hannibal left Gerunium and marched to Cannae in Apulia, where he captured the citadel and with it the Roman supplies stored in it. The citadel commanded the whole surrounding countryside so that any approach by the Romans would inevitably lead to a battle. The generals appealed to Rome for instructions, and the senate decided to put eight legions (40,000 men excluding allies) into the field. This was an unprecedented step, two legions being the usual complement or at most four legions. This huge force of around 80,000 men plus cavalry set out for Cannae under two consuls, the cautious L. Aemilius Paulus and the hasty Gaius Terentius Varro, who pitched camp by the river Aufidus a few miles from the Carthaginian camp. Hannibal, with a force numbering about half that of the Romans, had taken up a position on the right (south) bank of the river with the prevailing wind from the mountains behind him. This fact is not mentioned by Polybius, but Livy makes a great point of it. The wind drove over the sandy plain,

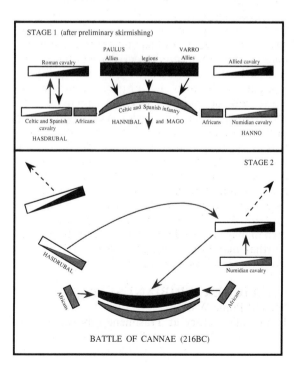

STAGE 1 (after preliminary skirmishing)

Roman cavalry

PAULUS
Allies   legions

VARRO
Allies

Allied cavalry

Celtic and Spanish infantry

Celtic and Spanish cavalry   Africans   HANNIBAL and MAGO   Africans   Numidian cavalry

HASDRUBAL   HANNO

STAGE 2

HASDRUBAL

Numidian cavalry

Africans   Africans

BATTLE OF CANNAE (216BC)

whipping up dust which would choke and blind his opponents. In accordance with custom, the consuls assumed command in turn on alternate days. On a day when Varro was in command – and against all the advice of Paulus – he led out his legions and drew them up facing the enemy with the legionaries in close formation in the centre and cavalry on both wings. Hannibal had drawn up his line in a crescent with the centre foremost. Here, in the middle, he had placed his weakest and most unreliable troops, the Celts and Spaniards. They were strengthened on either side by African infantry with cavalry beyond on the wings. In the engagement the Roman centre forced the Celts and Spaniards back, as Hannibal is said to have intended. When, under further pressure, they continued to give ground, the Carthaginian line ceased to be a convex arc and became concave. The Roman infantry had now penetrated deeply into the enemy centre where they found themselves flanked by the African troops at either end of the enemy line. These divisions turned inwards and attacked the Roman flanks. Meanwhile the Carthaginian cavalry was getting the better of the Roman horse. On the Carthaginian left, Hasdrubal with his cavalry had virtually destroyed the opposing wing and, being unengaged, he led his squadrons round behind the Roman position to assist the Numidian cavalry on the right. When they had routed the enemy horse, Hasdrubal turned and attacked the Roman infantry in the rear. The legions were now completely surrounded and were almost annihilated. Estimates of their total casualties range from 50,000 to 70,000. The consul Varro managed to escape, but the gallant Paulus was killed. On the Carthaginian side the losses were about 6,000 all told.

Livy tells a dubious story about some Numidians who pretended to be deserters to the Roman cause but had secreted swords under their tunics. Appian and Zonaras have a very similar tale about some Celtiberians. These accounts read rather like fabricated excuses for the Roman disaster, blaming it on dirty work. From the sketchy account of Zonaras it is difficult to recognize the battle as that of Cannae.

As a matter of perspective, it may be noted that Livy's lower estimate for the Roman casualties would still represent the worst losses suffered by any single western army on a single day up to the present time.

Polybius, 3: 110–117; Livy, 22: 43(10)–49; Plutarch, Fabius Maximus, 15–16; Appian, Hannibalic War, 19–26; Zonaras, 9: 1

NOLA (216) – Second Punic War

Hannibal's overwhelming victory at Cannae (above) opened the way for an immediate march straight on Rome, but he did not take it. His force was not a large one, and Rome still held the allegiance of the centre and north of Italy. The disaster of Cannae brought out the best in the Roman temperament. Peace was never mentioned. The senate proclaimed a levy and raised four legions, enlisting even boys. In addition, they armed 8,000 volunteers from among the slaves. There were also in excess of 10,000 fugitives who had managed to escape after Cannae.

Instead of attacking Rome, Hannibal roamed about mainly in Campania, receiving towns which were handed over to him or attacking them with or without success. When he presented himself at the gates of Nola, about 9 miles north-east of Vesuvius, Marcus Claudius Marcellus was holding the place with his army. The senators of Nola reported to Marcellus that the citizens were secretly plotting with the enemy to seize control of the town when the Romans moved out to battle. They would seize the Roman baggage, shut the gates and man the walls. Acting on this tip, Marcellus divided his army into three sections and positioned them at the three gates which faced the Carthaginian camp. The baggage was supervised and no citizen was allowed to approach the walls or gates. For several days Hannibal had lined his men up in battle order without obtaining any response. He then assembled all the gear needed for an assault and had started to advance when the middle gate was flung open. The pick of the Roman infantry charged forth followed by the cavalry. The Carthaginian centre was reeling under the shock when the allied horse and light infantry charged out of the other gates and attacked the enemy's wings. They were driven back to their camp and subsequently withdrew from Nola. The Carthaginians are reputed to have lost 2,800 men (Plutarch says 5,000) against a Roman loss of 500. But even Livy, whose accounts are frequently coloured with patriotic embellishments, hesitates to adopt these figures and clearly does not regard the result as more than a minor victory. It was, he says, a hard enough task at that time to avoid defeat by Hannibal.

Livy, 23: 16; Plutarch, Marcellus, 11

GRUMENTUM (215) – Second Punic War

In an action near Grumentum in Lucania, Tiberius Sempronius Longus defeated the Carthaginians under Hanno. Over 2,000 of the enemy were killed

with a Roman loss of 280, and 41 standards were captured. Hanno withdrew into Bruttium.
Livy, 23: 37(10–11)

NOLA (215) – Second Punic War

Hannibal decided to make another attempt at Nola, following his defeat there by Marcellus in the preceding year (Nola, 216). He was joined there by Hanno, who arrived from Bruttium with reinforcements from Carthage. Between them they surrounded the town. The proconsul Marcellus marched his men out, and a battle took place on flat ground between the town and the Carthaginian camp about a mile away. Plutarch records that Marcellus had armed his infantry with long spears for use at long range, whereas the enemy had only short weapons for close fighting. As a result, the Carthaginians turned and fled. No amount of praise or abuse from Hannibal could prevent his men from breaking. He lost 5,000 men killed against 1,000 Roman casualties. A few days later nearly 300 Spanish and Numidian cavalrymen deserted to the Romans.

This account by Livy, repeated by Plutarch, is at variance with the statement of Polybius that Hannibal remained unbeaten before the battle of Zama (202). If Polybius' assertion is accepted, it is necessary also to accept that Livy (and Plutarch) have exaggerated the Roman victory, presumably to offset the Roman disaster at Cannae (216).
Livy, 23: 44–46(6); Plutarch, Marcellus, *12(2–3); Polybius, 15: 16(5)*

CARALES (215) – Second Punic War

In Sardinia, the Roman presence was small and its control of the island was tottering. A certain local magnate, Hampsicora, was stirring up revolt and beckoning to Carthage. Hasdrubal the Bald was sent there with a force of about 12,000 foot and 1,500 horse, but the fleet was damaged and they were delayed by bad weather. On the other side, the Romans sent 5,000 foot and 400 horse under Titus Manlius Torquatus, who now controlled a total force of 22,000 foot and 1,200 horse. He marched upcountry and encamped near the position occupied by Hampsicora. Shortly afterwards Hasdrubal arrived, causing Manlius to withdraw to Carales [*Cagliari*]. Hasdrubal joined forces with Hampsicora and together they advanced toward Carales but were met and engaged by Manlius. The action lasted for four hours during which numerous Sardinians were either killed of fled. The Carthaginians put up a stiffer resistance but eventually they too turned

and started to flee, only to find that their retreat was cut off by the Roman wing which had routed the Sardinians. What followed was butchery. The enemy lost a total of 12,000 men killed and 3,700 captured. Among the prisoners were Hasdrubal himself and two other commanders, Hanno and Mago. Hampsicora, learning that his son was dead, killed himself.
Livy, 23: 40–41(4)

IBERA (215) – Second Punic War

In 216 or 215 Hasdrubal Barca, the Carthaginian commander in Spain, received orders to follow in the footsteps of his brother Hannibal and march to Italy. When the Scipio brothers, Gnaeus and Publius, heard of this, they joined forces in an attempt to abort the threat to Rome. They crossed the river Iberus [*Ebro*] and prepared to attack the town of Ibera just south of the river. Hasdrubal countered by assaulting a Roman-held town, probably Dertosa [*Tortosa*] on the north bank of the river, to which the Romans repaired. When the two armies lined up for battle, the Spanish contingents in Hasdrubal's centre gave way almost immediately and were completely routed by a vigorous charge. His wings fared better and partially encircled the Romans, forcing them toward the centre where they found themselves fighting in a massed body and in both directions. However, with the rout of the enemy centre the Romans had become superior in numbers, and they forced the enemy's wings to give way with heavy losses. Few Carthaginians survived. The enemy cavalry had already fled the field when they saw their centre give way. The Roman victory forced Hasdrubal to postpone his march to Italy, which eventually took place nine years later. An additional Roman gain was a resulting swing to Rome on the part of many of the Iberian tribes.
Livy, 23: 28(7)–29

ILITURGI (215) – Second Punic War

Iliturgi [near *Cabanes*], a Spanish town in the east which had joined the Romans, was besieged by Hasdrubal, Mago and Hamilcar (son of Bomilcar). Starvation was looming when Publius and Gnaeus Scipio forced their way in between the three armies, bringing supplies. The Scipios then made a sortie against the main enemy position under Hasdrubal, who was promptly joined by the other two armies. The Romans were grossly outnumbered with only 16,000 men against the combined enemy force of 60,000. Nevertheless, in spite of the mismatch, the Romans won an

undoubted victory which cost the enemy more casualties than the total Roman strength. All three enemy camps were captured.
Livy 23: 49((5–11)

INTIBILI (215) – Second Punic War
After their defeat at Iliturgi (above) the Carthaginians marched northwards to attack Intibili [near *Benicarlo*]. Here the story was much the same as at Iliturgi. The Romans engaged them and killed more than 13,000 of them as well as capturing 2,000 men and several elephants. These successes encouraged most of the local tribes to go over to the Romans.
Livy, 23: 49(12–14)

BENEVENTUM (214) – Second Punic War
In Italy, the Carthaginian general Hanno and the Roman Tiberius Sempronius Gracchus converged with their armies on Beneventum [*Benevento*]. When Gracchus learnt that Hanno was encamped about three miles away, he took up a position a mile away from him. After the two sides had lined up and engaged, there resulted one of the most extraordinary battles in the war. The troops of Gracchus consisted largely of slaves who, following the disastrous Roman losses at Cannae (216), had volunteered to enlist in exchange for their freedom. Now, two years later, they were wondering if that day would ever come. Gracchus sensed their resentment and told them that freedom would be granted immediately to any man in the coming battle who brought him a Carthaginian head. This nearly lost Gracchus the battle. The slaves were so busy decapitating corpses and running around with heads that they were incapable of fighting the living. When Gracchus was alerted to this, he told his men to forget the heads and proclaimed that no man could hope for freedom unless the enemy was utterly defeated. This turned the scales. The onslaught was so furious that the Carthaginian front was driven in and routed. The enemy were pursued to their camp where the slaughter continued unabated. Less than 2,000 escaped alive out of Hanno's total force of 18,000; the Romans lost around 2,000. Gracchus kept his promise and liberated every one of the slave-volunteers.
Livy, 24: 14–16

NOLA (214) – Second Punic War
The senators of Nola were loyal to Rome; the commons were hostile and had previously tried to hand the town over to Hannibal. When Hannibal arrived again in the vicinity, the commons sent envoys promising that the town would be surrendered to him. The senators called in Marcellus, who arrived hotfoot and sent 6,000 infantry and 300 horse into the town for immediate protection. Marcellus then summoned the troops stationed at Suessula about seven miles away to try to force an engagement. He also ordered a detachment of cavalry to leave the town through the far gate at night and to make a wide detour to the enemy's rear. This part of the plan failed as the detachment got lost and failed to sight the enemy. In spite of its absence the Romans had the upper hand and killed around 2,000 of the enemy for a loss of 400. But Marcellus did not want to press the pursuit without the cavalry. The following day he again lined up for battle but Hannibal did not accept the challenge.
Livy, 24: 13(8–11) and 17

ILITURGI (213) – Second Punic War
In Spain, the Roman garrison in Iliturgi [near *Andujar*] in Baetica was besieged by the Carthaginians and nearing surrender on account of starvation. Relief arrived in the form of Gnaeus Scipio with one legion, which forced its way into the town after inflicting heavy losses. The following day Scipio made a sortie. Over 12,000 of the enemy were killed in total.
Livy, 24: 41(8–10)

MUNDA (213) – Second Punic War
After failing to take Iliturgi (above), the Carthaginians decided to try their luck at Munda, a town in the extreme south, the precise site of which has not been defined. Gnaeus Scipio followed and engaged them in an action which lasted several hours. The Romans withdrew when Scipio was wounded, but only after 12,000 of the enemy had allegedly been killed, as well as 39 elephants.
Livy, 24: 42(1–4)

AURINX (213) – Second Punic War
The Carthaginians proceeded from their defeat at Munda (above) to Aurinx, again followed by Gnaeus Scipio. Mago, one of the Carthaginian generals, had been sent out to raise fresh troops and bring the Carthaginian strength up to scratch. This was of little avail. The Romans won their third victory in succession, in which they are said to have slain a further 8,000 of the enemy.
Livy, 24: 42(5–8)

CAPUA (212) – Second Punic War
The consuls, Appius Claudius and Quintus Fulvius, were bent on capturing the enemy-held city of Capua, 15 miles north of Neapolis [Naples]. When they arrived in the neighbourhood, they started devastating the crops for miles around. The Capuans, supported by Carthaginian cavalry, made a sortie and overwhelmed the Romans before the consuls had time to recall their troops and line them up. They lost more than 1,500 men through their lack of caution.
Livy, 25: 18(1)

CAPUA (212) – Second Punic War
A few days after the incident above, Hannibal moved to Capua to protect it and offered battle in what proved to be an abortive action. The Roman infantry were faring badly at the hands of the enemy cavalry until their own mounted troops were ordered into the fray. During this cavalry battle an unidentified body of men was seen approaching in the distance. Both commanders favoured discretion and disengaged, returning to their respective camps.
Livy, 25: 19(1–5)

HERDONEA (212) – Second Punic War
Hannibal was looking for easy victories when the news reached him that the forces under the praetor Gnaeus Fulvius were in the neighbourhood of Herdonea [Ordona] in Apulia and that they and their commander had become very lax and undisciplined. Hannibal proceeded there and concealed a force of 3,000 men by night, placing them in nearby farms and woodlands. Mago with 2,000 horse was instructed to cover all possible escape roads. The next morning Hannibal drew up his infantry in battle order, a challenge which was impetuously accepted by Fulvius and his men. They failed to stand up to the first onslaught and were surrounded and hacked to pieces. Not more than 2,000 escaped out of the force of 18,000. As for Fulvius, he galloped off the field in the early stages of the encounter.
Livy, 25: 20(5)–21

HIMERA (211) – Second Punic War
In 212 Marcellus captured Syracuse, thus bringing virtually the whole of the island of Sicily under Roman control. But there was still a sizeable active pocket of opposition at Agrigentum [Agrigento] under the Carthaginian generals Hanno and Epicydes and an African half-caste called Muttines, who had been trained and sent out by Hannibal. Muttines, who was the driving force of the party, persuaded his colleagues to leave the protection of the city and to take up a position on the river Himera [Salso]. Marcellus replied by camping a few miles away. For two days Muttines and his Numidian cavalry inflicted severe damage on the Roman outposts. On the third day Muttines was called away to deal with a mutiny of the Numidians at headquarters, and he adjured the other two commanders not to engage the enemy in his absence. They, however, were beginning to find him insufferable and, moreover, they wanted the credit for any success. Accordingly, they crossed the river and offered battle. At that point a few of their Numidian cavalry rode up to Marcellus and told him of their grievances and their sympathy with their mutinous colleagues. They would, they said, stay out of any fight. In the absence of this – the most feared branch of the enemy forces – the battle was short and the Roman victory was overwhelming. It is said that many thousands were killed or captured.
Livy, 25: 40(5)–41(7)

UPPER BAETIS R (211) – Second Punic War
The Scipio brothers, Gnaeus and Publius, had gained control of Spain north of the Iberus [Ebro], thereby fulfilling their principal aim of preventing Hasdrubal from departing for Italy. In 212 they advanced south of the river and, at the end of the year, went into winter quarters, Publius at Castulo and Gnaeus at Orso (also known as Urso [Osuna]). There were still three Carthaginian armies opposing them, but during the winter the Romans were strengthened by the addition of 20,000 Celtiberian mercenaries. With these reinforcements they decided to start a major offensive in the spring. They also decided – unwisely with hindsight – to split their forces, Publius taking two thirds of the total for action against Mago and Hasdrubal (son of Gisgo), Gnaeus with the rest against Hasdrubal Barca. Publius is believed to have headed for the upper reaches of the Baetis [Guadalquivir], where he fell foul of the young Masinissa and his Numidian cavalry. This awe-inspiring opponent hung onto him like a leech, harassing him day and night and preventing him from leaving his camp to obtain supplies. Moreover, Publius knew that Indibilis, the prince of the Ilergetes, was on his way to join the Carthaginians with 7,500 of his people. Yielding to necessity, he determined to try to stop this reinforcement. Leaving his camp at night, he met the enemy and was engaged in a running battle with Indibilis when the Numidian cavalry

suddenly appeared on both his flanks. As if this was not enough, the Carthaginian generals also put in an appearance in his rear. Publius was killed in the fighting, after which the Romans broke. They were slaughtered in the process of trying to escape, only a few being saved by the onset of darkness.
Livy, 25: 34

ILORCI (211) – Second Punic War
The background to this battle has been outlined in the preceding entry. Publius and Gnaeus Scipio had decided to go their separate ways and Gnaeus was taking one third of their total strength for action against Hasdrubal. When the Carthaginian was in sight, the Celtiberians serving with Gnaeus, said to be 20,000 in number, suddenly deserted him and departed. Livy says that Hasdrubal had bribed them to abstain. Whatever the motive, the effect left Scipio too weak to match the enemy. He determined to move away, but they followed close-ly on his heels. The outlook for Gnaeus reached its lowest ebb when Hasdrubal Barca was joined by Mago and Hasdrubal, son of Gisgo, after their defeat of Publius (above). The only course open to Gnaeus was to get away as far and as fast as he could. He withdrew during the following night and got well away undetected, but the Numidians caught up with him before the end of the day. They harassed him so hard that he was forced to stand and defend himself. Toward nightfall he withdrew to a nearby hill. This proved to be so bare and stony that the Romans were forced to pile their pack-saddles as a makeshift rampart. It sufficed only to cause a temporary delay and was quite inadequate to hold off three armies and to prevent the inevitable. Some of the Romans escaped into the woods but Gnaeus Scipio was among those killed. Livy gives no indication of the site of this battle; it is to Pliny that we are indebted for the name of Ilorci [*Lorca*] in the hinterland behind New Carthage.
Livy, 25: 32(3)–33 and 35–36; Pliny, Natural History, *3: 9*

CAPUA (211) – Second Punic War
In Italy, the whole of the Roman war effort was devoted to the siege of Capua. This caused Hannibal to abandon, with reluctance, the capture of the citadel at Tarentum [*Taranto*] in favour of an attempt to save Capua. Having established himself in a valley out of sight of that city, he managed to get messages into the city so as to co-ordinate his attack from outside with a mass sortie of the

Campanians, supported by the Carthaginian garrison. To deal with this situation, the consul Appius Claudius opposed the town while his colleague Quintus Fulvius confronted Hannibal. In the action, Claudius had little difficulty in keeping the Campanians at bay and eventually forcing them back into the town. In Fulvius' sector, on the other hand, a Spanish cohort broke through the Roman lines and penetrated with three elephants right up to the ramparts. Realizing the gravity of the situation, Fulvius rallied his men and directed them to wheel inwards and attack the Spaniards on both flanks. They were cut to pieces and the elephants were killed. When Hannibal saw that his Spanish cohort was being mauled, he broke off the assault and withdrew. According to Livy, the early accounts varied greatly in their assessment of this battle. Some regarded it as a major encounter with heavy casualties; others as noise and confusion rather than death and destruction. Capua fell to the Romans shortly afterwards.
Livy, 26: 5–6

COLLINE GATE (211) – Second Punic War
After withdrawing from Capua, Hannibal made tracks for Rome. It was Fabius Maximus Cunctator who soothed the frayed nerves of his countrymen by pointing out that Hannibal's move was an obvious feint to draw the Roman armies away from Capua. In the event, Quintus Fulvius returned to Rome with a force of 15,000 from Capua, leaving the rest *in situ*. He encamped outside the City between the Colline and Esquiline Gates. Hannibal, for his part, established himself on the river Anio [*Aniene*] 3 miles away. He then rode up to the Colline Gate with 2,000 horsemen to inspect the City's defences. This piece of effrontery so infuriated Fulvius that he sent his cavalry against Hannibal. The engagement was successful and the Carthaginians were driven off.
Livy, 26: 10

ANIO R (211) – Second Punic War
A military non-event occurred the day after the skirmish at the Colline Gate (above) when Hannibal crossed the Anio and lined up for battle. Fulvius accepted the challenge. As the two armies confronted each other in readiness for a fight for Rome itself, a torrential downpour washed away any thoughts of battle and both sides returned to camp. When the same thing happened again on the following day, Hannibal accepted the omen and moved away.
Livy, 26: 11(1–4)

SAPRIPORTIS (210) – Second Punic War
In 212 the city of Tarentum [*Taranto*] was betrayed into Hannibal's hands but he failed to capture the citadel, to which the Roman garrison withdrew. They were still holding out two years later although starvation was nigh. Supplies were on their way from Sicily, escorted along the Italian coast by a fleet of 20 ships under Decimus Quinctius. This squadron fell in with a pro-Carthaginian fleet of Tarentine ships off Sapriportis, about 15 miles from Tarentum but now unknown. The Tarentine vessels were similar in number to the Romans' and were under the command of Democrates. The fleets met head on, beak to beak, resulting in much grappling, boarding and hand-to-hand fighting. The outcome centred around the first two ships to engage. In one was Quinctius fighting valiantly; the opposing vessel was commanded by a Tarentine named Nico, who ran Quinctius through with his spear. When the Roman flag-ship was captured, the rest of the fleet took fright and fled. Most of the supply vessels, which were outside the battle zone, managed to escape to sea but their contents never reached the beleaguered garrison in the citadel at Tarentum.
*Livy, **26**: 39*

HERDONEA (210) – Second Punic War
The proconsul Gnaeus Fulvius was camped near Herdonea [*Ordona*] and was hoping to wrest the town from the Carthaginians while Hannibal was out of the way in Bruttium. Hannibal heard of these plans and was also aware that Fulvius was characteristically negligent. With a lightning forced march he made a totally unexpected appearance before Herdonea in battle order. Fulvius hurriedly assembled his forces and accepted the challenge. When the infantry battle was in full swing, Hannibal sent his cavalry round the flanks, some with orders to attack the Roman camp and the rest to take the Romans themselves in the rear. The Romans, who up to that point had stood their ground, now gave way and tried to flee, but many were killed, including Fulvius and 13 military tribunes. The Roman losses have been variously put at between 7,000 and 13,000.

Before the battle Hannibal, having inflicted an ignominious defeat on the praetor Gnaeus Fulvius at Herdonea two years earlier, joked contemptuously about his impending defeat of the praetor's namesake at the same place. The quip was only accurate up to a point. The praetor was

Gnaeus Fulvius Flaccus whereas the proconsul was Gnaeus Fulvius Centumalus.
*Livy, **27**: 1; Appian, Hannibalic War, 48*

NUMISTRO (210) – Second Punic War
In Lucania, Hannibal was encamped on a hill near Numistro when Marcellus arrived and took up a position on level ground not far away. In spite of his disadvantageous position, it was Marcellus who issued the challenge by adopting battle positions, which Hannibal accepted. In the engagement, both sides were evenly matched and on both sides fresh forces were periodically sent forward to relieve the exhausted front lines. The battle raged in this way from dawn to dusk, when the opposing armies were forced to separate with the issue still undecided. On the following morning the Romans again formed up, but there was no enemy to fight. Hannibal had crept silently away during the night. Although pursued by Marcellus, Hannibal studiously avoided any major confrontation while his pursuer cautiously avoided any trap.
*Livy, **27**: 2; Plutarch, Marcellus, 24(4–6)*

NEW CARTHAGE (209) – Second Punic War
In Spain, the young Publius Cornelius Scipio (later Africanus) had assumed the command of the Roman forces following the death of his father at the Upper Baetis (211) and of his uncle at Ilorci (211). He found himself opposing three separate armies. He decided to give them all the brush and to attack their key base at New Carthage [*Cartagena*], from which they were all at least 10 days' march away. He took up a position a quarter of a mile away from the city and drew up his men in front of his camp. The hostilities began with an open battle when the garrison commander Mago opened the city gate and launched a charge by 2,000 armed citizens (Appian says 10,000) against the Romans. The fighting was stubborn, but the odds were heavily in favour of the Romans. Scipio had deliberately positioned his forces at a distance from the city so that the enemy had to cover the intervening ground, while the Roman reserves were close at hand. The enemy were forced back by sheer weight of numbers. They broke and fled back to the gate where many were trampled to death in the crush. Scipio proceeded to assault and capture the city from the land and sea.
*Polybius, **10**: 12; Livy, **26**: 44(1–4)*

CANUSIUM (209) – Second Punic War
Quintus Fabius Maximus was intent on retaking from Hannibal his one last remaining stronghold

in Italy: Tarentum [*Taranto*]. He asked Marcellus to dog and divert the Carthaginian with all his might. When Marcellus met up with Hannibal near Canusium [*Canosa*], the Carthaginian moved away and did his best to avoid a battle. But the Roman stuck close to his heels and eventually caught and harassed him while Hannibal was fortifying his camp. A general engagement was inevitable and continued until dusk with no decision. Both sides again took the field next morning. The struggle was resumed and was evenly balanced until the Roman right wing started to weaken. Marcellus brought another legion up to the front to replace the exhausted men, but the execution of this manoeuvre went awry. With one legion moving forward and another retiring, muddle and confusion set in and turned into a general rout. The Romans lost 2,700 men.
Livy, 27: 12(7–17); Plutarch, Marcellus, *25(2–4)*

PETELIA (208) – Second Punic War

The consuls hoped that it might be possible to make an assault on the Carthaginian-held town of Locri Epizephyrii [*Locri*] near the extreme south in the 'toe' of Italy. They ordered a detachment to be sent to Locri from the Roman garrison at Tarentum. Hannibal's spies informed him of these moves, and he sent 3,000 cavalry and 2,000 foot to conceal themselves under the hill of Petelia [*Strongoli*] along the Romans' route. The Romans walked straight into the ambush. Two thousand or more were killed and almost as many taken prisoner.
Livy, 27: 26(5–6); Plutarch, Marcellus, *29(1)*

VENUSIA (208) – Second Punic War

Hannibal was encamped near Venusia [*Venosa*] in the direction of Bantia about 12 miles away. Marcellus moved up and stationed himself nearby. Between the two camps was a wooded hill, to which Hannibal sent a detachment of Numidian cavalry with orders to conceal themselves. The Romans, also, considered that it was a key feature which deserved investigation. Marcellus decided to reconnoitre the hill himself and he rode out with his consular colleague, Quinctius Crispinus, and 220 horsemen, 40 of whom were from Fregellae while the rest were Etruscans. Their approach was spotted by the Numidian lookout. When the Roman party drew close, the men in ambush sprang up, hurled their spears and charged. The Etruscans fled straight away, but the men from Fregellae stayed to fight until both consuls were struck. Marcellus was run through with a lance

and killed; Crispinus was wounded but managed to get away with the survivors from Fregellae. He died of his wounds at the end of the year (not within a few days, as Plutarch relates).
Livy, 27: 26(7)–27; Plutarch, Marcellus, *29*

LOCRI EPIZEPHYRII (208) – Second Punic War

In the ambush at Petelia (208), Hannibal had thwarted the Roman attempt to assault Locri by land. But the place was still being besieged from the sea by Lucius Cincius, who had sailed a fleet over from Sicily with men and much equipment. Hannibal now marched to relieve the siege, preceded by his Numidian cavalry. As soon as Mago, the garrison commander, heard that the Numidians were arriving, he marched out against the Roman besiegers and caught them unawares. The encounter was nevertheless indecisive until the Numidians actually appeared, at which point the Romans broke and fled to their ships.
Livy, 27: 28(13–17)

CLUPEA (208, summer) – Second Punic War

During the summer, Valerius crossed from Sicily to Africa with a fleet of 100 ships. He landed near Clupea [*Kelibia*] and was devastating the surrounding territory when he heard that a Carthaginian fleet of 83 ships was approaching. After a hurried re-embarkation Valerius engaged the enemy fleet in a successful action. Eighteen enemy vessels were captured and were taken to Lilybaeum [*Marsala*] as prizes.
Livy, 27: 29(7–8)

BAECULA (208) – Second Punic War

In Spain, Hasdrubal, son of Hamilcar and brother of Hannibal, was aware that the Spaniards were going over to the Romans in considerable numbers and he was determined to fight a battle before the imbalance became too great. Scipio, too, wanted to fight – before the three Carthaginian armies could amalgamate. He marched to Baecula [*Bailen*], where the Carthaginians were encamped. Hasdrubal was camped on a high plateau with a river behind, which protected his rear. The plateau was bounded in front by a flat ridge at a lower level so that the whole formation was stepped, while the front edge of the ridge was steep and rock-strewn. This highly advantageous position gave Scipio cause for deliberation. When he attacked, he sent forward some light-armed troops to climb the ridge and make a direct frontal assault on the enemy's light troops who were covering the ridge.

The going was exceedingly tough, but they carried out the order so successfully that Hasdrubal, seeing the heavy losses among his own men, started to lead out his troops onto the plateau. Scipio responded by sending more light troops to reinforce the centre while he divided his main body into two parts. With one half he worked his way round the ridge to the left and attacked the enemy in the flank. The other half, under the command of Laelius, did the same thing on the opposite flank. These manoeuvres took Hasdrubal by surprise in his confidence in his unassailable position, and they gave him no time to deploy. The Romans charged from both sides before the enemy had formed up, and forced them to turn and flee. It is said that the Carthaginian losses totalled 8,000 dead and 12,000 captured, but these are dubious figures which would have amounted to around 80 per cent of the total force. After the battle, Hasdrubal collected the fugitives together and headed for the Pyrenees in the first stage of his march to join his brother in Italy.
Polybius, 10: 38(6)–39; Livy, 27: 18

CARMONE (207) – Second Punic War
The action at Carmone [*Carmona*] consisted of two engagements, both of which have been reported only by Appian. He recounts that after the departure of Hasdrubal Barca for Italy, Hasdrubal (son of Gisgo) assembled all the remaining Carthaginian forces in Spain at Carmone. These included large numbers of Spaniards under Mago and the Numidians under Masinissa. The cavalry of Mago and Masinissa bivouacked in the open in front of Hasdrubal's fortified camp. When Scipio arrived on the scene, he sent Laelius to attack Mago while he himself took on Masinissa and the Numidian cavalry. The Numidians severely embarrassed him with their usual hit-and-run tactics, in which they discharged their darts then speedily withdrew to form up for another charge. Scipio countered this by ordering his cavalry to level their spears and advance steadily regardless of the enemy tactics. This robbed the enemy of any chance of turning round within their striking range, and they withdrew.

After these preliminaries, Scipio encamped in a strong position a little over a mile from the enemy. His total strength was barely a third of the enemy's numbers, which are said to have been 70,000 foot alone, a superiority which caused Scipio to hesitate. When his supplies began to run short, he decided to fight. He ordered his men to eat and then led them in a rapid advance against the enemy, who were only a little over a mile away and were caught unprepared and fasting. The Roman cavalry got the better of the Numidians by using similar relentless tactics to those employed in the preliminary engagement. The infantry, however, were heavily outnumbered and were hard pressed all day. Eventually, Scipio seized a shield and dashed into the space between the armies, shouting out to his men to rescue him. This brought about such a furious charge that the Carthaginians were utterly unable to resist. Their collapse was followed by a terrible slaughter in which 15,000 of them are said to have been slain. The Roman casualties numbered 800.

It is now thought that Appian's battles at Carmone may have been the actions at Ilipa (206) in a different guise.
Appian, Spanish Wars, 25–27

GRUMENTUM (207) – Second Punic War
Hasdrubal, son of Hamilcar, was bringing a fresh army from Spain to Italy to join his brother Hannibal. He had already crossed the Alps in his brother's footsteps and was besieging Placentia [*Piacenza*]. The two consuls for the year left Rome in opposite directions, Livius marching northwards to intercept Hasdrubal while Nero's task was to oppose Hannibal in the south. Hannibal collected all the forces he could muster and proceeded to Grumentum in Lucania, where he set up camp almost against the walls of the town. Nero followed him cautiously and took up a position about one and a half miles away. His entire aim was to pin his adversary down. Hannibal, on the other hand, was so intent on getting away that he lined up repeatedly in battle formation in the hope of inflicting a quick rebuff. This prompted Nero to set a trap for the master of traps. On the Roman right were some bare hills which provided no cover and aroused no suspicion. Nero ordered a detachment to cross them after dark and to take up a position on the far side. Next morning he led out his army, to which the Carthaginians responded. They started pouring out of their camp gates in such a random fashion that they were flung into disorder by a Roman cavalry charge. At this point Hannibal emerged with his main force, which started to join in the undisciplined fighting and could not be brought into proper order before the concealed Roman detachment charged down upon them from the flank. The Carthaginians turned and fled back to their camp, losing more than 8,000 killed in spite of the proximity of the camp. The Roman losses were about 500.

As in a previous instance (Nola, 215), this account is at variance with Polybius who asserts unreservedly that Hannibal remained undefeated until 202. Disorderly and undisciplined troops under Hannibal defy the imagination. Livy has probably amplified a minor Roman success.
Livy, 27: 41–42(8); Polybius, 15: 16(5)

VENUSIA (207) – Second Punic War

After the engagement at Grumentum (above), Hannibal refused to accept a further challenge but slipped away during the night and made for Apulia. Nero caught up with him near Venusia [*Venosa*], where there was a running battle in which the Carthaginians lost a further 2,000 men. Hannibal again moved on – by night over the mountains – with Nero always in pursuit.
Livy, 27: 42(14–17)

METAURUS R (207, June 23) – Second Punic War

The decisive Roman victory at the Metaurus came about through the extraordinary initiative of one man, the consul Claudius Nero. Hasdrubal had crossed the Alps in the spring of 207 and had worked his way down to Sena Gallica [*Senigallia*] in Umbria, near which he had camped. The consul Livius had been sent north to oppose him and was encamped 500 yards away. Hasdrubal sent a letter to his brother Hannibal about a meeting in Umbria, but the bearers were captured and taken to Nero, who had been assigned the task of pinning Hannibal down in the south. Nero forwarded the letter to the senate and informed them at the same time of his intentions. He then detached his best 6,000 infantrymen and 1,000 horse from his force and left the rest with his second-in-command at Canusium [*Canosa*] to continue the watch on

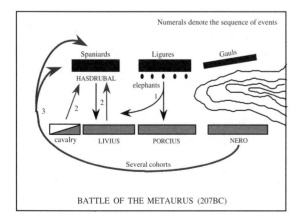

Numerals denote the sequence of events

BATTLE OF THE METAURUS (207BC)

Hannibal as if nothing had changed. Nero departed at night and is reputed to have made a forced march of about 250 miles in six days to join his colleague Livius in Sena. When he arrived at Livius' camp under cover of darkness, the two consuls shared the camp and took every measure to ensure that Hasdrubal was unaware of the proceedings. The next morning Nero refused to entertain any idea of a rest for himself and his men, insisting that they must strike at once. Hasdrubal, however, had got wind of the truth by noticing, for example, that the trumpet had sounded twice in the consul's camp. He recalled his men back to camp. After dark he silently withdrew northwards to the Metaurus [*Metauro*] in the hope of putting the river between himself and the Romans. But he missed the track and reached the banks of the river at a point where there was no chance of crossing it. Here the Romans caught up with him and Hasdrubal was forced to draw up his men and fight. The battle commenced with a bloody fight between Livius on the Roman left and Hasdrubal who was opposing him with his veteran Spaniards. There was great slaughter on both sides but no advantage to either. The antagonists were well matched and the result hung in the balance. Meanwhile Nero, on the Roman right, was unable to advance owing to the hilly nature of the terrain in front of him, which separated him from Hasdrubal's Gauls. Wondering why he had come so far to no purpose, Nero displayed another stroke of genius which saved the day. Wheeling several cohorts from his force, he led them speedily round behind the Roman lines to the opposite side of the field where they charged the Spaniards in the flank and rear. The movement was as successful as it was unexpected. The enemy were cut to pieces where they stood. The Gauls, who were on the Carthaginian left and had taken no part in the strife up to this point, were now surrounded and butchered in their turn. Even the elephants, which Hasdrubal had placed in front of his line, were of no help to him. They did no more than cause confusion on both sides. When Hasdrubal saw that the day was irreparably lost, he galloped straight into the midst of a Roman cohort and died fighting valiantly. Polybius estimates that the Carthaginians lost no less than 10,000 killed in the battle as against 2,000 Roman casualties. Livy's figure of 57,000 Carthaginian dead is unacceptable, being almost certainly larger than Hasdrubal's entire force.

Nero started back for Canusium on the night after the battle, arriving on the sixth day according to the reports. He took with him the head of

Hasdrubal and ordered this to be thrown into Hannibal's camp, the first intimation Hannibal received of his brother's defeat and death. The supreme initiative of the consul Claudius Nero had saved Italy and Rome. The victory, of which he was the ultimate architect, was the truly decisive event in the whole campaign against Hannibal. It defeated the Carthaginian aspirations once and for all and shattered them irreparably in readiness for the final dénouement at Zama.

Livy, 27: 43–49; Polybius, 11: 1–3 (fragment); Zonaras, 9: 9

ILIPA (OR SILPIA) (206) – Second Punic War

In Spain, Hasdrubal (son of Gisgo) and Mago (son of Hamilcar) collected together a force estimated at 50,000–70,000 foot and 4,000 horse and established themselves near Ilipa [*Alcala del Rio*] in open country at the foot of the hills. When Scipio (later Africanus) heard about the size of this force, he raised 3,000 extra Spanish auxiliaries who brought his total numbers up to 45,000. While they were fortifying their camp on a low hill opposite the enemy, Mago and Masinissa seized the opportunity to attack with their cavalry in force. Scipio had foreseen this probability and had stationed his cavalry out of sight behind a hill. The

unexpectedness of their charge disconcerted the enemy, who broke up and retired after a brisk struggle. For several days after this preliminary engagement Hasdrubal led out his forces each morning and lined them up in battle order. Each time, Scipio followed suit after an interval but, as the day wore on, nothing further happened. Scipio, however, noticed that Hasdrubal always emerged at a leisurely hour and that he invariably placed his best troops, the Libyans, in the centre, while he himself had opposed them with his Roman troops and put the Spaniards on the wings. On the day on which he intended to give battle he changed everything round. He ordered his troops to breakfast early, and then he sent the cavalry and light troops ahead to harass the enemy camp. He led out the main forces at sunrise and lined them up with the Spaniards in the centre and the Romans on the wings. Hasdrubal was caught unprepared. He had to send out his own cavalry and light troops to counter the enemy's and then hurry to line up his hungry men in their usual formation. For some hours the engagement was restricted to intermittent skirmishing on the part of the cavalry and light troops. Eventually Scipio allowed the skirmishers to withdraw and, having placed them in the rear of the wings, the whole

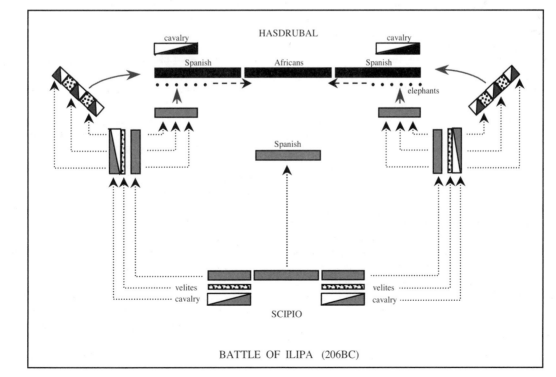

Based on a diagram in B.H. Liddell Hart, *Scipio Africanus*, 1926

BATTLE OF ILIPA (206BC)

force advanced to within about half a mile of the enemy. At this point the wings were ordered to execute certain manoeuvres, the objects of which were to extend them so as to cover the enemy wings and to advance them out in front to within striking distance of the enemy. The Spaniards, in the centre, were withheld and were told to move forward only slowly. The cavalry were on the extreme wings. As Scipio had intended, the battle devolved entirely round the two wings, where the enemy were attacked by the Roman infantry from the front and by the cavalry on the flank. Moreover, the Roman veterans were opposed by raw recruits. On the Carthaginian side, on the other hand, the veteran Africans in the centre had been inactivated by Scipio's tactics. They dared not turn to assist their wings because they would have presented their flanks to the Spaniards. Hungry and outmanoeuvred, the Carthaginian wings began to retreat, then finally broke and fled back to their camp. Hasdrubal's elephants, as so often, did as much damage to friend as foe and did not influence the result either way. At the end of the struggle, the Romans looked set to capture the enemy's camp but a torrential downpour intervened.

Scipio's masterly strategy achieved one further object. He could not completely trust his Spaniards, particularly after the Celtiberian desertion of his father, Publius, and uncle, Gnaeus, which led to their respective defeats and death at the Upper Baetis and at Ilorci in 211. Placing the Spaniards in the centre of his line discouraged a repeat of any such infidelity.
Polybius, 11: 20–24; Livy, 28: 12(13)–15

ASTAPA (206) – Second Punic War

After the crushing defeat of the Carthaginians at Ilipa (above), the Romans were set on subduing any Spanish tribes who had not capitulated. Marcius Septimus, one of Scipio's officers, had already received the peaceful surrender of two wealthy settlements, but at Astapa [*Estepa*] the community had a seething hatred for the Romans which far outweighed their allegiance to Carthage. They decided to do or die and piled up all their possessions in the forum. On top of this pyre they forced their women and children to sit, prepared to fire it if matters went against them. When the gates were flung open, they rushed out with a roar. The Romans had not expected such a sortie and sent for two or three troops of cavalry and some light infantry. In the words of one historian, there was 'a battle of sorts'. The onslaught of the inhabitants

was so frenzied that the leading Roman horse were driven back, inducing panic in the light infantry behind. But they rallied and formed into line. When the townspeople persisted in hurling themselves onto the Roman swords in blind fury, the Romans extended their line and with their superiority in numbers encircled the townspeople. Every man of them was killed, just as he had wished. In the town, the pyre of possessions and people was ignited. The final act in this macabre scene was played by those who had been deputed to light the fire, who then hurled themselves into the flames.
Livy, 28: 22

CARTEIA (206) – Second Punic War

The Carthaginian Adherbal was sailing from Gades [*Cadiz*] to Carthage with eight triremes and a quinquereme, the latter containing some conspirators who had plotted to hand Gades to the Romans. They were just entering the Straits when Gaius Laelius sailed out of Carteia in a quinquereme accompanied by seven triremes. Livy gives a graphic but uninformative description of the effect of the strong tides, which tossed the ships around out of control and turned the action into a chaotic matter of chance. In view of these hazards, it is surprising that the Roman quinquereme managed to sink two of the enemy triremes and to disable a third, while Adherbal succeeded in escaping with his remaining five vessels.
Livy, 28: 30(3–12)

SALAECA (TOWER OF AGATHOCLES) (204) – Second Punic War

Publius Cornelius Scipio landed in Africa at Cape Apollinis [*Cape Farina*] and moved down the coast to nearby Utica where he camped about a mile from the town. His presence caused extreme consternation in Carthage. Hanno, son of Hamilcar, had been sent out to raise reinforcements and was in Salaeca about 15 miles from the Roman camp with 4,000 men. Scipio wanted to put a brake on his activities. He asked Masinissa, who had by then changed sides and joined the Romans, to ride up to the town with a detachment of cavalry and to draw the enemy out, gradually retiring as the pressure on him increased. Scipio then followed with the bulk of the cavalry, which he concealed behind some hills. Masinissa did as instructed and managed to lure the entire enemy cavalry out of the town. They forced him to withdraw, but he achieved this in a gradual orderly way until he had lured them to the scene of the ambush. Scipio and the cavalry then appeared and surrounded the

enemy, while Masinissa turned round and joined the fray. About a thousand of the enemy were killed, including Hanno. The rest managed to escape, but 2,000 more were killed or captured in the pursuit. Appian, whose account differs in several respects from Livy's, says that the ambush occurred near a tower built by Agathocles about 3 or 4 miles from Utica. Modern scholars hold that this site is identifiable and that the geography conforms precisely with what is known about the battle.
Livy, 29: 34; Appian, Punic Wars, 14

CROTON (204) – Second Punic War

In Italy, the consul Sempronius came upon Hannibal on the march in the region of Croton [*Crotone*] in Bruttii. A running fight ensued, in which the Romans lost 1,200 men. The following night Sempronius joined forces with the proconsul Licinius, after which he challenged Hannibal to fight again. The Carthaginians were routed and suffered over 4,000 casualties. This Livian account of the second engagement is suspect, like some earlier accounts of Hannibalic defeats (Nola, 215; Grumentum, 207), in view of the statement by Polybius that Hannibal remained undefeated until the battle of Zama (202).
Livy, 29: 36(4–9)

UTICA (203) – Second Punic War

Scipio had problems. He had camped for the winter on a promontory, later known as the Castra Corneliana, close to Utica. The problems arose because Hasdrubal and his ally Syphax, the chief of the Numidian Masaesylii, had both set up camp not far away where they could hem him in with forces superior in number to his own. Furthermore, the Carthaginians were keeping a fleet in readiness to cut off his supplies by sea. Scipio's solution to the problem was a well-researched incendiary attack on both enemy camps simultaneously. This was not strictly a battle since it was entirely one-sided. The enemy had no time to pick up arms; they either perished or fled, mostly the former.
Polybius, 14: 4–5; Livy, 30: 3(8)–6; Appian, Punic Wars, 21–23

GREAT PLAINS (203) – Second Punic War

Hasdrubal escaped from the blazing inferno of his camp (above) with about 2,000 infantry and 500 cavalry. He set about raising fresh troops. Syphax, an ally of Carthage, also escaped after the incendiary attack and was on his way home to his capital, Cirta [*Constantine*], when he encountered 4,000 Celtiberian mercenaries on their way to join the Carthaginians. Within a month of the burning of the camps, Syphax and the Celtiberians had joined the forces raised by Hasdrubal and had congregated on the Great Plains, around *Souk el Kremis*, on the upper reaches of the Bagradas [*Medjerda*] river. Their combined strength is quoted by Polybius and Livy at around 30,000 men. Here, 75 miles west of Utica, they were quietly organizing themselves at leisure when Scipio appeared. As soon as he had heard of the enemy congregation, he had detailed some of his men to continue the siege of Utica while he set out with the rest (perhaps 15,000), arriving at Great Plains five days later. He encamped on a hill about 4 miles from the enemy and descended on the next day into the Plains, where he drew up his forces within a mile of the enemy and engaged in some skirmishing. But it was not until two more days of skirmishing had elapsed that both sides went into battle. Scipio advanced with his infantry in the centre in the usual Roman order. The cavalry were on the wings: Italians on the right wing and Masinissa with the Numidians on the left. The enemy's centre was held by the redoubtable Celtiberians; the cavalry were again on both wings. In the first charge both Carthaginian wings were routed by the Roman cavalry. The Celtiberians, on the other hand, stood fast, but their flanks had been exposed by the flight of the cavalry. Scipio's front line (*hastati*) continued to engage them while the second line (*principes*) and third line (*triarii*) turned, half to the right, half to the left, and marched out to outflank the enemy on both sides. The Celtiberians were soon surrounded and cut to pieces, but their resistance gave Hasdrubal and Syphax time to escape.
Polybius, 14: 7(9)–8; Livy, 30: 8

AMPSAGA R (CIRTA) (203, winter) – Second Punic War

When Syphax fled from the battlefield at Great Plains (above) he made for his capital of Cirta [*Constantine*], where he assembled and armed all the able-bodied men. In the meantime Masinissa obtained from Scipio a third of the Roman force, under the command of Laelius, to supplement his own Numidian cavalry. Together they set out in pursuit of Syphax whom they encountered somewhere near Cirta. The resulting battle is sometimes referred to by that name. Appian, however, records that Syphax gave battle near a certain river and this would almost certainly be the Ampsaga

[*Rummel*], on which Cirta stood. The engagement began with a cavalry skirmish, which gradually escalated until the entire cavalry strengths on both sides were in operation. The large numerical superiority of Syphax's horse was telling in his favour until the Roman light infantry intervened and checked the enemy. At this point the legionaries advanced, whereupon Syphax's Masaesylians decided to stay on the field no longer. While trying to encourage his men, Syphax was thrown from his horse, taken prisoner and put in chains. The casualties suffered by his side are put at less than 5,000 by Livy but at 10,000 by Appian. Masinissa and Laelius between them lost only a few hundred men.

Livy, 30: 11–12(5); Appian, Punic Wars, *26*

UTICA (203) – Second Punic War

With Carthage itself now the prime objective, Scipio occupied Tunes which had been abandoned by its garrison. It afforded a good view of the capital which was only about 15 miles away. From Tunes the Romans spotted the enemy fleet sailing out of Carthage in the direction of Utica. Scipio immediately hastened there with his men to organize his ships which had been left in no sort of order and with no thought of an impending attack. His subsequent actions were, as so often, unorthodox. He ordered all the warships to be brought close inshore. Then, on their seaward side he lined up the transports four deep. These he lashed together (with gaps between the groups of four), securing planks on top to provide a passageway down the line. Although the Carthaginians had naval superiority, they were dilatory in pressing their attack, deferring it until the morning after their arrival. As Livy says, what followed bore no resemblance to a sea-fight. The Roman transports were taller than the enemy's ships, giving the Romans the advantage of height in firing missiles at their adversaries. After a period of Punic unsuccess, the enemy started to grapple the transports in an attempt to tow them away, forcing the Romans to cut the bonds between their ships. About 60 of the transports were towed away in this fashion, a feat which the Carthaginians regarded as a source of much rejoicing in view of their recent string of disasters.

Livy, 30: 10

ZAMA (202) – Second Punic War

The defeat and capture of Carthage's ally, Syphax, at the Ampsaga river (203) and Scipio's occupation of Tunes caused the Carthaginians to seek

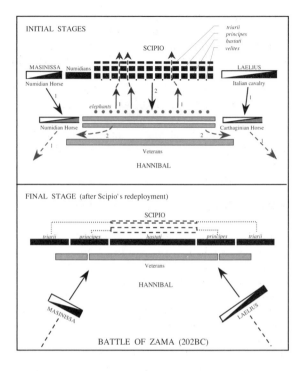

Adapted from a diagram in B.H. Liddell Hart, *Scipio Africanus*, 1926

peace terms, while at the same time they ordered Hannibal to return at once from Italy. Their envoys were still in Rome asking for peace when their brethren at home violated the armistice. Scipio sent urgent messages to Masinissa in Numidia to collect as large a force as he could and to meet up with him. He then set off westwards up the Bagradas [*Medjerda*] valley and eventually encamped at Naragara [*Sidi Youssef*], 50 miles west of Zama, where the reunion with Masinissa and his Numidian forces took place. In the meantime, Hannibal had landed near Hadrumentum [*Sousse*] and had proceeded after an interval to Zama, about 80 miles south-west of Carthage. He sent to Scipio requesting a conference. Scipio promptly moved a few miles to the east and encamped on a hill with a plentiful supply of water nearby. He invited Hannibal to meet him there. Hannibal moved westwards out of Zama and encamped on a hill opposite Scipio. His hill was short of water, a factor which played a part in the battle to come. At the conference the negotiations came to nothing; the only possible outcome was a battle – on the following day.

Both armies were drawn up for battle in three

lines. Hannibal's first line consisted of 12,000 mercenaries, and his second line, at a distance behind, comprised the Carthaginians and Libyans. Considerably further in the rear were the veterans whom Hannibal kept as a reserve force. The cavalry were divided between the wings. In front of the whole force were the light-armed troops and some 80 or more elephants, the largest number Hannibal had ever fielded. The grand total would be around 40,000. Facing them, the Romans were drawn up in their usual three lines but with an unusual formation. The maniples of the front line (*hastati*) were drawn up with the usual intervals between them. The unusual feature was the deployment of the second line (*principes*), the maniples of which were aligned immediately behind those of the first line, while the deployment of the third line (*triarii*) was a repetition of the other two. This formation aligned the intervals between maniples as corridors to allow elephants to pass through the lines while inflicting minimal damage. Initially, light-armed troops were stationed in the front of these gaps. The cavalry were on both wings.

After some preliminary skirmishing on the part of the cavalry, Hannibal ordered a charge of the elephants to terrify the enemy. Scipio adroitly turned the tables by ordering all the trumpeters and buglers to blow, and the resulting cacophony created panic in the beasts. Some turned round and collided with their own cavalry; others charged the Roman light troops among whom they did inflict heavy damage. The surviving beasts escaped by way of the corridors between the Roman maniples and stampeded off the field. It was at this moment of confusion that Laelius on the left wing and Masinissa on the right launched charges against the enemy's cavalry, driving both wings off the field and pursuing them. Both flanks of the Carthaginian infantry were therefore exposed. Meanwhile the two opposing bodies of infantry were advancing steadily towards each other until the Romans charged and engaged the enemy in hand-to-hand fighting. The Carthaginian mercenaries gained the upper hand initially, but the Romans remained steadfast and forced them to give ground. Moreover, the enemy's second line failed to give any support to the mercenaries in their hour of need. When the mercenaries did fall back, they were repelled by the Carthaginians behind them, against whom they then turned in anger. Although these Carthaginians had to contend first with their own mercenaries and then with the Romans, they put up a spirited fight and even managed to cause some confusion in the Roman ranks. But most of them were cut down by one side or the other. By this time the space between the armies was a slippery, blood-soaked, corpse-ridden mess, which made any advance difficult. In the final phase of the battle the Romans faced Hannibal himself in charge of his formidable reserve body of veterans who were still some distance in the rear. Up to this point they had had no part to play and were fresh and full of energy. To deal with this new situation Scipio calmly redeployed his force, extending his front by placing the *principes* and *triarii* on the wings, the *hastati* remaining in the centre. The opposing forces then closed for the final round. The antagonists were evenly matched and the issue hung in the balance in breathtaking suspense. At the crucial moment Laelius and Masinissa returned from the cavalry pursuit and launched themselves into the Carthaginian rear. This tipped the scales heavily and brought the contest to a rapid end. The Roman losses amounted to a total of 2,000 men, but more than 20,000 Carthaginians are said to have been killed and almost as many were taken prisoner. These figures for the dead and captured together account for virtually the whole Carthaginian force with no leeway for any escapees, although Hannibal was one.

Zama brought the Second Punic War to an end. The Carthaginians had little option but to capitulate, and Scipio forced the point by parading his legions, his navy and himself in the environs of the city.

Polybius, 15: 9–14; Livy, 30: 32–35; Appian, Punic Wars, *40–47*

MUTILUM (201) – Gallic Uprising

Throughout the Second Punic War the Gauls had caused little trouble to the Romans, who had contained them without much difficulty. After the war, however, the Gallic tribes began to reassert themselves. Hostilities commenced with a minor incident – not a full-blown battle but a prelude to worse to come. When the consul Publius Aelius arrived in Gaul, he learnt that the Boii had raided the territories of some of Rome's allies. He enrolled two scratch legions, adding four cohorts from his own forces, and ordered Gaius Ampius to invade the territory of the Boii. Ampius started plundering their land and found, near a place called Mutilum (now unknown), some crops ready for harvesting, but he failed to detail sufficient armed pickets to protect the reapers. The Gauls made an unexpected attack and surrounded the

harvesters, whereupon the pickets fled. As many as 7,000 scattered reapers were slain, including Ampius himself.
Livy 31: 2(5–9)

CREMONA (200) – Gallic Uprising

In a major uprising, the Insubres from around Mediolanum [*Milan*] joined up with the Cenomani from Brixia [*Brescia*], Bergomum [*Bergamo*] and Verona, and the Boii from Cispadana together with various other tribes whom they had incited. There were 40,000 of them under arms and under the leadership of the Carthaginian Hamilcar, who had stayed behind from the army of either Hasdrubal or Mago. They began by sacking and burning Placentia [*Piacenza*] and were intending next to attack the Roman colony of Cremona. The praetor Lucius Furius advanced against them and encamped, and the next day both sides came out prepared for battle. Furius stationed a squadron of allied troops in the front line, supported by two Roman legions. The Gauls made a mass attack on the front squadron but were repelled and decided instead to use their superior numbers to outflank and encircle the Romans. To counter this move, Furius extended his line by bringing forward the two legions, one to each wing. He also threw in the mounted troops, directing the legionary cavalry to one wing and the allied horse to the other. In their determination to encircle the Romans, the Gauls had weakened their centre. Furius observed this and ordered his infantry to charge. The Gauls, pushed back along their whole front by the infantry and cavalry, gave way and fled to their camp with the Romans in pursuit. It is said that only 6,000 escaped, 35,000 being killed or captured. The dead included Hamilcar. The Roman casualties amounted to around 2,000.
Livy 31: 10 and 21

ATHACUS (200) – Second Macedonian War
Described under *The Greek World*, p. 125.

OTTOLOBUM (200) – Second Macedonian War
Described under *The Greek World*, p. 126.

AOUS R (198) – Second Macedonian War
Described under *The Greek World*, p. 126.

CYNOSCEPHALAE MS (197) – Second Macedonian War
Described under *The Greek World*, p. 126.

MINCIUS R (197) – Gallic Uprising

Three years after their massive defeat at Cremona (above), the Boii crossed the Padus [*Po*] and combined again with the Insubres and the Cenomani. At that time a report that one of the consuls was devastating the lands of the Boii split the *entente*. The Insubres refused to desert their possessions to help their allies and so the Boii departed alone to defend their territory, leaving the Insubres and the Cenomani encamped on the banks of the river Mincius [*Mincio*]. The consul Gaius Cornelius arrived and established his position 2 miles downstream on the same river. When he discovered from the local Cenomani villagers that their men had joined the revolt without any official backing, he tried to persuade the warriors to detach themselves from the Insubres and either to go home or to join the Romans. They refused to depart but did give assurances that they would at least remain inactive. The Insubres somehow came to suspect that their allies were backsliding and so they stationed the Cenomani in reserve, refusing to trust them on either wing. In the encounter, the Insubres failed to stand up to the first Roman assault. Some sources have even reported that the Cenomani attacked their former allies in the rear. The Insubrian casualties are given as 35,000 killed and 5,200 captured, including Hamilcar. As these figures are virtually the same as those reported for the battle of Cremona (above) in which Hamilcar was said to be killed, they are clearly suspect. Nevertheless, as a result of the Roman victory many Gallic towns which had joined the revolt subsequently surrendered to the Romans.
Livy, 32: 30

COMUM (196) – Gallic Uprising

In the year following the slaughter of the Insubres on the Mincius (above) the consul Claudius Marcellus was devastating the territory of the Boii, who refrained from being drawn into a pitched battle. Marcellus decided to cross the Po and advance instead against the Insubres in the region of Comum [*Como*]. They joined battle with him immediately and with such vigour that his front line was forced back. Marcellus responded to this threat by sending all the Latin cavalry against the enemy. A couple of charges from this quarter blunted the Gallic zeal and put heart into the Roman line. After one vigorous charge by the infantry the enemy gave up the fight and fled in disorder. The enemy losses were heavy – 40,000 according to Valerius Antias (although as Livy

observes, this historian was usually prone to exaggeration). The enemy camp was plundered and Comum was captured. This was followed by the defection to the consul of 28 walled towns.
Livy, 33: 36(9–15)

SPARTA (195) – War against Nabis
Described under *The Greek World*, p. 128.

TURDA (195) – Spanish Wars
During the Second Punic War the Spanish tribes fought for one side or the other (or both in turn). Soon after the cessation of hostilities they began to fight for themselves – against the Romans. In 197 the Romans divided the administration of the conquered part into two praetorian provinces, Hispania Citerior (Hither Spain) in the east and Hispania Ulterior (Further Spain) in the south. In the same year there was an insurrection in Hither Spain in which a Roman army was routed at an unknown place and the praetor Tuditanus died of his wounds. After this, the Spaniards appeared to simmer down until, two years later, the praetor Minucius routed two Spanish commanders in a pitched battle near Turda (probably Turba), inflicting 12,000 casualties and capturing one of the commanders. It is unsaid but may be presumed that the Spaniards started the fight.
Livy, 33: 44(4–5)

ILITURGI (195) – Spanish Wars
Marcus Helvius was retiring from Further Spain with 6,000 men at the end of his tour of duty. A large force of Celtiberians, estimated at around 20,000 in number, fell upon him in the vicinity of Iliturgi [near *Cabanes*]. About 12,000 of the Celtiberians were said to be killed. The town was seized and all the adults were put to death.
Livy, 34: 10(1–2)

EMPORIAE (195) – Spanish Wars
The senate decided that the escalation of the war in Spain necessitated a commander of consular rank instead of a praetor. The province of Hither Spain was assigned to Marcus Porcius Cato, who landed at Emporiae [*Ampurias*] just south of the Pyrenees and encamped nearby. While he was there, representatives of the Ilergetes, who were allies of Rome, came to complain that they were being continually attacked by hostile tribesmen and they asked for help. Cato was in a dilemma. He was unwilling to refuse aid to his allies but thought it equally unwise to weaken his modest force. He solved the problem by ordering the embarkation of a third of his force in full view of the delegates. When the latter had departed to report the 'facts', which were also certain to reach the enemy ears, he ordered the disembarkation of the troops. After a period of intensive training, he took his men out one night and led them past the enemy position. At daybreak he drew his men up in battle order and sent three cohorts up to the ramparts. When the enemy saw them, Cato recalled them as if in flight. The ploy succeeded in enticing the enemy out of their defences, whereupon Cato ordered the cavalry to attack them on both flanks while they were still in disorder. Even with this advantage, the fighting was indecisive. The cavalry on the right were driven back, causing some panic, and so the consul sent two cohorts to outflank the enemy on that wing and attack them in the rear. This redressed the balance. When his men became exhausted, the consul put in fresh reserves who made a vigorous charge in wedge formation. This forced the enemy back and then put them to flight back to their camp. When Cato saw this, he ordered the second legion to advance at full speed and attack the camp. The fighting was still robust and the camp was vigorously defended until the consul noticed that the left gate was only thinly manned. He directed the *principes* and *hastati* to the weak point, where they burst inside the camp. After that, it became a massacre as the Romans cut down the enemy who jostled and scrummed at the approaches to the gates. The enemy losses were 'heavy'. In consequence of the battle the Spaniards in that area surrendered, as did many other towns along the consul's route until the whole country north of the Ebro had been subdued.
Livy, 34: 11–16(2); Appian, Spanish Wars, 40

MEDIOLANUM (194) – Gallic Uprising
In Gaul, the Insubres and the Cenomani had been subdued by the battles on the Mincius (197) and at Comum (196) and had been granted peace. The Boii, in Cispadana, were still insurgent and disruptive. They crossed the Po and incited the Insubres to take up arms again. Valerius Flaccus fought and won a pitched battle with them near Mediolanum [*Milan*]. About 10,000 of the enemy were killed.
Livy, 34: 46(1)

MUTINA (193) – Gallic Uprising
In spite of frequent expeditions against them, the Boii remained unsubdued. The consul Lucius Cornelius marched against them, plundered their

territory and offered battle, but they persistently refused to engage in the open. After he had finished wreaking havoc, the consul withdrew toward Mutina [*Modena*]. The Boii followed silently, intent on an ambush. They stole past the Roman camp at night and occupied a defile on the enemy's route ahead, but their movements had not passed unnoticed. In the morning the consul detailed a troop of horse to reconnoitre, and a battle subsequently took place in the open with both armies in proper array. Initially, the Roman front line failed to hold the Gallic attack, and an urgent message was sent to the consul for help to prevent a humiliating defeat. The second legion was sent forward and this infusion of fresh troops restored the equilibrium, after which the original frontliners were brought back. It so happened that it was a scorching hot day and the Gauls began to suffer. When the consul noticed this, he sent in the auxiliary horse at full gallop with the legionary cavalry in support. This equestrian hurricane threw the Gauls into disorder, and their attempts to reform were defeated when the cavalry got in among them. A final concerted push by the infantry settled the issue and put the enemy to flight, pursued by the cavalry. Fourteen thousand of the Boii were slain and 1,092 were taken captive, but this was at a cost to the Romans and their allies of more than 5,000 men, including two military tribunes, four allied commanders and 23 centurions.
Livy, 35: 4–5

ILIPA (193) – Spanish Wars

When Marcus Cato returned home after the battle near Emporiae (195), many of the local communities began to rebel again. There were a number of unrecorded battles which achieved nothing and brought no credit to the Romans. Prestige was restored by the unsung successes of P. Cornelius Scipio Nasica, the son of Gnaeus who had been killed at Ilorci [*Lorca*] in 211. Soon after these events Nasica, as praetor in Further Spain, attacked a column of the Lusitani near Ilipa [*Alcala del Rio*]. They had been marching home all night from Further Spain with a vast haul of plundered booty. The Romans were greatly outnumbered, but they had the advantage in every other respect. The enemy were tired, straggling in column and embarrassed by their beasts of burden. In spite of these handicaps, the Lusitani held the Romans in a well-matched confrontation until, after five hours, Scipio exhorted his men to make a final effort. The enemy gave way and fled, losing

12,000 of their number slain in the pursuit against a Roman loss of 73.
Livy, 35: 1(5–12)

TOLETUM (193) – Spanish Wars

Matters were proceeding well for the Romans in both Spanish provinces. Marcus Fulvius had won two battles (unspecified) and had captured four towns, when he came to Toletum [*Toledo*]. He was besieging the city when a large force of Vaccaei, Vettones and Celtiberi came to assist the Toletani. Fulvius engaged them in a pitched battle and routed them before reducing the city.

A battle which appears to be this one has been recorded again by Livy under the following year. The small variations in the two accounts have been amalgamated here.
Livy, 35: 7(8) and 22(6–8)

PISAE (192) – Ligurian Wars

Not infrequently the Roman battles with the Ligures took place at sites unnamed or now unknown in their uncharted territory. This is one of the exceptions – it took place outside Liguria near Pisa where Quintus Minucius engaged the Ligures in a pitched battle. Nine thousand of the enemy were killed and the rest were driven into their camp. The Romans failed to take the camp before nightfall and the Ligures abandoned it silently during the night. Minucius pursued them into their territory and laid waste their towns.
Livy, 35: 21(7–9)

THERMOPYLAE P (191) – War against Antiochus

Described under *The Greek World*, p. 129.

CORYCUS PR (191) – War against Antiochus

Described under *The Greek World*, p. 129.

PANORMUS (190) – War against Antiochus

Described under *The Greek World*, p. 130.

PHOENICUS (190) – War against Antiochus

Described under *The Greek World*, p. 130.

SIDE (190) – War against Antiochus

Described under *The Greek World*, p. 130.

MYONNESUS PR (190) – War against Antiochus

Described under *The Greek World*, p. 131.

MAGNESIA-AD-SIPYLUM (190) – War against Antiochus
Described under *The Greek World*, p. 131.

LYCO (190) – Spanish Wars
In Further Spain, the Romans suffered a severe setback when an army under Lucius Aemilius was defeated by the Lusitani at a place called Lyco (now unknown) in the country of the Bastetani, the south-eastern region around and behind New Carthage [*Cartagena*]. Six thousand Romans were slain. The rest were forced back behind their ramparts, which they held with difficulty, and they were subsequently led back like sheep to safe country.
Livy, 37: 46(7–8)

CUBALLUM (189) – Galatian Expedition
Described under *The Greek World*, p. 132.

OLYMPUS M (189) – Galatian Expedition
Described under *The Greek World*, p. 132.

ANCYRA (189) – Galatian Expedition
Described under *The Greek World*, p. 132.

MAGABA M (189) – Galatian Expedition
Described under *The Greek World*, p. 132.

CYPSELA (188)
Described under *The Greek World*, p. 132.

TEMPYRA (188)
Described under *The Greek World*, p. 133.

HASTA (186) – Spanish Wars
In the extreme south of Spain, Gaius Atinius won a victory but lost his life. In a pitched battle with the Lusitanians near Hasta [near *Jerez de la Frontera*], about 6,000 of the enemy were killed and the rest were put to flight. Atinius then captured the town with little difficulty but, in the process, he was hit by a missile and died a few days later.
Livy, 39: 21(1–3)

CALAGURRIS (186) – Spanish Wars
In Hither Spain, Lucius Manlius Acidinus engaged the Celtiberians in an action which was so indecisive that both sides withdrew. The Celtiberians moved camp during the night but returned with reinforcements a few days later and challenged the Romans to battle near Calagurris [*Calahorra*]. Livy remarks on the paradox that greater military strength can lead to greater weakness, as exemplified in this battle. The augmented Celtiberian force was defeated with the loss of about 12,000 men killed and 2,000 captured.
Livy, 39: 21(6–10)

TOLETUM (185) – Spanish Wars
In early spring the praetors, Gaius Calpurnius and Lucius Quinctius, led their men out of their winter quarters and joined forces. They marched into Carpetania and headed for the enemy camp not far from Toletum [*Toledo*]. Foraging parties from the two sides came into contact with each other and a fight broke out. Reinforcements from both camps kept joining in until the entire armies were involved. The Romans showed up particularly badly, especially in view of the fact that they had two armies in the field. Both were routed with a loss of about 5,000 men and were driven back to their camps, which they proceeded to abandon silently during the night. The enemy looted the camps and then moved away to the Tagus.
Livy, 39: 30(1–6)

TAGUS R (185) – Spanish Wars
After their bitter defeat near Toletum (above) in the spring of this year, the praetors recruited Spanish auxiliaries from the allied towns as hard as they could. When they had got their forces up to strength and had repaired the shattered morale of their men, they marched down to the Tagus [*Tajo*] and saw the enemy encamped on a hill across the river. There were two fords across the river. Calpurnius and his army crossed by one of them and Quinctius by the other, in full sight of the enemy who failed to seize such a good opportunity for attack. By the time the Spaniards had rushed at them across the intervening plain, the Romans had formed up, putting all their strength in their centre. The Spaniards attacked in wedge (*cuneus*) formation and were causing some distress to the Roman centre, at which point Calpurnius took the legionary cavalry round the struggling lines and charged the enemy wedge in the flank. Quinctius, with the allied cavalry, executed the same manoeuvre on the other wing and attacked the opposite flank. The legions, emboldened by these actions, swept forward in an irresistible charge which overwhelmed the enemy and sent them fleeing to their camp. They were pursued by the cavalry, who forced their way inside the rampart and were followed by the legions. Only about 4,000 of the Spaniards escaped out of the original

force of 35,000. The Romans and their allies lost about 750 men all told.

Livy, 39: 30(6)–31

AEBURA (181, spring) – Spanish Wars

After a lull, war broke out again in Hither Spain. The praetor Quintus Fulvius Flaccus heard that the Celtiberians were mobilizing and he recruited as many Spanish auxiliaries as he could. But he could not match the 35,000 men that the enemy had under arms. Nevertheless, he marched into Carpetania and encamped not far from Aebura [probably *Cuerva*]. A few days later the Celtiberians arrived and set up camp about two miles away at the base of a hill. The praetor sent his brother with two troops of cavalry to ride up to the enemy ramparts to reconnoitre and to withdraw immediately if the enemy emerged. This was repeated on several consecutive days. Eventually the Celtiberians came out of their camp and lined themselves up midway between the two positions, and there they stayed for four days while Flaccus made no movement. Bored by the inactivity, the enemy gave up and returned to camp. When Flaccus judged that they no longer expected any Roman initiative, he ordered Lucius Acilius to take a squadron of cavalry and 6,000 auxiliaries by night to the far side of the hill in the enemy rear and to charge down when he heard a signal. Flaccus then sent Gaius Scribonius and his allied troops up to the enemy's rampart, which brought out their whole army. As soon as they were in the open, Scribonius retreated as ordered, bringing the enemy in pursuit. As the enemy approached the Roman ramparts, Flaccus sallied out with his army in three divisions, raising a shout which brought Acilius charging down on the enemy camp. This was captured with ease and it was then set on fire. The incendiary strategy may have been misguided. Its effect on the Celtiberians was one of initial panic which was followed by greater stubbornness at the realization that they had no haven of retreat. Their centre was hard pressed, but they were on the point of forcing back the auxiliaries on the Roman left when the garrison in Aebura came out to help. In addition, Acilius was rapidly approaching from the rear. The Celtiberians became surrounded and were cut down on the spot. Those that escaped were pursued. Their casualties amounted to 23,000 killed and 4,700 captured. Nor did the Romans escape lightly. Over 200 legionaries were killed and more than 3,000 Latin allies and auxiliaries perished.

Livy; 40: 30–32

CONTREBIA (181) – Spanish Wars

From Aebura (above), Flaccus marched to besiege Contrebia [near *Albarracin*]. The inhabitants of this town called on the Celtiberians for help, but the relief was long delayed by the effects of torrential rains with the result that the town surrendered. The Celtiberians knew nothing of the surrender. When they reached the town and saw no camp, they assumed that the enemy had withdrawn. As they approached the walls in peaceful disorder, the Romans sallied out and scattered them in flight. About 12,000 were killed and 5,000 taken captive. Early in the following year much of Celtiberia surrendered.

Livy, 40: 33

MANLIAN PASS (180) – Spanish Wars

While he was waiting for his relief to arrive from Rome, Fulvius Flaccus took his army to the remoter parts of Celtiberia, which had not surrendered. He ravaged the countryside, which provoked the natives into mustering their forces on the quiet. At this point, Flaccus received a message telling him of the day of his successor's arrival, which caused him to turn round and begin his return to base immediately. His route took him through the Manlian pass, as the natives had foreseen and which they had blocked. When the Romans entered the pass, the enemy appeared on both sides and fell upon them. Flaccus coolly drew up his men in column and faced the charge. When the Celtiberians found that they were unable to make any headway against the legions, they formed up and attacked in wedge formation. The Roman line was on the point of breaking when Flaccus ordered the legionary cavalry to close their lines and to give the horses their heads without reins in a violent charge against the wedge. The cavalry did as ordered, not once but twice – out and back – inflicting heavy slaughter and breaking up the wedge. It was now the turn of the allied cavalry, who without waiting for an order charged into the disorganized throng. The Celtiberians turned in headlong flight and were cut down as they went, leaving 17,000 dead in the pass and 3,700 captives. The Romans, also, had their losses: 472 were killed and over 4,000 of the Latins and auxiliaries were slain.

The *saltus* Manlianus is thought to have been on the *Parameras de Molina* in the Idubeda mountain range in Celtiberia.*

*Livy, 40: 39–40; *W. Smith (ed.),* Dictionary of Greek and Roman Geography, *s.v. Idubeda, 1873*

COMPLEGA (179) – Spanish Wars

Tiberius Sempronius Gracchus took over from Flaccus and carried on trying to subjugate the further parts of Celtiberia. When he was encamped near Complega (site unknown), the inhabitants of that town, about 20,000 in number, came to him bearing olive branches and professing peace. As soon as they had been received, they attacked his camp. Gracchus immediately abandoned the camp and simulated flight, but he turned abruptly and fell upon the horde while they were busy plundering. Most of them were killed.

Appian, Spanish Wars, 43

ALCE (179) – Spanish Wars

Continuing his campaign to subdue the remoter parts of Celtiberia, Gracchus came to Alce [*?Alcazar de San Juan*], where the enemy were encamped, and began harassing their outposts. Every day he increased the scale of his skirmishes until they brought the enemy out in full force. When this had been achieved, he reduced the pressure and ordered his skirmishers to turn tail and flee back to their camp as if they had been overcome. The enemy followed in disorderly pursuit. The skirmishers had just reached the camp and were entering through one gate when Gracchus sallied out with his whole force through all the other gates. The surprise attack completely routed the enemy who were driven back to their camp, which was subsequently taken. Nine thousand of them were killed. Gracchus then began plundering and devastating a wide area, as a result of which 103 towns surrendered within a very short space of time.

*Livy, **40**: 48*

CHAUNUS M (179) – Spanish Wars

Livy retails other sources, which he does not name, but which relate that Gracchus fought a day-long pitched battle with the Celtiberians on the Chaunus mountain in the north of the country. The losses were heavy on both sides in what appears to have been an indecisive action. Two days later hostilities were resumed in a bigger battle in which the Romans were the victors. It is said that the enemy lost 22,000 men and that this action put an end to war with the Celtiberians. It is certainly on record that Gracchus received their surrender.

No mountain is known by the name of Chaunus. It is probable that Livy's sources were referring to Mount Caunus near Bilbilis [*Calatayud*] in the Idubeda chain in Celtiberia.

*Livy, **40**: 50*

TIMAVUS R (178) – Istrian War

When trouble broke out with the Istrians (Histrians), the consul Aulus Manlius set out from Aquileia and pitched camp at the source of the river Timavus [*Timavo*] about 5 miles from the sea. At the same time warships and transports were sent to the nearby harbour. To protect the traffic between harbour and camp the Romans established a string of outposts. The Istrians attacked some of these posts in the morning mist, which caused the attackers to seem like a veritable army in the eyes of the terrified guards. The guards fled to the camp, where their alarm caused even more panic and a general flight to the sea. The only human beings left in camp were a military tribune with three companies which had been abandoned in the turmoil. The Istrians burst into the camp and a fierce struggle ensued in which all the Romans were killed. In the officers' quarters the Istrians found everything ready for a banquet, and so the chief reclined and dined; his men followed suit. By the time the consul and his men had been recalled from the boats and had returned to the apparently deserted camp, the Istrians were all inebriated and presented no problem. A few escaped but about 8,000 of them were slain. No prisoners were taken, but the drunken chief managed to escape when two of his men hoisted him onto a horse. Apart from the three Roman companies which were annihilated in the camp, 237 of the others fell, mostly during the flight. Istria was subsequently pacified during the following year.

*Livy, **41**: 2–4*

SCULTENNA R (177) – Ligurian Wars

The Istrian War ended with the capture of its principal towns by the new consul Gaius Claudius. But as one war ended, the Ligurian Wars recommenced. It was suggested to Gaius Claudius that he might consider leading his army against the Ligurians to assist his brother, Tiberius, who was proconsul at Pisa with only one legion. The Ligurians had come down to the plains and had encamped near the river Scultenna [*Panaro*]. In the battle 15,000 of them were killed and over 700 taken captive. The rest fled to the mountains and kept out of sight.

*Livy, **41**: 12(7–10)*

CAMPI MACRI (176) – Ligurian Wars

The Ligurians did not lie low for long but rebelled again in the year after their defeat by Gaius Claudius at the Scultenna river (above). This time they decided to avoid the plains and they occupied

two mountains called Letum and Ballista, which were near the Campi Macri and which they surrounded with a wall. Claudius, now proconsul, was asked to meet the consul Quintus Petilius at Campi Macri near Mutina [*Modena*[, where the other consul Gaius Valerius also joined them. There they divided their forces into two armies and approached the enemy from different directions. It was Petilius who had all the action. With his camp facing the two mountains, which were joined by a ridge, he marched his men up the hills in two columns, one on each side. The column which he himself led made good progress, but the other one was forced back by the enemy. When Petilius rode over to the waverers, he did indeed restore order but he was struck by a javelin and killed in the process. The column managed to conceal the death of its leader from the enemy and proceeded to dislodge them and seize the mountain. The Ligurians lost about 5,000 men killed; the Roman losses were 52.
Livy, 41: 17(9)–18(13)

CARYSTUS (173) – Ligurian Wars

A multitude of Ligurians assembled near a town called Carystus, north of *Genoa* in the territory of Statellae. The consul Marcus Popilius marched against them but they remained behind their ramparts. Popilius made preparations to assault the town which, as he had hoped, brought the enemy out into the open where they formed up in front of their gates. The battle raged indecisively for more than three hours until the consul ordered the cavalry to divide into three squadrons and to charge simultaneously at different points with as much uproar as possible. When many of the horsemen had forced their way through the Ligurian centre and had reached the rear lines, the enemy panicked and fled. It is said that 10,000 were killed and 700 were captured; but the Romans lost as many as 3,000 soldiers, mostly in the initial stalemate. When the Ligurians counted their losses, they surrendered unconditionally. Carystus is now unknown.
Livy, 42: 7(3–10)

CALLINICUS (171) – Third Macedonian War
Described under *The Greek World*, p. 133.

PHALANNA (171) – Third Macedonian War
Described under *The Greek World*, p. 133.

USCANA (170) – Third Macedonian War
Described under *The Greek World*, p. 134.

SCODRA (168) – Third Macedonian War
Described under *The Greek World*, p. 134.

ELPEUS R (168) – Third Macedonian War
Described under *The Greek World*, p. 134.

PYTHIUM (168) – Third Macedonian War
Described under *The Greek World*, p. 134.

PYDNA (168) – Third Macedonian War
Described under *The Greek World*, p. 135.

NUMANTIA (153) – Spanish Wars

The consul Fulvius Nobilior marched against the Celtiberi with an army of 30,000 men and pushed on as far as Numantia [*Cerro de Garray*], a city of considerable natural strength. Here he was joined by 300 horse and 10 elephants which had been sent to him by Masinissa, Rome's ally in Numidia. When Nobilior moved against the city, he placed the elephants in the rear where they could not be seen by the enemy. As the armies came to close quarters, the right and left halves of the Roman army parted to reveal the beasts. The Celtiberians, who had never seen an elephant before, were terrified and fled back to their city. Nobilior proceeded up to the walls, where one of the elephants was hit by falling masonry and ran amok in rage. The other beasts followed suit and the whole herd turned and attacked the Romans, putting the army to flight. The Numantines sallied forth and pursued the Romans, killing 4,000 men and three elephants for a loss of about 2,000 of their own number.

This was the first engagement in the Numantine War, in which a few thousand people defeated assaults by four later Roman armies until the city was besieged and destroyed in 133, bringing the Spanish Wars to an end.
Appian, Spanish Wars, 46

CAUCA (151) – Spanish Wars

A new consul Licinius Lucullus – an aggressive brute – took up his command in Spain with a fresh army. Without the authority of the senate and with no incitement he invaded the territory of the Celtiberian Vaccaei, a people who had never offended the Romans. He pitched his camp near the city of Cauca [*Coca*] and gave some trumped-up excuse for war. There was a pitched battle in which the light-armed Caucaei were getting the better of it until they had expended all their darts. Being unaccustomed to withstanding an orderly charge, they fled back to their city where about 3,000 were

slain while they struggled to get through the gates. The next day the citizens asked for peace terms and complied with all of Lucullus' requests, but this did not prevent him from gaining access to the city by trickery and slaying all the adult males.
Appian, Spanish Wars, *51*

INTERCATIA (151) – Spanish Wars
At Intercatia, the consul Lucullus tried to make a treaty with the inhabitants but was reproached with his recent perfidy at Cauca (above). Angrily Lucullus drew up a line of siege and attempted to provoke a battle. The citizens as a whole did not respond, but one of their number, a large and distinguished man in splendid armour, rode into the space between the armies and challenged the Romans to single combat. When he jeeringly repeated the challenge, it was taken up by Lucullus' deputy – the young Scipio Aemilianus – who triumphed in spite of his small stature. The siege was pressed and the wall was broken, but when the Romans rushed in, they themselves were in such poor condition that they were overpowered. As both sides were suffering from malnutrition, Scipio made a treaty with the inhabitants and promised that it would not be violated, a pledge which the inhabitants accepted in view of his reputation for honour.
Appian, Spanish Wars, *53; Livy*, epitome *48*

NEPHERIS (149) – Third Punic War
The sole Roman object in waging another Punic War was the complete destruction of Carthage. Contrary to expectations, it took three years to achieve. In the early days the consul Manius Manilius undertook an expedition against Hasdrubal, the Carthaginian leader, whose camp was at Nepheris, south of Carthage, in wild and rugged territory. Scipio Aemilianus, who was then only a military tribune serving in the force, disapproved of the project because of the difficult terrain. Less than half a mile from their destination they had to descend into a river bed and climb out on the other side. Scipio again remonstrated on the grounds that they would cut themselves off from any base for a retreat. He was accused of cowardice. Manilius pressed on and met Hasdrubal on the other side, where there was much slaughter of both armies. Hasdrubal retired to his stronghold to wait for a better chance, leaving the Romans to withdraw to the river. This was Hasdrubal's chance and he took it, putting the Romans to flight and killing a great number of them. At this point Scipio collected a few hundred horsemen, divided them

into two troops and instructed them to take turns in charging the enemy, throwing their javelins and withdrawing in a continuous round of hit-and-run harassment. His action drew the enemy against him and allowed the other Romans to cross the stream, an operation which Scipio and his men then achieved only with great difficulty. That was not all. Four Roman cohorts had got separated from the main body and, being unable to cross the stream, had taken refuge on a hill where they were besieged by the enemy. Scipio again collected some cavalry and set out to rescue them or perish. The details of this operation are unclear but the result was entirely successful. It was all of two years later that Nepheris was actually captured, town and camp.
Appian, Punic Wars, *102–103; Livy*, epitome *49*

CARTHAGE (147) – Third Punic War
The siege of Carthage, which led to its capture and utter destruction, was conducted by Scipio Aemilianus who had by then been promoted to consul. He aimed to prevent anyone getting into or out of the place by land or sea. His naval blockade was not proof against the occasional runner and so he planned to block the harbour entrance. The harbour was formed by a long spit of land which projected from the shore below the city and then extended parallel with the shore, acting as a breakwater. The entrance lay between the end of the spit and the shore. Scipio proceeded to close this entrance by building a massive stone mole from the shore to the spit of land. The Carthaginians met this threat by digging a new exit from the harbour straight out to sea, an operation which they managed to conceal until the last minute. It was therefore with profound astonishment that the Romans suddenly noticed a Carthaginian fleet of 50 triremes and other craft sailing out into the sea. If at that point the Carthaginians had attacked the Roman fleet, which had not been properly maintained, they might well have captured or destroyed the whole fleet. But they contented themselves with 'showing their flag' and then retiring. The battle came three days later when the Carthaginians set out to fight and were met by the Romans with their ships by then in good order. The nimble Carthaginian small boats inflicted considerable damage to their adversaries by breaking off their oars and rudders and stoving holes in their sterns. Nevertheless, by evening the outcome was still undecided and the Carthaginians thought it prudent to withdraw and recommence on the morrow. As the small boats led the way and jostled to get

into the harbour through the new entrance, they became entangled and blocked the mouth. The larger ships were then forced to berth at the quay below the city wall on the sea front. The Romans attacked them with ease but found it less easy to extricate themselves, and they suffered much damage while they were turning round. Some friends of the Romans who were helping out provided the answer. They attached long ropes to the anchors of their five ships and dropped the anchors out at sea, using the ropes to haul themselves back stern first after each attack. The rest of the fleet then followed the same routine. After many such hit-and-run attacks the Carthaginian fleet had been sorely reduced in numbers and ceased to be a threat.
Appian, Punic Wars, *120–123*

TRIBOLA (147) – Viriathus' Uprising
About 10,000 Lusitanians who had escaped the perfidious massacres of Lucullus and his successor Galba, for instance at Cauca (151), assembled together. Marcus Vetilius marched against them with a force of around 10,000 men and bottled them up in a place from which there was no escape. The Lusitani asked for a truce, but a shepherd called Viriathus, a born leader, rose up in their midst as a champion and reminded them of Roman perfidy and broken pledges. With 1,000 men and some swift horses he managed to harass the Romans and hold them at bay while the rest of the Lusitanians escaped, with instructions to meet up at Tribola. Pursued by Vetilius, Viriathus himself then proceeded towards the town, near which he laid an ambush in a dense thicket. As the Romans passed the place, they were suddenly attacked by Viriathus from the front and the concealed men in the flanks. About 4,000 of the 10,000 Romans were slain; Vetilius himself was captured and then killed. The account of Orosius is basic and at variance with Appian in regard to the casualties and the fate of Vetilius.
Appian, Spanish Wars, *61–63; Livy, epitome 52; Orosius, 5: 4(2)*

ALPHEUS R (146) – Achaean War
Described under *The Greek World*, p. 137.

SCARPHEA (146) – Achaean War
Described under *The Greek World*, p. 137.

CHAERONEA (146) – Achaean War
Described under *The Greek World*, p. 137.

ISTHMUS (146) – Achaean War
Described under *The Greek World*, p. 137.

TERMANTIA (141) – Spanish Wars
Nearly a decade after the defeat of the consul Fulvius Nobilior at Numantia (153), the 'Numantine War' erupted in earnest. When Quintus Pompeius encamped against the city with an army of 30,000 men, he suffered a series of almost daily setbacks through skirmishes and guerilla warfare until he decided to move away and try his luck against an easier target, Termantia. Here, too, he suffered no less than three indignities in one day. The following morning he got his chance when the Termestini came out prepared for a regular battle. It lasted all day and was eventually stopped by nightfall, when neither side had gained the upper hand. After that Pompeius moved away against a smaller Numantine-held town!
Appian, Spanish Wars, *77*

ERISANA (140) – Viriathus' Uprising
In the process of chasing the redoubtable guerilla leader Viriathus round his native Lusitania, Fabius Maximus Servilianus invested the town of Erisana. Viriathus got into the town furtively at night, and at daybreak he fell upon the men who were digging the trenches and sent them flying. Servilianus drew up the rest of the army in battle formation. In the ensuing battle Viriathus was victorious, pursuing the fleeing Romans and driving them up against some cliffs where they were hemmed in. Regarding this as an apt opportunity for ending the war, he came to terms with the Romans and was declared to be a friend. The peace, however, did not last. The treaty, like so many of its predecessors, was broken by the Romans. Later in the year Viriathus was assassinated by his most trusted friends, whom he had sent as emissaries of peace to the Roman commander. The latter had bribed them to commit the fell deed.
Appian, Spanish Wars, *69*

LEUCAE (130) – Aristonicus' Uprising
When Attalus III of Pergamum died in 133, his kingdom passed at his bequest to Rome. A man called Aristonicus, who was probably an illegitimate relation, intended to usurp the kingdom and led a formidable popular uprising, chiefly among the slaves and depressed classes. The Romans sent an army against him under the consul Publius Licinius Crassus, who received much assistance

from the rulers of Bithynia, Pontus, Cappadocia and elsewhere. A battle was fought in the region of Leucae [near *Foca*], a town which had been caused to revolt by Aristonicus. In spite of the large size of the Roman and allied army, Crassus was defeated and his army was routed. He himself was surrounded by the enemy and was killed.
Strabo, 14: 1, 38; Orosius, 5: 10(1–3); Livy, epitome *59*

STRATONICEA (130) – Aristonicus' Uprising
At the time of Crassus' defeat and death at the hands of Aristonicus near Leucae (above), his relief had already been appointed. The successor, Marcus Perperna, set out immediately for Asia and engaged Aristonicus, whom he defeated. According to Orosius, Perperna took his adversary by surprise while he was resting after his recent victory, suggesting that the confrontation took place not far from Leucae. Aristonicus was forced to flee and took refuge in Stratonicea in the north of Lydia. Eutropius, however, says that the battle took place near Stratonicea, to which Aristonicus had fled. Perperna subsequently reduced the city and forced his enemy to surrender.
Eutropius, 4: 20; Orosius, 5: 10(4–5)

VINDALIUM (121) – Conquest of Narbonese Gaul
The Massiliotes were the most trusty friends of Rome. When they complained to Rome about the behaviour of the Saluvii, military action had to be taken. Complaints were also received from the Aedui, likewise Roman allies, to the effect that the Allobroges, who centred around Vienna [*Vienne*] on the Rhône, had devastated their land. In addition, the Allobroges had given refuge and all possible assistance to the Salluvian chief when he fled. As a result of these incitements an army, which included some elephants, was sent out against the Allobroges under the proconsul Gnaeus Domitius. He met the enemy in front of Vindalium [*Sorgues*], where they panicked at sight of the elephants and turned to flight in their myriads.
Strabo, 4: 1, 11; Livy, epitome *61*

ISARA R (121) – Conquest of Narbonese Gaul
After their defeat at Vindalium (above), the Allobroges received help from the Arverni [*Auvergnats*]. Between them they put up a force of 180,000 men under Bituitus, the king of the Arverni, and were opposed by the consul Quintus Fabius Maximus with a force of less than 30,000. Orosius

relates the scornful remark attributed to Bituitus that there were insufficient Romans even to feed the dogs in his own camp. In spite of his contempt, he suffered a massive defeat at the place where the river Isara [*Isère*] flows into the Rhodanus [*Rhône*]. As Bituitus had realized that one bridge across the Rhône was insufficient for the crossing of his huge force, he built a second one from small boats chained together. During the flight, the chains broke under the pressure imposed on them, drowning a multitude of the fugitives. Estimates of the enemy casualties range from 120,000 to 200,000!
Orosius, 5: 14(1–4); Strabo, 4: 1, 11; Livy, epitome *61; Florus, 1: 37*

NOREIA (113) – Invasion of the Northmen
From Germany there occurred a mass migration of Cimbri and Teutones who were driven out of their lands by the encroachment of the sea and were in search of new pastures. They roamed into Illyricum and Noricum, giving the Romans cause to fear an incursion into Italy. The consul Papirius Carbo moved to block their progress and seized the nearest Alpine pass. Although they made no hostile move, he still marched against them on the grounds that they had invaded a state friendly to Rome. The Northmen sent ambassadors stating that they were ignorant of this friendly relationship and giving an undertaking that they would desist from any molestation. Carbo nevertheless pressed on against them. A battle took place at Noreia [*Neumarkt*], according to Strabo, where the Romans were heavily defeated and routed. The action was eventually terminated by a thunderstorm and darkness but not before Carbo had lost the greater part of his army.
Appian, Gallic Wars, *fragment 13; Livy,* epitome *63; Strabo, 5: 1, 8*

SUTHUL (109) – Jugurthine War
After the destruction of Carthage in 146, Numidia was firmly in the hands of Masinissa's eldest son, Micipsa, who followed his father's tradition of friendship with Rome. The region was at peace until the death in 118 of Micipsa, who had left his kingdom jointly to his two sons, Hiempsal and Adherbal, and a nephew, Jugurtha, whom he had adopted. The able Jugurtha wasted no time in arranging the assassination of Hiempsal, followed by an attack on Adherbal, who was driven out of the country and went to Rome to air his grievance. Matters might have been settled amicably but for the subsequent actions of Jugurtha, which left the

Romans with little alternative but to go to war. Their campaigns against him were initially marked by a conspicuous lack of success. In 111 Calpurnius Bestia made no military headway and resorted to abortive negotiations. The following year, his successor, Spurius Postumius Albinus, achieved nothing and returned to Rome for the elections, leaving his brother Aulus in charge. In January of 109 this officer summoned his men from their winter quarters and marched them in appalling weather against Jugurtha's treasure-hold at Suthul. The place was virtually impregnable, not only because of its natural strength but also by virtue of the bad weather which had converted the surrounding terrain into a lake. A siege was out of the question but this did not deter Aulus from making the usual preparations. Jugurtha, arriving in the vicinity, feigned fear and withdrew into wooded country, luring Aulus with the prospect of a treaty into raising the siege and following him. At dead of night Jugurtha surrounded the Roman camp, in which he was assisted by a number of bribed traitors. One, a chief centurion, allowed the enemy to break into the camp through the section of rampart which he had been detailed to defend. The Numidians burst in; the Romans fled out to a nearby hill. The next day Jugurtha pointed out to Aulus that he had his men completely surrounded. He spared their lives on condition that they passed under the yoke in token of surrender, as in days of yore, and that they departed from Numidia within 10 days.

Sallust puts the date of this battle at the very beginning of 109 but there is evidence that it may have taken place a month or two earlier, at the end of 110, which is now more generally accepted.
Sallust, Jugurthine War, 37–38

MUTHUL R (109) – Jugurthine War
When Metellus assumed command in Numidia, his first task was to restore discipline and morale among the troops. Then he initiated a campaign of attack against Jugurtha's towns. Jugurtha noted his line of march towards the river Muthul [?*Melègue*] and got ahead of him. About 20 miles from the river and parallel with it there ran a range of barren hills from the middle of which projected a long spur populated with trees and thickets. The plain below was waterless as far as the river. On this spur Jugurtha positioned his men and elephants in an extended line. Metellus was unaware of the ambush until he had descended the hill, when he saw the enemy. Fearing the effects of thirst during prolonged skirmishing in the plain,

he sent his lieutenant Rutilius Rufus ahead to the river with light troops and cavalry to seize a position for a camp. Meanwhile, Jugurtha sent a force to block the track down the hill by which Metellus had descended and to prevent any retreat by that route. Then he signalled the Numidian cavalry to attack. Their method of fighting was one of fast and furious harassment, throwing missiles at long range then wheeling away and returning again. The Romans were powerless and unable to hit back. When they charged, the enemy retreated individually in different directions so that any pursuit was also an individual affair which broke the Roman ranks. The result was an utterly confused and random conflict, which proceeded in this way until late in the day. By this time the Numidian attack was weakening and Metellus managed to reform his ranks. As his men knew that they had no way of escape, they obeyed his order to storm the hill and they dislodged the enemy who turned to flight.

In the meantime Jugurtha's Numidian ally, Bomilcar, led some cavalry and the elephants down to the plain and followed Rutilius to his wooded camp site by the river. When the two sides closed, they both charged. Fortunately for the Romans, the elephants became entangled in the trees and presented easy targets for individual destruction. As soon as the Numidians saw that they had lost the beasts on which they relied for protection, they turned and fled. Forty of the elephants were killed and four were captured.
Sallust, Jugurthine War, 48–53

CIRTA (106) – Jugurthine War
After capturing a number of Jugurtha's valuable towns, the proconsul Marius, who had assumed command in 107, ventured to the western extremity of Jugurtha's kingdom. Here the river Mulucca [*Moulouya*] formed the boundary with the Moorish realm of King Bocchus, Jugurtha's brother-in-law. The aim of Marius was to take Jugurtha's treasure-fort situated near the river. By a stroke of luck, he succeeded in doing this, thereby depriving the king of the means to pay his mercenaries. Jugurtha, having lost his bases and much money, persuaded Bocchus to come to his assistance with an army, as a pitched battle now seemed to be inevitable. Marius, having completed his mission, decided to winter in the coastal towns to the east, a journey of at least 600 miles as the crow flies. During his progress Jugurtha and Bocchus set on him twice. Sallust says that the first attack occurred just as Marius was setting out. But

later he says that the second battle occurred on the fourth day after the first one, by which time Marius had covered most of his journey. The first engagement, in which Marius eventually routed the enemy and killed more of them than in any previous battle, is described by Sallust in some detail but the site of the battle remains obscure. The second attack was launched against Marius as he was approaching Cirta [*Constantine*]. Wary of the enemy's habits, he had adopted the precaution of marching in square formation, ready to receive an attack from any direction. At this juncture he saw no reason to change his deployment. The enemy were known to be in the offing but there was no indication of their position. In the event, Jugurtha had divided his forces into four sections in the certainty that one of them would catch Marius in the rear. At the outset of the engagement, the quaestor Sulla took some squadrons of cavalry and charged against the Moorish horse. Meanwhile Jugurtha himself attacked the Roman front lines with his best cavalry while Bocchus and his son with their infantry attacked the rear lines. The Romans were faring badly until Sulla returned after routing the Moorish cavalry and charged Bocchus and his infantry in the flank. Bocchus fled immediately. Jugurtha exhorted his men and tried to grasp the victory that was almost in his hands, but he was surrounded by cavalry and had to force his way out and escape alone, leaving his comrades dead on the field. The Jugurthine War was over. Bocchus was subsequently persuaded by Sulla to set a trap to catch the king, who was sent to Rome and executed in due course.

It is well-nigh impossible to reconcile Orosius' graphic description of the battle 'near Cirta' with that of Sallust. It seems more likely that he has recounted the first of the two battles, to which he has appended a brief mention of a second and final battle, the actual battle of Cirta.
Sallust, Jugurthine War, 101; Orosius, 5: 15(10–19)

ARAUSIO (105, October 6) – Invasion by the Northmen
The invasion by the Northmen, which had already led to the battle of Noreia (113), continued to cause alarm in Rome where it was feared that the invaders would cross the Alps and invade northern Italy. Nevertheless, after their overwhelming victory over the consul Carbo at Noreia, the Cimbri and Teutones refrained from pressing southwards but moved around the Alps into Gaul. Within a few years they had routed three more Roman armies at unknown sites outside Italy. Then, an army under Gnaeus Manlius and Servilius Caepio met them on the Rhône at Arausio [*Orange*], where the Romans suffered a catastrophic defeat. This was largely attributable to bad relationships between the two generals. The proconsul Caepio was jealous of the consul and refused to co-operate in a joint camp or a joint plan. Anxious to secure all the glory for himself, Caepio positioned himself between Manlius and the enemy, allowing the enemy to take on the two armies one at a time. Both their camps were captured and, according to Antias, 80,000 Roman soldiers were killed. Orosius goes so far as to say that only 10 men were left alive to carry the bad news, but it may be noted that this historian has confounded this battle with the rout and subsequent execution of Marcus Aurelius Scaurus at around the same time.
Livy, epitome 67; Orosius, 5: 16(1–4); Dio Cassius, 27: fragment 91(1–4); Eutropius, 5: 1

SCIRTHAEA (103) – Second Servile War
In both Sicily and Italy there occurred at this time a number of insurrections on the part of slaves. In Sicily one of these uprisings escalated into a major rebellion under the leadership of a man called Salvius. Having assembled as many as 30,000 picked fighters, he proclaimed himself king and assumed the name of Tryphon. His aim was to occupy Triocala [*?Caltabellota*], an almost impregnable ridge of rock on which he intended to build a royal palace. He strengthened the place further with a wall and a moat. Against the dissident slaves the Roman senate assigned Lucius Licinius Lucullus with an army of 16,000 men. Tryphon not unnaturally wanted to meet them at Triocala, but one of his generals, Athenion, advised against letting themselves in for a siege and advocated a fight in the open. The advice was accepted and they encamped near Scirthaea [*Castello Gristia*] with a force of at least 40,000. The Roman camp was about a mile and a half away. When the two armies closed, Athenion achieved miracles with the 200 horse at his command until he himself was wounded and had to drop out. After this, the slaves lost heart and were routed, Tryphon fleeing with them. At least 20,000 were killed; the rest fled to Triocala. Nine days later the praetor arrived to besiege the place but, after inflicting a few casualties, he was driven off. He was later called to account in Rome and was punished. His immediate successor did and fared no better.
Diodorus, 36: 7–8

AQUAE SEXTIAE (102) – Invasion by the Northmen

After the battle at Arausio (105), the Northmen again failed to follow up their victory with an invasion of Italy. Instead, they moved westward to Gascony and Spain before returning once again to threaten the Romans. Without even waiting for Marius to set foot on home soil on his return from Numidia, the senate re-elected him consul for the second year (and subsequently for four more terms) to deal with the threat in the north. Marius promptly set about assembling and training his army. As soon as he heard that the Northmen were approaching, he crossed the Alps and set up camp near the *Rhône*. The Northmen had divided themselves into two parts. The Cimbri were planning to move inland through Noricum and to force a way south through the mountains. Marius' colleague, Lutatius Catulus, would proceed there to head them off. The Teutones and Ambrones set out to take the coastal route through Liguria, passing close to Marius' camp. To the disgust of Marius' men, the consul let the Northmen pass by without making a move. Their number is said to have been so great that a steady stream passed by for six days. As soon as they had gone, he decamped and shadowed them on a parallel road, always setting up camp with the fullest precautions and with difficult ground between them, until they came to Aquae Sextiae [*Aix-en-Provence*] where he intended to give battle. Here, he occupied some high ground for his camp while the enemy were down by a river. Hostilities began immediately with an unscheduled skirmish when the Ligurians, allies of the Romans, rushed down and attacked some Ambrones who were crossing the river. The Romans charged down to help their allies and between them they routed the enemy, crossed the river and pursued the fugitives back to their camp. Throughout the following day the enemy showed signs of preparing for a regular battle. Marius, on his part, sent Claudius Marcellus with 3,000 infantry round to some wooded glens on the far side of the enemy position. His instructions to them were to lie low until they heard the fighting. At dawn on the morrow Marius lined up his troops in front of his camp. When the natives saw this, they were too impatient to wait or consider the situation but charged uphill against the Romans. With the terrain in their favour the Romans had gradually forced them back to the level ground when Marcellus took his cue and appeared at the double, charging their rear. The whole horde went into confusion, broke and fled.

In the pursuit more than 100,000 of them were said to have been killed or captured, including their king Teutobodus who was taken prisoner. Livy inflates the figures further to 200,000 killed and 90,000 captives. Orosius, at variance with Plutarch and Florus, puts the whole battle in the valley and says that Teutobodus was killed. Plutarch is the only source mentioning an ambush, which seems to have been a major factor in the Roman victory. *Plutarch*, Marius, *18–21(2); Livy*, epitome *68; Velleius*, *2: 12(4); Florus*, *1: 38(6–10); Orosius*, *5: 16(9–12); Eutropius*, *5: 1*

VERCELLAE (101) – Invasion by the Northmen

While Marius was waiting in Gaul to oppose the oncoming Teutones and Ambrones at Aquae Sextiae (above), the Cimbri had hived off inland toward Noricum with the aim of forcing an entry into Italy through the Alpine passes. To Marius' consular colleague, Quintus Lutatius Catulus, was assigned the task of blocking their progress. When it came to the point, he decided that he was not strong enough to hold the passes and he descended into the Italian plain and fortified a place on the far bank of a river. The arrival of the Cimbri and their preparations for crossing the river unsettled the Romans who started to flee, forcing Catulus to make a further withdrawal. Marius at that time was in Rome where he had been recalled for discussions. He set out north to join Catulus and sent for his own army to join him from Gaul. They crossed the Padus [*Po*] and confronted the Cimbri, who at first were hesitant to fight. It appeared that they were waiting for their friends the Teutones to join them. Marius disillusioned them on that score and brought forth the Teuton kings in chains as proof of the events at Aquae Sextiae. The king of the Cimbri then challenged Marius to make an 'appointment' for a battle, which was arranged for the third day thereafter on the Campi Raudii near Vercellae. On the appointed day the two armies drew up for battle with the combined Roman force of nearly 55,000 facing the west. Marius divided his men between the two wings with Catulus' force in the centre. The Cimbri moved first, their infantry advancing slowly in a square while their cavalry, 15,000 strong, moved to their right away from the square. The aim of the horsemen was to draw the Romans after them so that the square was on their flank. In fact, it appears that such a cloud of dust was raised by the horses that Marius, when he advanced, made no contact with the enemy at all. The enemy infantry bore down on Catulus in the centre, who carried the whole brunt.

Thanks to Marius' foresight, the Cimbri were fighting with the sun in their eyes and the dust blown into their faces. With the Romans well trained and in good fettle, the end result was the destruction of a large part of the enemy force. Nor did those who fled back to their camp escape – they were killed by the women, who then killed themselves. There is a fairly general agreement among the sources that 60,000 Cimbri were taken prisoner while double that number were slain. Florus puts the casualties at a much lower 65,000 killed against a mere 300 on the Roman side. Their losses, at any rate, ensured that the Northmen ceased to pose a threat.
Plutarch, Marius, *24–27(3); Livy,* epitome *68; Florus,* **1***: 38(11–18); Orosius,* **5***: 16(14–21); Velleius,* **2***: 12(5); Eutropius,* **5***: 2*

AESERNIA (90) – Social War
At the beginning of the first century there was increasing unrest among the Italians, who wanted equal rights with the Roman citizens. The anger grew until, in 90, it developed into a frank revolt and then an out-and-out war. There is a remarkable paucity of extant information about this Social, Marsic or Italic War, as it is variously called. Over a brief two-year period the battles were many; the details are almost non-existent. This and the following entries do little more than list those which took place at or near some identifiable site.

Vettius Scaton, a Samnite commander, defeated the consul Lucius Julius Caesar (sometimes called Sextus Julius) and killed 2,000 of his men. Appian says that Scaton then marched against Aesernia [*Isernia*]. According to Livy the siege of Aesernia was commenced at the outset of the war and probably in the year 91. It fell into the hands of the Samnites in 90 but the order of events is unclear. Caesar may have been trying to relieve it when the battle took place – *at* Aesernia, according to Orosius.
Appian, Civil Wars *1: 41; Livy,* epitome *72 and 73; Orosius,* **5***: 18(14)*

AESERNIA (90) – Social War
It is reported that while Aesernia was still held by the Romans, an attempt to relieve it was made by Cornelius Sulla who went to its aid with 24 cohorts. According to Orosius, Sulla lifted the siege after a tremendous battle with great slaughter of the enemy. If this is correct, the relief must have been short-lived before the Samnites captured the place in the same year.
Orosius, **5***: 18(16)*

GRUMENTUM (90) – Social War
Marcus Lamponius, one of the Italian leaders, engaged Publius Licinius Crassus and killed about 800 of his men. He drove the rest into the town of Grumentum, which suggests that the encounter took place in the vicinity.
Appian, Civil Wars **1***: 41*

ACERRAE (90) – Social War
Gaius Papius Mutilus, the Samnite commander of the southern rebels, captured many towns in Campania and put such fear into the others that they submitted. On demand, they provided him with 10,000 infantry and 1,000 horse, with which he laid siege to Acerrae [*Acerra*], now a suburb of *Naples*. Lucius Julius Caesar went against him with 10,000 foot and some African cavalry and he encamped near the town. Papius attacked him and breached the palisade of the camp but Caesar burst out through the gates with his cavalry, slaying 6,000 of the enemy. He then withdrew.
Appian, Civil Wars, **1***: 42*

TOLENUS R: I (90, June 11) – Social War
The consul Rutilius and his legate Gaius Marius built two bridges over the river Tolenus [*Turano*] (Appian says it was the Liris [*Garigliano*], which is further south). The bridges were sufficiently far apart to be out of sight of each other. Vettius Scaton, a Marsic commander, set up his camp on the opposite side of the river to the Roman encampment and close to the bridge of Marius. After dark he placed some men in ambush in some gullies opposite the bridge built by Rutilius. When Rutilius crossed the bridge, Scaton's men rose up in his rear and killed about 8,000 of his force. Others were driven back into the river. Rutilius himself was wounded and died soon afterwards.
Appian, Civil Wars, **1***: 43; Orosius,* **5***: 18(11–12); Livy,* epitome *73*

TOLENUS R: II (90) – Social War
When the consul Rutilius was defeated by Scaton on the Tolenus (above), Marius lower down the river saw corpses floating downstream and guessed the truth. He crossed the river and captured Scaton's camp, killing about 8,000 of the Marsi, according to Orosius, although the camp was said to be only lightly held. The enemy was forced to withdraw for lack of provisions.
Appian, Civil Wars, **1***: 43; Orosius,* **5***: 18(13); Livy,* epitome *73*

TEANUM SIDICINUM (90) – Social War
Lucius Julius Caesar was marching through a rocky gorge with 30,000 foot and 5,000 horse when he was attacked by the Samnites under Marius Egnatius. He was utterly defeated and lost most of his force. He himself was ill and was carried out on a litter, reaching Teanum [*Teano*] only with difficulty. Orosius and Livy mention the defeat but provide no further details.
Appian, Civil Wars, *1: 45; Orosius, 5: 18(11)*

FALERNUS M (90) – Social War
In the northern sector Gnaeus Pompeius was defeated near Mount Falernus (unidentified) by the combined forces of Vidacilius, Lafrenius and Vettius. He was pursued and fled to the city of Firmum where he was besieged by Lafrenius.
Appian, Civil Wars, *1: 47*

FIRMUM (90) – Social War
While Pompeius was being besieged by Lafrenius in Firmum [*Fermo*] after the battle near Mount Falernus (above), he learnt that another enemy force was approaching. He decided to make a dash for it and sent a lieutenant round to attack Lafrenius in the rear while he himself made a frontal sally. The fighting was bitter until Sulpicius set fire to the enemy's camp. Lafrenius had already been killed, and the leaderless army fled for refuge to Asculum which Pompeius proceeded to invest.
Appian, Civil Wars, *1: 47*

ASCULUM PICENUM (89) – Social War
When Pompeius extricated himself from the siege of Firmum (above), he in his turn set about besieging Asculum [*Ascoli Piceno*]. He was attacked by the Marsi in a fierce battle in the plain in which 18,000 of them were slain. Vidacilius, the leader of the Picentes, whose home town this was, also hastened to its relief with eight cohorts, having first sent word to the inhabitants ordering them to make a sally as soon as he arrived. Although they were too frightened to obey his instructions, he still managed to force his way in through the Roman forces. Realizing that he could not save the city, he built a large pyre, had a good meal and then took poison, after which the pyre was ignited as he had requested. The city fell to Pompeius.
Appian, Civil Wars, *1: 47–48; Orosius, 5: 18(18); Livy, epitome 76*

FUCINUS L (89) – Social War
Several sources baldly record the death of the consul Lucius Porcius Cato while he was fighting the Marsi. Orosius goes further in saying that the battle in question was fought at the Fucine lake and that Cato's death was no mere military matter. Cato, who had had much help from the Marian forces, is said to have boasted that Marius himself had never achieved greater deeds. It is alleged that Cato was surreptitiously killed in the battle by Marius' son, a charge which remains unconfirmed.
Orosius, 5: 18(24)

NOLA (89) – Social War
Lucius Cornelius Sulla was encamped near the Pompaean hills when Lucius Cluentius pitched his camp close by. Sulla attacked him impetuously with only a part of his force because many of his own men were out foraging. He got the worst of it. After assembling all his men, he tried again and defeated Cluentius, forcing him to move his camp further away. Cluentius received reinforcements and moved in again for another contest. It commenced with a challenge from a Gaul of gigantic proportions to any Roman who would engage him in single combat. A little man accepted the challenge and killed the Gaul, whereupon all the other Gauls fled. As a result of the gap in Cluentius' lines, the rest of his men failed to stand their ground and fled to Nola. They were pursued by the Romans who killed about 3,000 of them in the pursuit, but the main slaughter occurred outside the gates of Nola. The inhabitants would only open one gate for fear of letting the enemy in as well. Around 20,000 of the fugitives were killed outside the walls, including Cluentius.
Appian, Civil Wars, *1: 50; Orosius, 5: 18(23)*

CANUSIUM (89) – Social War
The praetor Gaius Cosconius laid siege to Canusium [*Canosa*]. A Samnite army came to its relief and there was a bitter struggle. After much slaughter on both sides Cosconius was defeated and withdrew to Cannae.
Appian, Civil Wars, *1: 52*

TEANUS R (89) – Social War
Two of the Italian leaders, Poppaedius Silo and Obsidius, were killed in a major battle against the Apulians, which Orosius places at the river Teanus. The Roman commander is variously given as Sulpicius (Servius Sulpicius Galba), Caecilius Metellus (Pius) or Aemilius Mamercus (Mamercus Aemilius Lepidus). The Teanus river appears to be unknown today but it might be expected to be in the vicinity of Teanum Apulum

[*San Paolo di Civitate*], possibly a tributary of the Frento [*Fortore*].
Orosius, 5: 18(25); Appian, Civil Wars, *1: 53; Livy,* epitome *76*

ESQUILINE FORUM (88) – First Civil War

The enmity between Gaius Marius and Lucius Cornelius Sulla, which *inter alia* led to the First Civil War, had its origins in the Jugurthine War. Marius won the battles; the diplomacy of Sulla reaped the ultimate goal and, in the eyes of Marius, the credit. Subsequently, Sulla had been appointed to command the campaign against Mithridates when, by a political fiddle, it was given instead to Marius. Sulla resolved to settle the issue by force of arms. With the exception of one quaestor, Sulla's superior officers deserted him because they would not subscribe to civil war. On the other hand, the rank and file of his army, prepared for the Mithridatic War, was solidly behind him. Moreover, he was joined by his consular colleague, Quintus Pompeius. Together with six legions, they marched on Rome where Sulla took possession of the Esquiline Gate while Pompeius occupied the Colline Gate. With two of the legions, Sulla entered the city. He met Marius and his associate, Publius Sulpicius, with some hastily assembled troops near the Esquiline Forum and here a battle took place – not a mere street riot but a proper battle with all the paraphernalia of war. When Sulla's troops started to waver, he grabbed a standard and stood out in front exhorting his men while at the same time he called up fresh troops to go round and take Marius in the rear. It was the Marians' turn to waver. Marius called to the citizens in the houses, proclaiming freedom to slaves who joined them, but answer was there none. In despair the Marians fled, Marius himself ultimately making his way to Africa. Sulla punished looters on the spot and began to restore order. In the following year he sailed with his army to Greece. It was not until his return in 85 that the Civil War was resumed in earnest.
Appian, Civil Wars, *1: 57–58; Florus, 2: 9(6–8)*

AMNIAS R (88) – First Mithridatic War

Mithridates VI Eupator of Pontus wanted more space. In the past he had gained control of Cappadocia but had been ordered by the Romans to give it back and keep his hands off it. When Rome became involved in the Social War, Mithridates saw his chance and expelled Nicomedes from Bithynia and Ariobarzanes from Cappadocia. Contrary to his expectations, the Romans sent

Manius Aquilius to reinstate the two kings with the assistance of the Roman troops in Asia. Mithridates remonstrated but, after the failure of talks, war was inevitable and Mithridates was the first to act. He sent a large force to seize Cappadocia, after which he collected further forces from all over Asia Minor until he had an army of 250,000 foot and 40,000 horse with Neoptolemus and Archelaus as his generals. On the Roman side, the Governor of Asia had at his disposal a total force of 120,000 men, which he divided into three equal divisions.

The first encounter took place when Nicomedes of Bithynia with his whole army of 50,000 foot and 6,000 horse met Neoptolemus and Archelaus, the generals of Mithridates, with a much smaller force of light infantry, cavalry and some scythed chariots. They met in a plain alongside the river Amnias [*Geuk Irma*] in Paphlagonia, where Neoptolemus sent a small force to seize a hill in the plain. When it was driven off, both sides sent in more men and the action escalated. Nicomedes put the enemy to flight but Archelaus then attacked the Bithynian pursuers, giving the fugitives time to rally and advance. At the same time the scythe-bearing chariots were sent in against the Bithynians with devastating effect. After that, the Bithynians were routed by the combined assaults of Archelaus on their front and Neoptolemus in their rear. Nicomedes fled and many prisoners were taken, whom Mithridates treated with great humanity. The battle caused considerable alarm among the Roman generals, who were disturbed that such a small force had defeated one so much larger.
Appian, Mithridatic Wars, *18*

PROTOPACHIUM (88) – First Mithridatic War

After the battle by the river Amnias (above), Neoptolemus met up with the legate Manius Aquilius at a stronghold called Protopachium. The Roman force consisted of 40,000 foot and 4,000 horse, but in an action about which nothing more is known Neoptolemus killed 10,000 of them. The prisoners were again treated humanely and released by Mithridates. Aquilius escaped to Pergamum. The Mithridatic forces were now virtually unopposed and made a clean sweep through Asia Minor, where Mithridates himself ordered the massacre of all Romans and Italians in what has been called the 'Asian Vespers'. The war was now to be war with a vengeance.
Appian, Mithridatic Wars, *19*

CHAERONEA (86) – First Mithridatic War

Not content with the control of Asia Minor, Mithridates prepared for an invasion of Europe. His henchman Aristion fomented a revolution in Athens and won the city over, while his general Archelaus occupied the Piraeus and then proceeded to gain control of the whole of the south and most of central Greece. In 87, Sulla landed in the south of Greece with five legions. It took him until the following year to break into Athens and seize Piraeus. Meanwhile, the Pontic army was advancing southwards from Thrace, and Archelaus moved northwards to join up with it. He assumed overall command of the combined forces, which are said to have numbered 120,000 men. Sulla, also, moved northwards into Boeotia and the two sides met near Chaeronea. Plutarch gives the size of Sulla's force as a mere 15,000 infantry but this appears to be a considerable understatement in view of the fact that he landed in Greece with around 30,000 and had received some reinforcements from Macedonia. Appian's statement that Sulla was outnumbered about three to one may be nearer the truth.

There are two accounts of the battle, neither of them very clear. The action took place in a narrow plain surrounded by craggy hills and mountains where a large force would have little advantage. The Pontic army had a heavily fortified encampment at the base of and between two mountains. They lined up their forces on the plain and Sulla deployed his men opposite them. He placed cavalry on both wings, with himself in charge on the right, and positioned a force in reserve on higher ground in the rear. As Sulla gave the order to advance, the enemy unleashed his scythe-bearing chariots. The distance between the two armies was not sufficient to allow these to get up an effective speed, and they were easily side-stepped or turned. Archelaus then extended his right wing in an enveloping movement. Sulla's reserve flying force charged to the assistance of his left but found itself being surrounded and hemmed in against the cliffs. Sulla, who had not yet engaged on the right wing, went across immediately to the assistance of the distressed left where he turned the tables. Archelaus then abandoned his assault against the enemy left and turned his attention to the opposite wing, which Sulla had left temporarily leaderless. Sulla, seeing the other's move, rode across and charged Archelaus while he was in the middle of executing his manoeuvre. This created confusion and broke the enemy's lines. When the wings collapsed, the enemy centre started to give up too

and the whole army rushed to their fortifications, losing many more men in the flight than the fight. It is reported in both accounts that only 10,000 of the enemy multitude survived whereas the Romans, it seems, lost only 12 men (Appian says 13).
Plutarch, Sulla, *15–19; Appian*, Mithridatic Wars, *41–45*

ORCHOMENUS (86) – First Mithridatic War

Sulla moved northward from Chaeronea (above) into Thessaly but, as he did so, a large enemy fleet put into Chalcis in Euboea with 80,000 of Mithridates' best troops on board. This army crossed the Euripus and invaded Boeotia, encamping near Orchomenus on a plain which extended from the city to the marshes of the river Melas. The site seemed to Archelaus, the general, to be ideal for cavalry, in which he excelled. Sulla turned about and marched to Orchomenus where he encamped close to the enemy. His first action was to get his men digging trenches down both sides of the plain in an attempt to deny the enemy access to the harder ground suitable for cavalry. This thought did not appeal to the enemy who charged out and routed not only Sulla's diggers but also the troops who were protecting them. At this point Sulla dismounted and dashed through the fugitives to the front, exhorting them to rally and to turn and face the enemy, after which he led an assault which sent the enemy fleeing back to their fortifications. On the following day, Sulla resumed his digging and the enemy reappeared but without any zest for fighting. They were routed easily, with the loss of 15,000 men, and their camp was captured as well. This action, combined with the previous one at Chaeronea, brought to an end the hostilities of Mithridates in Europe.
Plutarch, Sulla, *20–21; Appian*, Mithridatic Wars, *49*

TENEDOS ISL (85) – First Mithridatic War

Following the defeat of his forces in Europe, Mithridates retired to Pergamum and then escaped from there to Pitane on the coast of Aeolis. An unscrupulous Roman legate, Flavius Fimbria, who had murdered the consul Flaccus and had assumed command of his army, besieged Pitane by land but had no ships with which to prevent an escape by sea. He appealed to Lucullus to bring his fleet but the admiral refused to do so and continued his campaign against the king's ships. After defeating some of them off the promontory of Lectum in the Troad, he found

Neoptolemus waiting for him with a large armament off the island of Tenedos [*Bozcaada*]. Neoptolemus came out well in front of his fleet with the intention of ramming Lucullus but, as Lucullus' flag-ship was a heavy well-reinforced vessel, the enemy steersman refused to obey his instructions and minimized the collision. Lucullus proceeded to put the enemy fleet to flight and to give Neoptolemus a good run in the chase.
Plutarch, Lucullus, *3(8–10)*

CANUSIUM (83) – First Civil War

Sulla's return from Asia after the end of the First Mithridatic War signalled the resumption of the First Civil War in earnest, after a preliminary confrontation five years earlier in Rome itself (Esquiline Forum, 88). In the interim Marius had died, but his death did nothing to relieve the tensions between the opposing factions. According to Appian, Sulla's first encounter with the opposition, which could have occurred on his route northwards from Brundisium [*Brindisi*], is said to have taken place at Canusium [*Canosa di Puglia*] where he and Caecilius Metellus Pius met the consul Gaius Norbanus. They are reputed to have killed 6,000 of his men for a loss of 70 of their own. Norbanus retreated to Capua. Velleius, Florus and Eutropius, however, say that Sulla first met Norbanus near Capua (below), suggesting that Appian may have been in error in regard to the site.
Appian, Civil Wars, *1: 84*

CAPUA (83) – First Civil War

Sulla met Norbanus and the other consul, L. Cornelius Scipio Asiaticus, near Capua [*S. Maria Capua Vetere*], either by the river Volturnus (Florus) or on Mount Tifata (Velleius). Norbanus was promptly routed, whereas Scipio's army longed only for peace and the whole lot were enticed to desert *en masse* to Sulla. Norbanus lost 7,000 men killed and 6,000 captured; Sulla's losses amounted to 124 men. It may be noted that these casualty figures are comparable with those reported by Appian for Canusium (above), which was probably the same battle at an erroneously reported site.
Velleius, 2: 25(2); *Florus*, 2: 9(20); *Eutropius*, 5: 7

AESIS R (82, spring) – First Civil War

When fighting was resumed in the spring, the consul Papirius Carbo sent a large cavalry force under his lieutenant Carinas against a Sullan force on the banks of the Aesis [*Esino*], which forms the border between Umbria and Picenum. The commander of the Sullan force was the young Gnaeus Pompeius (not Metellus, as Appian states). Heavy fighting took place and continued for several hours until Carinas was routed. In the pursuit, Pompey drove the enemy onto difficult ground from which they could not escape and were forced to surrender.
Plutarch, Pompey, *7(3); Appian,* Civil Wars, *1: 87*

SACRIPORTUS (82) – First Civil War

The young Marius, son of the great general, was one of the consuls in 82. He was encamped near Setia [*Sezze*] in Latium when Sulla captured the town. Marius withdrew to Sacriportus where he was brought to battle. When his left wing gave way, five cohorts of foot and some cavalry deserted to Sulla. Marius and the rest of his army fled to Praeneste [*Palestrina*] pursued by Sulla. The Praenestines allowed the first fugitives to enter but they shut the gates as soon as Sulla appeared. As a result, there was another great slaughter outside the walls as Sulla's men despatched the unfortunates who could not gain admission. Marius himself was hauled up into the city by means of a rope.
Appian, Civil Wars, *1: 87; Florus, 2: 9(23);*
Velleius, 2: 26(1); Livy, epitome 87

CLANIS R (82) – First Civil War

As warfare was being waged vigorously in Etruria, Sulla set out there to deal with it. He began with a cavalry battle on the banks of the river Clanis (Glanis) [*Chiana*] against some Celtiberian horsemen who had been sent over from Spain by the praetors to reinforce the consuls. After Sulla had killed about 50 of them, 270 more deserted to him. The rest were killed by the consul Carbo, probably out of fear of further desertions.
Appian, Civil Wars, *1: 89*

SATURNIA (82) – First Civil War

Shortly after the tussle at the river Clanis (above), Sulla overcame another enemy detachment near Saturnia in Etruria. The details are unknown.
Appian, Civil Wars, *1: 89*

CLUSIUM (82) – First Civil War

A major battle was fought near Clusium [*Chiusi*] in Etruria between Sulla and Carbo. It went on all day without showing any clear advantage either way, according to Appian. Livy talks of a victory here by Sulla, along with several other victories, but this may refer to the second recorded

encounter at Clusium in the same year, which is entered below (Clusium, 82).
Appian, Civil Wars, *1: 89; Livy*, epitome *88*

SPOLETIUM (82) – First Civil War
In the plain of Spoletium [*Spoleto*], Sullan forces under Pompey and Crassus killed about 3,000 of Carbo's men and besieged his lieutenant Carinas, who was in command. Carbo sent some reinforcements but Sulla heard about this and set an ambush. He killed about 2,000 of them.
Appian, Civil Wars, *1: 90*

FAVENTIA (82) – First Civil War
Carbo and Norbanus planned to make an attack at dusk on the camp of Metellus in Faventia [*Faenza*] in Gallia Cispadana. They set out at the appointed time but the darkness was too much for them. The area was covered with vineyards, in which they got completely entangled. They lost 10,000 men in the escapade, after which a further 6,000 deserted.
Appian, Civil Wars, *1: 91; Velleius, 2: 28(1); Livy*, epitome *88*

PLACENTIA (82) – First Civil War
Marcus Lucullus, Sulla's lieutenant, defeated a body of Carbo's forces near Placentia [*Piacenza*] in Gallia Cispadana. This so discouraged Carbo that he fled to Africa in spite of his position as consul and the large forces which he still had at his disposal.
Appian, Civil Wars, *1: 92*

CLUSIUM (82) – First Civil War
When the consul Carbo fled to Africa, there was still an army of 30,000 of his men at Clusium [*Chiusi*] in Etruria. Pompey engaged this force and killed 20,000 of them.
Appian, Civil Wars, *1: 92; Livy*, epitome *88*

COLLINE GATE (82, November 1) – First Civil War
As a result of their losses in Etruria the remaining Marian forces joined up with a Samnite army of 40,000 under their chieftain Telesinus. The combined forces made an effort to relieve Praeneste [*Palestrina*] and to rescue the young Marius, but they failed in the attempt. They then turned their footsteps in the direction of Rome and encamped outside the walls. Sulla hurried after them and took up position by the Colline Gate where he gave battle. In the fierce fighting that followed, Crassus on Sulla's right wing crushed his oppo-

nents but the Sullan left was routed. The close and bitter contest persisted until the early hours of the morning, by which time the Samnite generals had been killed and their camp had been taken. The generals of Carbo's faction fled after their army had been destroyed. It was estimated that in all about 50,000 men were slain. In the aftermath of Sulla's narrow victory his enemies were rooted out one by one and eliminated, leaving him with the absolute power of a dictator.
Plutarch, Sulla, *29–30(1); Appian*, Civil Wars, *1: 93; Velleius, 2: 27(1–3); Orosius, 5: 20(9); Eutropius, 5: 8; Livy*, epitome *88*

BAETIS R (80) – Sertorian War
Quintus Sertorius was a military adventurer who supported the popular faction of Marius during the Civil War. When Sulla returned from Asia and the popular party lost its popularity, Sertorius sailed away to Spain where he trained a native army and became much respected locally. Sulla sent an army against him, and Sertorius then sailed to Mauretania. While he was there – and after many adventures and several battles – the Lusitanians in Iberia invited him to become their leader in their need for protection against Rome. Their confidence was not misplaced. Among other feats he opposed the governor of Further Spain, Lucius Fufidius, on the banks of the river Baetis [*Guadalquivir*] near Corduba [*Cordoba*] and routed him, killing 2,000 of his men.
Plutarch, Sertorius, *12(3)*

ANA R (79) – Sertorian War
Marcus Domitius, the governor of Hither Spain, was one of the first generals to oppose Sertorius. Domitius fought Lucius Hirtuleius, the Sertorian second-in-command, at the river Ana [*Guadiana*] and was defeated.
Florus, 2: 10(6–7); Plutarch, Sertorius, *12(3); Eutropius, 6: 1; Orosius, 5: 23(3); Livy*, epitome *90*

SEGOVIA (78) – Sertorian War
Sertorius' lieutenant, Hirtuleius, followed up his defeat of Domitius (above) by obtaining a victory at Segovia over another of the enemy commanders. The defeated general is said to have been called either Thorius or Thoranius but in all probability he was Lucius Manlius, who was governor of Transalpine Gaul in 78 and who crossed into Spain to help in the fight against Sertorius.
Florus, 2: 10(6–7); Plutarch, Sertorius, *12(4); Orosius, 5: 23(4); Livy*, epitome *90*

MILVIAN BRIDGE (77) – Lepidus' Revolt
No sooner had Sulla died, in 78, than the factions began to quarrel with each other. The consul Marcus Aemilius Lepidus, a former supporter of the Marian faction, wanted to repeal some of Sulla's decrees. His actions incited revolt and threatened to destabilize the constitution, as a result of which he was declared an enemy of the state. He repaired to Etruria, where he recruited forces and then marched on Rome. The other consul, Q. Lutatius Catulus, was waiting for him and, with the help of Pompey, had already seized the Milvian Bridge and the Janiculum. Lepidus was repulsed at the first onslaught and fled. He sailed soon afterwards to Sardinia where he died. Appian places the battle near the Campus Martius and ascribes no part to Pompey.
Appian, Civil Wars, *1: 107; Florus,* **2:** *11*

LAURO (76) – Sertorian War
The guerilla tactics of Sertorius and his largely local army met with so much success that he eventually held most of Roman Spain. Various generals were sent against him, notably Metellus Pius, who achieved little on his own, and in 76 the great Pompey. Pompey's first encounter with Sertorius turned out to be an utter humiliation. Sertorius was besieging the town of Lauro, and Pompey marched to relieve it with the whole of his army. A hill nearby appeared to be an important position, and both armies raced to get there first. Sertorius succeeded and occupied it. Pompey's chagrin at his failure to prevent the other from gaining the hill was completely offset by the realization that he had trapped the enemy – between the city and himself. But Pompey had not kept an eye on his rear and was unaware that it was he who was trapped until 6,000 of the enemy appeared behind him from Sertorius' camp, where they had been left as an ambush. As Pompey did not dare to attack and was ashamed to run away, he had to sit and watch the siege while Sertorius won a victory without a battle.
Plutarch, Sertorius, *18(3–6), and* Pompey, *18(3); Orosius,* **5:** *23(6–7)*

ITALICA (BAETICA) (75) – Sertorian War
It is reported that Hirtuleius, Sertorius' lieutenant, battled against Metellus and was heavily defeated. Orosius places the battle at the city of Italica [*Santiponce*] and says that Hirtuleius lost 20,000 men. He fled into Lusitania.
Orosius, **5:** *23(10); Livy,* epitome *91*

VALENTIA (75) – Sertorian War
Gaius Herennius and Marcus Perperna were two Roman exiles who had joined Sertorius and had been given commands by him. Pompey engaged them near Valentia [*Valencia*] and defeated them, killing Herennius and inflicting more than 10,000 casualties.
Plutarch, Pompey, *18(3)*

SUCRO R (75) – Sertorian War
Immediately after the battle near Valentia (above) Pompey hurried to challenge Sertorius himself and engaged him by the river Sucro [*Jucar*]. Pompey is said to have been anxious to get the credit for a victory before Metellus arrived to join him. This jealousy suited Sertorius, who was content to fight one army at a time. In the encounter, on each side one wing was winning and one losing until Sertorius, having routed the enemy wing opposite him, went to the assistance of his left wing which was being forced back by Pompey. He rallied his troops and launched a successful counterattack. Pompey found himself in a very difficult position and only managed to escape by abandoning his horse. Both armies lined up again on the following day but, as Metellus was by then approaching, Sertorius withdrew and his army scattered. This is Plutarch's account of events. Appian contends that Metellus was present from the start and that the battle was really a foursome in which Perperna, who had joined Sertorius from Italy in 77, was also leading a wing. According to this source, Metellus was defeating Perperna while Sertorius defeated Pompey so that the overall result was inconclusive. However, this account is so similar to Appian's ensuing description of the battle at Segontia (see Saguntum, 75, below) as to suggest an error of duplication. Appian's account of Sucro is suspect.
Plutarch, Pompey, *19(1–4), and* Sertorius, *19; Appian,* Civil Wars, *1: 110*

TURIA R (75) – Sertorian War
A brief comment by Plutarch refers to a battle near the river Turia in which Pompey and Metellus defeated Sertorius. Apparently Sertorius managed to extricate himself favourably, but no other details are given.

When was this battle fought in relation to the other Sertorian encounters? Plutarch asserts that Pompey hurried from Valentia to engage Sertorius in person at the river Sucro before Metellus arrived. On these grounds the action near the Turia must have taken place after Sucro when

Pompey and Metellus had joined forces. Plutarch implies this when he praises Sertorius' qualities on the Sucro and *again near the Turia*. The fierce struggles on the Sucro and the Turia (in that order) are also mentioned by Cicero. Finally, the opposing armies would have to cross the river Turia to get from the Sucro to Saguntum (below) – a direct progression northwards.
Plutarch, Sertorius, *19(1); Cicero*, pro Balbo, *2(5)*

SAGUNTUM (75) – Sertorian War
Plutarch briefly describes a battle in the plains of Saguntum [*Sagunto*] between Sertorius and the forces of Pompey and Metellus. Sertorius was winning the day until Metellus was wounded and was carried off the field. This so enraged his men that they redoubled their efforts and forced Sertorius to abandon the field. Appian cites a battle at about the same time – after the battle at the Sucro (75) and before winter – in which Sertorius defeated Pompey and killed about 6,000 of his men. At the same time Metellus worsted Perperna, slaying about 5,000 of his force. Appian places this battle near Segontia [*Siguenza*], also known as Saguntia. Confusion with Saguntum would be an easy matter.

It seems probable that these are two admittedly differing accounts of one and the same action. The site of Saguntum makes good geographical sense for a sequel to the battles on the Sucro and Turia. Moreover, Plutarch specifies the site as the *plains* of Saguntum, which was situated on the fertile coastal strip. It is unlikely that there was an action at this time near Segontia, a distance of 150 miles from Saguntum as the crow flies. The place name given by Appian may have been corrupted.
Plutarch, Sertorius, *21(1–3); Appian*, Civil Wars, *1: 110*

CALAGURRIS (74) – Sertorian War
The last recorded combat of the Sertorian War occurred after Pompey laid siege to Pallantia [*Palencia*]. Sertorius came on the scene and raised the siege, whereupon Pompey retired to join Metellus at Calagurris [*Calahorra*]. Sertorius attacked their encampment and killed 3,000 of their combined forces. By this time Pompey and Metellus were taking more and more towns and Sertorius was losing his hold. The war was brought to an end by the assassination of Sertorius in 72 by the jealous Perperna, who was himself defeated and slain by Pompey soon afterwards.
Appian, Civil Wars, *1: 112; Livy*, epitome *93*

CHALCEDON (74) – Third Mithridatic War
The First Mithridatic War was followed by a period of good relationship between the Pontic king and Rome but this was short-lived. The Second War was almost a non-event, an internal affair which did not involve Rome, but a Third War loomed rapidly out of the murk of mutual suspicion. When Nicomedes IV of Bithynia died, he bequeathed his realm to Rome. The Romans accepted it; Mithridates did not! To him, a Roman province down the road was an unpalatable threat, and so he invaded it. The unmilitary consul, Aurelius Cotta, who had been sent out with some ships to guard the area, fled to Chalcedon [*Kadikoy*] at the entrance to the Bosphorus, where he was besieged. When Mithridates advanced against the city, Cotta was afraid to go out and meet him. One of his officers, Nudus by name, did take a detachment and occupy a position in the plain but was driven back to the gates, which the guards were afraid to open. Nudus and a few others were hauled over the wall by ropes; the rest perished. Mithridates then assailed the harbour, burnt four of Cotta's ships and towed the other 60 away. In the action Cotta lost about 3,000 men against an enemy loss of only 20.
Plutarch, Lucullus, *8(1–2); Appian*, Mithridatic Wars, *71; Livy*, epitome *93*

RHYNDACUS R (74) – Third Mithridatic War
Mithridates proceeded to besiege Cyzicus by land and sea. In the meantime, the consul Lucullus had landed in Asia with an army to which he attached all the Roman forces in the area, giving him a total of 30,000 infantry. He pitched camp near Mithridates at Cyzicus. When Lucullus heard that the enemy amounted to 120,000 foot (Appian says 300,000) and 16,000 horse, he was struck by the logistical problems of feeding such a horde. The obvious way to defeat them was to starve them. To this end he encamped on a suitable hill from which he could obtain supplies while denying them to the enemy. Mithridates, ignoring all advice, pursued the siege with every means at his disposal until famine started to take its toll. At that point he sent away to Bithynia all his cavalry, beasts of burden, and disabled foot soldiers, who were of no use in the siege. Lucullus pursued them and overtook them at the river Rhyndacus [*Kocasu*], where he defeated them overwhelmingly. In addition to those that were slain, he captured 6,000 horses and 15,000 men.
Plutarch, Lucullus, *11(1–3); Appian*, Mithridatic Wars, *75*

AESEPUS R (74) – Third Mithridatic War
The starvation caused by Lucullus' blockade forced Mithridates to abandon the siege of Cyzicus. He fled to the sea, leaving his generals to evacuate the army to Lampsacus [*Lapseki*]. Lucullus fell upon them and killed 20,000 of them at one of the two main rivers in the area, which were greatly swollen and difficult to cross. A vastly greater number were taken captive. Appian names the river Aesepus [*Gönen*] nearer Cyzicus; Plutarch quotes the Granicus [*Kocabas*], further west. As it would be necessary to cross both rivers between Cyzicus and Lampsacus, the difference is of academic significance.
Appian, Mithridatic Wars, *76; Plutarch*, Lucullus, *11(6)*

LEMNOS ISL (73, spring) – Third Mithridatic War
Lucullus raised a fleet and sailed to the Troad, where he heard that enemy ships had been seen sailing from the harbour of the Achaeans near Ilium toward Lemnos. He proceeded to the harbour, where he caught the last 13 ships of the enemy fleet of 50 vessels and captured them before proceeding to chase the rest of the fleet. He met up with them off a small deserted island near Lemnos, where they had either beached their ships or dropped anchor close to the shore. Attempts to draw them out to sea failed; they preferred to defend themselves on land. Lucullus overcame them by sending some of his ships round the island to disembark and take the enemy in the rear. After suffering much slaughter, they took to flight. Their leaders were captured, including Marcus Marius, who had been sent to assist Mithridates by his ally Sertorius in Spain.
Appian, Mithridatic Wars, *77; Plutarch*, Lucullus, *12*

VESUVIUS M (73) – Third Servile War
In 73 a slave of Thracian origin called Spartacus escaped from the gladiatorial school at Capua with a handful of colleagues and proclaimed a revolt. His call to arms soon raised a force of around 10,000 fighters, at first men of Thracian and Celtic extraction, but this figure rapidly increased to at least seven times that number. Reports of his activities are both few and sketchy. His first base was on Mount Vesuvius, where the praetors Claudius Glaber and Publius Varenus with 3,000 men surrounded him and attempted to besiege him. Spartacus and his men rushed down from the heights and captured the Roman camp after putting their enemy to flight. Some say that the top of the mountain was covered with vines from which the rebels made ladders. With the help of these, they descended some precipitous slopes and appeared in the enemy's rear.
Orosius, 5: 24(1); *Appian*, Civil Wars, 1: 116; *Florus*, 2: 8(3–5); *Plutarch*, Crassus, 9(1); *Livy*, epitome 95

CABIRA (72, spring) – Third Mithridatic War
Lucullus, the general opposing Mithridates, spent the year 73 in chasing his quarry, wasting his land and winning over his cities. His soldiers criticized him for not pursuing the war but allowing his enemy to recoup. Lucullus replied that that was precisely what he wanted – a strong enemy who would fight rather than bolt into the wilderness. In the spring of the following year Lucullus crossed the mountains and marched against Cabira (Neocaesarea) [*Niksar*], where Mithridates had entrenched himself with 40,000 foot and 4,000 horse. The Pontic king crossed the river Lycus to meet the Romans in the plain, and a cavalry battle ensued in which the Romans were put to flight. Lucullus decided to avoid the plains in future as they were favourable to his adversary with his numerically superior cavalry wing. He retired into the hills and encamped at a well-provided spot which was directly above the enemy camp. While he was there, he sent out some men to get supplies of grain. Mithridates, hearing of this, sent a large detachment of his best cavalry to intercept the convoy, which it met as the convoy was coming through a defile. The enemy cavalry were too impatient to hold off until the Romans emerged into open country. They attacked immediately in a confined space, which rendered their horses quite useless. The Romans lined up in formation and won a complete victory in which few of the enemy escaped to tell the tale. This and one or two similar incidents, narrated by Plutarch, put such fear into Mithridates that he decided to decamp and move away, leaving Lucullus free to capture Cabira.
Appian, Mithridatic War, *79–81; Plutarch*, Lucullus, *15 and 17(1–2)*

GARGANUS M (72) – Third Servile War
By the end of 72 Spartacus, the leader of the slave revolt, had defeated four Roman armies, and yet the whereabouts and details of these contests remain obscure. At one named site, a Roman army under the consul Gellius Publicola defeated Spartacus' lieutenant, Crixus, and a force of 30,000 near Mount Garganus [*Gargano*] in Apulia.

Crixus himself was killed together with two thirds of his men (Plutarch says the lot). But this gain was offset by a heavy defeat of the other consul by Spartacus himself at a place unknown.
Appian, Civil Wars, *1: 117; Plutarch*, Crassus, *9(7); Orosius, 5: 24(4)*

CAMALATRUM (71) – Third Servile War
The propraetor M. Licinius Crassus, who had been placed in charge of the war, encountered Castus and Cannicus, the leaders of the Gauls in Spartacus' army, near a place called Camalatrum (unknown). Crassus sent 12 cohorts round a mountain with instructions to fall on the enemy in their rear as soon as the action began. The enemy were completely routed and fled.
Frontinus, 2: 4, 7

CANTENNA M (71) – Third Servile War
When Spartacus was encamped near Mount Cantenna (unidentified), Licinius Crassus fortified two camps in close proximity to the enemy. One night, he led all his forces out quietly, leaving his camp looking as if it was occupied. He divided his cavalry into two detachments and directed one half to engage Spartacus and to pin him down. The other half was to make a feint attack on the Germans and Gauls and then to withdraw with the object of luring them out into an ambush. The exercise proceeded according to plan. The cavalry fell back to the base of the mountain and then withdrew to the flanks, disclosing Crassus with the infantry arrayed in battle order. Thirty-five thousand of the enemy were slain, including their leaders Castus and Cannicus. (The battle against these leaders which is described by Plutarch seems to be a different one, probably earlier. The casualties were fewer and there is no mention of the deaths of Castus and Cannicus.)
Frontinus, 2: 5, 34; Orosius, 5: 24(6); Plutarch, Crassus, *11(2–3); Livy,* epitome 97

PETELIA (71) – Third Servile War
Spartacus retired to the 'mountains of Petelia', the city itself being perched on top of a lofty hill. He was followed there closely by two of Crassus' officers until Spartacus turned and attacked his pursuers. They were completely routed. As a result of this victory Spartacus' slaves became overconfident and refused to listen to reason. They forced their officers to lead them back through Lucania against the main Roman force.
Plutarch, Crassus, *11(4–5)*

SILARUS R (71) – Third Servile War
Crassus had asked that Pompey should be sent to assist him in the destruction of Spartacus. He now bitterly regretted his action and was determined to effect the kill himself before the arrival of Pompey, who would gain the credit. Orosius alone of the extant sources provides a specific indication of what may have been the site of the final showdown. He states that Spartacus was laying out a camp at the head of the river Silarus [*Sele*], which is in Lucania near the Campanian border. It is unclear whether the final battle actually occurred at this site. Some say that it may have taken place in Apulia. But it has been noted above that from Petelia the slaves forced their officers to lead them back through Lucania against the Romans, which suggests that the Silarus would be equally feasible. Wherever the encounter, Crassus was completely victorious, killing 60,000 of the enemy and capturing another 6,000 for the loss of 1,000 Romans. Spartacus himself was killed, his death marking the end of the war, but his body was never found.
Orosius, 5: 24(5–8); Livy, epitome 97; *Appian,* Civil Wars, *1: 120*

CYDONIA (69) – Third Mithridatic War
During the Mithridatic War, the Cretans supported Mithridates, to whom they gave considerable assistance against the Romans. When Rome declared war on them, they sent an embassy to treat for peace but were unwilling to accept the terms dictated to them. Q. Caecilius Metellus was sent against them and he defeated the Cretan leader Lasthenes at Cydonia [*Khania*]. Lasthenes fled, and Metellus proceeded to subjugate the whole island.
Appian, Sicily, *fragment 6*

TIGRANOCERTA (69, October 6) – Third Mithridatic War
After his defeat at Cabira (72), Mithridates took refuge with his kinsman Tigranes in Armenia. Lucullus demanded that he be surrendered. When this was refused, Lucullus marched with two legions against Tigranes at Tigranocerta [*?Silvan*]. Nobody dared to tell the king that Lucullus was approaching because the first man to do so was beheaded for his pains. When Tigranes did learn the truth, he sent Mithrobarzanes against Lucullus with 2,000 horsemen, while he himself went out and collected an army which is said to have comprised between 150,000 and 250,000 foot and 50,000 horse. In the meantime Lucullus had readily defeated Mithrobarzanes at the first

encounter and was now preparing to face Tigranes himself. Mithridates advised Tigranes not to come to close quarters with the Romans but to surround Lucullus and to cut him off from all supplies. But Tigranes scorned such ideas and advanced to meet his enemy. Behind the king there was a hill of which Lucullus took good note. He stationed his cavalry in front of the enemy with instructions to harass them and by withdrawing slowly to draw them gradually forward in pursuit. Meanwhile, Lucullus led his infantry in a detour round to the hill, which he occupied unobserved by the enemy. As soon as he saw that they were widely scattered in pursuit of the Roman cavalry, Lucullus charged down the hill onto the enemy's baggage train directly below. This caused chaos as the baggage personnel fled into the midst of the assembled horde of soldiery, setting everybody in collision with each other. At the same time, the Roman cavalry, having lured their pursuers after them, turned and hacked them to pieces. Tigranes and Mithridates fled, and the city of Tigranocerta fell to the Romans. It is said that more than 100,000 of the enemy infantry were slain and almost all of the cavalry. In contrast, 100 Romans were wounded while only five are reported as killed.
Appian, Mithridatic Wars, *84–85; Plutarch,* Lucullus, *25–28(6)*

ARSANIAS R (68) – Third Mithridatic War
Following his defeat and the capture of his royal city of Tigranocerta (above), Tigranes retired to his capital city of Artaxata [*Artashat*]. Almost a year later Lucullus set out against him. Tigranes led out his forces to meet the enemy and took up a position on the banks of the river Arsanias [*Murat*], which Lucullus would have to cross on his march to Artaxata. Undeterred, the Roman crossed the river with his troops deployed on a broad front to prevent any outflanking movement. He was confronted at the outset by mounted archers and lancers who covered the main body of the enemy troops. Although Tigranes thought highly of them, a brush with the Roman cavalry was all that was needed to send them flying in all directions. When Tigranes took their place at the head of his cavalry, matters took on a different hue for Lucullus who was taken aback by their numbers and splendour. He recalled his own cavalry from the pursuit of the light troops and confronted the enemy immediately in front of him, but they fled before he could even get close to them. That ended the battle, leaving the Romans engaged in a pursuit which lasted throughout the night. The

casualty figures are not recorded, but it is on record that Mithridates was among the first to make a shameful flight.
Plutarch, Lucullus, *31(3–8)*

COMANA (68, winter) – Third Mithridatic War
A certain legate, Marcus Fabius, who commanded a force of untrustworthy mercenaries, found himself besieged by Mithridates in Cabira [*Niksar*]. A legate of Lucullus, Valerius Triarius, was passing that way to join Lucullus and heard of these events. He collected as many men as he could and marched against Mithridates, who assumed that Triarius was advancing at the head of a full army. The king withdrew without ever setting eyes on his opponent. Triarius followed him as far as Comana Pontica [*Tokat*] where he found Mithridates encamped on the far side of a river. The king wanted to engage immediately while the Romans were fatigued, and so he crossed the river after instructing a part of his force to cross by another bridge further along. The second bridge collapsed under the weight of the soldiery, robbing Mithridates of his outflanking manoeuvre. He himself put up a stout fight for a considerable while but eventually he was forced to retreat after suffering a severe defeat. He retired into winter quarters.
Dio Cassius, **36***: 10*

ZELA (67) – Third Mithridatic War
Early in the year Mithridates encamped opposite the legate Triarius near Gaziura in Pontus and tried to provoke him into a battle before Lucullus arrived on the scene. When the Roman refused to accept the challenge, Mithridates sought to lure him out by sending a force to attack the town of Dadasa, which the Romans used as a store. This had the desired effect. As Triarius was reluctantly advancing toward the place, Mithridates' army fell upon him and surrounded his force, killing most of his men. It is said that over 7,000 Romans fell, including 150 centurions and 24 tribunes. The battle took place near a high hill a few miles from Zela [*Zile*]. The site of the battle is quoted in *The Alexandrian War* in connexion with the later and better-known battle of Zela in 47.
Dio Cassius, **36***: 12; Plutarch,* Lucullus, *35(1); Appian,* Mithridatic Wars, *89; (Caesar),* The Alexandrian War, *72*

CORACESIUM (67) – War against Pirates
During the Mithridatic War piracy on the high seas began to flourish, encouraged by Mithridates himself. There was a rapid increase in the numbers

of pirates and ships and in their marauding expeditions until eventually they controlled the whole of the Mediterranean. This state of affairs brought severe shortages and starvation to Rome. To deal with the menace, Pompey was given absolute command of the naval 'province' with a large number of ships and men which he divided into 13 sections, each with its own area of operation. His methods were so successful that he ridded the seas of piracy within three months. The pirates withdrew to their principal bases in Cilicia and awaited Pompey's attack. According to Plutarch, there was a battle off Coracesium [*Alanya*] in which the pirates were defeated. They were then besieged in their strongholds and eventually surrendered, more than 20,000 of them in number. Appian, however, says that there was not even a battle; the pirates merely capitulated in the hope of lenient treatment. Pompey did not put them to death. He decided sagely to disperse them inland, using them to colonize under-manned areas.

Plutarch, Pompey, *28; Appian,* Mithridatic Wars, *96*

NICOPOLIS (66) – Third Mithridatic War

After Pompey's final defeat of the pirates off Coracesium (above) , he was appointed commander of the Mithridatic War with absolute powers and control over all Roman forces outside Italy. In fact, his predecessor Lucullus had done all the work. Little was left apart from a final defeat of Mithridates, who was on the run with a much reduced army of 30,000 men. Pompey immediately moved northwards from Cilicia and caught up with Mithridates 'near the Euphrates'. A major battle took place, the site of which would be unknown if Pompey had not subsequently founded the city of Nicopolis [*Divriği*] near the site as a memorial. There are three versions of the battle. Plutarch maintains that Pompey's fear of letting his enemy escape during darkness prompted him to make a night attack on their camp. The enemy were caught off guard and fled in panic at the tricks played by the moonlight shadows. More than 10,000 of them were cut down, but Mithridates managed to escape. Dio Cassius, also, describes a night attack, but in his account Pompey eluded Mithridates in the daytime and created an ambush in a defile ahead of the enemy. When Mithridates' army marched in column through the defile at night, the Romans created an ear-splitting din, hurled rocks and javelins down onto them and then charged, killing many. Appian's battle was a daytime affair. It would be difficult to imagine that

this was the same battle were it not that Appian is one of the two sources to mention Nicopolis. Whichever account is nearest the truth, all are agreed that Mithridates suffered a crushing defeat, from which he managed to make a characteristic getaway. He headed for Colchis.

Plutarch, Pompey, *32(3–7); Dio Cassius,* **36***: 48–49; Appian,* Mithridatic Wars, *99–100, and* Syrian Wars, *57*

CYRUS R (66) – Third Mithridatic War

Leaving Armenia, Pompey went in pursuit of Mithridates towards Colchis. This took him through the territories of the Albanians and the Iberians in the region of the Caucasus. The Albanians granted him a free passage but, while he was in their territory, he was overtaken by winter. The Albanians then mustered 40,000 men and crossed the Cyrus [*Kür*] river (also variously called the Cyrnus or Cyrtus) against him. Pompey allowed them to cross and then attacked them, routing them and killing many. Appian states that Pompey drove the barbarians into a wood and set fire to it, causing them to emerge and surrender. Their king Oroeses begged for mercy and Pompey made peace with him. Then he marched against the Iberians, who were anxious to keep in favour with Mithridates. Pompey routed these people also, at some unknown place. After this, he proceeded to Colchis where, to judge by Appian's description, he indulged in what seems like a sightseeing spree.

Plutarch, Pompey, *34; Appian,* Mithridatic Wars, *103; Dio Cassius,* **36***: 54(5)*

ABAS R (65) – Third Mithridatic War

At Colchis, Pompey heard that the Albanians were up in arms again. Retracing his steps, he crossed the river Cyrus [*Kür*] and then, after a long march, the river Cambyses [*Iori*]. Proceeding further, he had reached the river Abas [*Alazani*] and had crossed it, without any interference, when he heard that Oroeses was coming up against him. Pompey was anxious to conceal the size of his army from the enemy for fear that it might give him second thoughts and cause him to withdraw. Accordingly, he positioned his cavalry in front and instructed the infantry to kneel motionlessly behind them under their shields. Oroeses was deceived and sent his cavalry into battle contemptuously. When Pompey's cavalry turned in simulated flight, the infantry rose up and allowed their cavalry to pass through their ranks but surrounded the enemy who were pursuing them. The Roman cavalry then wheeled round and attacked the enemy flanks with devastating result. Afterwards Pompey granted a renewal of peace to the Albanians.

Plutarch's account is sketchy and gives none of the tactical details of Dio's readable version; nor does he give any result save that Pompey killed the enemy leader, a brother of Oroeses and not the king himself.
Dio Cassius, 37: 3(6)–4; Plutarch, Pompey, 35

PISTORIA (62) – Catiline Conspiracy
Lucius Sergius Catilina sought election to the consulship in 63 and 62 and was thwarted on both occasions by Cicero. His frustrated ambitions caused him to initiate a conspiracy aimed at causing riots, incendiarism and other disturbances in Rome while he marched on the City with an army from Etruria. The plot was discovered and Catiline's fellow-conspirators were arrested and executed. His army, which had been built up to two full legions, dwindled through desertions to a few thousand men, only about a quarter of whom were properly armed. With this band he headed northwards intending to slip through into Gaul. The senate sent the consul Gaius Antonius after him, and Catiline found himself trapped near Pistoria [*Pistoia*] between Antonius and the army of Metellus Celer. Metellus, who had been in Picenum with three legions, had moved to block Catiline's advance. Catiline decided that his only course was to risk a battle. He elected to fight Antonius, even though the latter's army was the larger of the two, probably because Antonius had played a part in the conspiracy and might hold his punches. This general, however, was either ill or pretending to be so, and his army was entrusted to Marcus Petreius. The battle took place on a plain at the foot of the mountains. Here Catiline posted eight cohorts consisting of all his picked men in the front line. The rest he placed in reserve. Petreius likewise placed his cohorts of veterans in his front line. When the signal was given, the two sides closed so rapidly that spears were discarded and opponents resorted to hand-to-hand fighting. In spite of their great inferiority in numbers, Catiline's men resisted with the utmost bravery and vigour, yielding not an inch. Petreius then led his picked bodyguard against the enemy centre, which was thrown into confusion, and he followed this up with attacks on both flanks. When Catiline saw that resistance was at an end, he plunged headlong into the enemy mass, fighting to the bitter end. Only then could it be seen that practically every man in the conspirator's force lay dead at his post

– 3,000 of them. The government forces did not get off lightly either. All their best fighters were either killed or badly maimed.
Sallust, War with Catiline, 57–61; Cassius Dio, 37: 39–40; Appian, Civil Wars, 2: 7

SOLONIUM (61) – Gallic Uprising
An uprising among the Allobroges, who inhabited the north-eastern corner of the Roman Province, was responsible for the devastation of much of Gallia Narbonensis. The legates Lucius Marius and Servius Galba crossed the Rhône and attacked a place called Solonium or Solo (now unknown), where they defeated the enemy and set fire to parts of the town. They were prevented from capturing it by the arrival of Catugnatus, the chief of the Allobroges. The job was completed by Pomptinus, the governor, who then proceeded to subjugate the other districts.
Dio Cassius, 37: 48; Livy, epitome 103

ADMAGETOBRIGA (61) – Germanic Incursion
Around the year 71, Ariovistus, king of the Germanic Suebi, was invited by the Gallic Sequani to help them in their feud against the Aedui. The Germanic 'visitors' developed such a liking for Gaul that more and more of them arrived. Not content with defeating the Aedui, they started occupying the land of their 'hosts', the Sequani. The Gauls united in an attempt to throw the Germans out but they were defeated at Admagetobriga, after which they appealed to Julius Caesar for help.
Caesar, Gallic War, 1: 31(12)

ARAR R (58) – Gallic War
The Helvetii, who numbered around 300,000 in all, were cramped for space in their small mountain-locked country and decided to migrate *en masse*. The plan had been instigated by their leader Orgetorix, but he died before it could be put into practice. Undaunted, the Helvetii resolved to proceed all the same. They burnt their homes and moved westwards through the territories of the Sequani and the Aedui, heading for the Roman Province. Caesar decided that they would not be the most desirable neighbours. He did not forget that one of their tribes, the Tigurini, had humiliated a Roman army 50 years previously by sending it under the yoke. He immediately collected five legions and crossed the Alps into Gaul, where he came upon the barbarians as they were crossing the river Arar [*Saône*]. Three quarters of

them had already crossed, but Caesar took three legions and attacked the rest, destroying most of them. It was gratifying to Caesar that the group which he had slaughtered comprised the Tigurini, the tribe which had so humiliated Rome in the past.

Caesar, Gallic War, *1: 12; Plutarch,* Caesar, *18(1–2); Dio Cassius,* **38***: 32(4)*

BIBRACTE (58) – Gallic War

After the battle on the Arar (above) Caesar crossed the river and doggedly followed the Helvetii for about a fortnight, resisting any contest with them. As the Romans were running short of provisions, Caesar decided to turn off toward Bibracte [*Mont Beuvray*], the largest town of the Aedui, and to stock up there. The Helvetii heard of this and turned to follow him. Caesar withdrew to a nearby hill and stationed his four veteran legions in three lines halfway up the hill. The two raw legions of recent recruits he placed on top of the hill with the auxiliaries. When the enemy arrived they formed themselves into a compact body and started to march up the hill. They were met by a shower of *pila* from the legionaries, who then charged down with drawn swords. The enemy were falling back to a hill about a mile away, when 15,000 tribesmen from the rear of the enemy's column marched up and attacked the Roman right flank. This put heart into those who were withdrawing and they turned and resumed the attack. The battle was a long and hard one, fought on two fronts from midday till evening. The fighting was particularly fierce around the waggons, which the enemy had converted into a laager. Here the battle continued well into the night. Caesar records that not a single man of the opposing force was seen in flight. Eventually, however, they were forced to yield, and about 130,000 of them marched off through the night. Subsequently, short of supplies, they sent envoys to Caesar offering surrender and were told to return to their own country and to resettle themselves there. Caesar's motive behind this humane decision was the fear that if that country was left unpopulated, the Germanic tribes might cross the Rhine and appropriate it.

Caesar, Gallic War, *1: 23–26; Plutarch,* Caesar, *18(2–4); Dio Cassius,* **38***: 33*

PLAIN OF ALSACE (58) – Gallic War

Ariovistus, the leader of the Suebi from north of the Rhine, was a cruel and arrogant tyrant. Having invaded Gaul and conquered the neighbouring tribes at Admagetobriga (61), he appropriated their land and generally enslaved them. More Germans poured across the Rhine every day, ravaging the Gallic territories, until it seemed that there would be no end to the influx. The Aedui appealed to Caesar, whose remonstrations with Ariovistus elicited only an insolent rebuttal. The situation was also of concern to Caesar himself because of the mounting threat to the Roman Province. Accordingly, Caesar advanced at top speed against Ariovistus. On hearing that the latter was hurrying to occupy the valuable city of Vesontio [*Besançon*], Caesar pushed ahead by forced marches and occupied the place. From there he marched for six days until he was within 23 miles of his quarry. In a large plain – the plain of Alsace – there was a mound where the two leaders held a conference. Caesar repeated his previous demands and received the usual arrogant replies. On the following day Ariovistus moved closer to the Romans and camped at the foot of the mountains in a position which would allow him to cut off the Romans' supplies. But day after day he refused Caesar's challenge to fight. Caesar ascertained the reason for this from prisoners: Ariovistus had been told by his diviners that he was not destined to win before the new moon. The next day Caesar forced the issue on his adversary by drawing up his five legions in three columns and advancing right up to the enemy camp, compelling them to come out and line up. The engagement was started by Caesar who, noticing that the enemy left looked the weaker wing, led his right wing against it. The enemy responded immediately with such a rapid dash that the Romans discarded their spears in favour of swords. The enemy adopted their usual phalanx formation, which helped them to ward off the attack until the Romans threw themselves onto the shields, wrenched them out of the enemy hands and stabbed the unprotected owners. These tactics confounded the enemy and put his left wing to flight. On the opposite flank, the enemy right was pressing hard on the Romans by sheer weight of numbers. Publius Crassus, in charge of the cavalry, noticed this and sent the third line forward to relieve the harassed wing. This caused the pendulum to swing the other way, and before long the whole enemy horde was in flight and heading for the Rhine a few miles away. Ariovistus himself managed to find a boat and escape across the river, but most of his forces were hunted down and slain by the Roman cavalry. Plutarch quotes a figure of 80,000 dead.

The battle took place in the plain of Alsace at the foot of the Vosges and, according to Caesar,

about five miles from the Rhine, but the exact site is not known. The vicinity of *Cernay* is thought to be likely if Caesar's 'five miles' is assumed to be a corruption.
Caesar, Gallic War, *1: 51–53*

AXONA R (57) – Gallic War

In the winter of 58/57 rumours reached Caesar, who was in Italy, that the tribes of the Belgae were conspiring against the Romans and were mobilizing their forces. Caesar raised two new legions and set off immediately for the Belgic frontier. When he learnt that the various tribes had already joined forces and were advancing, he crossed the Axona [*Aisne*], 8 miles from Bibrax [*Bièvres*], and encamped with the river protecting his rear. He did not have long to wait for the enemy, who encamped barely 2 miles away. Both sides marched out of their camps and deployed for action, but between them there was a marsh. Each side waited in the hope that the other would be prepared to advance over unfavourable terrain, but neither side moved and a pitched battle never materialized. Instead, some of the Belgae marched straight to the river and began to cross it at a ford. When Caesar heard about this, he crossed the river by a bridge which was guarded by his men, taking all his cavalry and the light-armed troops. With this force he attacked the Belgae as they attempted the crossing and killed many of them. Others who attempted to cross over on the corpses of their mates suffered a similar fate. The Belgae then decided to return to their homes and to await future developments.
Caesar, Gallic War, *2: 5–10*

SABIS R (57) – Gallic War

After expelling a number of Belgic tribes and receiving the surrender of several others as a result of the encounter at the Axona (above), Caesar marched against the Nervii, the most warlike of the Belgae. They had been joined by two neighbouring tribes, the Atrebates and the Viromandui, and the whole horde had massed together on the north side of the river Sabis [*Sambre*], awaiting Caesar's arrival. The Romans chose for their camp a hill on the south side of the river, which sloped gently down to the river bank. Across the river there was another hill with a densely wooded summit. Here the main body of the enemy lay concealed, while some cavalry on the low ground acted as a decoy. While the six Roman legions were engaged in fetching materials and building their camp, the enemy suddenly debouched from

the wood opposite and raced down the hill, crossed the river and started climbing the Romans' hill with a surprising speed and agility. The Romans were caught completely off guard. There was no time to don full armour or to find one's own legion. The men just fell in under the nearest standard. The ensuing battle was no set piece. Co-ordinated command was impossible as the legions faced in different directions and fought separate fights as and where the threat presented itself. The only bright spot for the Romans was on their left, where Titus Labienus and the famous Tenth legion forced back their opponents and drove them down to the river. After slaughtering them, the Romans charged up the enemy's hill and captured their camp. When they looked back and saw that Caesar and the rest were in dire straits, the Tenth legion rushed back again over the river to their assistance. This completely changed the whole face of the battle. Romans who had given up hope were reinvigorated, while the cavalry which had fled returned to the fight. What promised to be a catastrophic disaster turned into a resounding victory. Caesar himself writes that the Nervii were almost annihilated and their name was virtually blotted out. The enemy reported that of their survivors only 500 were fit to bear arms out of a force of 60,000. Caesar told them to keep their territories and ordered their neighbours to leave them in peace.
Caesar, Gallic War, *2: 16–28; Plutarch, Caesar, 20(4–5)*

OCTODURUS (57) – Gallic War

Caesar wanted to open a safe trading route through the Alps. To this end he sent Servius Galba with one legion and some cavalry up into the region of *Haute Savoie*. After a few minor encounters he made peace with the tribes and decided to winter in the village of Octodurus [near *Martigny*]. Some days later the Romans woke up one morning to find that the surrounding heights were densely occupied by an immense swarming horde of the Seduni and Veragri, who had also blocked all the roads. The Roman force was small enough at the best of times but, in addition, two cohorts were absent on a search for supplies. From their commanding position the enemy charged down the slopes and hurled missiles at the encampment. The Romans responded well at first but they lacked any reserves to back them up and take over, in contrast to the attackers with their almost unlimited manpower. After more than six hours of fighting the Romans were in a desperate

state, exhausted and almost out of ammunition. The enemy had broken through the palisade and were filling up the ditches. Galba, prompted by his chief centurion, decided that their only feasible course was a sudden sortie. After a period of passive resistance to give themselves a rest, they suddenly charged out of the camp and surrounded the enemy. Of the 30,000 or more tribesmen who had been active in the attack, over a third were killed. The rest fled in panic. The next day, Galba led his men back to safe territory without further incident.
Caesar, Gallic War, *3: 1–6*

JERUSALEM (57) – Jewish Revolt

On the death of Salome Alexandra, the widow of King Alexander (of Judaea), the succession was fought for by her two sons, Aristobulus II and Hyrcanus II. At this point the Romans arrived on the scene, and Pompey the Great attempted to mediate. He ended up by making a prisoner of Aristobulus and sending him to Rome; Hyrcanus was made High Priest. Pompey then captured Jerusalem. In 57, Alexander, the son of Aristobulus, made his bid for the throne. He assembled a force of 10,000 infantry and 1,500 horsemen, which brought the Romans against him. Aulus Gabinius, the commander in Syria, sent his cavalry commander, Marcus Antonius (better known as Mark Antony), in advance while he himself followed with his legion. Alexander fell back on Jerusalem, where the adversaries met in a pitched battle near the city. Three thousand of Alexander's men were killed and a similar number were taken prisoner.
Josephus, Jewish Antiquities, *14: 5, 2 (82–85) and* Jewish Wars, *1: 8, 2–3 (160–165)*

MORBIHAN GULF (56) – Gallic War

Caesar was satisfied that he had pacified Gaul for the time being. Leaving his troops in their winter quarters, he was in Illyria when war broke out again, this time on the Atlantic seaboard. Publius Crassus, who was encamped in those regions, had sent tribunes to the neighbouring tribes to seek provisions. The Veneti, a powerful maritime tribe in the Brittany area, detained the tribunes sent to them and persuaded their neighbours to do likewise. When Caesar was informed, he instructed his officers to build warships on the river Liger [*Loire*] pending his return. Bad behaviour must be punished as an example to others.

The strongholds of the Veneti were difficult to attack. They were built on headlands in the tidal estuaries and could only be approached by land at low tide and by sea at high tide and in fair weather. When the Romans did succeed in making life difficult, the occupants merely decamped to other strongholds. Because of these natural features, the boats of the Veneti were of unusual design. They were exceedingly strong, made of oak, with flattish bottoms for negotiating shallow waters and with high sides as a protection against high seas. Against them, the Roman vessels had but two advantages – speed and oars. When the Roman fleet assembled off the Liger estuary under the command of Decimus Brutus and headed for the enemy, 220 enemy ships sailed out against him. But Brutus was confronted not only by an enemy fleet; there were tactical problems to face as well. Ramming would do no serious damage to the oaken enemy, and the disparity in height of the ships favoured the enemy's missiles. The Romans, however, had given some thought to these matters and had equipped themselves with long poles, each fitted with a hook at the end. Armed with these, they contrived to ensnare the halyards of the enemy ships and bring down their sails. As these ships were dependent on sail and could not be rowed, they found themselves immobilized and were ripe for boarding by the crews of two or three Roman ships attacking simultaneously. After losing a number of vessels in this way the Veneti turned to escape, but a providential calm brought a complete victory to the Romans. The enemy lay like sitting ducks ready to be plucked. Very few of them made it back to land after a battle which had lasted all day. The survivors surrendered and received harsh treatment from Caesar.

It is generally accepted that the battle probably took place in the *Gulf of Morbihan*, on which the Veneti had established their capital, Dariorigum [*Vannes*]. The Liger [*Loire*] estuary with its similar geographical features has been suggested as a possible alternative. This was not in the territory of the Veneti, but the Namnetes who occupied the territory between *Morbihan* and the Liger were probably in league with them.
Caesar, Gallic War, *3: 7–16*

SOTIUM (56) – Gallic War

Before the battle off *Morbihan* (above), Publius Crassus was sent by Caesar to Aquitania with 12 cohorts and a strong cavalry force to prevent any reinforcements reaching the Veneti from that quarter. When he arrived in the territory of the Sotiates, these people assembled a force and attacked his column on the march with their cavalry. When this was repulsed, their foot soldiers who were concealed in a valley sprang up and fell on the Romans while they were in a disordered state. After a fierce struggle the Sotiates were routed and fled to their town of Sotium [*Sos*], which Crassus proceeded to besiege until the inhabitants capitulated. A modern authority* states that the battle took place near the source of the river *Ciron*, a tributary of the Garonne. No evidence is quoted, but the *Ciron* does arise not far from *Sos*.

Caesar, Gallic War, *3: 20–21; Dio Cassius, 39: 46(1–2); Orosius, 6: 8(19–20) and translation by *R.J. Deferrari, Catholic University of America Press, Washington DC, note 25 (p. 246)*

TABOR M (55) – Jewish Revolt

Alexander, son of Aristobulus, having been defeated in his first revolt against the Romans (Jerusalem, 57), struck again. This time he collected an army of 30,000 Jews with which he encountered his former antagonist Gabinius. A battle took place at Mount Tabor, in which Alexander was again defeated and lost 10,000 of his men.

Josephus, Jewish Antiquities, *14: 6, 3 (101–102) and Jewish Wars, 1: 8, 7 (177)*

CARRHAE (53, June 9) – Parthian War

M. Licinius Crassus Dives was an ambitious man who, in spite of his advancing years, was loath to play second fiddle to Pompey and Caesar in achievement and reputation. He obtained the province of Syria and set himself to beat the Parthians. It was his private war, uninstigated by the senate. He crossed the Euphrates with seven legions, 4,000 cavalry and some light-armed troops, and with little knowledge of the country or of the Parthian army and its methods. He stubbornly refused to take advice from his quaestor Cassius to maintain the protection afforded by the river. Lured on by a treacherous, wily Arab chieftain, he allowed himself to be led into the plains, which deteriorated into a waterless sandy desert devoid of any sign of life. In this way he marched on until his scouts reported the approach of a considerable Parthian force. Crassus hastily formed his men into an open square, with the cavalry distributed equally on the four sides, and marched to meet the enemy. They did not appear to be nearly as numerous as the scouts had implied, but this was because Surenas, the

greatest of the Parthian generals, had hidden the bulk of his force behind the front lines and had told them to cover themselves with skins to prevent any tell-tale glitter from the armour. When they advanced, they created a terrifying noise of drum-beats, after which the hidden troops dropped their camouflage and revealed themselves as a magnificent glittering host composed entirely of cavalry. After that it was a matter of superb and deadly archery from horseback against foot soldiers who were inadequately armoured against the slender, sharp and very fast arrows of the enemy. A charge by the Roman light-armed troops achieved nothing but suicide. With nobody to stop them, the Parthian cavalry surrounded the square and poured a continual shower of arrows into a target in which they could not fail to find a mark. The Romans endured it in the hope that the enemy would run short of arrows, but they lost hope when they realized that there was a camel train loaded with fresh supplies. Crassus asked his son Publius to try to effect a breakthrough. The enemy whom Publius attacked turned and appeared to flee, luring him away from the main force, only to turn and to surround him. The Parthians then stationed a body of armoured cavalry with long spears in front of the Romans and subjected them to the same treatment with long-range archery as the square had received. They were literally shot through. In a last gesture Publius charged the heavy-armed Parthian cavalry with his Gallic horse, but they had no chance – they carried only short light spears which were no match for the long pikes of the enemy. The force was annihilated apart from 500 who were captured and who killed themselves with their swords. Publius Crassus was unable to despatch himself on account of a wounded arm. He asked his shield bearer to do the job for him. The Parthians carried his head on a spike back to the main body, vaunting it and taunting his father, whose spirit was finally broken. The fighting, such as it was, carried on until dusk when the Parthians retired for the night. Crassus and the few ambulant survivors set out and were picked up by the garrison from Carrhae [*Harran*]. Following further treachery and deception, Crassus was killed. The 4,000 wounded who had been left behind mostly died from their wounds or from exhaustion or by suicide, according to Dio. Plutarch says that the Parthians returned and slaughtered them all and picked off any stragglers or isolated groups that they could find.

Plutarch, Crassus, *23ff.; Dio Cassius, 40: 20(3)ff.*

NOVIODUNUM BITURIGUM (52) – Gallic War

In the later stages of the Gallic war a young Avernian called Vercingetorix emerged as a Gallic champion and worthy adversary for Caesar. Their first spar took place when Caesar was besieging Noviodunum in the territory of the Bituriges [*?Neuvy-sur-Barangeon*]. The garrison had sent envoys asking for peace, but at this point the cavalry vanguard of Vercingetorix was seen approaching in the distance. The townsmen changed their minds about peace and manned their wall. Caesar sent his Gallic cavalry to engage the advancing horse, but as his men were faring rather badly he sent out his 400 German horsemen to reinforce them. Their charge caused heavy losses and sent the enemy flying back to their army, causing the defendants of the town to change their minds again. Although this was no more than a cavalry skirmish, it was sufficient to stop the advance of Vercingetorix. As a result of this and other reverses he decided that he would have to change his plan of campaign.

Caesar, Gallic War, *7: 12–13*

GERGOVIA (52) – Gallic War

Caesar successfully besieged Avaricum [*Bourges*] – another setback for Vercingetorix. He then divided his army into two parts. Four legions under the command of Labienus were to move northwards while Caesar and the other six legions proceeded to Gergovia [*Gergovie*]. Situated on the summit of a steep high mount, this town was difficult to attack. Opposite the town another steep hill, which rose up from the base of the mount, was garrisoned by the enemy. At dead of night Caesar dislodged this garrison and built a small camp on the summit. He connected this by a trench with his main camp further back. While he was at Gergovia it was heard that Rome's most loyal allies, the Aedui, were stirred into revolt and there was fear that this would spread into a major uprising. Caesar was anxious to disengage himself from Gergovia without losing face in order to deal with the situation elsewhere. Within the enemy's lines there was a wooded ridge which gave access to the far side of the town. The enemy were anxious about its security and had been fortifying it. Caesar sent some men in that direction with instructions to make themselves conspicuous and to move around the whole area with an air of purposeful intent. This brought all the Gauls to the threatened area to complete the fortifications. In the meantime, Caesar had moved his legions

surreptitiously from the main camp to the small one via the connecting trench. From there they were sent to climb the hill on which the town stood, a distance of about one mile up to the ramparts. The lower part of the hill was undefended; the upper half was covered with the enemy's camps, which were protected by a high stone wall coursing around the hillside. The Romans climbed over the wall and captured three of the camps, a gesture sufficient for Caesar's purpose and enough to prevent any suggestion of a cowardly retreat. Unhappily, the legions – apart from the Tenth – got carried away and continued the ascent up to the ramparts. When the Gauls hurried to the scene from the other side of the town, there was fierce hand-to-hand fighting in which the Romans, who were already exhausted, were also greatly outnumbered. They were driven down and pursued, but the pursuit was checked by the Tenth legion which was lined up at the bottom against such an eventuality. Nevertheless, the over-zealous legions lost nearly 700 men including 46 centurions.

Caesar, Gallic War, *7: 41–51*

LUTETIA PARISIORUM (52) – Gallic War

Caesar divided his army and put Labienus in charge of four legions with instructions to proceed against the Senones and Parisii. Labienus set out for Lutetia [*Paris*], a town which was built on an island in the middle of the Sequana [*Seine*]. When he was close to it, the neighbouring tribes assembled against him in large numbers under the leadership of Camulogenus and contrived to stop him advancing. He retraced his steps for about 30 miles upstream to Metlodunum [*Melun*], where he crossed the river to the right bank and again advanced downstream to camp near Lutetia. The tribes encamped on the left bank opposite him. Meanwhile, news of a Gallic uprising to the south forced Labienus to change his plans. His overriding aim was to get away safely back to his base at Agedincum [*Sens*]. He ordered his main body of three legions to move silently downstream at night and to cross the river, while five cohorts were to move upstream and make as much commotion about it as they could. The remaining five cohorts were to guard the camp. The Gauls were confused by the news coming in from all sides. They, too, divided their force into three divisions, but Labienus and the legions were already across the river before they encountered Camulogenus with the larger part of the enemy. At the signal to attack the Seventh legion on the Roman right put their

opponents to flight. On the left, the Twelfth legion was having a much tougher fight against Camulogenus himself, in which the Gauls showed no sign of breaking. The issue was in the balance until the Seventh legion, having cleared the field in front of it, turned and took the Gauls on the other wing in the rear. Even then, no Gaul considered flight. The legions surrounded and killed the lot including Camulogenus. After that, the other enemy detachments were easy prey, and Labienus returned in safety to Agedincum.
Caesar, Gallic War, *7: 57–62*

ALESIA (52) – Gallic War
Alesia [*Alise Ste Reine*] was the site of Caesar's most famous siege. As such, it does not come within the scope of this work, but an open battle qualifies for inclusion. Vercingetorix had made a fatal mistake in withdrawing within the walls of this city. Caesar laid siege to the place but found himself besieged in his turn by the arrival of a combined Gallic relief force, allegedly of 250,000 men and 8,000 cavalry. They encamped on a hill outside the Roman lines and about a mile away. The following day they occupied the whole of the plain with their cavalry interspersed with archers and light-armed troops. Caesar ordered his cavalry to engage them, and the battle went on from midday until sunset with no clear advantage either way until Caesar's German horse made a mass charge at one point. This threw the Gauls back and they broke and fled. The rest of Caesar's cavalry then took up the pursuit as far as the enemy camp, allowing the enemy no chance to resume the offensive.
Caesar, Gallic War, *7: 79–80*

UXELLODUNUM (51) – Gallic War
Within a year of the siege of Alesia all organized resistance had come to an end throughout the whole of Gaul. Isolated tribal insurrections still occurred and were dealt with, only to be superseded in many areas by localized bands of guerillas. One of these bands, which was led by two brigands called Drappes and Lucterius, was operating close to the Roman Province and was causing some anxiety. Drappes, a Senonian, had been raiding Roman convoys with a bunch of desperadoes and slaves while Lucterius, a Cadurcan, had previously tried to invade the Province. They joined forces and started to march toward the Province with about 2,000 men. When they heard that Caninius, one of Caesar's generals, was after them, they occupied Uxellodunum, a town

situated on top of precipitous rocks. Caninius camped nearby and started to make entrenchments. The townspeople feared starvation and so Drappes and Lucterius went out and collected a large quantity of grain. While Lucterius was trying to smuggle the load into the town in the dark, the noise alerted the Romans. Caninius led out some cohorts against the convoy and gave no quarter. Lucterius got away with only a handful of his men and was unable to rejoin his colleague. Caninius then learnt that Drappes was encamped about 12 miles away. He led out his cavalry, his German infantry and one legion. When he approached, he found that Drappes was encamped by a river and that the cavalry and German foot were already attacking it. Caninius seized all the surrounding high ground with his legionaries, who charged down on the enemy from all sides. All the Gauls were killed or captured, Drappes being among the prisoners.
Hirtius: In Caesar, Gallic War, *8: 32–36*

ANTIGONEA (51) – Parthian War
Following the destruction of Crassus and his army at Carrhae (53), the Parthians were able to win back the whole of the country east of the Euphrates, but they did not advance beyond the river. It was not until two years later that they invaded Syria in force under the leadership of Osaces, who was acting as regent for the infant Pacorus. They reached Antioch [*Antakya*] but were repulsed by Gaius Cassius. He had been Crassus' quaestor and so was in command of the diminished Roman forces in Syria pending the arrival of Crassus' successor, Bibulus. From Antioch the Parthians turned their attention to Antigonea. They made little progress there too and decided to move on to some easier prey, but Cassius heard about their intended route and set an ambush. He met them with a few men and lured them into pursuing him – straight into the arms of his whole force. Osaces was killed, after which Pacorus abandoned any further intentions against Syria.
Dio Cassius, 40: 28–29

AMANUS M (51)
In the summer of 51, Cicero, the famous orator, took up an appointment as governor of Cilicia and proconsul for one year. Soon after Cassius had repulsed the Parthians from Antioch and ambushed them near Antigonea (above), Cicero mounted an offensive against the hostile people of Mount Amanus. This formed the boundary

between Cilicia and Syria. Taking advantage of defiles and other contours, he took the enemy by surprise and killed or captured many of them. He then captured and burnt their strongholds. After being hailed as *imperator* at Issus, he proceeded to besiege the fortified town of Pindenissus. When he returned home at the end of his term, he hoped to be awarded a triumph; instead, he found himself embroiled in the nastiness of the Civil War.
Cicero, Letters to his Friends, *2: 10*

MASSILIA (49) – Second Civil War
While Caesar was fighting the Gallic War, a power struggle was taking place in Rome in which Pompey in essence gained complete control of the state. In January 49, Caesar, having subdued the Gauls, crossed the Rubicon with his army and invaded northern Italy in defiance of an order that he should relinquish his command. The civil war between himself and Pompey had begun. Caesar 'escorted' Pompey from Rome to Brundisium [*Brindisi*] where Pompey embarked for Illyria. Caesar, unable to pursue him for lack of ships, turned and headed for Spain where Pompey's lieutenants were active. *En route* he stopped at Massilia [*Marseilles*] where the Massiliotes refused him entry. Caesar responded by bringing up three legions and making preparations for a siege. He also ordered the construction of 12 ships and put Decimus Brutus in charge. While Caesar was in Spain, a naval battle took place off Massilia. Domitius, in charge of the Pompeian forces in Massilia, had 17 ships, many of them decked. He manned them with a large number of archers and proceeded confidently against the 12 ships of Brutus, which were heavier and slower than his own. Moreover, Brutus' crews were hardly trained. But Caesar had manned his ships with veteran fighters and they were equipped with grappling irons. The Massiliotes with their superior numbers kept making attempts to surround the enemy. They were also adept at nimbly evading close contact. In spite of this, Brutus' crews managed to use their grappling equipment to good effect. Whenever an opportunity presented itself, an enemy ship found itself held fast, and on occasions one ship would grapple two of the enemy, one on each side. In this way the Massiliotes lost nine ships sunk or captured and the rest were driven into harbour. Brutus' losses are not recorded.
Caesar, Civil War, *1: 56–58; Dio Cassius, **41**: 21(3)*

SICORIS R (49) – Second Civil War
Caesar continued his advance from Massilia to Spain, having sent Gaius Fabius ahead with three legions to seize the passes over the Pyrenees. These were in the hands of Pompey's lieutenant Afranius, who was dislodged. Afranius linked up with Petreius, who was in command of a second Pompeian army in Spain. This gave them a combined force of five legions and about 5,000 cavalry with which they encamped near Ilerda [*Lerida*] on the west bank of the river Sicoris [*Segre*]. Altogether Caesar's force comprised six legions and 6,000 cavalry, half of them Gallic. Fabius had built two bridges about 4 miles apart across the Sicoris. With a shortage of food, he had taken to crossing the river to the west bank and foraging. On one of these expeditions, two of Fabius' legions sent to guard the foragers had crossed the bridge, when a sudden squall carried the bridge away, cutting the legions off from the cavalry who were on the point of crossing. The flotsam carried down the river told the enemy what had happened. Afranius immediately led four legions and all his cavalry against the distressed legions of Fabius. These had taken up a position on some higher ground and were managing to hold out when, according to Caesar's account, two more legions came to their assistance. They had been sent over the second bridge by a far-sighted Fabius, and their arrival put an end to the fighting. Dio and Appian both put a less favourable interpretation on the events, holding that many of Fabius' men were killed. They make no mention of a relieving force.
Caesar, Civil War, *1: 40; Dio Cassius, **41**: 20(1–2); Appian,* Civil Wars, *2: 42*

ILERDA (49, August 2) – Second Civil War
Two days after the battle at the Sicoris (above), Caesar arrived with 900 cavalry and marched with his whole force towards Ilerda [*Lerida*]. He camped about half a mile from Afranius and fortified his camp with a trench on three sides. Afranius and Petreius, who were encamped on a hill close to the town, marched down to the foot of the hill in the hope of provoking a battle but Caesar ignored them. Between the town and the enemy camp there was a hillock in the middle of a small level plateau, which appeared to Caesar to be an ideal objective. He led out three legions and then sent one line at the double to occupy the hillock. Afranius saw what he was up to and sent some cohorts, who managed to get there first by a shorter route. The Pompeian legions then charged down from their camp and created confusion among Caesar's

vanguard and right wing. Caesar led the Ninth legion to their support and turned the tables, forcing the enemy to withdraw right back to the walls of the town. However, the men of the Ninth legion got carried away by their success and pressed the pursuit too far. They found themselves on a flat ridge which had steep sides and which led to the final climb up to the town. The enemy were above them, showering missiles down on them and receiving fresh reinforcements from their camp through the town, while the steep sides of the ridge made it extremely difficult for Caesar to get any help to his men. When they tried to withdraw, the enemy pressed down on them with renewed vigour. After five hours of fighting the Ninth legion had used up all its missiles. As a last resort they drew their swords and charged uphill against the enemy, killing some and forcing others back and some even into the town. At last this gave them a chance to withdraw. Seventy of Caesar's force were killed in the initial charge and 600 were wounded. Afranius lost 200 men and five centurions killed.

The war in Spain became a war of attrition. Petreius and Afranius, finding it dangerous to forage, decided to move south to Celtiberia. Caesar pursued them, continually harassing them, preventing them from foraging and depriving them of water. Eventually, the Pompeians sued for peace, which was granted on the one condition that their armies should be disbanded.

Caesar, Civil War, *1: 43–46*

UTICA (49) – Second Civil War

Gaius Curio, one of Caesar's generals, landed near Clupea [*Kelibia*] in Africa and marched with his two legions and 500 cavalry to Utica, where he encamped near the town. The enemy camp of Attius Varus was right up against the town walls and was sandwiched between the walls on one side and a massive edifice on the other. As the only approach was a narrow passageway, the encampment was highly secure. While Curio was fortifying his camp, his scouts reported that a large army had been sent by King Juba of Mauretania to reinforce Varus and that it was approaching. Curio sent out his cavalry to delay the enemy while he himself organized the legions; but they were not needed. The king's forces were not expecting an encounter and were in such disorder that Curio's cavalry routed their horse and killed many of their infantry. On the following day, before Juba's army reached Utica, Curio and Varus led out their men and confronted each other. Between the two

armies there was a small valley with steep sides which were difficult to scale. Both sides were waiting to see who would be the first to attempt a crossing when the cavalry of Varus accompanied by some light-armed troops suddenly appeared in the valley on Curio's right and trotted down the centre of it. Curio sent in his cavalry, who routed their opponents at one charge and sent them flying back to their base, leaving the light-armed troops to be slaughtered to a man. Curio himself then followed in the steps of his cavalry, leading his legions down into the valley. That was enough for Varus' troops, who turned about and bolted back into their camp, blocking the entrance with their numbers and being crushed in the stampede. About 600 of them died and 1,000 were wounded. Curio did lose one man, an ordinary soldier who got caught up with the retreating enemy and sought out Varus in a suicidal dash. Varus managed to ward off the blow but his assailant was inevitably killed.

Caesar, Civil War, *2: 26 and 33–35*

BAGRADAS R (49, August 24) – Second Civil War

Curio heard that a large force of King Juba's was approaching Utica under the command of his general Saburra. The king had been detained by a border dispute and would be following shortly. The young and enthusiastic Roman, spurred on by his previous success at Utica (above), decided that he would give battle before Juba arrived with the rest of the Numidian forces. Saburra was encamped by the river Bagradas [*Medjerda*] some distance away, and Curio sent out all his cavalry after dark. Arriving around dawn, they caught the unsuspecting Numidians sleepy-eyed and slew a great number of them. The cavalry returned toward their camp and met Curio, who had left in the early hours and had already marched 6 miles. Spurred on by the good news, he marched as fast as he could, ordering the weary cavalry to follow although they were unable to keep up with him. On the other side, Saburra suspected that the cavalry attack had been a mere preliminary and that the whole force would follow. He had his men lined up and ready for the enemy, with instructions to withdraw gradually as if in fear. Curio took the bait, brought his men down into the plain and pursued the enemy for around 16 miles. At this point Saburra gave the signal and turned to face the enemy with his cavalry in the front line. Curio's principal weakness was his shortage of cavalry. He had only 200 with him; the others had stopped to rest the horses some way back. The enemy, by contrast, had received a reinforcement of 2,000 Spanish and Gallic cavalry which had been sent in advance by Juba. As a result, the Romans were easily surrounded, while further instalments from Juba were adding to the Numidian numbers all the time. In desperation, Curio ordered his men to seize a nearby hill, but Saburra anticipated them and got there first. Every infantryman was killed. Curio himself dismissed the suggestion that he might try to escape. He preferred to die with his men. The exhausted cavalry who had ridden all the previous night and arrived too late for the battle were just about the only survivors.

Caesar, Civil War, *2: 38–42; Appian*, Civil Wars, *2: 45*

SALONAE (48) – Second Civil War

When Pompey was forced out of Italy, he crossed the Adriatic and eventually retired to Dyrrhachium where he built up a base for a future invasion of Italy. Caesar followed him there after the end of hostilities in Spain. While they were there, Marcus Octavius, one of Pompey's admirals, sailed to Salonae [*Split*] and tried to stir up the Dalmatians against supporting Caesar. The Roman community at Salonae were uncompromising and so Octavius laid siege to the place with a ring of five camps around it. When the inhabitants became desperate for lack of corn, they made a sudden sortie and stormed the nearest camp so successfully that they proceeded to attack the remaining four, one after the other. They drove the besiegers out of all the camps, killing many of them, and forced Octavius to flee to his ships with the rest. He sailed to Dyrrhachium to join Pompey.

Caesar, Civil War, *3: 9*

DYRRHACHIUM: LESNIKIA R (48) –
Second Civil War

When Caesar heard that Pompey was at Asparagium, he moved there and camped nearby. The next morning he offered battle. Pompey was anxious to avoid this in spite of his overwhelming numerical superiority as his troops were inferior in training to Caesar's veterans. When the offer was refused, Caesar decided to make for Dyrrhachium [*Durrës*], Pompey's base. By heading off in a different direction and making a detour, Caesar outwitted his foe and got there first as Pompey appeared in the distance. Pompey, excluded from the town, built a strong camp south of the town on a hill called Petra close to the Bay of Dyrrhachium,

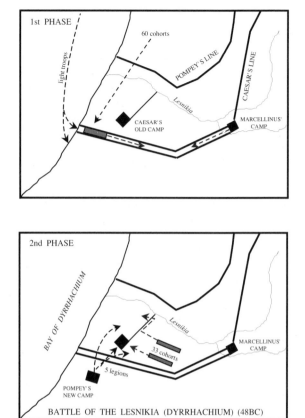

Based on a diagram in J.F.C. Fuller, *Julius Caesar*

where he established a well-stocked base. Caesar camped further inland and started blockading Pompey by constructing a line of forts with entrenchments between them, stretching from sea to sea over a distance of about 12 miles. Pompey retaliated by making a similar but shorter line of fortifications inside Caesar's line. Military activities in the early stages were confined to harassment and attempts to confine the other and deny access to supplies and provisions. Caesar mentions that in one day alone there were six engagements which accounted for enemy losses of about 2,000 casualties. When Pompey decided to attempt a break-out, a bigger battle did ensue.

In the middle of the night he led 60 cohorts to the southern end of the encircling fortifications where they joined the sea. At the same time he embarked a large force of archers and light-armed troops, whom he sent to the same shoreline accompanied by his warships. At this point Caesar's line was a double wall consisting of two parallel lines of ramparts and trenches a few hundred yards apart. They extended from the sea for about 2 miles inland at which point there was a camp, occupied at the time by Lentulus Marcellinus. These fortifications had been built by Caesar in the early stages of the campaign but had not been quite completed. The cross wall connecting the two ramparts by the sea had never been built, and Pompey had heard about this deficiency from deserters. At the time of Pompey's attack, two cohorts of Caesar's Ninth legion were camping by the sea. The attackers started hurling missiles from outside the outer rampart while others attacked the inner rampart from the other side. The defenders, between the walls, had only stones with which to retaliate. They were already suffering badly when the enemy noticed that there was no cross wall and managed to get into the space between the ramparts from the shore. Taken on the flank as well as in the front and rear, the defenders turned to flight. Some cohorts which were sent to the rescue from Marcellinus' camp failed to achieve anything except to increase the confusion and to get in the way. Finally, Antony arrived with 12 cohorts and drove the enemy back. The final disgrace was avoided when a legionary standard bearer just managed to hand on his eagle, the supreme emblem, before he expired. After his victory Pompey built a new camp, situated on the shore to the south of the circumvallation, outside the blockade.

This battle consisted in fact of two distinct engagements and what has been described was only the first. The second phase took place in the same area and centred round an old camp of Caesar's situated in the plain between his double fortification and the southern end of Pompey's line of works to the north. A river, the Lesnikia [*Gesnike*], ran on the north side of this camp through the plain to the sea. Caesar heard that Pompey was moving troops into this camp and he sent 33 cohorts in two columns to attack it. The left column got into the camp and forced the occupants back; but the right column encountered a rampart which they thought was the camp wall. In fact, it ran from the camp to the river. Unable to find a gate, they broke through the rampart near the river and got into the plain on the other side. Pompey then led five legions and some cavalry to the relief of the camp. When Caesar's right column tried to retire they came up once more against the rampart which led to the river. Unable to get through *en masse*, many of them jumped from the top of the rampart into the trench and were trampled down by those that followed. When the

left column saw that the right was in rout, it too turned and fled. Caesar himself attempted to halt the headlong flight but no one paid any attention to him. In the two engagements taken together Caesar lost 960 men and 32 military tribunes and centurions; the Pompeian losses are unknown.

These encounters are now known as the Battle of the Lesnikia. Caesar, however, does not name the river and neither Appian nor Dio Cassius mention a river at all.

Caesar, Civil War, *3: 62–64; Appian*, Civil Wars, *2: 61; Dio Cassius, *41: 50(3–4)*

PHARSALUS (48, August 9) – Second Civil War

Caesar's reverses at Dyrrhachium led him to pull out and give himself time to boost the morale of his troops. He met and joined forces with Gnaeus Domitius at Aeginium and they proceeded into Thessaly. Caesar was looking for a suitable base with ample crops for fodder and he decided to halt near Pharsalus [*Farsala*] and wait for Pompey there. Pompey had meanwhile joined forces with Q. Caecilius Scipio. He arrived a few days later

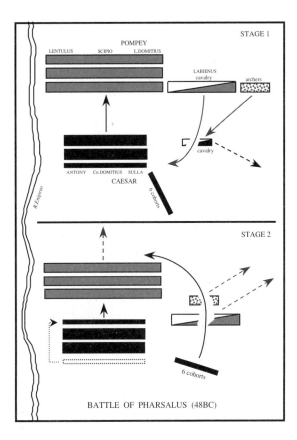

BATTLE OF PHARSALUS (48BC)

and encamped at the foot of a mountain. In spite of his large numerical superiority Pompey was at first loath to commit himself to a pitched battle, but he was eventually persuaded to settle the issue. He led his men out in battle array and Caesar followed suit. Pompey's right wing was protected by the river Enipeus and so he put all his cavalry and light-armed troops on the opposite wing. His force totalled at least 40,000 infantry and 7,000 cavalry. Against them, Caesar lined his troops up in the usual three rows but, on noting the enemy's dispositions, he withdrew one cohort from each legion from the third line and stationed them as a fourth line opposite the enemy cavalry. His total force amounted to 22,000 men and a mere 1,000 horse. The engagement began on Caesar's side with an infantry charge which was met and matched by their opponents. At the same time Pompey's cavalry, supported by the archers, charged forward with the intention of attacking Caesar's right wing in the flank and rear. They made short work of his cavalry but were brought up sharply by his fourth line, which had been formed specifically for the purpose. This corps ran forward with their javelins aimed at the faces of the enemy, who failed to withstand the unnerving experience. They turned and fled to the hills, leaving their supporting archers and slingers exposed and unprotected against the butchery which followed. Meanwhile, Caesar's fourth line continued its charge round Pompey's left wing and attacked it in the rear. At this point Caesar threw into the fray his third line, which had so far seen no action. The Pompeian force could not stand up to this new assault by fresh soldiers. They turned and fled as a whole and were pursued to their camp, which was stormed, after which they occupied a hill. Caesar's men started to besiege the hill but the Pompeians retreated over the hills behind. They were finally rounded up and forced to surrender. Caesar spared them all. Pompey himself left the field after the defeat of his cavalry. He stayed in his tent until the camp was attacked and then rode off to Larissa. It is thought that about 15,000 of his men were killed in the battle, while more than 24,000 were taken prisoner. The losses on Caesar's side were said to number no more than 200.

Caesar, Civil War, *3: 85–99; Dio Cassius,* **41:** *52(3)–61(1); Appian,* Civil Wars, *2: 70–82; Plutarch,* Caesar, *42–45 and* Pompey, *68(3)–72*

SALONAE (47) – Second Civil War

Pompeian pockets of resistance to Caesar were growing in Illyria, and the propraetor Quintus Cornificius was having a hard time holding his own. Caesar sent Aulus Gabinius with some new levies to join him but Gabinius, too, had a hard time as the weather was bad and the country was bare. After frequent defeats in his attempts to storm places, he withdrew to Salonae [*Split*] on the Adriatic coast, where the Roman citizens were loyal. One source states that he was attacked on the march and lost 2,000 men including 38 centurions and four tribunes. Dio, however, makes no mention of this. He reports that Octavius had been besieging Salonae for a long time without success until, one night, Gabinius and the inhabitants attacked the camp of the besiegers and captured both the camp and the harbour. Octavius escaped, gathered another force and returned to take the town, by which time Gabinius had died there of some disease. Dio places these events in the year 48 – before Pharsalus.

(Caesar), Alexandrian War, *43; Dio Cassius,* **42:** *11*

TAURIS ISL (47) – Second Civil War

At about the time of the above events at Salonae, the propraetor Cornificius in Illyria was sending urgent appeals to Vatinius in Brundisium [*Brindisi*] to come and help. Vatinius had only a few battle ships and so he fitted beaks to a number of his smaller craft and embarked many veterans, of whom there were large numbers at Brundisium as a result of the war. At that time Marcus Octavius was attacking Epidaurus. He was forced to abandon the siege and withdrew to moorings by the island of Tauris [*Torcola*]. There, Vatinius opposed him and both sides deployed for battle. Vatinius with his quinquereme sailed straight for the quadrireme of Octavius and the two ships became entangled. The other ships on both sides rallied to the support of their flag-ships so that they became packed in a concentrated mass. This suited Vatinius, whose smaller vessels were less appropriate for naval warfare but whose seamen were better motivated for boarding and hand-to-hand fighting. The enemy flag-ship sank and Octavius boarded a small craft, which promptly went down under the weight of escaping seamen. He managed to escape in spite of wounds but 11 of his decked ships were captured. Vatinius' fleet remained intact.

(Caesar), Alexandrian War, *44–47*

ALEXANDRIA (47) – Alexandrian War

After his crushing defeat at Pharsalus (48), Pompey fled to Egypt, where he was murdered.

Caesar, who had followed him there, got embroiled in local politics and the regal succession, and gained the enmity of the king and of the Alexandrians, who besieged him. From the military point of view most of the action was in the form of street fighting and similar urban episodes. But the Alexandrians decided that if they built up their fleet, they might effectively complete the blockade against Caesar. They built small boats and called in every old ship for restoration, completing 5 quinqueremes, 22 quadriremes and a number of undecked vessels. They manned them with troops and prepared for battle. Caesar had 34 ships from Rhodes, Pontus, Lycia and Asia, under the command of Euphranor, who sailed round Pharos and drew up opposite the enemy. He placed 17 ships in the front line with the remainder in reserve. The Alexandrians had 22 in their front line and, in addition, a large number of dinghies equipped with fire-darts. When the engagement started, the Rhodians displayed their skill in that they never presented themselves broadside on; nor did they allow their oars to be sheared off. The outcome of the battle was hardly dramatic but it was a definite victory for Caesar's men. A quinquereme and a bireme were captured and three other enemy ships were sunk, while the rest fled to the protection of the townspeople. Caesar's fleet suffered no losses.

(Caesar), Alexandrian War, *12–16*

NILUS R (47) – Alexandrian War

At the start of the Alexandrian War, Caesar had asked his friend Mithridates of Pergamum, a reputed son of the great Mithridates, to bring reinforcements from Syria and Cilicia. Mithridates marched with a large force to Pelusium on the eastern side of the Nile delta and captured the place. The king, Ptolemy XIII, sent a large force against him, but those of his troops who were first across the river were too eager to attack and claim the credit for the victory. They lost it and many were killed. The king himself then sailed down the Nile to check Mithridates, while Caesar set out by sea at the same time to meet up with him. The king encamped in a strong position on some high ground which adjoined the Nile on one side and was protected by a marsh on another side. To reach it Caesar had to cross a narrow tributary of the Nile which had high banks. The king sent out all his cavalry and some light troops to stop him, but Caesar's German cavalry scouted around and found some places where the banks were lower, while his troops felled tall trees and bridged the

river. When they had effected a crossing, they engaged and killed nearly all of the enemy cavalry. The king had built a fort in a nearby village and had connected it to his camp with walls. The next day, Caesar captured this fort and proceeded with his whole force up to the camp's fortifications. There was a space between the camp and the Nile which offered a possible opening for an attack on the fortifications. Here the Romans made no headway. They were targets for missiles both from the fortifications and from boats full of archers and slingers on the river. At this point Caesar noticed that the highest – and most naturally secure – part of the camp was the most lightly defended. He sent some cohorts round there, and they had little difficulty in dealing with the few guards. This caused a panic and rout which spread rapidly throughout the camp, allowing the Romans to capture it with ease. The king escaped and embarked on a ship, but the crowds trying to scramble aboard capsized it and the king was drowned. As a result of the Roman victory, the Alexandrians submitted to Caesar, who gained control not only of the town but also of Egypt.

(Caesar), Alexandrian War, *26–32*

NICOPOLIS (47) – Revolt of Pharnaces

Pharnaces, son of the great Mithridates, took advantage of Roman involvement in the Civil War to seize Armenia Minor and Cappadocia. Domitius Calvinus, to whom Caesar had assigned the administration of Asia, took one of his legions and two native legions with which he marched to the vicinity of Nicopolis [*Divriği*], where Pharnaces had installed himself. Pharnaces dug two parallel trenches leading out from the town and drew up his battle line between them. His cavalry, which greatly outnumbered the enemy's, was divided between the flanks outside the confines of the trenches. Domitius deployed his force opposite the enemy and both sides launched a fierce charge simultaneously. Domitius' Thirty-sixth legion on the right wing charged the enemy cavalry so successfully that they forced them back to the town walls. After that, the legion crossed the ditch and attacked the enemy infantry in the rear. On the other wing, however, Domitius' Pontic legion attempted to cross the trench in order to attack their opposite numbers on the flank, but they were overcome when they were negotiating the ditch. In the centre, Domitius' native forces failed to make any stand, with the result that Pharnaces' right and centre were both free to join in against the Thirty-sixth. This legion, surrounded by the whole enemy army, formed itself into a circle and withdrew to the foothills of the mountains where the enemy was unwilling to pursue the attack. The Romans escaped with a loss of no more than 250 killed. The native legions, on the other hand, were almost annihilated. With this victory behind him, Pharnaces occupied Pontus with a devastating display of cruelty and despotism.

(Caesar), Alexandrian War, *34 and 38–40*

ZELA (47, August 2) – Revolt of Pharnaces

After gaining Egypt, Caesar proceeded via a roundabout route to Pontus against the rebellious Pharnaces. He had four legions and the remains of a fifth legion of veterans. Pharnaces asked for terms and gave many pledges but clearly had no intention of abiding by them. About 3 miles from Zela [*Zile*] there was a high hill, which was almost connected to the town by a ridge. Here Pharnaces installed himself – in the place where his father had camped before winning a victory against the Romans two decades previously (Zela, 67). At dawn the next day Caesar surprised him by capturing some neighbouring heights which were only about a mile from Pharnaces' camp across an intervening valley. Caesar was amazed when Pharnaces drew up his forces in front of his camp and proceeded to descend into the valley and then advance speedily towards him over the rising, rough and uneven, intervening ground. Caesar assumed that his enemy was merely flexing his muscles in a display of strength, and so he carried on with his fortifications. When it became apparent that Pharnaces was intending to fight, Caesar had to move quickly to assemble his men and get them into some sort of order. A charge by some scythed chariots caused additional confusion but they were readily driven off with missiles. The two armies then came to grips. In hard fighting the veteran Sixth legion on Caesar's right forced its opponents back down the slope. Elsewhere along the line, victory came more slowly but the outcome was similar. Once the enemy had been dislodged, the downhill flight was as rapid as had been their spectacular initial uphill charge. Their camp was captured and Pharnaces fled, but the whole of his army was either captured or killed. When he was celebrating his triumph in Rome, Caesar referred to the battle with his now famous utterance *'Veni, vidi, vici'*. It was all in a day's work!

(Caesar), Alexandrian War, *72–76*

HADRUMENTUM (46) – Second Civil War

The Civil War did not come to an end with the death of Pompey. Large numbers of his supporters were in control in Africa with very considerable forces, which were further augmented by troops from the Numidian king, Juba. Caesar proceeded against them and embarked an army of six legions and 2,000 cavalry. He landed near Hadrumentum [*Sousse*]. Appian maintains that he intended to attack the town but that he himself was attacked and badly beaten by Labienus and Petreius. Against this, it is reported in the *African War* that Caesar's ships became separated during the crossing and that he landed near Hadrumentum with only 3,000 infantry and 150 cavalry. He knew that he was not in a position to attack such a strong town and was starting to move away when the townspeople sallied out, reinforced by 2,000 of Juba's cavalry who had just arrived. They attacked the rear of Caesar's column and were driven off by his cavalry but returned and repeatedly harassed him for some distance. He encamped that night at Ruspina.

(Caesar), African War, *3–6; Appian*, Civil Wars, *2: 95*

RUSPINA (46) – Second Civil War

While Caesar was at Ruspina [*Monastir*], the rest of his ships arrived. When the whole force had encamped, Caesar went off on a foraging expedition with a force of 30 cohorts, 400 cavalry and 150 archers. They had gone but 3 miles when a much larger enemy force of cavalry and light troops under Labienus arrived and deployed. The enemy tactics were novel to Caesar. The Numidian light troops would rush forward between their horsemen and throw their javelins. When the Romans charged, the cavalry would retire. But any pursuit by the Romans would expose their flanks to the light troops, who held their ground until the cavalry returned for another round. In the meantime the enemy numbers were such that their cavalry had no difficulty in surrounding Caesar's force. Caesar countered this by extending his line as far as possible and getting the alternate cohorts to turn about and face in the opposite direction – an extended back-to-back deployment. Showers of missiles thrown in both directions kept the enemy at a distance while the Caesarian line gradually fell back toward its defences. At this point a force of 1,600 Numidian cavalry arrived to reinforce the enemy, and so the battle started up again. Caesar's troops were utterly exhausted but fortunately the day was nearly at an end. With a last desperate effort they forced the enemy back off the plain and

behind a hill, which the Romans then possessed. After this the enemy withdrew.
(Caesar), African War, *12–18*

THAPSUS (46, April) – Second Civil War

Caesar spent some time in the vicinity of Ruspina, where he received a second convoy of troops from Sicily. The enemy was not far away and so there was a seemingly endless succession of forays and skirmishes. It seemed evident that Quintus Caecilius Scipio, the Pompeian commander, had no intention of risking a full battle in spite of his numerical superiority. He had eight legions of his own, 20,000 horse, 30 elephants and numerous light troops. Additionally, his ally Juba had 30,000 foot, as well as 20,000 horse and 60 elephants. Caesar had 10 legions. It was Caesar who forced the issue by moving 16 miles after dark and camping near the Pompeian-held coastal town of Thapsus [*Ras Dimas*]. Inland from the town there was a lake about 7 miles long. The arc of land between the lake on one side and the coast and town on the other side was about one and a half miles wide. Caesar positioned his camp near the town, in the middle of the arc, and set about investing the town. When Scipio arrived, he found that he had been debarred from entering the southern end of the arc by Caesar, who had erected a fort there and installed a garrison. Scipio was forced to march right round the far side of the lake, and he camped in the northern entrance to the arc. Caesar withdrew his troops from the siege and proceeded to deploy his forces in battle array. Scipio drew up his line with his elephants on both wings, and Caesar opposed them with cavalry, archers and slingers. The archers and slingers on the right wing sent such a volley of missiles at the elephants that the terrified beasts turned and charged through their gates to the protection afforded by the ramparts. After this overture, the infantry engagement was started by Caesar's troops, who were so eager for battle that they refused to be held back and acted entirely without orders. A trumpeter was persuaded to sound the call to charge, whereupon the legions unleashed themselves. The Moorish cavalry on the enemy left failed to withstand the charge and followed the example of the elephants so that Caesar's legions readily seized the rampart. After this the opposition crumbled completely along the whole line, and Scipio's army took to flight with Caesar's men in hot pursuit. The Pompeians fled back to their camp only to find it deserted. They went on to Juba's camp, but

that was already in Caesar's hands. Finally, they retreated to a hill and made gestures of surrender. Even this did not halt the angry victors, whose blood was so high that, in spite of Caesar's protestations, they massacred them to a man. Five thousand (Plutarch says 50,000) were killed for a loss of 50 on Caesar's side. Apart from some mopping up, organized resistance to Caesar in Africa was at an end.

Plutarch makes the interesting comment that according to some sources Caesar was not on the battlefield at Thapsus because of a recurrence of his illness (epilepsy). If that is true, it might explain the impetuousness and impatience of his troops. Appian provides another variation when he says that Juba had to remove his forces and return home before the battle to defend his capital Cirta against an attack.
(Caesar), African War, *79–86*; Dio Cassius, **43**: *7–9(1)*; *Appian*, Civil Wars, **2**: *96–97*; Plutarch, Caesar, *53*

HIPPO REGIUS (46) – Second Civil War

Scipio fled from Thapsus (above) with a number of senators and other officers. They were on their way to Spain in a convoy of 12 ships when they were driven by bad weather into Hippo Regius [*Bône*]. It so happened that the fleet of Publius Sittius was in port at the time. This mercenary captain had previously routed Juba's army somewhere in Mauretania and killed its general Saburra, the victor at the Bagradas River (49). He had also ambushed and captured Afranius during his attempted escape to Spain. On this occasion, Sittius' ships surrounded and sank the whole of Scipio's fleet. Scipio and the other officers were all drowned. Appian says that Scipio stabbed himself and then jumped into the sea. Another variation is given by Dio, who holds that Scipio was cast ashore in Mauretania and committed suicide out of fear of Sittius.
(Caesar), African War, *96*; Appian, Civil Wars, **2**: *100*; Dio Cassius, **43**: *9(5)*

CARTEIA (46) – Second Civil War

Pompeian supporters were crossing from Africa to Spain and were rallying to Pompey's son and namesake, who retired to Baetica to consolidate. Caesar's lieutenant Didius sailed against them and defeated Pompey's legate Varus in a naval battle off Carteia [near *San Roque*]. Varus would have lost his whole fleet if he had not got ashore and embedded a row of anchors in the mouth of the harbour. These wrecked the foremost of the

pursuing ships before the rest of the fleet was alerted to the danger.
Dio Cassius, **43***: 31(3)*

MUNDA (45, March 17) – Second Civil War

Caesar travelled to Spain to put an end to the last bastion of Pompeian resistance, which flourished under the banner of Gnaeus Pompeius, the eldest son of Pompey the Great. When Caesar arrived in Spain, he began attacking the Pompeian-held towns and fortifications, but he was unable to draw the enemy out to battle until he reached Munda, where Pompeius had encamped under the town's fortifications in a strong position. The town was on high ground, which sloped down to a plain across which there flowed a stream. Caesar camped opposite the enemy in the plain convinced, it is said, that Pompeius would descend to his level where the flat terrain would be ideal for the Pompeian cavalry. He was proved wrong. The enemy army showed no sign of moving. In consequence, Caesar was faced with a literally uphill task which, most uncharacteristically, he accepted. The enemy infantry were deployed under 13 standards, with cavalry and 6,000 light-armed troops divided between the wings. Caesar had eight legions and 8,000 cavalry. It was a long, hard struggle which, according to one source, lasted all day. The issue remained in doubt with no advantage either way until the Tenth legion in its customary place on the right wing managed to push the opposing forces back. To avoid being attacked on their flank, the enemy directed a legion to move across from their right wing. Caesar's cavalry then seized the opportunity to push hard on this now weakened wing which gave way, causing the rest of the line to crumble and flee into the town. A major additional reason for the Pompeian defeat is given by Dio Cassius. He recounts that Bogud, king of Mauretania and an ally of Caesar's, was not directly involved in the conflict and decided on his own initiative to attack the enemy camp. Labienus left the enemy line to go against him and was thought to be fleeing, to the detriment of Pompeian morale. About 30,000 of the enemy were killed; Caesar's losses were 1,000. A macabre note was sounded when the victors had to erect a palisade against escapers from the town. The only materials they could find were corpses and heads, which they impaled on lances. Gnaeus Pompeius did escape but he was subsequently found and killed.

Munda was in Baetica, but the quoted distances and landmarks do not add up and the site is uncertain. It is now thought to have been near Urso [*Osuna*].
(Caesar), Spanish War, *28–31; Dio Cassius,* **43***: 35(4)–38; Appian,* Civil Wars, **2***: 104–105; Plutarch,* Caesar, *56(1–3)*

FORUM GALLORUM: I (43, April 14) – War of Mutina

The issue which triggered this and the next action was the command of Cisalpine Gaul, which was held by Decimus Brutus until Mark Antony enacted a law assigning it to himself and authorizing him to transfer Caesar's legions to his new province. He promptly effected the take-over before the end of the current term and penned Brutus up in Mutina [*Modena*], which he besieged. There are two good accounts of the ensuing events. One is Appian's; the other is contained in a letter to Cicero from Sulpicius Galba, who was with the consul Vibius Pansa and who wrote within a few days of the actions. When Brutus started to suffer from hunger, Octavian and the consul Hirtius marched toward Mutina but waited at a little distance for Pansa, who was coming to join them. They sent Carfulenus (Appian calls him Carsuleius) with Galba and the Martian legion and two praetorian cohorts to reinforce Pansa. At this point Antony sent out his cavalry and some light troops against Pansa, while holding his two legions back in reserve. The opposing forces met in some marshy country near Forum Gallorum [*Castelfranco*] where, according to Appian and Dio Cassius, Pansa was ambushed. Pansa's Martians on the right wing advanced on their own initiative and were forging ahead when Antony suddenly charged out of Forum Gallorum with his legions. At first the Martians repulsed one of Antony's legions, but they were then outflanked by the cavalry and became surrounded. Galba summoned help from two legions of recruits, which were still coming up, and managed to retreat toward their camp. Meanwhile, Antony's praetorians confronted Octavian's in the road, while Pansa's left wing in the marshy ground alongside the road was outflanked by more of Antony's cavalry and was forced to retreat. Galba admits to heavy losses in the praetorian cohorts and Martian legion. According to Appian, Octavian's praetorians perished to the last man, but Pansa's troops held out until the consul himself was wounded and carried off the field to Bononia [*Bologna*].
Cicero, Letters to his Friends, **10***: 30; Appian,* Civil Wars, **3***: 67–69; Dio Cassius,* **46***: 37(5–6)*

FORUM GALLORUM: II (43) – War of Mutina

After the battle near Forum Gallorum (above), Antony tried to capture the enemy camp but was repulsed. When Hirtius, who was near Mutina, heard that a battle had taken place, he hurried there with 20 veteran cohorts and attacked the weary and disordered Antonians as they were withdrawing to their own camp. According to Galba, Hirtius routed and annihilated Antony's men on the same ground as the previous battle.
Cicero, Letters to his Friends, *10: 30; Appian*, Civil Wars, *3: 70; Dio Cassius*, *46: 37(7)–38(2)*

MUTINA (43) – War of Mutina

The outcome of the encounters at Forum Gallorum dissuaded Antony from a further general engagement. He preferred to bide his time until Brutus, besieged in Mutina [*Modena*], surrendered. On the other side, Octavian and Hirtius wanted to settle the issue by lifting the siege. They made a pass with their cavalry at the least defended part of the city, while their infantry prepared themselves for battle. Antony parried the cavalry attack with his cavalry alone but then had second thoughts and sallied out with two legions, as the enemy had hoped. He sent for other legions from various camps, but they failed to arrive in time to prevent his defeat at the hands of Octavian. Hirtius even broke into Antony's camp, but he was killed in the process. Against the advice of his friends, Antony abandoned the siege and headed for the Alps.
Appian, Civil Wars, *3: 71–72; Dio Cassius*, *46: 38(5–7); Plutarch*, Antony, *17(1)*

LAODICEA (42) – Campaign of Cassius

The command in Syria had been assigned to P. Cornelius Dolabella, but he blotted his copybook when he killed one of the tyrannicides, C. Trebonius, who had previously held the command. C. Cassius Longinus immediately seized control of Syria and was given authority by the senate to make war on Dolabella. Cassius had the Syrian forces at his disposal. Moreover, the Roman troops who had been left in Egypt by Caesar and were on their way to Syria were easily persuaded to desert to his side. With these reinforcements Cassius joined battle with Dolabella, defeated him and then besieged him in the port of Laodicea [*Al Lādhiqīyah*]. Dolabella still had power on the sea, partly by virtue of ships which had been sent to him by Cleopatra. This situation was dealt with by L. Murcius Staius, who sailed into the harbour and defeated any ships that opposed him. Devoid of hope and fearing betrayal, Dolabella killed himself.
Dio Cassius, *47: 30(1–5)*

MYNDUS (42) – Campaign of Cassius

Brutus and Cassius had gained control of all the eastern provinces but there were thorns in their flesh – the Rhodians and Lycians. These peoples were friendly to Octavian and Antony and constituted a potential threat in the rear of the conspirators. It was decided that Brutus would deal with the Lycians, Cassius with Rhodes. The Rhodians under the command of their leaders, Alexander and Mnaseas, struck first. They sailed their best 33 ships against Cassius at Myndus [*Gümuslük*], hoping to take him by surprise. The Roman numbers are not known, but the Rhodians were heavily outnumbered and were surrounded. The Roman ships were the heavier and were therefore superior at close quarters when it came to ramming, while the swiftness of the Rhodians was of little benefit to them. Three of their ships were captured with their crews and two were sunk. The rest fled back to Rhodes in a damaged condition. Many of the Romans' ships also were damaged but they suffered no actual losses.
Appian, Civil Wars, *4: 71*

RHODES (42) – Campaign of Cassius

When Cassius had repaired the damage inflicted to his ships off Myndus (above), he sailed against Rhodes with 80 ships and transported some foot soldiers across from the mainland. The Rhodians sailed out to fight but were forced to give up with the loss of two ships after being completely encircled. The city was not prepared for a siege and was soon forced to capitulate.
Appian, Civil Wars, *4: 72*

SCYLLAEUM PR (42) – War against Pompeius

After the battle of Munda (45) which ended the Second Civil War, Sextus Pompeius, the younger son of Pompey, became the rallying point for Pompeians from all parts. Following the murder of Caesar in 44, Sextus was given command of the sea, which provided him with ships as well as men. He sailed to Sicily and obtained the surrender of the island, which prompted Octavian, Caesar's adopted son and heir, to send Salvidienus with a fleet to destroy him. Sextus sailed out against Salvidienus with a large fleet and they met off the Scyllaeum promontory [*Scilla*] at the entrance to the *Straits of Messina*. Sextus' ships were lighter and swifter than those of his adversary and his crews were much better trained and more capable of negotiating the heavy seas of the straits. Salvidienus was the first to withdraw. Appian is somewhat ambivalent in his assessment of the outcome. He says that both sides suffered about equally but then refers to what was left of Salvidienus' damaged fleet.

Appian, Civil Wars, *4: 85*

PHILIPPI: I (42, October 3) – Wars of the Second Triumvirate

Marcus Brutus went through the Balkans collecting an army in Greece, Illyria and Macedonia. Cassius meanwhile was doing the same thing in Asia Minor. The two conspirators met up together and set up camp near Philippi [*Krinides*] in Macedonia, where they fortified an impregnable position on two hills a little over 2 miles from Philippi and about a mile apart. Cassius set up camp on one of the hills, Brutus on the other, and they built a fortification joining the camps across the intervening space. There were marshes on one side of the hills and gorges on the other. To complete the defences, Cassius fortified the narrow gap between his camp and the marsh. When Mark Antony and Octavian arrived they encamped in the plain about a mile from the enemy. Each side had 19 legions but those of Brutus and Cassius were under strength. On the other hand, they had 20,000 cavalry as against Antony's 13,000. Brutus and Cassius had all they wanted in the way of supplies and they were keen to spin out the confrontation to their advantage. Antony, by contrast, feared delay and planned accordingly. Every day he led out his forces, apparently entire, while a part of his force worked surreptitiously by day and night to make a causeway over the marsh and to erect some forts to protect it. When this had been completed, he attacked the enemy's fortifications between their camp and the marsh, demolished their palisade and forced a way in through the gate. Relying on the natural strength of the place, Cassius had detailed only a few men to guard the camp, which was taken with little difficulty. In the meantime the rest of Antony's forces, who had lined up as usual, were surprised to find that Cassius was prepared to risk an open battle. In a long, hard struggle the forces of Antony proved victorious. At the same time, in what was virtually a separate encounter, the forces of Brutus charged down of their own initiative against Octavian's troops, put them to flight and captured the camp which he and Antony shared.

The defeated Cassius, however, deprived of his camp and unaware – according to most sources – that Brutus had triumphed, persuaded his shield bearer to kill him. It is thought that about 8,000 of Cassius' men were killed; Octavian is believed to have lost about double that number. But since each side had won one round and lost another the score was broadly even.

Appian, Civil Wars, *4: 107–112; Plutarch*, Antony, *22(1–3) and* Brutus, *40(10)–43; Dio Cassius, 47: 42–46*

PHILIPPI: II (42, October 23) – Wars of the Second Triumvirate

After the first battle Antony and Octavian remained encamped opposite Brutus. News that a large fleet which was bringing them supplies had been destroyed in the Adriatic gave them considerable anxiety. Hunger was beginning to be felt and they wanted a quick military settlement. Brutus, on the other hand, was well stocked and had complete control of the seas. He was content to watch the enemy starve to death. His troops, however, were becoming restive, and eventually he gave in and lined them up for battle. Appian's and Dio's versions give the impression of a very ordinary battle, devoid of strategy, in which the two armies simply engaged with drawn swords in hand-to-hand fighting. The forces of Brutus were slowly pushed back and gave way to flight. Plutarch's account is more clarifying. Brutus, in his own sector on the right wing, overcame the enemy left and drove it back with the help of the cavalry. His left wing, however, had been extended to prevent it from being outflanked by the enemy's superior numbers. This left a weak centre which was unable to hold its ground but broke and fled, leaving the victorious right wing open to encirclement. Brutus himself fled and later killed himself. None of the accounts gives any casualty figures.

Plutarch, Brutus, *49; Appian*, Civil Wars, *4: 128–129; Dio Cassius, 47: 48(4–5)*

CILICIAN GATES (39) – Parthian War

After Philippi (above), Antony proceeded eastwards with the intention of waging a war against the Parthians. He sent Publius Ventidius ahead to pave the way. On the way Ventidius encountered Quintus Labienus, who had fought with Brutus and Cassius on the losing side and had not dared to return home for fear of the consequences. Labienus had not yet received some Parthian troops that he was expecting, and he was so

terrified of Ventidius that he ran away through Syria with Ventidius on his heels. Ventidius overtook him near the Cilician Gates [*Gülek Boğazi*]. It was here that the expected Parthian troops caught up with Labienus, but at the same time Ventidius received a reinforcement of heavy-armed infantry. Ventidius remained judiciously encamped on the heights for fear of the Parthian cavalry. They, on the other hand, were utterly fearless and self-confident. They did not even wait to join Labienus but approached the heights and charged straight up them. The Romans on top had little difficulty in hurling them back down the hill, killing many of them. Even more were killed by their own people when those fleeing downhill charged into others who were still ascending. The survivors fled into Cilicia. Labienus himself offered no opposition but attempted to escape after dark. His plan became known to Ventidius, who set ambushes and either killed his men or won them over to his own side, but Labienus managed to get away. He was later found and killed.
Plutarch, Antony, *33(4); Dio Cassius,* **48***: 39–40*

AMANUS M (39) – Parthian War
After recovering Cilicia, Ventidius proceeded to Mount Amanus [*Nur Dağlari*], having first sent Pompaedius Silo ahead with the cavalry. Pompaedius tried to occupy the exceedingly narrow Amanic Gates but he was defeated by Phranapates, who was in charge of the Parthian garrison at the pass. Pompaedius would have lost his life if Ventidius had not happened to arrive at that time and fallen unexpectedly upon the enemy. With his superior numbers he killed many of them, including Phranapates.
Dio Cassius, **48***: 41(1–4); Plutarch,* Antony, *33(4); Strabo,* **16***: 2, 8*

GINDARUS (38) – Parthian War
Publius Ventidius heard that Pacorus, the son of Orodes of Parthia, was preparing to invade Syria. This worried him because his troops were still in winter quarters and nothing was in place for a reception. He resorted to subterfuge by getting a friendly 'confidence' to the ears of Pacorus to the effect that his men would do better to cross the Euphrates at their customary place rather than further down where the river ran through a plain. Pacorus was deceived by what he assumed was deliberate misinformation and he crossed the river lower down, as Ventidius had intended. This route was the longer of the two, which gave the Romans more time to prepare. They allowed the Parthians to cross the river without opposition and were conspicuous by their absence on the far side. Consequently, when the Parthians reached the Roman camp at Gindarus, they attacked it immediately, expecting to take it with ease. A sudden sally took them by surprise, and as the camp was on high ground they were easily defeated by the heavy-armed Roman soldiers charging down on them. When Pacorus was killed, the Parthians gave up the struggle and were either killed or fled. The battle came to be regarded as settlement in full for the disaster at Carrhae (53) and the death of Crassus, which had been such a bitter humiliation to the Romans.
Plutarch, Antony, *34(1); Dio Cassius,* **49***: 19–20(3); Strabo,* **16***: 2, 8*

CUMAE (38) – War against Pompeius
Octavian engaged in a campaign to rid himself of his opponent Sextus Pompeius, the younger son of Pompey, who had gone from strength to strength. Sextus had been deserted by his admiral Menodorus, who had defected to Octavian. In his place, Sextus gave the naval command to Menecrates, the bitterest enemy of Menodorus, and ordered him to sail up the Italian coast and intercept the enemy fleet. When Octavian's fleet under Calvisius Sabinus and Menodorus caught sight of Menecrates at dusk, they retired into the Bay of Cumae for the night. The next morning they deployed their ships in a crescent formation as close to the shore as possible. Menecrates could not lure them out to sea and so he adopted the alternative tactic of driving them onto the rocks. As they were prevented by the hostile terrain from moving, Menecrates was able to draw off and renew his attack with fresh ships as he pleased. When Menodorus was still afloat, he caught sight of his arch-enemy Menecrates. They charged at each other, grappled and fought in what amounted to a single combat at sea, oblivious to all around. Menecrates was wounded in the thigh, and when his ship was captured he threw himself overboard and was drowned. This was the only bright spot in the gloom on Octavian's side.
Appian, Civil Wars, *5: 81–83; Dio Cassius,* **48***: 46(5)*

MYLAE (36) – War against Pompeius
Octavian was sailing with his fleet to the Lipara [*Lipari*] islands off north-east Sicily when he noticed considerable Pompeian naval forces off the Sicilian shore. Reckoning that Sextus Pompeius was there in person, Octavian sailed away

with the intention of attacking Tauromenium [*Taormina*], leaving Agrippa in command. This brilliant admiral took half of his ships and sailed forth against the Pompeian commander Demochares (some say Papias) and his 40 ships off Mylae [*Milazzo*]. Meanwhile, according to one source, Sextus had sent a further 45 ships to the area and was himself following with another 70. Agrippa immediately summoned the rest of his fleet to join him at top speed. Both of the ancient sources proceed to a dissertation of the relative merits of the opposing ships and the quality of their seamanship. Whatever these may have been, the outcome was such that the Pompeians are said to have lost 30 of their ships and sunk only 5 of the enemy's. When the remaining Pompeian ships withdrew in good order, Agrippa continued to harass them until they took refuge among the shoals, where his larger ships would be unable to navigate. He was intent on blockading the enemy but he reluctantly accepted advice to retire.

Appian, Civil Wars, **5**: *105–108; Dio Cassius*, **49**: *2–4(1)*

TAUROMENIUM (36) – War against Pompeius

Octavian sailed to Tauromenium with three legions, 1,000 light troops and 2,000 allies. He was laying out his camp when, to his amazement, Sextus Pompeius arrived with a large fleet from Messana having guessed the intentions of the other. The next day Octavian left his infantry in the charge of Cornificius and sailed out to sea to forestall any attempt by the enemy to blockade him. Sextus put to sea against him and a battle ensued which went on until nightfall. Octavian's fleet was utterly broken and dispersed. Some ships were captured; others were set on fire; yet others fled to the Italian coast. Octavian spent the night in a small boat and eventually reached the shore with one attendant.

Appian, Civil Wars, **5**: *110–111; Dio Cassius*, **49**: *5(1–4)*

NAULOCHUS (36) – War against Pompeius

In the Sicilian war between Octavian and Sextus Pompeius, the latter became afraid of Octavian's troops, of which there were 21 legions with 20,000 cavalry. Sextus had more confidence in his naval forces and decided to stake everything on a major battle at sea. One source says that he challenged Octavian to a naval duel and that a date was fixed for an engagement off Naulochus. On each side 300 ships lined up, fully armed with towers,

missiles and the best of machines. The device which in practice proved to be the most successful was a novel grab which had been devised by Agrippa, Octavian's brilliant admiral. This consisted of a long pole, bound with iron to prevent it from being cut or broken and on the end of which there was a claw. Long ropes were attached to the pole, which was propelled by a catapult at long range. When one of these devices grabbed a target, the victim was hauled in by the ropes as the attacking ship backed water. As the prey also backed water, the result was a tug-of-war in which the heavier ships of Octavian were likely to win. After that it was a matter of boarding and fighting on deck. When Agrippa had overpowered a number of the enemy ships, 17 of them escaped toward the straits. The rest were cut off, and some which were driven aground were either pulled off or set on fire. According to one source, Demochares killed himself to avoid capture, while Sextus' other captain, Apollophanes, deserted to Octavian. The Pompeian ships which were still resisting surrendered. In the battle, Sextus lost 28 ships at sea; the rest were captured, burnt or beached apart from the 17 escapees. Only three of Octavian's ships were sunk. Sextus hurried away leaving behind most of his forces, who surrendered to Octavian, and bringing the Sicilian campaign to an end.

Appian, Civil Wars, **5**: *118–121; Dio Cassius*, **49**: *8(5)–11(1)*

PHRAASPA (36) – Parthian War

The successful campaign of Publius Ventidius in Parthia (Cilician Gates, 39, *et seq.*) might have aroused some feelings of jealousy in Mark Antony. In consequence, Ventidius diplomatically postponed further activities as a precaution. Antony eventually set out for Parthia himself two years later, after Phraates had killed his own father and seized the kingdom. He received reinforcements from Artavasdes of Armenia, which brought his forces up to 60,000 Romans with 10,000 cavalry and 30,000 other nationals. Winter was approaching but Antony was impatient. Antony marched on from Armenia through Atropatene in such a hurry that he refused to wait for his 300 waggons of siege-engines, which were to follow behind in the care of a large force under Oppius Statianus. When Phraates heard about this, he sent a strong force of cavalry which surrounded Statianus, killing 10,000 of his men and destroying the siege equipment. Meanwhile Antony was besieging Phraaspa [*Takhti Suleiman*], the royal city of Media, and was bitterly regretting his folly over the engines. When the Parthian army arrived, Antony tried to draw them off to a pitched battle by making an expedition with 10 legions and all his cavalry. The Parthians started to encircle his camp and so Antony pretended to be in retreat. He marched his men in perfect formation past the barbarian lines but had given instructions for a charge as soon as the legions were within attacking range. The barbarians repelled the initial cavalry charge, but their horses were terrified and bolted when the legions followed up the attack, creating as much noise as they could. The Roman cavalry pursued them for many miles but, at the end of the day, the enemy losses were estimated to have been a mere 80 killed and 30 taken prisoner. On their way back to Phraaspa, the Romans were again attacked and managed to reach their camp only with great difficulty. The siege of Phraaspa had to be abandoned.

*Plutarch, Antony, 38–39; Dio Cassius, **49**: 25–26(2)*

ACTIUM PR (31, September 2) – War against Cleopatra

By 33, war between Antony and Octavian had become inevitable. The balance in the popularity of the two runners in Rome had been shifting in Octavian's favour. The scales were given a further push when Antony, while still married to Octavian's sister, agreed to become Cleopatra's consort. The implications for Rome were grave. The last straw came when Octavian unscrupulously got hold of Antony's will and read the contents to the senate. Rome was outraged, and war was declared against Cleopatra. Octavian, as consul, was directed to promote it.

At the end of 32, Antony moved down through Greece and sent his fleet ahead to moor in the strait leading into the Ambracian Gulf [*Arta*]. He had assembled around 500 ships, many of them very large ones (*deceres* or decimemes). Meanwhile, Octavian gathered his forces off Brundisium [*Brindisi*] before crossing the sea to Epirus, where he disembarked his army on the northern side of the strait. He is said to have had 250 ships but modern estimates double this figure. When Antony arrived with his army, he encamped at the base of the Actium [*La Punta*] peninsula, the southern side of the strait. For many months the two sides just watched each other. In the meantime Agrippa, Octavian's admiral, had been putting his fleet through its paces. An attack upon the enemy fleet was abandoned but he did succeed in cutting

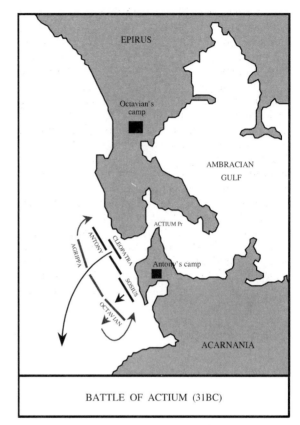

BATTLE OF ACTIUM (31BC)

their supply routes. Faced with shortages and desertions, Antony eventually decided to give battle and lined up his much reduced fleet in open sea outside the straits with Cleopatra and her 60 Egyptian ships as a rearguard. Octavian confronted them. But Antony's fleet remained stationary and showed no sign of engaging. Antony had given orders that the sails were to be stowed on board – a most unusual event in naval battles – which suggests that he may have contemplated a break-out if the wind was favourable. Similar implications can be drawn from the fact that he had taken all his treasure on board. Moreover, both Plutarch and Dio put heavy emphasis on disease, death and desertion in the Antonian camp. These factors had reduced Antony's manpower to the extent that he had superfluous ships, which he burned before the battle. Those that were in service were under-manned, badly crewed and ripe for further desertions. When this fleet showed no sign of movement, Octavian eventually sailed against it in a crescent formation with the aim of outflanking the enemy, who reluctantly got under way. According to Plutarch, Octavian on the right wing backed water to lure the enemy left on and then turned to the attack in an outflanking movement. Apart from these snippets of information the two principal accounts of the battle are deficient and give no clear impression of events. Dio's is essentially a stereotyped discourse on the naval tactics of the time which could apply equally to many other naval encounters. The unusual feature of this battle was provided by the sudden departure of Cleopatra, who hoisted her flag and proceeded to sail from her place in the rear of Antony's lines right through the battle zone, heading for Egypt. Antony promptly transshipped to a smaller vessel and followed as fast as he could, abandoning his own fleet in a manoeuvre not calculated to bolster confidence in his crews. This fiasco ensured that the loss of life was small in proportion to the numbers involved and that the number of captured ships and desertions was comparably great. It is said that not more than 5,000 lives were lost but that 300 ships were captured. The survivors surrendered to Octavian and the army followed suit soon afterwards.

In the past century there have been a number of reconstructions of these events with various interpretations. It has even been mooted provocatively that Cleopatra may never have sailed away at the critical moment, nor that her besotted lover abandoned his fleet to follow. These stories could have been the propagandist fabrications of Octavian to denigrate his adversary.* Such speculations and interpretations are outside the scope of this work. Actium, whatever did or did not happen, was the turning point which led to Octavian's mastery of Rome.

Plutarch, Antony, *61–68(3); Dio Cassius, **50:** 12–35; *M. Rostovtzeff, A History of the Ancient World, Oxford, 1928, vol. 2, p. 157*

BIBLIOGRAPHY
INDEXES

Select Bibliography

GENERAL

Bury, J.B. and Meiggs, R., *A History of Greece*, 4th edn. (Macmillan, 1975)

Cary, M. and Scullard, H.H., *A History of Rome*, 3rd edn. (Macmillan, 1974)

SPECIFIC TOPICS

Alton, E.H., 'The Roman Army,' in Sandys, J.E. (ed.), *Companion to Latin Studies*, 3rd edn. (Cambridge, 1921)

Bickerman, E.J., *Chronology of the Ancient World*, revised edn. (Thames & Hudson, 1980)

Connolly, P., *Greece and Rome at War,* revised edn. (Greenhill, 1998)

Connolly, P., *The Roman Army* (Macdonald Educational, 1975)

Cook, A.B., 'Ships', in Whibley, L. (ed.), *Companion to Greek Studies*, 4th edn. (Cambridge, 1931)

Cottrell, L., *Enemy of Rome* (Evans, 1960)

Fuller, J.F.C., *The Generalship of Alexander the Great* (Eyre Spottiswoode, 1958; Wordsworth, 1998)

Fuller, J.F.C., *Julius Caesar: Man, Soldier & Tyrant* (Eyre Spottiswoode, 1965; Wordsworth, 1998)

Grant, M., *Greek and Roman Historians: Information and Misinformation* (Routledge, 1995)

Green, P., *Alexander of Macedon, 356–323 B.C.* (University of California Press, 1991)

Hackett, J. (ed.), *Warfare in the Ancient World* (Sidgwick & Jackson, 1989)

Lazenby, J.F., *The Defence of Greece 490–479* (Aris & Phillips, 1993)

Lazenby, J.F., *The Spartan Army* (Aris & Phillips, 1985)

Lazenby, J.F., *Hannibal's War* (Aris & Phillips, 1978)

Liddell Hart, B.H., *Scipio Africanus: Greater than Napoleon* (William Blackwood, 1926; reprinted Greenhill, 1992)

Oman, C., 'War', in Whibley, L. (ed.), *Companion to Greek Studies*, 4th edn. (Cambridge, 1931)

Scullard, H.H., *Scipio Africanus: Soldier and Politician* (Thames & Hudson, 1970)

Sekunda, N.V., *The Ancient Greeks* (Osprey, 1986)

Tarn, W.W., 'The Roman Navy', in Sandys, J.E. (ed.), *Companion to Latin Studies*, 3rd edn. (Cambridge, 1921)

Warry, J., *Warfare in the Classical World* (Salamander, 1980)

Index of Persons

Praenomina: A.: Aulus; Ap.: Appius; C.: Gaius; Cn.: Gnaeus; D.: Decimus; L.: Lucius; Mam.: Mamercus; M'.: Manius; M.: Marcus; P.: Publius; Q.: Quintus; Ser.: Servius; Sex.: Sextus; Sp.: Spurius; T.: Titus; Ti.: Tiberius

The Romans in this index are entered under their *nomen* (family name), not *cognomen*, in accordance with logical practice. Cross-references from *cognomen* to *nomen* (e.g. Scipio: *see* Cornelius) are given for those individuals who are either generally or seem to be the most likely ones to be known by their *cognomen*.

Index of Places

C: Cape; Isl(s): Island(s); L: lake; M(s): mountain(s); P: Pass; Pr: Promontory; R: River

The bracketed figures are the dates of battles. All the dates are B.C. The names in italics before the dates are the modern names ('[*id*]' if the modern and ancient names are the same) of the sites or of nearby places. The names of the present provinces, departments or districts are also given in italics. Page references for maps are given in **bold** type.